AF254852

BICENTENNIAL CHIC

Bronx Bombers, Son of Sam, **KISS**teria & the Birth of Saturday Night Fever

MIKE DERRICO

Hardcover ISBN: 978-1-7354767-7-3

Paperback ISBN: 978-1-7354767-6-6

eBook ISBN: 978-1-7354767-8-0

Cover & Interior formatting by Abbey Suchoski.

This book is dedicated to the memory of my cousin, Peter Crincoli, and also, to the memories of Donna Lauria, Christine Freund, Virginia Voskerichian, Valentina Suriani, Alexander Esau, and Stacy Moskowitz.

CONTENTS

INTRODUCTION

The early years of the 1970s, as tumultuous as they seemed at the time, were always filled with the constant reminder that America's two hundredth birthday was coming up in 1976. As the decade began, committees were already being formed to plan for the worldwide events that would simultaneously take place when that day finally arrived. Even in the year of this publication, 2026, the Bicentennial has never been surpassed as the most talked-about and widely anticipated day in American history. You heard about it in '72, '73 and '74. But around '75 it really began to take hold of the public conscience. If you were a student during the 75-76 school year, rarely did a day go by where you didn't hear about something in preparation for the Bicentennial, so as one might imagine...by the time of the Bicentennial, we were sick to death of the Bicentennial.

Growing up in Central New Jersey, we were always collectively cognizant of two things...the approaching Bicentennial and the hovering presence of New York City. Somehow, we were always reminded of the goings on in the city, and most of it wasn't good. Sure, there was the Yankees and the overwhelming majesty of the skyscrapers made famous to Generation X kids through the 1976 Dino DeLaurentis remake of *King Kong* and its 1933 original...but there was crime and danger that we only heard about in the news and often joked about because New York City was not a place where you really went to if you were in New Jersey...you only heard about it and most people were afraid of it. And if God forbid you had to go into the city for the Ice Capades or a baseball game or to visit the Empire State Building, you took the dreaded train into Penn Station and then used the subways while your friends and family told you that you were going to get mugged. Mugged was always a word used in reference to the city. And if your parents chose to drive in instead, you got buckets of soap thrown on your car by the squeegee men. New York City to New Jerseyans was a place that haunted you from the sidelines of your peripheral vision, and no matter how much you tried to avoid it, it always let you know it was there.

But then there were those of us who saw beauty in the chaos, and art in the profane. There was indeed turmoil in those years. And yet there's something about being young and missing out on the adults' full experience that causes us to romanticize this very particular period that we encapsulate and shroud both in scorn and reverence...this period when America pushed toward the biggest birthday celebration in its history, and landmark events in Hollywood, professional sports, rock and roll music and the underground dance floors of New York City merged black, white, straight and gay subcultures into mainstream living rooms.

This book, *BICENTENNIAL CHIC: Bronx Bombers, Son of Sam, Kissteria & the Birth of Saturday Night Fever* emphasizes that the heart of the 1970s as we know them exists within the space of 18 months. For the most part, it happens in New York City, while the effects reverberate across America long into the twenty-first century. Some of the main subjects of this book have long been unanimously championed through history as a small handful of usual suspects in replaying 1976 and 1977 for the sake of acknowledging and stressing how popular culture changed immensely during this period...and some of them have not. I suppose it would be up to the reader to determine which is which while surveying topics like the New York Yankees, aka Bronx Bombers who enter the new age of free agency under the leadership of George Steinbrenner, whose only mission is to restore the faltering baseball team back to its former glory at any price.

Or the rock band, Kiss. Why Kiss? Why not the usual script of the tired CBGBs thread that accompanies the New York City story of this era? Well, that's there too, but it's Kiss whether the critics like it or not who contributed to shaping how we remember the 1970s in the overall Big Picture. Kids growing up in Possumdick, Middle America weren't listening much to Television in 1977, they were painting their faces up like this godforsaken Kiss. And so, there's Kiss adjusting to their newfound success with the rollercoaster of sudden stardom illuminating the cracks in the foundation of a band already breaking apart from within.

Or disco thriving in the city's black and gay communities and finally reaching mainstream white suburbia with producer Robert Stigwood setting out to make *Saturday Night Fever*, the film that will spark a full-scale cultural revolution. There are also the presidential and mayoral elections, the NBA-ABA merger along with the tragic arc of Dr. J, Julius Erving's last days in a New York uniform, Rupert Murdoch's acquisition of the *Post*, the bitter cold, the scorching heat, and of course the night when the lights went out. And all the while, in an era of widespread crime, when it's difficult to tell one day from the next, much less, one shooting from the other...it's rather easy to understand why the first victims fell away and blended in with everything else while nobody knew a serial killer was roaming the streets...when it took months before anybody realized what was happening and suddenly everything changed.

The advent of cable television in the suburbs of New Jersey in the early 1980s helped create the foundation for the cinephile in me at a very early age. One of the first movies I remember watching was *Somewhere in Time*, a 1980 film starring Christopher Reeve and Jane Seymour. In the film's opening scene, Reeve in the role of playwright Richard Collier is given an antique gold pocket watch by a frail, elderly woman who approaches him at an after-show party. She tells him "Come back to me" and then abruptly leaves. What Richard doesn't know that night is that the woman immediately goes home and drops dead. Years later, Richard checks himself into the old Grand Hotel for an extended stay in order to concentrate on a new project. In the hotel museum, he spots a photo of Elise McKenna, a local actress who starred in productions in the hotel theater...many many years ago. In fact, the photo is dated 1912. Richard becomes transfixed by the photo, returning to it over and over again, becoming obsessed with it, and ultimately falling in love with McKenna. His obsession leads him to research McKenna, leading him to her former assistant who he meets and speaks to. When she shows him the last picture taken of McKenna before she died, Richard realizes Elise McKenna was the woman who gave him the pocket watch. Determined to see her again, especially given her last words to him "come back to me," Richard begins looking into the concept of time travel and is told by a former college professor that it's possible through the power of suggestion and a complete manipulation of one's environment, though the chances are highly unlikely...and even if he were able to get back to 1912 from 1979, he would only be there for a fraction of a moment. Richard spends the next few days altering his appearance and wardrobe and everything in his hotel room that may be a reminder of the present day. He dresses in early twentieth century attire and into a tape recorder feeds himself the suggestion of 1912 as the current year. From there we tell ourselves, "if only time travel were this simple!" In a spiraling sequence we watch Richard travel back to 1912 for several minutes as he lay on his hotel bed. Back in the present, he's unsure if it really happened or if he were dreaming. During some further research, Richard gets his hands on the Grand Hotel guest book all the way back to 1912, and when he checks the logs for that particular date, he sees his own name registered as a guest. In that startling moment it dawns on him that his experience was real as he exclaims to himself in an enthralled whisper, "I was there. I...was...there!"

When I was 11 years old, I was naïve enough to believe I could achieve time travel through the same method. It was 1981 and I was trying to get back to 1977 convinced I might be able to attend a Kiss concert or something ridiculous like that. I can't remember my exact motives behind the half-hearted attempt at going back in time.

Every generation rides its own nostalgia wave. Sadly, I believe we spend too much time wishing we could go back to something...some particular time and place without realizing we're already back there in mind and heart, and sometimes without warning, the simple sound of a piece of music will be our transport and make it as real as it was back then. Because of this, it's probably more likely that time travel happens much more than we think, and far more times than we're even aware of. It happens in those moments when we hear that song that delivers us directly into the backseat of our parents' car and suddenly, we're seven years old again. A simple smell could put us back in our grandmother's kitchen. These are the brief flashes that serve as far as I can tell, as the only physical conduits to the past. But we can't always control or predict which sound or song we're going to come in contact with, just as we can't predict or control what smell, scent or stench will waft in from somewhere to take us back to a time or place that we'd either love to visit again or would do anything to avoid experiencing again. Depending on how one looks at it, it's all in the heaven and hell of memory.

In 2021, I published a novel called *The Locker Notes,* and in a chapter called "The Feast," I wrote extensively about the relation between music and memory, and how our senses are the only real direct connection back to the past, and how sound and smell especially can help us locate lost time and space. In 2025, the final year I worked on this book, a family member said I was stuck in the 1970s. It made me think about how I spend a lot of time mentally in that decade. Two and a half of my books take place in the 1970s and I've returned there time and again because it's necessary for my writing projects. Then I thought of that Brian Wilson line "I just wasn't made for these times." It was then that I realized that I was staying in the 1970s by choice...and that I wasn't stuck there at all. It was 2025 that I was stuck in.

Though all my books so far have touched on the same timelines that all take place during the final 25 years of the twentieth century, none of them have anything to do with each other, and they all first and foremost serve as standalone projects, which they are. That said, *Bicentennial Chic* does in fact inadvertently constitute the third and final book of what's become an unofficial 1970s memoir trilogy that began with *The Locker Notes*. Does this mean I'll never write another Seventies-related book again? Absolutely not. But the content stemming from my own personal memories ends with this one. At this point, let me be clear and establish...this is not a memoir, though at times it acts like one.

Let's draw some comparisons. First, let's acknowledge that Christopher Reeve's character was driven by a deep urgency to meet Elise McKenna. He traveled back to a time long before he himself was born...a time that he had no personal experience or memory attached to. He didn't give a shit about nostalgia. But those glimpses of Reeve realizing that he'd somehow, someway gone back in time are tantamount to the glimpses we get from our senses that often put us back in places whether we intend them to or not. Though unlike Reeve who gets there through the power of suggestion and not quite sure of what to expect when he does get there, we get to those places with a full sense of having lived it already because we're dealing with our own personal memories...and so the setting is already familiar and often more welcoming than our present setting. I suppose this is exactly what nostalgia is, though not everyone gets nostalgic and many would much rather stay in the present as much as possible. But aside from the occasional encounters with sound and smell that often take us back...what if we could do it through words? And I mean just words...without the usual narratives via the typical past tense history? What if we could move through that history in present tense? All that power of suggestion bullshit happens in present tense anyway. So, as we revisit America in the years 1976 and 1977, we'll do it in present tense. When we go through these pages of *Bicentennial Chic*, we're not looking backwards at history. We're there right this minute, and we're living it... right now. This entire book will be right now, and it will remain in present tense. We'll focuses on everything going on in and around New York City during a very particular 18-month period, though it pays specific attention to the details of four influential storylines across American popular culture that take place simultaneously...the rise of a young rock band, a baseball team, a murder spree and a magazine article that becomes one of the biggest films of all time...in short, the things that greatly influenced or changed pop culture in the years that followed. But it doesn't go much beyond that in terms of furthering our understanding of what's taking place at any given time. We are not looking at these things the way we're used to viewing them as history. These things are being thrown at us from all directions...*as they happen*...so we really don't have time to think about what we later learn about them as history...we're too busy *experiencing* them...and as quickly as we experience them, they're over. This book does not spend long-winded amounts of time with any one particular subject or event with respect to our simultaneous stories. It does not analyze or philosophize ideas around the events covered, nor does it look for answers let alone offer them. In other words, *Bicentennial Chic* is not intended to deliver any new revelations regarding the topics presented here. Nor does it aim to further our knowledge with new information. What it does is take everything we already know about said subjects... and presents it all in real time. Everything we know about these events as well as everything we talk about with respect to these events is everything we know *at the time* of these events. And that is the only perspectives presented in this book...how things looked and seemed *at the time*.

What else can I say here? I'm supposed to write an introduction for this project, but honestly, once I finish something, I go blank. Or to put it more into a spiritual or cyclical light, it's like shedding a skin. I really don't have much to say about these things I write once I'm finished with them. They spend years in my head and once I get it out, like any other creative work, it belongs to whoever encounters it. But if you like the idea of time travel, then you should consider this book a time travel. For context, the people in this book don't all know each other. Most don't cross paths with each other. Their stories often get interrupted by the other stories and then even those stories are interrupted by other stories...but we always return to each story. I invite you to think of each chapter as an episode in a series or a soap opera where the scenes play out visually. Think about those chapters. What is going on in those chapters in conjunction with their corresponding music and pop cultural events? It's all deliberate and nothing is by chance. Every last bit of *Bicentennial Chic* is chronological, and the sights and sounds that accompany the backgrounds of each event is how it all went down. All that said, *Bicentennial Chic* is not *about* these events nearly as much as it's about the backgrounds and the set pieces *behind* these events. If nothing else, this book is meant to serve as an exhaustive and intricate timeline with chapters instead of brief captions for each milestone marker.

At the outset, it is imperative to note to you, the reader, that the stories told in these pages, at some point, will be abruptly cut off. They are not resolved. There is nothing in this book that comes full circle or contains any meaningful ending. This book is a snapshot of a period that came and went. You will experience it in chronological real time. And when you reach that stage where you think there might be resolution or something that has a feeling of completion, you will be swiftly transported back. But in the end, you'll know you've been there.

Mike Derrico

February 1, 2026

PART ONE

“Break out the flags, strike up the band, light up the sky...”

— President Gerald Ford

1

BUYCENTENNIAL SELLABRATION

In the glistening New York City night, darkness has fallen in the inevitable evening on the longest day of the year. The summer solstice of 1976 has been approaching for weeks through the rapturous buoyancy of a spring more festive than recent memory allows, and an equinox that couldn't wait to tip the balance and stretch daylight again.

In the wake of the blue hour, the stars that may align in the sky are concealed by the obscuring lights of Lower Manhattan where the twin towers stand like sentinels over the canyons Downtown and the cluster of collective concrete and glass skyscraping structures provide their own illumination to the airspace above. The city is the great metropolis...at one time, the nation's capital, but now the nerve center of the world. Everything, for better or worse, begins here.

Sometime just after nine on the summer solstice which happens on Monday, June 21, King Kong falls from the top of the World Trade Center and descends to his death, creating a ground-quaking jolt to Lower Manhattan, prompting some five thousand New Yorkers from all directions to surge past police lines in search of what the hell has just taken place. A giant ape has run rampant on the city, escaping the shackles and chains that bound him to the steel cage forced down upon him by his unlikely captors, the greed-driven Petrox oil company. He's ripped through the bars quite easily. They've proven no match for his strength as he tosses the twisted remnants aside and walks forth, plowing through the streets of New York City in search of Jessica Lange. In the process he demolishes an elevated subway platform, pounding it into oblivion, derailing a train and crumbling it to bits when he can't find the actress. Lange is hiding out in a hotel bar with Jeff Bridges when the "nice monkey" reaches through a window and grabs her while Bridges isn't looking...big mistake on the part of Bridges.

It's not long before the airplanes come. Kong has grabbed the girl and is headed up the south tower. Then he leaps to the north tower, the thump of his feet heard and felt below. The towers haven't been there long...maybe a few years since opening, although New Yorkers and New Jerseans watched them go up for several years. The whole project was first announced way back in 1962 and then they had years of red tape and bureaucratic bullshit before they cleared out a neighborhood called Radio Row where a bunch of poor bastards lost their livelihoods and saw their buildings and businesses get dug up...the earth below it excavated and packed tightly into the Hudson River...the future foundation of Battery Park City...a place that doesn't exist yet and won't for another two decades. Kong has actually fallen from the tower on a Hollywood soundstage, but with director, John Guillermin sitting on a 30-foot hydraulic crane directing the crowd with a megaphone under two dozen 40,000 watt arc lights, the unpaid extras get to crowd up to the Styrofoam ape which lays at the bottom of the plaza oozing fake blood that's occasionally touched up by assistants. This shoot is for the post-fall close-ups of Kong. It's shot multiple times, and because of the nature of the scene, engulfed by the disorder of the movie's climax, most of the night is spent in preparation, cleaning up the shot and getting every extra back in place behind police barriers...only to have those barriers rushed again during the next take. The shoot called for 5000 extras but some 30,000 are said to have shown up around the World Trade Center area. This is the second time in a week these skyscrapers are attracting attention. Just four nights ago, New Yorkers and New Jerseans alike all marveled at the mysterious lights hitting and bouncing off the twin towers over a period of two hours on June 17. Laser technology of some sort and that is all most people knew. By midnight on June 22, the novelty of Hollywood has worn off and people begin to disperse. The colossal Dino DeLaurentis production, a remake of the 1933 classic, *King Kong*, will return to lower Manhattan for the next two nights to shoot the same scene.

The film has become synonymous with the Empire State Building in Midtown and vice versa. With the recent addition of the new tallest buildings in the world, Downtown has stolen the skyline like a new baby that gets all the attention. Aesthetically, the twin towers of the World Trade Center have nothing on the majestic Art Deco of New York's most beloved building and many regard them as an eye sore that rudely interrupts the architectural language of Lower Manhattan. That is nothing new though. New York City is notorious for pissing off virtually every generation of human existence that has ever tried to lay claim to the city as its own. It is a setting of inevitable change, and Downtown is no stranger to that. Even as the towers were going up in the late Sixties and early Seventies, the Singer Building, one of the neighborhood's most unique gems, was demolished in favor of a glass cereal box that contained more floor space for offices. Office space is prime real estate, and the twin towers offer it...especially floor space, despite the central core that imposes itself straight down the middle of the structures... the type of layout that would allow for those floors to pancake on top of each other just two and a half decades later. The city has become accustomed to change throughout its entire history, although each generation curses it. So, the towers assume all the attention in the mid-Seventies as Manhattan's new big tourist attraction, even if the morale and reputation of the city is at an all-time low. Still, it doesn't stop King Kong from passing through, and he will now be associated with the World Trade Center as well as the Empire State Building...at least to the Baby Boomers and Generation X.

Philippe Petit, a French high wire artist was probably the first person to feel any sort of personal claim on the towers, having formed a kinship while the north tower was still being completed. On the morning of Wednesday, August 7, 1974, New Yorkers were treated to a 45-minute show as Petit walked on a wire strung between the tops of the two towers some 1350 feet in the air. The young man just days away from his twenty-fifth birthday dazzled the stunned crowds below as well as police officers who clapped along with everyone else once it was all over. And then Petit was arrested and taken to Beekman Downtown Hospital where he was examined before going to the Ericsson Place station house where he was booked. A few hours later, the Manhattan District Attorney announced that the charges were dropped and that Petit was free on the condition that he agreed to do a free performance at a park for the children of the city. Petit is in attendance for the *King Kong* shoot, remarking to a reporter that he had probably drawn a bigger crowd.

The day after Petit walked between the towers, President Richard Milhous Nixon resigned from office. The stink from two years of Watergate along with the overall Nixonian stench had put a damper on America's faith in its government a faith that was perhaps naïve up to that point in time, but nonetheless shattered in the collective experience of a decade marked by the murder of John F. Kennedy, Vietnam War and a scandal that reached the highest levels, thus putting the final exclamation point on an era of lost innocence.

The week King Kong falls from the top of the World Trade Center, Jones Beach out on Long Island is closed to bathers with toxic material washing up. Anyone who has swum off Fire Island this month has been given an inoculation against hepatitis. No cases are being reported but the incubation period is 10-50 days. With the biggest Fourth of July Weekend in American history fast approaching, life begins to imitate art. Last year in the summer of '75, a movie called *Jaws* was released. It was the moment when all of America discovered the horrors of the Great White shark, and Long Island beaches were closed because people were getting eaten very close to Fourth of July Weekend. Now in real life, it isn't a shark keeping the beaches closed and threatening to ruin the climax of summer, but rather the influx of sewage. Residents count on the South Shore beaches for income during the summer months. The rich, however, will be getting their two-day sneak away, mostly to the New England coast, so the suburbs of Long Island and their economic ruin aren't of much concern to those who can buy their way into some alternate scenery. This isn't the first time livelihoods are muted. A few years earlier in Nassau County waste balls of tar and oil closed beaches for a short period of time. That same summer saw 24 miles of the North Shore closed when an oil spill at Port Jefferson occurred on a Sunday morning in mid-July with oil being transferred from the 741-foot tanker the Nepco Courageous to a barge owned by the McAllister Towing Company and some 34 gallons of it being pumped into the Sound. We can continue tracing these occurrences backwards, but that's neither here nor there. Beaches closing to the fuckups of mankind are nothing uncommon. They just aren't feasible with the party of the century a few weeks away, and with the commercial peak of summer magnified to such enormous proportions, the prospects of losing business that weekend are an unprecedented nightmare. Bicentennial advertising began long before the Bicentennial...months before...years before! And now America's two-hundredth birthday is fast approaching along with the birthday party. The question that has been common for the past few years is what you are going to be doing on July 4, 1976. Where are you going to be when it happens?

The hype...the anticipation...all the big to-do is enough to dwarf the totality of every New Years Eve blowout you'll ever have in your life. It's going to be one fuck of a party...that's for sure.

On a corner in Midtown on the evening of the summer solstice, an attractive woman of 39 named Mandy is standing with two teenage girls...her daughter, Heather, and Heather's friend Stacy, both 13, in front of a Sam Goody record store across the street from Radio City Music Hall. It's a Monday night in mid-June and the three are making their way up the Avenue of the Americas to catch the 9 PM showing of *That's Entertainment* at the Ziegfeld. After a lovely dinner, the three stand waiting at the red light, while crosstown traffic and the choking fumes of bus exhaust spray the intersection. From a transistor radio someone carries in the awaiting crowd comes the repeated phone number 976-3838...numbers that have become a mantra in Bicentennial-era New York City advertising the marketing brilliance of Dial-a-Joke. If you need a laugh, all you have to do is pick up the phone.

"Oh my God, it's Barbarino!" Heather, wide-eyed, is glancing upward.

"Oh my God, what is this?" Stacy follows.

Mandy cuts in. She's up on the news but matter-of-factly informs the girls of what they're looking at. The enormous square cardboard cutout of actor John Travolta's new record leers out at them from the Sam Goody window. It is surrounded by at least a dozen smaller squares all containing the same album photo...the 22-year old actor in a light blue turtle neck sweater, feathered shoulder-length hair, arms crossed in a relaxed pose and smiling that dimpled-chin, irresistible twinkly-eyed smile that has become the key luring features that have won the hearts of many a teenage girl and young adult female by the summer of 1976.

"Oh yeah," mom recalls. "He has a record album now. He was just on the *American Bandstand* talking about this."

"And you didn't tell me?" dismayed daughter inquires.

It's true. John Travolta, the hottest new heartthrob for girls in their teens and twenties made a recent appearance on *American Bandstand* to perform his new single "Let Her In" and to show the world he's not just a mumbling monosyllabic punk in a leather jacket like Vinnie Barbarino, the character he plays on the hit show *Welcome Back Kotter*. The ABC sitcom premiered in September 1975 and has propelled Travolta to superstardom almost overnight in the nine months since. On the episode in question, Dick Clark introduces Travolta as the "man who plays Barbarino" to a mass squeal reminiscent of those old Elvis and Beatles films of rabid females in grainy black and white... crying, pulling their hair and peeing themselves. In a pair of brown bell bottoms and a skin-tight yam-colored turtleneck, a smiling, youthful Travolta is quite animated, at least in facial expression, though his movements are few and probably instinctive and habitual by now... back arched, hips gyrating, weight shifted to one leg with his thumb clipped inside his belt much like Barbarino. This kind of slender, lanky S-shaped movement hasn't been seen on a male vocalist much since Jim Morrison, although Travolta's moves are more exaggerated and self-conscious. Still, he exudes a relaxed confidence in being in front of a crowd. Some sentiment in the audience is that of surprise as many watching the performance express to Clark that they had no idea Travolta sung. The truth is, he is no stranger to live audiences and performing outside the television show that has made him a star. The actor has half a decade behind him of TV commercials and a role in the Broadway production of *Grease* prior to his big break. He's just recently completed production of two films...one, a major motion picture called *Carrie* based on a little-known book by a new author named Stephen King... the other, a made-for-TV movie called *Boy in the Plastic Bubble* which will air later in the year. Travolta is clearly the *it* person going into the summer of 1976. "Let Her In" enters the Billboard Hot 100 that week where incidentally, the theme from *Welcome Back Kotter* sung by John Sebastian happens to be the number one song. By mid-June, "Let Her In" has climbed to number 26. It climbs steadily while "Welcome Back" has dropped, knocked out by the Sylvers' "Boogie Fever," which in turn was knocked out by Diana Ross's "Love Hangover," which in turn was knocked out by a Beatle singing "Silly Love Songs." All the while, Vinnie Barbarino is slowly and steadily inching toward all of them.

By mid-June, the New York Yankees are slated to outdraw the New York Mets in attendance for the first time since 1963. An illustrious new era of New York sports history has been underway since millionaire, George Steinbrenner purchased the Yankees in 1973, though it's been a slow-moving beginning to that era...one that's taken precisely since then to get moving, and let's remember...we're in 1976, so it's been three years of inching, and I mean inching toward getting them to look and feel like a winning baseball team.

When the Yankees held a press conference in January 1973, many were scratching their heads over the purchase of the team from the Columbia

Broadcasting System by a shipbuilder from Loraine, Ohio for ten million dollars. The price was odd as well, considering CBS bought the team for 13 million dollars eight years earlier. Who was this stranger, an outsider from the suburbs of Ohio coming in to take responsibility for the success or failure of the biggest team in baseball and perhaps the greatest sports franchise in all of sports history? Steinbrenner, the president of American Shipbuilding was one of those movers and shakers...the kind of people of such wealth, success and grandiosity in upper echelon human ambition and achievement that money magazines showcase in their issues that list the top young money makers and business giants in the world. He grew up rooting for the Indians, but the Yankees were always an attraction when they came to town. Sitting in Municipal Stadium watching this visiting team in their gray road uniforms which always had that blue hue to them always left Steinbrenner awestruck. As a kid he was very aware of the Yankees' status in the league along with the history that he, even as a Cleveland fan, revered.

The Steinbrenner era began with the last season played inside Yankee Stadium's original incarnation as a full-scale renovation began in 1974 with the team subletting Shea Stadium over in the Flushing section of Queens where the other New York team played. The Mets, the disadvantaged little cousins of the Yankees, shared their home for two full seasons while Yankee Stadium was dismantled and profoundly restructured and reshaped into a homerun-friendly castle in the Bronx. If only the Yankees had homerun power! The next moves on the part of the new owner were not that of homerun power, but of pitching. In the inaugural year at the new stadium, the next renovation is being performed on the team itself, though the changes are merely subtle at first...a managerial shift that actually occurred the previous season...and then a major shakeup as the Boss's right hand man and Yankees president, Gabe Paul begins to alter the pitching staff with a handful of stars and some prospects added to the gutted rotation. We get into the nitty gritty of these crucial players a little further ahead, but at the outset, let's note that controversial former Yankee, Billy Martin is onboard as the new manager, and he's done something crazy. He's promised Steinbrenner the pennant.

Win the pennant?

George Steinbrenner laughs in Billy Martin's face.

"Like hell you will."

He then proceeds to tell Martin of the tugboats he owns and promises the new manager his very own tugboat if the Yankees win the pennant.

Well, the Yankees have a noticeably safe lead in the American League Eastern Division, occupying first place in mid-June, the same month as a scandalous pitching deal that would all but guarantee them to extend and prolong that noticeably safe lead...again, details will be unraveled in further pages...though what is noteworthy here in terms of the team's troubles during this stretch of the season, is not related to issues with players or performance, but rather with logistics and public relations.

By mid-June of 1976, the Yankees find themselves in a dispute with Consolidated Edison over a ticket agreement that goes back almost a decade. The team has just suspended a program that allows 3000-5000 underprivileged kids to attend some 25 games for free through a deal with Con Edison whereby the power company distributes tickets upon request to the children. The Yankees organization argues that violence and unacceptable fan behavior in the upper left field stands where the Con Edison seats were reserved has become an issue. The Yankees call the suspension temporary until the team along with Con Edison can work out better security arrangements. Yankees security guards are reported to have faced violent incidents and threats from gangs in the restrooms and outside the reserved sections. While there is no age limit on the tickets, most of the kids attending the games are said to be under the age of 15. In the newly refurbished stadium, attendance is much higher than it has been in previous years, though they argue that the ticket suspension has nothing to do with increased attendance. Con Edison argues that rowdy and violent fan behavior is nothing new nor different than what was acceptable in the old stadium. Very quickly, a court order stops the suspension, but Steinbrenner suggests that the future of the program is in the hands of the children. It's difficult to fathom that such behavior is limited to some underprivileged kids though...especially with alcohol-fueled adults in the equation. An incident earlier in the month when someone tossed a pack of firecrackers out of the right field upper deck indicates that it wasn't all the

Con Ed ticketholders. The violence and hostility has been on record and reported on since the season began and it's coming from all over the stadium...not just the cheap seats. During a weekend series against the Oakland Athletics (A's), the opposing team's relief pitcher, Rollie Fingers was given a ride from the bullpen to the mound, as is customary at the Stadium and in most major league ballparks. The white Toyota was pelted with cans, cups and garbage from the stands along the third base line as ground crew driver Danny Colletti drove Fingers to his destination, so this kind of shit is nothing new in the Bronx. Regarding the Boss's passing off the fate of the kids to be in the hands of the kids...it is the typical buck-passing that comes along with the bureaucratic measures that those truly responsible takes to dismiss certain petty responsibilities as gravity issues that are out of their hands. He'd made it clear that owning the Yankees would not be his everyday job. The day-to-day decisions of running a baseball team were to be done by people who worked for him...the president, manager, coaches, etc...He wasn't going to pretend he was something he wasn't. He was a shipbuilder, so he would stick to building ships. That was what he said.

In mid-June 1976 the proud New York City institution known as the New York Knickerbockers, aka the Knicks basketball team is seething and so is Madison Square Garden, the world's most famous arena which owns the Knicks. At the moment, another New York team...one that has never been taken too seriously, and to many, never proven legitimate, is creeping in on Knicks territory and invading their turf. The Knicks feel threatened by this and have quickly let it be known that the organization is not happy. The Knicks have been the only New York basketball team in the National Basketball Association until now. That other team, the New York Nets never really counted, because, well...they're part of that inferior league known as the American Basketball Association. They also play all the way out on Long Island. They couldn't possibly be spoken of in the same sentence as New York's premier teams, the Knicks and National Hockey League Rangers. The ABA is not the NBA...not even by a fraction. The ABA doesn't have nearly half the resources for success that the NBA has. And yet, the insecurity over the ABA that has always plagued anyone involved with the NBA has always remained. The ABA is their competitor with its three-point plays and slam-dunking luring fans in ways that the traditionally safe and orthodox NBA cannot... and the NBA knows it. The NBA knows that the ABA is far more adventurous, energetic and unpredictable, and without much speculation needed, more appealing overall. Yet, the ABA is no match for the superior bigness of the NBA. The ABA, now on the verge of folding, was never a hell of a whole lot of threat to the NBA financially though there is something to be said about the general common knowledge that one league is just more exciting than the other.

The ABA began as a rebel league...a second option for fans to enjoy, and players to gain exposure on the national stage, even if that stage was considerably smaller. The underlying not-so-secret secret intent was to merge with the NBA and after several years of NBA players and owners trying to prevent the inevitable, the inevitable finally happens on Thursday, June 17. Some teams do in fact fold, while the owners of one team, the Spirits of St. Louis, strike an historic deal that will make them millions of dollars for doing nothing. Spirits owners Ozzie and Daniel Silna will be paid a cut of the future television revenue of the four remaining teams that get absorbed into the NBA... the San Antonio Spurs, Denver Nuggets, Indian Pacers and New York Nets. The agreement is that the Silna's will get paid this money for basically the rest of the NBA's existence. They are offered this deal just to go away and not have the Spirit of St. Louis take part in the merger. The irresponsibly stupid people who offered them this deal obviously didn't have much faith in the merger or in the NBA and probably didn't expect the league to be around much longer, nor did they consider that the Silna brothers would still be collecting millions in TV revenue well into the next century.

For immediate context going into the merger, the Nets have just won the ABA championship, their second in the past three years. Their biggest asset is small forward Julius Erving. He has just won the Finals MVP. They call him Dr. J, and Dr. J is not only the best ABA player, but he is by far better than any player currently in the NBA. No bullshit, no debate. The Doctor is the Shit, and the Shit. Is. It. There are many reasons for this, and once again, for our own astonishment, enjoyment and further knowledge of details, we'll explore the trajectory of Julius Erving during this pivotal period of months further ahead. What is most important at this stage in our little time capsule back to 1976 is that Julius Erving and the Nets will now be major players on the basketball stage. The Nets, already a New York team, will not only be on the same New York stage as the Knicks, but also in the same league, same conference and same division. Is there room enough for two basketball teams in New York? The Knicks don't seem to think so. Consequently, the Nets must indemnify the Knicks for moving in on their territory. The Knicks feel their turf being invaded, and so they demand close to five million dollars in reparations...or extortion depending on how one looks at it. Nets owner, Roy Boe offers Julius Erving to the Knicks much to the chagrin of his team and his team's fans. This should cover the ransom. The Knicks decline the offer in one swift rejection that will prove to be one of the worst decisions in Knicks history, and one that will quickly destroy the Nets.

On the evening of the day the merger takes place, June 17, a Yes concert is going on at the dilapidated Roosevelt Stadium in Jersey City. Yes, a progressive rock band that has been part of the rotation on FM radio stations since first appearing on the scene half a decade ago has built up enough of a following to fill sports arenas for multiple nights. Yes is a popular band and their shows are as visually stunning as their music is aurally appealing or challenging, depending on your nervous system's tolerance for progressive rock. On this warm evening in New Jersey however, the routine of touring and the expectations of shows going off without a hitch prove elusive throughout. In the audience, the spirit is ugly in an Altamont sort of way. Little pockets of fighting break out throughout the crowd, much of it agitated after having camped out and waited since the night before...just to get a good spot to stand in this general admission event. At one point closer to show time, one of the giant laser mirrors on the stage comes crashing down, resulting in slicing and dicing injuries to fans down front. No fatalities inside the stadium though, and the concert, broadcast live on WNEW-FM goes off successfully with the now-misguided lasers extending out of the stadium and reaching well into New York City...those same mysterious lights bouncing off the World Trade Center and Empire State Building that caused a head-scratching metropolitan area to wonder just where in the hell these lasers were coming from. Outside Roosevelt Stadium, a 17-year-old Bayonne kid named Guy Porzelt is stabbed and listed in critical condition.

By Thursday, June 24, the *King Kong* shoot is history, and the lower tip of the island is restored to its natural flow...whereas some fifty blocks north of the World Trade Center, a photo shoot is happening at the top of the Empire State Building. There are no gawkers on Fifth Avenue...nobody with their heads tilted back in vertigo-inducing neck bending with eyes focused upward...nobody pointing and nobody spreading word-of-mouth babble that results in crowds flocking to the happening. There is nobody to say "Look up there! It's a bird! It's a plane! It's Kiss!"

Why?

Because nobody can see them.

The mighty Kiss, New York City's hottest band, growing (even as we speak) more popular by the week, is perched on a private landing one floor above the observation deck where the public would normally gaze out at the ocean of concrete, steel and glass, and beyond. The Empire State Building boasts a view of up to ten miles out on a clear day.

Kiss has been out and about throughout the city today...taking pictures with photographer Barry Levine, posing and walking casually in the streets among the public until arriving by horse and carriage at Thirty-Fourth and Fifth. The New York City background is no stranger to Kiss photography, as the band has been inhabiting these streets, mostly in black and white, since they first appeared in 1973, though the public didn't really catch a glimpse of them fully realized until 1974 when the debut album was released in February of that year. Why "fully realized" you ask? Because Kiss is not your ordinary group. Even in this age of glitz and glam and theatrics, nobody has seen the likes of Kiss. It's been about five or six years since Alice Cooper burst on the scene in full makeup and a stage show to haunt your dreams. David Bowie became Ziggy Stardust a few years back but has since evolved out of that character, morphing into Aladin Sane and then into some form of Philadelphia-influenced plastic soul. Even now, his latest album is *Station to Station* and doesn't resemble much of anything he's done in the past, although seems much more in line with *Young Americans*, his previous record, than anything else. There's no indication yet that he's about to spend the next three years in Berlin making music with Brian Eno while getting more detached from whatever they thought he was. Peter Gabriel, to be fair, was theatrical with makeup before all of them, but he split from Genesis about a year ago. There's also Little Richard who arguably started glam. Incidentally, Gabriel will be entering the studio soon with Bob Ezrin, the guy who just produced Kiss's latest record, *Destroyer*.

But Kiss is something completely different.

Kiss displays four distinctive faces covered in kabuki makeup designs and accompanying outfits custom-made to correspond with each unique stage identity. In full costume, the members of Kiss stand nearly seven feet tall. Their concerts are loud, bombastic spectacles of lights, explosions, smoke, fire and blood. The first year of their existence, they did gymnasiums, cafeterias, clubs, theaters and small arenas mostly as an opening act, often on bills consisting of at least three bands. As word began to spread almost instantly, they took on some headlining gigs in certain cities toward the end of 1974. Going into 1975, they had a decent amount of nationwide exposure from three major television appearances...ABC's *In Concert*, the *Mike Douglas Show* and the *Midnight Special*. Touring persisted with a joyous homecoming at New York City's Beacon Theater. What Kiss was lacking, however, was radio airplay, record sales and a hit song. Introduced nightly as "the hottest band in the land," they lived up to it by all accounts of those who witnessed it. The reputation they earned over those first fifteen months was built on consistent touring. But that didn't come without its problems... especially since they weren't selling albums. Manager, Bill Aucoin had been financing the band's expenses on his personal American Express card, and with their record label showing signs of time running out on Kiss, everything pointed to a band about to blow their one big shot, which began to seem like some purgatorial trial and one colossal clusterfuck of financial ruin. The decision to record a double live album as a last-ditch attempt to save themselves...themselves meaning the band, label and Aucoin...proved to be masterful in a time when nobody gave a shit about live albums and nobody was doing them. Kiss did one though. And by the end of 1975, they had a hit song in "Rock and Roll All Nite," which climbed the charts this past winter and peaked in February at number 12. What has become known as *Kiss Alive!* has gone gold and the band is now a nationwide headliner. In March, they released *Destroyer* followed by some European dates in April. Though *Destroyer* has been out three months, the European shows were played on the success of *Alive* and an extension of the 1975 *Dressed to Kill/Alive* stage show, although they did premiere some new material from *Destroyer*. Now in June, Paul Stanley, Gene Simmons, Peter Criss and Ace Frehley in their new attire are stalking the city with Barry Levine for promo shots as they prepare for the *Destroyer* tour proper. The new costumes have not been worn in concert yet, and have only been seen on the album cover, though they were worn for a prior photo shoot in early April just before embarking on the final *Alive* shows in Canada and Europe with the '75 costumes and stage show. Again, to address these April and May dates for 1976, revisionist history for one convoluted reason or another has reassigned these European shows as part of the *Destroyer* tour. Revisionist history is wrong here, as there is nothing in the costumes, stage show or even set list that remotely resembles the actual *Destroyer* shows. Kiss fans will nitpick though, and that is one of the expected and accepted laws of the universe.

As Kiss perches themselves along the grated landing of the Empire State Building, band members are petrified with fear. Still, it's all for rock and roll and they make it look cool and effortless as Levine shoots the images that will become among the most iconic in the band's long illustrious history.

At this time in the third week of June, they have already been a growing fixture in rock magazines with Creem paying special attention early on along with Circus being supportive, beginning in the post-*Alive* surge that would sprawl out before the rest of America. The current issue of Circus on the newsstands features a look at Bob Ezrin's involvement on *Destroyer*. On the cover are Mick Jagger and Keith Richards. Over the course of the next few years, Kiss will be featured on the cover several times, collectively and often individually.

On the same newsstands right next to Kiss, disco music is staring them in the face. A few weeks earlier and still circulating around the print media and literary community, is the first issue of *New York Magazine* for the month of June. It sits among the most recent magazine issues atop tables in the waiting rooms of doctors' offices and dental offices. The issue has people talking. Most notably, film producers are particularly aware of the cover story that jumps off the paper in white letters against a royal blue cover background, and illustrated in the brown, gold, green and pinks that might adorn a Byzantine painting. The painted picture however is absolutely modern in its appearance and in its contents...young men and women on a dance floor...polyester clothes, high heels, mustached, permed and decked out in the latest fashion. British writer, Nik Cohn is the author of the cover's corresponding article. The intriguing headline flaunts *Tribal Rites of the New Saturday Night*.

If you are a Baby Boomer or belong to Generation X in America, the two biggest and most anticipated events of your lifetime are the Bicentennial and the Millennium. Being a Boomer or Gen Xer means that you get to witness America's two hundredth birthday party and you get to watch one century end and another begin.

In our timeline, we are now in 1976. For the past year, the Bicentennial has become the biggest story in America and rarely has a day gone by where it hasn't been crammed down our throats in some form. Events commemorating this milestone have been planned for the past several years. Early in the decade, a commission was formed by the government to outline and put the Bicentennial in place. Commemorative stamps are produced by the U.S. Postal Service and special coinage is issued by the U.S. Treasury. A federally appointed group is created to issue similar collector's edition mementos like Bicentennial medals, posters, pillows, calendars...you name it. By 1972 the commission couldn't even decide on an official logo let alone plan nationwide activities and events...and then the debate became whether they should allow commercial use of the logo by corporations and their marketing campaigns. Private companies see the Bicentennial as a marketing opportunity, and everyone has gotten in on the action. The ephemera is endless and exists in forms that even the most visionary of imaginations in a twenty-first century mindset couldn't conceive of. Zippo gets in on the red, white and blue. Poulan introduces the Model 76 chainsaw that promises that we'll never see another chainsaw quite like it. It brags of its super lightweight prowess and boasts of having every possible feature needed to make cutting a breeze...claiming an all-position carburetor that'll allow for you to cut at any angle and buzz through a four-inch log in less than six seconds! The ten-inch sprocket nose cutting bar offers less wear than the average bear and the best part about the entire saw is its muffler. It's a multi-chambered muffler that keeps cutting activity incredibly quiet. But 1970s culture always offers one more thing and Poulan is no exception. So, in "wait there's more" fashion, the Bicentennial chainsaw comes with a free carrying case for a limited time at certain participating Poulan dealers.

Young America for '76 claims itself as the most outstanding youth Bicentennial program, and they're selling t-shirts in much the same manner most every other marketing campaign aimed at youth presents itself...in magazines and comic books...those ads showing you the miniature secret spy camera for only $2.25...the jackpot bank to store your coins for only $2.98...the learn-at-home karate course that revealed hundreds of deadly self-defense secrets which will enable you to protect yourself from attackers, and before you spend your hard-earned money, they send you an easy-to-read brochure for free. All you have to do is send a quarter to cover the postage and handling costs to Universal, Department 5 in Detroit, Michigan and they'll handle the rest. For serious-minded kids, these ads offer you the chance to train at home for a big career in accounting, including a 24-page book entitled *Your Career in Accounting* that you receive for free if you simply state your age and mail your request to the North American School of Accounting at 4500 Campus Drive, Newport Beach, California. It promises that you too can be a leader on your company's management team and that the skills you'll develop will enable you to be a key player in making corporate decisions and handling large affairs. Plant World in Newark, New Jersey tries to lure kids into having a Venus fly trap for hours of guaranteed fun and experiments to amuse their friends with. *Is it an animal or a vegetable?* they ask. Two dollars will get you a complete set of five bulbs and growing instructions. Ads from Estes sell solid propellant rockets. There also remains the classic "get a body like Charles Atlas in just seven days" spin.

To commemorate the big birthday party, Cadillac has made a Bicentennial Eldorado Convertible Edition for 1976, Gibson has turned out a '76 Bicentennial Edition Thunderbird guitar and Harley Davidson has issued a Bicentennial Edition Sportster XL 1000. *One Time for Old Glory* is a trademarked slogan advertising the official Bicentennial condom, which is still subtitled as a "prophylactic," possibly to offer another more scientifically appropriate name for what is otherwise referred to in slang as a rubber. It warns in a disclaimer that it's sold as a novelty only.

The underlying moral dilemma here with respect to the federal government is one of a rarely held position of morality and priority. With unemployment and inflation rising, politicians are more concerned about spending during this period, and the growing consensus is that the government is getting too big while the government itself is somewhat self-conscious about it. The government doesn't see fit to celebrate itself during a period of financial tumult and following the national embarrassments of Vietnam and Watergate. The government doesn't think it has any place throwing itself a party...that's at least the perception it wants to create. But the consensus by now, is that the Seventies are one long mindless party. And what about the idea that America is not just the government? Why does it have to be the government we're celebrating? What about just the idea of America itself? America is far bigger than the government. The government doesn't define America. America for better or worse defines America.

While the biggest party on a national scale is prepared for New York City, where some of our founding fathers' footprints are indelibly imprinted and George Washington remains on the steps of Federal Hall and his chair remains in St. Paul's Chapel and Alexander Hamilton remains buried outside Trinity Church, the city's reputation with America is one of a shithole, and a very dangerous shithole. Yet, they keep talking about the party. It's happening in thirteen days, though the festivities may as well begin right now, as everyone has been talking about it nonstop while the news media can't help but remind New York City how dangerous New York City is. In the wake of a fiscal crisis that brought the city to the verge of bankruptcy and back, along with a simultaneous crime wave that has all but assured the deterioration of the city's image in the eyes of the nation over the past half decade, not many think the city can pull it off, this nationwide hosting of the Bicentennial that's been planned for New York Harbor. New York outside the city is known as the most hellish place on Earth, though most people who believe that have never left New Jersey. It's known for crime and murder and stabbings and shootings and rapes and gangs and arson and hookers and pimps and swindlers and drug addicts and panhandlers and homeless vets and runways who get kidnapped, sold and never heard from again. It's a glamorous place, the city is. Just a year ago, the police started handing out pamphlets in the airports and train stations for people arriving in New York. The pamphlets greet them "Welcome to Fear City: A Survival Guide to Visitors of New York City." Then they proceed to list nine survival tips...

1. Stay off the streets after 6PM
2. Do not walk
3. Avoid public transportation
4. Remain in Manhattan
5. Protect your property
6. Safeguard your handbag

7. Conceal property in automobiles
8. Do not leave valuables in your hotel room and do not deposit them in the hotel vault.
9. Be aware of fire hazards.

As the government is consumed by self-inflicted demoralization and defeatist judgment, New York tries to get its act together while private companies have long been capitalizing on the Bicentennial regardless of what the government or the commission itself has been doing. There is more than enough of this historic event to go around, and it will indeed be spread throughout the country. It is much too big for any one entity to take on by itself. Nobody has a monopoly on the Bicentennial, nor does anybody want one.

2

THIS WHOLE DISCO THING

Regine Zylberberg is one of those oversized egos who go by one name... by which in high society she is known simply as Regine. Regine is the queen of the French nightclub scene, or as the *New York Post* dubs her, the queen of the night. Born in Belgium, she spent much of her childhood ducking the Nazis and hiding out in French convents during World War 2. Her father ran a café in Belleville where she waited tables. By 1953 she was running the Whiskey a GoGo where she trashed the jukebox in favor of two turntables, and in 1959 she opened the Chez Regine club, her first, and the one that raised the bar for what rich entertainment could be. She has raised an empire over the past two decades with establishments on three continents and no sign of stopping. Gratuitous overindulgence and partying for millionaires has often seen its backdrop in the form of one of Regine's hotspots. What do we credit Regine for? We credit her for basically inventing the modern nightclub and something called the discotheque.

Amid New York City's financial turmoil while Mayor Abe Beame was pleading to President Gerald Ford for a bailout last year, Regine felt that the city needed mouth-to-mouth resuscitation. She's 46 years-old when she opens Regine's on the ground floor of Delmonico's on Fifty-Ninth and Park Avenue. She believes in the power and the energy of New York, and she believes the city will bounce back. She loves New York City, partly because it's a place where one can make a lot of money and Regine loves money. With her new club only a month old, Regine's immediate plan is to spend at least six months of each year in New York City living in the penthouse of Delmonico's. Her opulent new $500,000 night spot exists just below on the ground floor of the building in lavish Art Deco décor. The lifestyles of the rich and famous are not so much a pop cultural fascination in nearly the same way as they will be during the 1980s, though some journalists inquire about where Regine got her financing to build this sought-after attraction. She only offers that she did not use her own money. In fact, she never uses her own money...just her name. Every day some businessman is in there with an offer to build her a club in some other remote part of the world. She can franchise her name if she wants to. This is an option that is certainly discussed these days, though she seems content not to. Regine presents herself with absolute confidence. Reporters call attention to her weight loss...she has recently dropped 40 pounds, though she remains slightly on the plumpish side. She has bright red hair, thin penciled lines where her eyebrows used to be and she delivers her new venture to the city as if on a rescue mission. She's come to help, she repeatedly told reporters upon first announcing the establishment late last year. Whether or not she could ever be successful in New York City was a question. She was told years ago that she couldn't make a go of it in Monte Carlo either...that there were too many old people. She's since opened three clubs there. She prides herself on not liking easy things, having nerves of steel and always being driven by challenge. Regine, however, contrary to her opinion, is not breathing new life into the city, nor is she catapulting any groundbreaking new trends aside from providing a new establishment for the rich and famous to be photographed as they make the scene. The average slob from the outer boroughs will not be seen in Regine's but that won't stop anyone from dancing, as Regine's is just one of many discotheques that have appeared in New York City in recent months...places like Infinity at Broadway and Bleecker in the Village, Murray the K's Hustle at 242 East Seventy-Second, Cecil at 161 East Fifty-Fourth, and a new private club called Doubles in the basement of the Sherry-Netherland Hotel.

Discotheques are viable establishments in these days of debauchery and hedonism. Even as the city falters and sputters into failure economically, socially, ethically and morally, the collective feeling across the entire spectrum of humanity making up Gotham is one of complete indifference. One observer of the thriving club scene anonymously likens it to a sense of fiddling while the entire shithouse burns to the ground, and nobody gives a rat's ass. If it's all going to hell, we're going to party while it does. The decade didn't begin this way, but this is certainly where we've ended up. Dancing hasn't been this popular in a few generations...at least on a mass scale of people going out to public places where dancing is the main reason for being there. This whole disco thing that can be traced all the way back to the Stonewall in the late Sixties and possibly further has now gained mainstream acceptance where dating as well as married couples seeping from the woodwork of the suburbs are bringing the bandwagon fascination to the ever-increasing dance floors of the city. This whole disco thing has also brought a lot of music to the pop charts over the past year, as dance beats now characterize most hit songs that make up the Billboard Hot 100...and not just the dance charts.

But just who is surfacing from out of the suburbs and into the realm of this abhorrent world? It is no secret that discotheques in the past half decade have been associated with homosexuals and African Americans. It's where the queers hang out on Saturday nights... or more to the point, black queers. This is not at all lost on the mentality that underlines the mainstream suburban male of European decent that make up the interweaving lines of streets in developments consisting of houses that all look the same in their cookie cutter architecture adorned by dandelion-infested front lawns, stoops with ornate railings and a slab of concrete for a driveway...nor is it lost on the homophobia and racism that will fuel the anti-disco backlash that inevitably creeps in as a result of the subculture reaching the white heterosexual universe by 1976.

If we refer to the origins of the discotheque, we find it in the French vocabulary serving as a library of phonograph records, much in the same way as bibliothèque is a library for books. In this respect, Regine has a head start on the latest fad in America by at least a decade and a half. But this type of establishment known as discotheques in the city has indeed been part of the contemptible underground, and this music has been cut from the cloth of its derived word...disco is indeed associated with blacks and gays. But now straight young white women of the suburbs have taken a liking to the sound they hear on the radio...all those disco hits of the past few years...and they too want to dance. They drag their boyfriends and husbands to these god-forsaken places where most never even go anywhere near the dance floor. And so disco in the suburbs is now also starting to be associated with women. Rock fans criticize it for being too conventional as if there is such a thing in anything about the genre. Conservatives, aside from hating it precisely because of those black and homosexual associations, see it as an escalation of deviant sexuality. And there is nothing macho or even manly about disco dancing, as some pharisaic phallic-sensitive males would have you believe. In their eyes and ears, it's musically inferior to rock and roll, and the entire genre is invalid as anything remotely in good taste or in the realm of decency. Yet, visually, at least in the underground places, the garb worn by some rather hardcore looking men is much more intimidatingly male than most straight males will dress on any normal day...bearded men in lumberjack shirts and leather pants...whips...studs...chains...things that will fuck you up in a fight are now fashionable to at least the queers who live in that world...though it is not that world that informs the fashion on the few suburban guys courageous and secure enough to get out on the floor under the lights with their wives. But then there are the ones who are brave enough. These guys who dance wear quirky choices like red and pink floral patterned ilk shirts with large collars and the top four buttons undone to expose vast fields of chest hair under gold medallions and crucifixes with Jesus swinging from their sweaty pasty necks reeking of Musk...sharp obtrusive seams running straight down the middle of bell-bottomed, Dacron periwinkle pants... something the crotchety older people call slacks.

The leisure suit is exclusively a phenomenon of the Seventies...a time when the surplus of polyester availability informs the trends.

The leisure suit is a far-out combination piece of matching jackets and flared slacks, often in informal shades of powder blue, burnt umber and burnt sienna. How sharp a man looks in his leisure suit! Look at those slacks! You look like a million bucks! A look that says you're about to get laid and at the same time go out and fuck up a motherfucker! But the night is young and you're all ready for the disco...your leisure suit worn over a turtleneck if not an open bare-chested sea of hair protruding between huge spread-out collars draping over wide floppy lapels. Real men wear their lapels wide.

But not really.

Most men in leisure suits are guys from the other side...not at all authentic to the culture revolution. They're just dabbling...getting a feel of this look...this life. Some even question how cool and together they really look, most unsure and insecure. But by this time in 1976, people are already starting to get sick of polyester and its rough staticky off-putting texture, not conducive at all to sweating. When your clothes are made by Dupont, serious re-evaluation is highly in order. But in the time being, for the less affluent, the jackets come from the suburban outlets and department stores...herringbone jackets...worsted wool with suede elbow patches and wool flannel dress slacks! And now, the latest fashion ideas are coming into reality...suit separates made for each other, but you have the freedom to add or subtract at your own will they say. New cut-away jackets that hug your curves and align themselves with the contours of your body. Dacron polyester and wool gabardine for better or worse. The good thing about this is it strikes a happy medium between heaviness and lightness...clothing made from all-climate fabrics, they say...and it's all aimed at the regular people...people from the same places where those suburban girls all thanks to television aspire to be Charlie girls...living for Sunday brunches at sidewalk cafes, flying to Paris on a whim, preferring daisies to orchids, hating to admit when she's sick and being the first on her block to wear a strapless dress to a disco.

In 1976, there are said to be over 200 public places to dance in the city and over 100 more in the suburbs...twice as many as there were in 1974. This spike in popularity is owed largely to the Hustle, which has given birth to the Latin Hustle, New York Hustle and L.A Hustle, and suddenly people from all walks of life and race, young and older are coming out...even the men who dare. Variants on the Hustle and other dances like the Line, the Walk, the Roach and the Chicago Bus Stop are more in vogue these days than older vestiges of the dance floor like the Watusi, Monkey, Jerk, Shake, Hully Gully, Lindy, Bostella, Madison and the Shag. Even professional dancers are frequenting discotheques. Some from the New York Ballet see it as a refreshing means of expression as opposed to always having to dance to someone else's work. The success of Van McCoy's "The Hustle" during the summer of 1975, peaking at number one on the Billboard Hot 100 was the catalyst that ignited white suburbia's interest and participation in the growing disco trends one year ago. Still, it's mostly all stigma attached in that world where white non-gay manhood feels threatened.

In 1976 Robert Stigwood is a name most associated with music management and theater production. His early label Reaction Records put out the Who's first single, "Substitute," and he managed Cream during their very brief existence during this time when Stigwood for the most part made his home in the UK since arriving there from Australia in the mid-Fifties. Though Cream broke up early, Stigwood still manages guitarist/vocalist Eric Clapton. His biggest act these days is the Bee Gees who he signed in 1967 when their manager was still Brian Epstein. The group, comprised of brothers, Barry, Robin and Maurice Gibb are Australian natives like Stigwood. They had worldwide success in the late Sixties and early Seventies until hitting a slump in 1973. Most of their hits during that first era were ballads of a very particular kind of sound. Last year's *Main Course*, however, was one of the surprise albums of 1975, not just because it was a new success for the Bee Gees, but because it brought the group into this new world of dance music and rendered them almost unrecognizable compared to what they had previously sounded like. The album put them back on the charts with two disco hits, "Jive Talkin'" and "Nights on Broadway." The group has gone in this direction partly on Stigwood's insistence, and they've got a new album coming out in September called *Children of the World* that follows in the same style as they hope to continue on the popularity of *Main Course*. With respect to the brief disappearance of the group on the pop charts, their new sound has been accompanied by their inclusion on Stigwood's newly founded RSO label. The Robert Stigwood Organization's record label was formed in 1973 at a time when all Stigwood associates were hitting career or personal lows, though clients Tim Rice and Andrew Lloyd Webber were hot off the Broadway hit *Jesus Christ Superstar*. Aside from the dip in popularity the Bee Gees were experiencing, Eric Clapton was strung out on junk, and the Stigwood Organization was barely surviving. This period, just a few short years ago, was the era of famous musicians becoming tax exiles and leaving the UK for France and America.

Stigwood, a closeted gay man at the age of 42 has his finger on the pulse of a new emerging cultural milieu. This is not an uncommon attribute among those he is most associated with...the dominating figures behind some of the world's biggest rock acts...managers...Svengalis whose visions all aspire to breaking barriers, finding and doing the next big thing and continually pushing the art forward...names like Larry Parnes, Brian Epstein, Kit Lambert, Simon Napier-Bell, Billy Gaff, Ken Pitt and Barry Krost...an interwoven community known notoriously as the gay mafia or velvet mafia. He's been to the discos in Paris and around Europe. He sees where the underground disco movement is going, and he sees the potential in translating it back to the public by way of Hollywood. On top of his entrepreneurial instincts is an understanding of how the marketing and merging of music and film is a viable coalescence. At the outset, he has an ambitious vision in mind with some sporadic groundwork being laid out in pieces and spread vastly enough for those around him to question and scratch their heads over. He has just purchased the rights to Nik Cohn's *New York* magazine article, "Tribal Rites of the New Saturday Night." Cohn has gotten multiple offers from Hollywood and the article is on the lips of people in the music, film and literary worlds. Cohn saw the emergence of a Fifties revival and his first book assessing that first generation of rock and roll, put him on the map.

But what are the Seventies going to look like?

What is the original art form that will define what writer Tom Wolfe would later refer to as the "me" decade?

Where is it happening?

Where do we look for it?

Where do we find it?

Cohn reporting from England is onto something happening and has an idea of some of the places he'll have to visit, even if he has to fabricate some of it. Moving from neighborhood to neighborhood and disco to disco, he is a self-professed explorer out of his depth, trying to learn the patterns, moves and the old/new tribal rites. He settles in on one close-knit group of friends who frequents one particular club.

This generation and its sensibilities are not all that difficult to understand within the harrowing circumstances that the decade has provided for it. The economy is for shit, and the sense of risk-taking and carefree experience sprawl that teenagers and those in their early twenties pursued during the 1960s have been replaced by the obedience of a structured life marked by a sense of responsibility. It centers around the workweek, the hourly wage, the stress of money and the need to save it. But the kids in Cohn's article are not the privileged kind in any capacity, though they are not yet adjusted to a world of adult concerns. The kids in "Tribal Rites" are working class Italian Americans in their late teens. They live at home with their parents, work jobs from Monday through Saturday and blow their paychecks on the latest disco fashions and Saturday nights at the 2001 Odyssey discotheque in Bay Ridge.

Cohn's focus is Vincent who works in a paint store and has bigger dreams than his friends who seemingly have no plan in life, not that Vincent really has much of one either. The dead-end world these kids live in is illuminated only by a few choice rituals...cruising around the borough looking for trouble, and they often find it, random sex and of course the local disco. Vincent and his friends speak in the latest trendy Bicentennial era language of lower to middle class whites...raw profanity sprinkled with racist, misogynist and homophobic slurs. It is a world of urban grittiness, territorial disputes, gang activity and retribution. Still, nothing stands in the way of Saturday night.

Nothing can touch them on Saturday night. None of the troubles and worries of their trivial lives matter on Saturday night. On Saturday night, they mark their territory by claiming their table in 2001 Odyssey and then their spot on the dance floor. Cohn refers to these kids as the Faces. Not Faces as in the rock band...but Faces as in the beautiful ones...the popular ones... the It crowd. When the Faces arrive, the place knows it. The people know it. And it's Vincent who is the Face amongst the Faces...the one everybody wants to see dance...the Star.

While Vincent's friends seem to be indifferent to the stagnant treadmill of day-to-day life and have no real ambitions for improvement, he yearns for something more. He's desperate and hungry to find something else that gives him the same thrill and rush that he gets from dancing. His dancing, however, is exceptional to the point where he clears the floor with just a few signature moves to indicate that he's taking over...and so everyone moves aside to stand and observe in astonishment. 2001 Odyssey is the only place where he feels like he has some say in his life...the only time when he feels like he has a purpose...a rare feeling of life having some meaning. It's Saturday night, and Saturday night is the metric that measures and marks the rhythm of the passage of time. The time in between...those wasted days of nothingness, of watching the clock and bearing it while they count and count and count and count and wait and wait and wait with butterflies of anticipation and that remaining glimmer of hope that still exists when you're that young... the promise of Saturday night...even on Monday night and Tuesday night when the dreadful feeling of *tomorrow's only Wednesday* and the knowledge that the grind is groveling in gut-wrenching lethargy...even then, there's that jolt of excitement in the pit of the stomach that happens when you suddenly remember something you're looking forward to that's getting closer and closer. By Thursday, cruise control has already set in and you're just coasting with the weekend creeping up. And so, they wait and wait and wait and wait as the creep creeps closer. It creeps and creeps and crawls and creeps. But then even Friday becomes too much to bear. If they had more money, they could afford to go out both nights, but who has money for that? And plus, Friday is still a work night in Vincent's world, and so Friday and Saturday afternoon need to pass. And they wait and wait and wait and wait...and the clock creeps laboriously, dragging and pulling them simultaneously under its own weight as time plays Tug of War with itself. Waiting and waiting and waiting and watching...and watching and waiting and waiting and watching seven sunrises in between and the passage of hours...those final hours until the clock says it's time to close. Vincent steps out onto the streets in the expressive exaltation of freedom...headed home to get dressed. The sun is setting over Brooklyn in a pinkish purplish blend of infinite possibility. It's Saturday night again.

As Cohn's article hits the streets in June 1976, it's well understood within the unwritten rules and laws that define and inform pop culture that Manhattan and Manhattan alone encompasses what is known as New York City. The other boroughs are viewed, at least in terms of significance...as a joke and in some cases, worse, as if they don't exist at all. In other words, New York City is Manhattan. The Bronx may boast the Yankees, but it's not Manhattan. Queens may house the Mets, some World's Fair ruins and Archie Bunker, but it certainly isn't Manhattan. Brooklyn may claim fourth largest city in America, but it sure isn't even so much as a speck on the ass of Manhattan's cultural imprint. And Staten Island may be a holding cell for ex-Brooklynites who really want to move to Jersey, and so we know that sure isn't Manhattan. Especially in the world of rock and roll in addition to the arts in general... museums, theater, film, publishing, fashion, food and any sports held in the Garden, this all prevails as gospel.

But another generation is growing up around Manhattan though...a generation of nobodies in the outer boroughs...the regular people.

Manhattan is still rooted in the 1960s and full of itself as the manmade island finds itself in the mid-1970s...dying out and sitting in its own shit as consequence of its own decadence. These kids of the outer boroughs are not intellectuals or even intelligent. They don't strive to "make it." They don't want to hang out with celebrities or even be celebrities. They don't attend art openings, nor do they go to wine and cheese parties. They don't frequent cafes or restaurants. Eating out is White Castle and coffee is the Maxwell House brewing from the percolator in their mother's kitchen with the white speckled Formica countertop and linoleum floor and round florescent tube light on the ceiling. These are the floors and lights that the regular people have in their kitchens. Nothing in their routines of life and excitement is dependent on the smug uppity culture of Manhattan. They're not even gutter trash or street punks. They're the product of parents who have lived blue-collar lives and tried to live within the family unit and within the confines and constraints of the boxed-in accepted narrative that many of Manhattan's subcultures rejected. Sure, the punks had similar upbringings...but these are kids who will inevitably become their parents within another decade. And yet, even in its narrow little world, its own subculture has formed outside of Manhattan, and you don't have to be rich and famous to enter, nor do you have to be gay. Still, the kids who inhabit Cohn's world consider themselves to be the elite in a world of nobodies. They have their spot and their table at 2001, and when they walk in, everybody knows them and everybody respects them and it's all part of the ritualistic tribal rites of Saturday night. Except for the occasional scuffle which is often more than just occasional. The cocksure braggadocio demeanor is often invitation to trouble in the everyday lives of streetwise youth, but divisions of class and race always play into the equation of these outer borough neighborhoods.

We see the word tribal used frequently in describing the layered dynamics of disco. Cohn is not the first writer to assign the adjective to the genre, though where he uses the word in association with racial and ethnic barriers among his violent and racist characters and their tribal rites, Vince Aletti of *Rolling Stone* three years earlier compared characteristics in sound to that of a tribal rallying cry...tribal in a completely different context...tribal in connection with the music...and it's the music that is the backbone of this entire subculture. What he was referring to was Manu Dibango's "Soul Makossa," a song that seeped into the public conscience by way of a DJ named Frankie Crocker who had gotten ahold of an undistributed record from an African import company in Brooklyn. The French pressing of the 45-rpm on the

Fiesta label was played by Crocker on WBLS. Crocker gets the credit with breaking "Soul Makossa," and it became a staple in the discos to the point where the groundbreaking mesh of African vocals and hypnotic grooves got Atlantic Records interested enough to purchase the U.S. rights and quickly had the song released as a single in 1973. While Barry White's Love Theme is largely credited as the first big disco hit, many argue that "Soul Makossa," not quite the smash "Love Theme" was, preceded it in terms of what the first disco song was, but that is all neither here nor there. Cohn translates the lives of these kids...these Faces and their stories through a literary piece of New Journalism that has movie written all over it.

In the case of Robert Stigwood, he secures the rights to Cohn's article with a clear vision that includes John Travolta. While Travolta is the It person now, Stigwood has had his eye on him since he was a young kid doing commercials in the earlier part of the decade. The actor had auditioned for Stigwood's production of *Jesus Christ Superstar* but wasn't right for the part. Stigwood then remembered Travolta when he saw him in the Broadway production of *Grease* in 1972. A few years pass and now the actor's superstardom looks promising for the Organization. Stigwood sees Travolta as a key component of a larger vision for RSO. It is already known by the summer of '76 that Travolta has been frequenting the Brooklyn dance clubs, though nobody really thinks too much about it aside from the usual gossip about stars being seen in local public places. By the end of summer, Travolta casually mentions to Dick Clark that he'll be dancing in a movie soon. What nobody knows yet is that Stigwood has also gotten the rights to the film version of *Grease* and is in the process of signing Travolta to a million-dollar contract for three films.

Kevin McCormick, a 23-year-old executive assistant for Robert Stigwood has just been put in charge of the development of film and television productions for RSO. Ever since Stigwood started the company, McCormick has been unsure what his role will be, as talks begin to solidify the film production of Cohn's "Tribal Rites" article. After living in Europe for a few years attending school, McCormick came back to New York to find a thriving disco scene. Though Stigwood has almost twenty years on him, he agrees with the RSO mogul...his youth and penchant for what's hot are a perfect gauge for the cultural zeitgeist and he knows the time is right for this kind of film.

John Travolta at 22 also has a sense that this is the right film at the right time, though that would only be from having seen the unfolding trend in the clubs himself. The purists who have been dancing for the better part of a decade in the underground black parties and gay bars swear this type of dance music has long peaked and is dying out. They already recognize some unfolding bastardization as whitey is now pulling all the punches to put his own stamp on it...the man...the machine...the capitalist pig at the top of Hollywood and at the top of fashion and at the top of the radio stations and TV networks and literary intelligentsia...the movers and shakers who are the real motherfuckers who dictate the culture who are all putting their claws and having their hand in the prize, and that's not to mention all those suburban white kids who resented their older brothers and sisters a few years ago for being space cadets for Ziggy Stardust who have all found their own niche in something inherently black and inherently homosexual, though none of them are sucking cock and even remain vocally and aggressively homophobic racists who John Travolta really doesn't come all that much in contact with. His character as one of the Saturday night Faces will no doubt wear his own bigotry on his sleeves and have it dripping out of his slimy mouth once that role is adapted into a script. But that's all in the hands of Kevin McCormick.

McCormick's first responsibility as per Stigwood is to go out and find a director. In Hollywood, he goes through agency after agency with Cohn's article...all to no avail. He's told they do films in Hollywood, not articles. There is one phone call of interest that he receives however, and he is quickly hooked up with John Avildsen, a low-key name in the industry who got his start as an assistant to Otto Preminger and Arthur Penn and is mostly associated with the low budget 1970 film, *Joe*. Avildsen at 40, has just wrapped up his new film, *Rocky*, slated for a November release. Stigwood and McCormick hire Avildsen after a private screening of *Rocky*, still in its final stages of post-production. The film was written by its lead actor, Sylvester Stallone, another up and coming artist taking big risks, though it is the studio taking the real risk by letting Stallone, a little-known face and name, play the lead role. Stallone's original screenplay is about a local Philadelphia boxer who is given a rare once in a lifetime shot at the heavy weight title against the world champion. It's an underdog story and America loves underdog stories. Avildsen is excited about it as is United Artists, though everyone involved is crossing their fingers.

In the meantime, Travolta bides his time, having finished up a short touring production of *Bus Stop* after having done *Boy in the Plastic Bubble*, which we now know will be shown on ABC in November. He does some magazine cover shoots and TV appearances but doesn't say much about the next project...only that he's got two films coming out in November and that he'll be "dancing in something" in 1977. The dancing is slowly moving in to share his time with everything else in his life, though his only focus in terms of hobbies or pastimes has been flying. Once his first big payments from *Welcome Back Kotter* came in, he deposited his first $5000 into the bank and then bought a single-engine Aircoupe for $2500. That's not happening though...at least not while he's trying to really make it in Hollywood. Nobody will insure any Hollywood project that has Travolta in it as long as he's flying his own airplanes. So, he keeps his plane grounded and usually as untouched as his Honda 350 or his 1955 T-Bird sitting in the garage of his 450 dollar a month high rise apartment in West Hollywood. He even owns a Mercedes 450 SL, but being shuffled around doing deals and interviews and checking in and out of hotels and limos and sitting in makeup chairs and being fitted in wardrobe departments and living the high-paced life of someone for whom it's happening to so quickly, it all becomes just another set of props and then you have to ask yourself...do these things really belong to me.

Travolta is already a major star in the sense of celebrity popularity, though he is not anywhere near the caliper performer he dreams of being. He wants to be this generation's Marlon Brando...another Robert DeNiro... Al Pacino. He just needs the roles. Maybe Stigwood will be his ticket. He knows *Grease* is coming up next summer and that he'd also be getting the starring role as Danny Zucko. He' s already played Kenickie on Broadway.

But this one might be bigger. Hell, it's *Grease. Grease* is huge on Broadway... it will be huge in Hollywood, and it will be the big one that Travolta needs. That's in one year though. He still has to do this little disco movie first.

THE FLAG ON THE BRIDGE

Unless you are crossing over from Staten Island into Brooklyn or vice versa over a three-day period in late June, chances are you will probably miss the flag on the Verrazzano Bridge. Most of the world ends up missing it and most people on the planet have no clue that it even happens. For decades, it remains a forgotten piece of New York City history...unless of course you actually remember it. In the summer of 1976, the largest flag in the world is an American flag...one of glorious red, white and blue...and it's going to hang on the longest suspension bridge in the world to mark America's two hundredth birthday. The plan is to unfurl and raise the enormous flag over the bridge the following week as the citywide celebrations are getting underway. On Friday, June 25, workmen gather 250 feet above the water for a test hoist. The world's largest flag is an enormous piece of nylon taffeta sailcloth stretching out longer than a football field. The double zigzag stitching of 200 denier material has been designed to handle winds of up to 30 miles per hour. This Friday sees rain and wind gusts of up to 25 mph and it's enough for the Triborough Bridge and Tunnel Authority which operates the bridge to cancel the test run. The hoisting of the flag is scheduled for the following Wednesday at 1 PM and whether the flag will still see a test run will remain to be seen in the next few days. In the meantime, the flag under heavy winds and sideways rain is tied to the trusses along one side of the Verrazano, this in itself a sight to behold.

The two visionaries behind the flag are Len Silverfine, a Brooklyn native, and Pierre Leduc, an advertising executive with offices in New York City and Montreal. Arm and Hammer Company has paid nearly $30,000 in manufacturing and other costs while the Triborough Authority has paid for the rigging crew on the bridge. The various components of the flag such as the stars measuring eleven feet from tip to tip, were made in different places, namely by Hood Sailmakers in Marblehead, Massachusetts and The Annin Flag Company in Verona, New Jersey.

The merger between the NBA and ABA comes right on the heels of the NBA championship, occurring a week and a half after the Boston Celtics win the finals against the Phoenix Suns...a series that saw one of the most memorable games in NBA history. Though game five didn't decide the series, it's being talked about as the single greatest game ever played...a brutal marathon consisting of triple overtime, Boston fans rushing the court prematurely with two seconds on the clock and a ref getting assaulted in the melee. Boston pulled it out anyway and won the title the next night.

In addition to the obvious factors already mentioned, a clear measure of the success of both leagues in relation to each other is the amount of money received by the winner and loser of the championship. The winning team of the ABA championship receives $95,000 whereas the NBA winner gets $250,000. The losing ABA team takes $75,000 while the NBA loser gets $185,000. In other words, it pays more to lose the NBA championship than to win the ABA championship. In the case of the ABA, the Nets are champions, having just beaten the Denver Nuggets in May. Winning doesn't go without its drama and mystery though. In Denver, someone took it upon themselves to steal the ABA championship trophy, forcing the league to present the Nets with a trophy they had already won in 1974. The 1976 model cost $900 and fortunately would not have to be replaced once it was returned to

ABA headquarters at 1700 Broadway. The package containing the trophy also had a return address with the name C.J. Flynn, 2619 Lark, Denver. Authorities in Denver confirmed there was no such person or location, though it was announced with amusement by Jim Bukata, the ABA's PR director, that the thief had to pay $7.80 postage to ship it back.

The merger between the two leagues happens after the merger was prevented for half a decade by the class action anti-trust lawsuit against the NBA and its 14 teams taken out by Oscar Robertson and the National Basketball Players Association in April 1970. Robertson, who represented the players union as president also represented his own team, the Cincinnati Royals. Also involved in the suit were 13 other player representatives from the other NBA teams with a focus on ending the increasingly unpopular reserve clause...that part of a contract that said a player was doomed to play and stay and go gray with one team...the team they were drafted by with no chance of playing elsewhere unless said player was traded to another team. The reserve clause bound a player to a team for his entire career and then for the rest of eternity. This was the case throughout professional sports. Though the players of Major League Baseball were slightly ahead of the NBA in veering toward any progress of officiality in free agency while the end result of what becomes known as the Oscar Robertson Rule clears the path to free agency in the NBA, Andy Messersmith became the first official free agent in baseball just weeks before the Robertson case came to an end early in the spring. Messersmith at 31 is already an established veteran, having pitched successfully for the 1974 Dodgers. He won a championship with them but held out on re-signing a contract after his team failed to meet his one request...that he not be traded. So, while he wished to remain a Dodger, the organization could not accommodate him, forcing his hand which held out...and so now Messersmith has signed with the Atlanta Braves. New owner Ted Turner has given Messersmith a handsome figure of one million dollars for three years but has assured the media that the pitcher will remain a Brave as long as he owns the team. While Messersmith is often highlighted as the first free agent, Jim "Catfish" Hunter is also a name that is eternally attached to the subject. Hunter, the central figure in the Oakland A's dynasty of the early 1970s...the team that went to three consecutive World Series and won two of them...the ace pitcher on a team consisting of an intimidating handful of aces. After a disagreement with A's owner, Charles Finley over his contract, Hunter ended up signing with the Yankees near the end of 1974 after the dispute went before an arbitrator during the last dying days of baseball under the reserve clause. Catfish signed for 3.5 million dollars. Not every owner is happy about the on-coming free agent marketplace. Most aren't. While it largely benefits the player, it seems to be designed for the extremely wealthy who are willing to invest millions of dollars to secure coveted high-priced players. It is designed for men like George Steinbrenner.

The Yankees weren't always perceived as the team that buys the post-season, though such beliefs weren't born at the outset of the Steinbrenner era. The overall bigness of the New York Yankees and the legend of forty years of dynasty that began in the 1920s and finally ended during the 1960s, has lent itself not so favorably to the idea that it was always money behind the team's success. Yes, it's true Babe Ruth was purchased. Though people tend to forget that the majority of Yankees legends throughout their history prior to 1976 were homegrown prospects...Lou Gehrig, Joe DiMaggio, Mickey Mantle, Phil Rizutto, Yogi Berra, Lefty Gomez, Whitey Ford, Tony Lazzeri, Joe Gordon, Bill Dickey...Sure lots of money was invested in the team...but it was in infrastructure...the elements that build a team from the ground up... farm clubs and quality scouts that could spot talent. But as we digress here, it is important to pick up on the larger point that the lawsuit years only delayed the basketball merger, which was inevitable, though Robertson won the case, thus freeing players from the reserve clause after a specific amount of time before free agency. Pending the outcome and resolution of the anti-trust issues, the injunction prevented a merger from happening. With the case recently ending in April, the NBA, now 18 teams deep, was able to proceed with the much-anticipated merger that came right on time for the dead-in-the-water ABA.

Just behind Yankee Stadium runs the Major Deegan Expressway which passes below the Macombs Dam Bridge. The bridge, connecting the Bronx with Manhattan, passes over the Harlem River and empties out onto One Hundred Fifty-fifth Street where at the intersection with Frederick Douglass Boulevard just to the north is Holcombe Rucker Park. Named after Holcombe Rucker, a father figure to countless youth all over Harlem, the park is a monument to a giant in the community who mentored young basketball players through tournaments, fostering the importance of education in their lives, ultimately helping many of them get scholarships for college. Rucker died at the age of 38 in 1965, and since then, the pro-am tournaments and the crowd of notable players who have emerged from the park's court over the years have ascended into legendary, almost mythic status...guys like Tiny Archibald, Ollie Taylor, and most recently Dr. J himself, Julius Erving. Julius and his slam dunk alone had this park and its surrounding vicinity packed with people in places where people don't belong...in the trees, hanging off the 155th Street overpass, and students sitting and standing on the roof and out the window ledges of their nearby classrooms.

If you're a basketball player or even just a fan, the Rucker is sacred ground.

The Rucker is one of two parks of significance in the life of Julius Erving, the first being Campbell Park from which he lived right across the street in Hempstead, Long Island during his early years of childhood...a public housing apartment building called Parkside Gardens. Born in Meadowlark Hospital on February 22, 1950, Julius Winfield Erving lived with his mother Callie, older sister Freda, and younger brother Marky. The three kids shared a bedroom as Callie worked to support her family. Julius's parents divorced when he was three years old and Callie was left a single mom raising three kids. She had a teaching degree from Batesburg, South Carolina that was invalid in New York, so she supported the family cooking and cleaning for another family. Young Julius spent a lot of very early childhood looking out his bedroom window down at Campbell Park with Marky, watching the basketball players that occupied the court daily, right up until the day he walked into the park himself and his life in basketball began. Noticeably tall as a teenager, he had already been nicknamed Dr. J through his reputation in total command of the ball at Roosevelt High School. The tragic untimely death of Marky at the age of 16 during Julius's freshman year of college serves as a turning point...one that would transform a timid and introverted teenager into a fearless and driven powerhouse Years later, players and spectators on and around the Rucker court would refer to Julius as Black Moses. After stints in the NCAA playing for the University of Massachusetts, a trip to Munich playing for Team U.S.A. in the Olympics and his first two professional seasons with the ABA Virginia Squires, that kid, now at 6 foot 7 with his graceful ability to jump unusually high and simultaneously handle and control the ball in the air is now considered an alien...something superhuman and as many sports journalists say, the coming of a new age.

It is rather fitting that Julius in 1973 ended up playing at Nassau Coliseum not very far at all from Campbell Park where his entire basketball story began in Hempstead under the shadow of the big blue water tank. It's the playground that still exists in Julius, and for much of the league for that matter. And compared to the conventional NBA, the upstart ABA had always been that playground version of basketball that the NBA has really known nothing about. There are things Erving does that nobody has seen before, and it's become part of the universal charm...how he can move like a guard, a forward and a center with equal precision. And now with the merger, the Knicks know he's coming...and the Knicks don't have him, the Nets do. This little team that plays all the way out on the Island that calls itself New York and plays for this little ABA league and will now be part of the NBA and it's no longer the Knicks who will get all the attention, it's the Nets. The Nets will be New York's premier team because they've got the Doctor, and the Doctor is now by default the greatest player in the NBA. In fact, the Doctor is probably the greatest player to ever play the game. They can't ignore those moves...those feats of superhuman abilities that not many in the game of basketball have matched. And the Nets are being penalized for it by having to pay the entrance fee, not into the NBA, but into New York to exist as a team...the extortion if you will, and why the NBA couldn't come up with a reasonable welcome into the league for the Nets is beyond human understanding.

Knicks Shmicks.

Anything Earl Monroe can do, Julius Erving can do better, and he can do it in the air. The Doctor seems to have been made for the air! Oh, the things he does in the air! Nobody so seamlessly and nonchalantly moves a ball from the right hand to the left the way the Doctor does it in midair... that midair prowess and power of the mystic that Julius Erving possesses when he's flying more than fifteen feet from the basket out behind the foul line and straight to the net to dump and dunk and slam that ball down like the hammer of Thor crashing down to fuck up your day. But aside from the primal aspect, there's also the elegant finesse of Erving...the art of his very demeanor on the court bordering on poetry and performance art. Erving is a language unto himself. And now, finally, as a New York Net in their red, white and blue uniforms, so fitting in this Bicentennial year, Julius Erving, already the biggest name in basketball, will have his premier season in the NBA. Make no mistake...the summer ahead will be one of sheer excitement and anticipation for Nets fans.

While basketball is merging, Gabe Paul, the man behind the Yankees pitching makeover flies into Chicago when he hears the Baltimore Orioles are in town to play the White Sox. He also knows A's owner Charles Oscar Finley operates out of his insurance company in the Windy City and the occasion becomes an opportunity to kill two birds with the same airplane ticket. Two months after trading two of his stars, Reggie Jackson and Ken Holtzman to the Orioles, Finley begins auctioning off more stars from his Oakland A's dynasty. Paul is instinctive and tries never to miss the possibility of business. He positions himself in the key places as soon as he catches word where team owners are going to be...and so with no hotel reservations or even a toothbrush, he takes off to Chicago on behalf of the New York Yankees and returns 36 hours later with Holtzman, Vida Blue, Doyle Alexander, Grant

Jackson and Elrod Hendricks on his team. The Red Sox also scored famously by obtaining Joe Rudi and Rollie Fingers. The biggest sales in baseball history have just taken place. The question over Finley's sale of his three biggest players for a total of 3.5 million dollars with no players in exchange arises with speculation that he's about to sell the A's. He meets such speculation with denial of any intention to sell his American League franchise. Not many people are taking him at his word though. Trading Jackson and Holtzman for Don Baylor and Mike Torrez was one thing...a trade is a trade...value lost, value gained. The loss of Vida Blue, Rollie Fingers and Joe Rudi, however, amounts to nothing more than a financial sale where the team's owner makes some money and the team itself gains nothing. Ill health has doctors on record as having advised Finley to get out of sports altogether. In recent years he has sold his hockey team and basketball team. There is also a divorce settlement in the picture as well as rumors of problems related to back taxes. There's so much speculation going on with this guy that aside from the specifics of who got who in this deal, the rest is merely gossip...albeit local gossip a little more conducive to headlines in Oakland and the Bay area as opposed to New York City. But if Charlie O is selling, George Steinbrenner is buying...and so Gabe Paul comes back to New York with a much richer pitching staff. Baseball Commissioner, Bowie Kuhn has a hearing on the controversial sale that now seems to have rocked the entire sports world. He orders the players involved to stay in place until he investigates the matters at hand. The rest of the league is concerned.

What is going *on* here? Why is Finley *doing* this? How is he even *allowed* to do this? All this talent being diverted to two of the biggest powerhouse teams in the American League. How is any of this *fair*? *Should* it be fair? Was it *ever* fair? What is fair *anyway*? This Finley can just auction off his team at *will*? And this Steinbrenner guy is allowed to *buy* people just because he *can*? Who the fuck *does* that? And what about all these other players who will suddenly be up for free agency now that free agency is going to be a *thing* in baseball? What about *that*???????? Does anybody wanna talk about *thaaaaat*????

This will ruin the *leeeeague!*

"I only regret that I didn't sell more of them," Finley says at the Commissioner's 90-minute hearing. "I hope to wake the stupid owners to the facts of reality."

Kuhn perhaps knows the inevitable and sees the writing on the wall though on the surface he appears to be acting in the best interest of the league. It is clear though...there is a money revolution going on in major league baseball and it's going to be a case of survival of the fittest where the ugliest elements of American capitalism will prevail and inform the game for the remainder of the century and into the next. The baseball world is momentarily beside itself.

The New York press, though mixed, marvels on what Steinbrenner and Paul have done, assembling a collection the way a museum might acquire paintings, and in several bold moves have amassed an all-star team, thus doing what most owners refuse to do and that's spending money on a winning team. Most will still argue that winning should be built on raising a farm club and selecting and developing talent. The Mets have often taken this approach and thus have paid the price in other more profound ways, such as mediocrity at best when such talent is few and far between. This is obviously not the first and only time we've seen players bought and sold. It's certainly been done before, though on much smaller scales and degrees of shock value...most notably, as previously mentioned, when the Yankees purchased Babe Ruth from the Boston Red Sox for $100,000 in 1920...though even that is relative.

With the Yankees already securely in first place in June 1976, it seems this will guarantee the post-season. Still, as good as the Yankees are and can still become, there is also criticism that they should have focused more on a shortstop like the A's unsigned Bert Campaneris. Though Fred Stanley has been around and still occasionally having his moments, he is not the future. The Yankees need a shortstop.

What is certain within the midst of the circumstances surrounding these A's deals with the Yankees and Red Sox is that Bowie Kuhn has the final say, and Bowie Kuhn orders Vida Blue, Rollie Fingers and Joe Rudi back to Oakland in the interest of baseball. The 3.5-million-dollar sales are cancelled.

Regarding the *best interest of baseball* mumbo jumbo, Kuhn as Commissioner reserved the right to investigate anything he sees as a threat to the best interest of baseball. Finley has done his homework however, and he sees it this way: When it comes to violating the best interest of baseball, there are penalties imposed on the offending party including something as minute as a reprimand to an organization's exclusion from a joint meeting to a fine of up to $5000. Kuhn's ruling does not include penalties on Finley other than the voiding of the sales. Kuhn doesn't see any reason for further penalty. Finley argues that no additional penalties eliminate him from the idea that his sales hurt the best interest of baseball, and so Kuhn, who he believes has overstepped his authority, will either have to step aside and get out of the way of these transactions or he'll need to hit Finley with some penalties. Or at the very least, for the love of Christ stop with the *best interest of baseball* bullshit. A judge will investigate the matter. In the meantime, Charles Finley, on a mission of self-sabotage is about to take his annual first place dynasty and willingly dismantle it into a last place team within a period of weeks. Within a few swift transactions, the Oakland A's will go from being the most feared and revered club in baseball (equaled only by the Cincinnati Reds) to one of the worst. While Finley dumps his team player by player, Steinbrenner's long-range plan is dominance. Rebuilding has required not only the key components on the field, but someone at the helm with as much passion and will to win as the boss himself.

When Billy Martin, a Berkeley, California native, came back to New York to manage the Yankees, he did it reluctantly...not particularly thrilled about working under the clutches of Steinbrenner. The contract offered could have deterred a man of Martin's hothead temperament and he could have easily rejected it. It was the same amount as he was given in Texas where he was fired. Martin spent a couple of years each managing the Rangers, Detroit Tigers and the Minnesota Twins. In New York, there were additional clauses in his contract that were designed specifically for him...things like no criticizing the front office or that he could be fired without pay if a situation arose where he wasn't always promptly available to management. Having been a Yankee from 1950-1957 with five world championships, he knew what the legacy meant, and he didn't take it lightly. He believed like Steinbrenner that he was the man for the job, and despite his reluctance, he really wanted the job... though he did play hard to get, sparring hesitantly with Steinbrenner who himself was playing chess in a *my offer is right now and it may not be here tomorrow* stance in order to get Martin on board. He made it clear that the offer was a one-time, one-shot deal. It would not come again. The Yankee owner knew Martin's reputation, so he spelled out the terms...take it or leave it.

Steinbrenner's goal is to restore the Yankees to their past glory. From 1923-1962 the franchise won 20 world championships, with the last one being 14 years ago. He envisions a future of World Series wins and another generation of dynastic rule in baseball. Coming in from Ohio...coming in as an outsider to own this team, it's a privilege to put on the pinstripes and it's his commitment to New York...to tradition...to the past...to those who came before and enshrined the Yankees into permanence and eternal legend...it is his obligation to bring the World Championship to his new city. The idea of saving money and developing a grassroots team doesn't appeal to him. He wants it all and he wants it now. So, with the restoration of past traditions, has to come some familiar faces. Enter Martin in the summer of '75. Coinciding is a simple twist of fate in Flushing, Queens where the Mets play. It seems the Mets had dismissed Yogi Berra from his managerial duties just four days after Martin was hired by the Yankees. That was one year ago. Long story short...the Yankees eyed Berra, the Yankees talked to Berra and the Yankees got Berra. There's a running joke in baseball that managers are merely ex-players whose coaching staff is usually made up of old drinking buddies, and that's precisely what Martin has in mind with Steinbrenner's blessing.

As a player, Martin was a fighter, often combative and aggressive...the type who would deliberately slide hard into a base to break up a double play and fuck up his opponent in the process. And this is how he is going to manage his team. He is exemplary of that philosophy that a manager's style will mirror the way he played the game. New York press along with fans will refer to it as Billyball.

Martin has never been a content person. He's prone to depression, anxiety, insomnia and hypertension. He goes long stretches without eating, mostly because his stomach is usually upset. When he does eat, he often doesn't hold it down. He has a steady diet of sleeping pills and scotch. His inability to cope with the circus of the public eye comes from his time in the major leagues...both as a player and as a manager. Steinbrenner knows his reputation. Guys who know him and been around him know his insecurities. Yankee announcer and ex-player Phil Rizutto used to play and room with Martin, and he knows his explosive temper. All who know him know that Billy's worst enemy is Billy. He's a devoted practicing Catholic who's been seen praying in his office. But even the Bible sometimes can't help him come to grips with his hostile violent temper...especially on the field, where throwing punches is a common thing. Turn the other cheek, the teachings say? Really? The Bible and God obviously don't know shit about baseball.

Although intense, Martin is fearful and paranoid...always afraid he's going to lose it all. There's always someone more powerful, someone younger, someone better who's going to come and take it from him. Maybe he got lucky and didn't have to suffer for long in his firing from the Rangers, as Steinbrenner hired him quickly after that, kind of like a rebound relationship. But this is the Yankees, and this is where it's all at stake.

In the pre-Martin nowhere land that saw the Yankees ousted from their home turf during the stadium renovations, the displaced team was subletting Shea Stadium for a few seasons. Bill Virdon was their manager then. Bill Virdon was a nice guy but didn't know much about pitching and apparently had no problem admitting it. His use or misuse of ace reliever Sparky Lyle was testament to this. Lyle had a few bad outings early in the '75 season, so Virdon left him sitting around not utilizing the reliever very effectively. This didn't work very well psychologically for Lyle because every ten days or so, he'd reappear on the mound only to have his ass beat. Virdon had come from the Pittsburgh Pirates. The Pirates were known for power...guys like

Roberto Clementi, Willie Stargel, Al Oliver. The Yankees didn't have power hitters, but Virdon managed as if they did. He wasn't a guy who wanted his hitters to bunt...no hit and runs and no moving the runners. Small ball wasn't his game, and he treated the Yankees as if he were surrounded by home run hitters. Players like Chris Chambliss and team captain Thurmon Munson had the potential to hit homeruns here and there, but they were scattered and few and far between up until 1976. The only batter who could hit over 20 homeruns in a season was third baseman, Graig Nettles. Nettles had come to the Yankees by way of a curious and suspect trade with the Cleveland Indians late in 1972...just weeks before Steinbrenner officially purchased the team. Why was this curious and suspect? It was curious and suspect because it didn't make any sense. The Yankees got a steal...Cleveland's most powerful hitter for four unknown prospects which quickly proved a bad deal for the Indians. It didn't make any sense, although Cleveland's general manager told the press that it was the right deal after 11 clubs came at him for Nettles and he rejected them all. Within a few weeks though, it would all make sense. It would make sense especially when we consider that Cleveland's general manager was Gabe Paul who would also arrive in New York with Steinbrenner to run the Yankees.

Then it made perfect sense.

So, while the Yankees played the *give up tomorrow for today* angle on the trade while eliminating their youth program in favor of older stars, Paul was seemingly already building a Yankee roster for Steinbrenner while still being paid by the Indians. In fact, there was no indication whatsoever...not on his team, not by the Cleveland press...nowhere that remotely suggested that Paul would be working for Steinbrenner and the New York Yankees within six weeks. This is the beginning of accusations of impropriety surrounding the Steinbrenner-owned Yankees where they become by a large margin the most hated team in baseball...perhaps the most despised in all of sports over the coming decades when they repeatedly exhibit a modus operandi of sending away prospects and/or spending unheard-of sums of money to purchase the best players in the league.

Steinbrenner often used the occasion of Old Timers Day as an opportunity to make a major announcement and shock the crowd in the process. This was the case at Shea Stadium on August 1, 1975, when Billy Martin trotted onto the field...announced not only as a legendary piece of the past... but as the new Yankees manager. He couldn't help the '75 Yankees much more than Virdon could during the short remainder of the season, but he seemed certain of 1976 and expressed that he was looking forward to getting this team for a full season...one in which he guaranteed a post-season.

In the off season, Gabe Paul traded Bobby Bonds to the California Angels for pitcher, Ed Figueroa and centerfielder Mickey Rivers. Figueroa is a native of Puerto Rico who performed remarkably well for the Angels, winning 16 games in his second season in the majors. Rivers is the fastest runner in baseball who led the league in stolen bases. Paul also sent George "Doc" Medich to the Pirates and got three players out of the deal...Willie Randolph, a rookie second baseman, Ken Brett, and Doc Ellis

Aside from the hostile incidents of unruly behavior by fans in Yankee Stadium, the season is a smooth drift toward the playoffs. Everything seems to be falling into place regarding Martin's promise of the pennant to George. Steinbrenner and Paul came in at the beginning of 1973 with some bold and controversial moves in the few years since, and now it's as if it were all in the stars all along...or in the cards...or in their plans...whatever prophesied predicament of fate or prediction...it all seemed to make sense by the summer of '76...transform the team...secure the ingredients...trade some players... buy some players...renovate the stadium to a shining gleam and present it all in a revamped package in the spring of the Bicentennial year. Now, in the inaugural season of the newly refurbished stadium, the Yankees dominate the American League East in a way they haven't in years. They dominate against a backdrop of dissolution in human behavior, a decaying infrastructure in the surrounding environment outside the stadium walls, and an overall decline in morale as a city and a country push their way toward a massive birthday party when the state of the nation at best is drained and demoralized. Even President Ford acknowledged in his State of the Union Address... the "state of the union is not good."

Yankee Stadium is indeed a sparkling jewel in a sea of shit...aerial views of the newly redone ballpark make it stand out in its surroundings of urban decay and abandonment, much like a single tiny Band-Aid attempting to cover multiple stab wounds. It was a project that was protested when first announced in the early part of the decade. Season ticket holders of the Yankees and football Giants organized together once it was announced that the Yanks would spend their 1974 and 75 seasons in Queens and the Giants would spend at least one season there...and when it was all over, the Yankees would move back in the spring of '76, while the Giants would move to New Jersey to play in their newly-built home in the middle of a swamp. The Meadowlands Sports Complex is a brand-new facility set to open in September. Owned by the New Jersey Sports and Exposition Authority, the space was approved and passed by the New Jersey legislature in 1971 with ground broken in 1972 on a track for horseracing and the crowning achievement of New Jersey sports venues...Giants Stadium, set to open just a few weeks after the racetrack, and it's about damned time! The New York Mets and Jets have been sharing their home turf with the Yankees and Giants, and they want it back! But the opening of the Meadowlands has already lead to a Pandora's Box of sorts... prompting Leon Hess, owner of the Jets to express an interest in taking his football team to New Jersey when the Mets organization becomes problematic in sharing Shea Stadium during the months when baseball and football are both played, leading to scheduling conflicts that ask the Jets to play on the road until the baseball season is finished. The bureaucratic red tape and politics behind the creation of the Meadowlands is enough to fill a book of its own, and it no doubt plays a major role in 1976 being the last summer for concerts at Jersey City's Roosevelt Stadium, where a non-related murder becomes the scapegoat for ending rock shows that would seamlessly and conveniently transition to Giants Stadium, which just happens to open weeks after the last Roosevelt Stadium concert.

But Yankee Stadium...

Yankee Stadium is a different story all the way around. Yankee Stadium is a treasured piece of architectural history that was just given the love of millions of dollars to update, upgrade and renew the Yankee tradition for a new era...though the 300,000 dollars set aside for community redevelopment was scrapped of its original intention and used for the Yankees team. What remains of the project gets left undone and the neighborhood remains reminiscent of a war zone, seen specifically around the nearby Grand Concourse. The Grand Concourse hotel...once a majestic building is now boarded up after being run for a while as a welfare hotel. The Grand Concourse itself has gone to shit with gangs, homeless, drugs, crime and arson. The ongoing fires around here have come to define the Bronx for the rest of America. Besides the obvious white flight, the fires being set deliberately have assured a high vacancy rate as entire neighborhoods are devalued as they burn. As a landlord in the South Bronx, it pays more to torch your building to collect on the loss and blame it on the tenants who the media and police refer to as welfare arsonists. The South Bronx has seen ten square blocks burned each year with 5000 housing units lost to arson. Over 1200 buildings have been burned or abandoned in the immediate area surrounding the stadium. Empty lots with weeds have grown chest-high...buildings are now empty skeletal shells. Entire stretches resemble Dresden in the aftermath of the Second World War. This is the home of the New York Yankees where their newly refurbished stadium has become notorious as a dangerous place to be. New Yorkers who have learned to navigate the experience are perhaps more streetwise and vigilant, but those from the outer suburbs, who God forbid have to drive to Yankee Stadium dread it and very often fear it. If you are lucky, the worst that will happen on most days or nights is your inevitable run-in with the squeegee men...guys who are out there trying to earn some money with an honest effort...but much to the chagrin of many drivers, the squeegee men don't ask if you would like your car cleaned. If you get the red light, you've barely got your car at a complete stop when before you know it your windshield is engulfed in a torrent of soapy water. It's one of those streets off the Major Deegan exit where the traffic has slowed to a ride-the-brake creep-along and fearful white people reach to their side to lock their door and roll up their window....because God forbid they may hit that light...and if they get that light, some black dude might ask them for money...or demand their money...or pull a gun on them...or...

SPLOOOSSSSHHHH

...like a back-of-the-hand slap upside the head but only it's your windshield and not your head. Still, it stuns you...the soap...suds and suds of white bubbly foamy soap and then the squeegees hitting the glass from both sides of the car. You can smell the soap...it's quite pleasant though you can't enjoy it because the stench of Squeegee Man's armpits reaching over the frame of the driver's side door is wafting into your car like trailing smoke as he reaches over the top to catch the uppermost edges of the glass. He's bare-chested with a shiny tan moistened by trailing beads of sweat that trickle down his side and into the folds of his love handles that droop over his shredded denim cutoff shorts with one hairy testicle hanging out the side. His legs are soaked and caked with wet matted down hair from constant contact with the side panels of car after car that he leans into while stretching across windshield after foamy windshield...his testicle peeking out shamelessly...bulging tightly as if it's going to burst. How can he work like this? Doesn't he feel pain? Does he even know it's there for all to see? Or must he not have any shame, opting with full knowledge to let his ball fall out like that?

The red light is a long one. Coming off the Major Deegan Expressway into the Bronx on game day should teach everyone a valuable lesson in work ethics.

Built in 1923, Yankee Stadium is as Howard Cosell suggests, the most renowned arena in the world, except for the Coliseum in Rome. The ballpark seems wider now, with the many support poles that once stood between each seating section now eliminated, giving fans an unobstructed view no matter where they sit. Those poles often blocked people's views especially if you got stuck sitting behind one. The dark blue seats have been replaced by a lighter and much cleaner shade of blue. With the trademark white façade that once adorned the top of the upper deck also removed, there is nothing to draw the eye upwards anymore thus putting the focus on the line of the stadium and its dominating sea of blue. The contour of the bleachers, now unrecognizable, has been radically re-shaped to hug the new outfield dimensions. The bleachers section is now the most unique and characteristic part of Yankee Stadium, and where they once curved around the outfield, the short porch of the right field stands now force an asymmetrical layout for the bleachers to seemingly face the third base line. New modern electric scoreboards rest above the bleachers, with a retained section of the famous white facade transplanted above the scoreboards. This minimal portion of the facade that once wrapped around the entire upper level now exists as a majestic crown...a subtle yet powerful reminder of the past and the overall magnanimity of the New York Yankees. The less-is-more approach to aesthetics provides an overall balanced look that the original stadium did not have. Any new additions as opposed to alterations only happen where they count. The new Monument Park for example, serves a convenient purpose, taking the monstrous monolithic plaques that existed more as obstacles to players in the Death Valley hinterland of the outfield, and moving them behind the fences where they're given a much more dignified location.

The *placing an advertisement in every fucking empty inch of space* that we will see in twenty-first century sports is not even a conceived idea in 1976, so the stadium is not plastered with commercial billboards other than the three that stay for years...Manufacturers Hanover, Marlboro cigarettes and French's mustard. Aside from Brut by Faberge and the Canon AE-1, which will become the "official camera" of the Yankees in another few years, these are the sole participating advertisers.

The flags above the façade top off the crowing ornaments on the renovation each flag representing one of the 24 teams of Major League Baseball and their respective logos the Yankees, perhaps the most American at least in design and the only team to feature the stars and stripes of the American flag...not at all lost on the patriotic sentiment of the Bicentennial spirit engulfing the country. American flags are everywhere this summer...so the Yankees, in as far as their logo, do not need to hop on that trend.

At 10:30 on Monday morning, June 28, the flag on the Verrazzano Bridge is carefully lowered from where it has been tied over the weekend. Winds are only six miles per hour, and it looks as if the test hoist can proceed. That's until the winds increase to 12 and then 16 miles an hour...after which, the flag becomes unrestrained and no match for the men who try to contain it. The flag, amidst the struggle of human hands, pins itself to the Verrazano's steel framework. Wind gusts hitting it on the Brooklyn side cause the horizontal stitching on the already-frayed ends to separate. Within minutes the red and white stripes on the flag are shredded and flapping individually and uncontrollably over the Narrows. The Eastbound side of the bridge is then closed to traffic for the next eight hours while the flag, completely wrecked, is carefully captured, collected and pulled back in, and then off the bridge. Not many pictures of the flag in place on the bridge exist. There are a few floating around that can be found on the Internet, but not many. The gist of this nearly forgotten piece of New York City history is that the biggest flag in the world suddenly appeared one day on the Verrazzano Bridge and only stayed there for three days. Anyone riding along 278 or the Belt Parkway on those days surely caught a glimpse of it during this very specific period of time...one weekend comprising the various stages of the flag's short and stunted life.

4

SPIRIT OF '76

Flags aren't just on the bridge...flags are everywhere. The latest Kiss poster is lovingly known as Sprit of '76 and was shot by Barry Levine. It showcases the group around the Bicentennial theme...Paul, Gene, Peter and Ace banded together as if wearily but proudly marching onward in this Continental Army-like scene with a 13-star Colonial American flag in the background and Peter in a bloody headdress, rapping on a snare drum. We can almost hear fifes and "Yankee Doodle" when we look at this photo, which will also become a tour advertisement for the summer. This will be one of five posters (Mega Alive poster, Chopper, Spirit of '76, Empire State Building, live Destroyer stage shot) commonly seen in shopping malls and Korvettes and Two Guys stores in the Bicentennial era, adding to the lure and mystique of Kiss, as suburban kids begin encountering their images more and more, eventually buying the albums and getting hooked. They learn the words to the songs, even if the youngsters have little clue what those words even mean. They learn the makeup designs and costumes. They learn the names of the band members and who plays and sings what. Kissteria is just on the horizon.

Paul Stanley, the main lead vocalist and rhythm guitarist, exhibits a single black star covering his right eye while white paint covers the rest of his face otherwise adorned by nothing else but red lipstick. His attire is head-to-toe black, dressed in an all-over leotard embellished with sporadic trails and bursts of rhinestones. A wide-open front reveals a naked torso...something that has become the consistent characteristic of Paul's costumes, always showcasing the hair on his unmistakable chest. Paul stomps and prances in knee-high boots and seven-inch heels. He poses and puckers his lips for cameras, androgenous mannerisms embodying his very presence and being.

There are no formal names to the Kiss characters, though Paul has recently become described as the "lover."

Everything about Paul Stanley screams behold, I'm a star!

Everything about bass player Gene Simmons is sinister. In fact, he described himself as *evil incarnate* on the *Mike Douglas Show* a few years back. If anything, Gene is known as the demon, or as *Creem* journalist Robert Duncan will refer to him...the bat lizard. Surveying his head-to-toe appearance, it is Gene's face that stands out above everything, and when it comes down to all the Kiss faces, it is perhaps the most striking of the four. His long frizzy hair is pulled back into a tail that rests several inches above his head revealing a forehead divided by a black V-shaped spike that separates two symmetrical curvilinear designs over his eyes. These eye patterns have developed in the two years since Kiss first appeared on the scene, as Gene has fine-tuned them over the course of four albums and four costume evolutions (one for each album), perfecting his look going into the summer of 1976. His outfit, like the rest of the band, consists of an underlying tight black stretchy material of a spandex nature, though that material is covered by an armor-plated jacket-like addition that covers his shoulders, arms and chest. Intimidating spikes protrude from the armor coming off his arms. A studded belt and codpiece is prominent in drawing attention to the crotch area...a glaring feature of both his and Paul's costumes... although Paul doesn't wear a codpiece but rather uses all pattern streams on his leotard to converge in the same crotch area in a sprawling explosion of rhinestones, turning it into the focal point of his outfit. The bottom of Gene's outfit is completed by bat wings and knee-high boots made up of scales and menacing gargoyles for feet.

While all members of Kiss possess a memorable presentation, the visuals of Gene Simmons exceed those of his band mates for three additional elements that distinguish his very existence in the rock and roll world. The first reason is a long tongue that quite often protrudes from his black-lipped mouth...shaking, stretching, curling and wiggling in reptilian motion. The second is the fire. One of Gene's signature stage rituals is to breathe fire at the conclusion of their song, "Firehouse," a Paul Stanley composition off their debut album. The third is the one that is quickly becoming the talk of the outside world that has not yet seen or heard Kiss. Yet, word of mouth has it that there's this band out there with a guy who spits blood onstage. Nobody has really seen it yet, except for those who have seen it. But pictures exist...pictures of this demonic bat lizard vampire creature of some sort with a bass guitar...leering down in maniacal frenzy over his audience...his face and tongue soaked in blood while it all drips and waterfalls out of his mouth...and supposedly into the crowd. The Kiss mythology has begun by the summer of '76. Kids of all ages are discussing and arguing these myths. The youngest ones haven't seen the band live and most of the oldest ones haven't either. Most of the hearsay at this point is just that. Does he really spit blood into the audience? Is that his real tongue? There's talk that it's really a cow's tongue that's been grafted on. All kinds of talk and speculation going on now in the suburbs about this band, Kiss.

Who *are* they?

What are they?

Peter Criss is the drummer. His face paint design is that of a cat, though the photographer who directed the band's photo session for the first album misunderstood the look and intention of Kiss and had Peter painted up as a clown. Peter quickly modified his makeup once the misleading album cover was unleashed on the world. The cat design is now unquestionable. His cat suit outfit is not unlike Paul's...an open-chest, tight black full-body leotard with very specific patterns of diamonds and rhinestones. The black and silver platform boots are also similar to Paul's look. With his image being the most identifiable in terms of character, Peter, to those who don't know his name yet, has become known simply as "the cat." Peter is the one with the raspy voice. We hear him often in raucous rock and roll screaming mode in the background of "Nothin' to Lose" as well as unmistakable leads like "Strange Ways" and "Black Diamond." The latter has become their epic showstopper.

Epic not in the traditional sense of length (it is roughly only five and a half minutes long), but in the bombastic climax sense. "Black Diamond" is the peak of a Kiss concert when Peter's drum riser extends upward to an additional 15 feet above stage level...something unseen in rock and roll theatrics, and part of the word-of-mouth surrounding Kiss. There are people who suggest that the drums go up 30 feet in the air, but that is merely part of the Kiss lore. With the Kiss members standing close to seven feet tall in their boots, one member could stand on the shoulders of another member and almost reach the top of the drum riser while it's extended. This never happens and seems quite foolish, but it's an easy way to get an accurate depiction on the height of the drum riser during the final seconds of "Black Diamond." The drums go up on a scissor lift that's hidden by a tapestry that drops down the length of the entire riser. Woven into the obscuring cloth material is a sparkling emblazoned cat. On *Destroyer*, Peter has a new song called "Beth"...an orchestrated piano ballad so far removed from the high-energy hard rock that it has become part of the talk among purists who are not so enthusiastic about the new album, suggesting *Destroyer*'s penchant toward slower songs, hokey choruses and over-production is a sellout.

Ace Frehley (pronounced Fray-lee), the fourth member of Kiss and the last to join, has some sort of outer space theme going on. At first, he appears to be obsessed with the lightning bolt, but by his third costume in 1975, it is clear that his outfit serves as a model of the universe, garnished with rhinestones forming little galaxies, stars, constellations, Saturn-like rings around his shoulders, silver and black moonboots and symmetrical lightning bolts that travel around his side to his back. Symmetry is everything in the Kiss visual in both costume and makeup design. Ace's new outfit for 1976 is equal parts silver and black...the black of course being the underlying tights that all members wear under the defining components. Ace now fits a giant V triangle that comes down around his neck and over his shoulders, ending at his waist. The triangle is decorated by rhinestone solar systems, much like the previous getup. His boots are all silver this time, and much bigger and awkward, going slightly above the knees. Ace is known in the Kiss camp to have bad balance, so while these boots may look aesthetically badass, they don't seem very conducive to keeping him upright. His face paint is perhaps the most complex, taking in a much more disciplined geometry than even Paul's perfect star. Unlike the rest of Kiss, Ace's eye makeup is silver with the only black makeup on his face being the outline of the eye design and the lipstick he wears. He has recently eliminated the curve of his lips, opting to no longer simply apply the lipstick, but to exaggerate the shape of his lips into angular zigzags. As seen in the lips, pointed eye patterns and lightning bolts, the zigzag is consistent in Ace's visual. Ace is the lead guitarist and the only member of Kiss who doesn't sing lead vocals. Onstage he remains slightly in the background except to play his solos and to occasionally share a microphone with Paul or Gene for background vocals. He moves in an elongated rubbery manner, swaying back and forth to the music as he plays...his eyes often closed as he gets completely immersed and enraptured in the experience. At mid-show he stands alone onstage for an extended solo that climaxes in his Gibson Les Paul billowing smoke from its upper pickup. There is an air of mystery and inaccessibility to Ace's entire demeanor. Perhaps it is the fact that Paul and Gene are always up front and in the spotlight...or possibly just his laidback behavior. Whatever the case, there is just something about Ace that is at least on the surface much cooler than the other guys, and fans seem to have a special affinity for him.

One of the problems for Kiss is most critics of any relevance are unable to take them seriously let alone have anything to do with them. The gimmicks as they see it are beyond gimmicks. Whereas some can look past the shock value of say, Alice Cooper or the glam of Bowie and Bolan and even the New York Dolls for a few weeks in 1973 because there is something in the music lending a significant amount of validity to said artists, there is no redeeming value in Kiss. Jann Wenner doesn't even want them reviewed in *Rolling Stone* magazine. There is something about Kiss that the Baby Boom generation of critics take personally, and the vitriol is quick to come, almost right out of the gate. They know there are lots of kids who are suddenly flocking to their shows due to the word-of-mouth of 1975. They know these are not the same kids who grew up on Dylan and the Beatles, but younger kids. But *Rolling Stone* has been in the process of moving out of San Francisco to New York

City where Wenner has his eyes on his own prize...the chance of evolving from a hippie rag to a respectable newsstand publication and he can hobknob with the establishment that his publication once railed against. That whole philosophy of never trust anyone under thirty went away quickly once everyone was in their thirties and had made their money, and now here they are...ready to rub elbows with politicians in the Democratic Party and Hollywood and the fashion world and the rest of the publishing industry. This is no longer the time to start acknowledging let alone suggesting anything relevant by anyone in their early to mid-twenties unless you're Bruce Springsteen and even he's taken some shit because some say he hasn't delivered on the hype, and at the moment, he's locked in a lawsuit that prevents him from recording. The people who love Kiss so far say they deliver on the hype.

Behind the hype is manager Bill Aucoin and slightly more in the uncredited background, Sean Delaney...a gay couple in a time when the homosexual closet is bursting at the seams. Aucoin, 32, born in Ayer, Massachusetts and a film graduate out of Northwestern University has been in and around the entertainment industry since working at WGBH in Boston along with various cinematography roles and a production role in the short-lived TV series, Flipside, an inconsequential show that boasts of once having John Lennon and Yoko Ono as guests. Delaney, 30, born in Tempe, Arizona came out to the East Coast after living as a musician in New York City. He'd scored two record deals with two different acts...one with Elektra and one with Columbia...both of which were unsuccessful. It was Delaney who opened the invitation to a showcase at the Hotel Diplomat in the summer of 1973. The showcase invite, sent out by Paul Stanley and Gene Simmons, was a ballsy move in Delaney's eyes, because it aimed at portraying Kiss as something so big and eventful, and how lucky anyone would be to be witness to such greatness. He saw the whole presentation as over-the-top, and so he appealed to Aucoin who probably would have ignored it...persuading him to attend the performance. Aucoin was impressed, though Delaney was only half impressed. The songs were good, but these guys who had potential with underdeveloped makeup designs all stood in place like four uptight squares who sorely lacked any sort of charisma or ability to move their bodies. Delaney saw what Kiss was, but he also envisioned what Kiss could be. Aucoin quickly got Kiss a record deal with the newly formed Casablanca, a new venture of Neil Bogart whose prior Buddha label had recently folded. That was three years ago.

If Aucoin brought opportunity to Kiss, Delaney brought vision. It's his vision that has enabled Kiss to develop into full fruition from the mere ideas put forth by Paul and Gene. Upon first meeting the band, the guys were tight asses who barely moved onstage. If they were going to have this look and exist in makeup, whatever these characters were developing into, Delaney felt they needed to go all the way and inhabit these characters...or more accurately, let these characters inhabit them. Delaney offered a choreography unique to each member of the band as well as a collective body of movement in unison. Take the ritualistic rocking back and forth in the final thirty seconds of "Deuce," for instance. This wall of three guitarists at center stage swaying in lockstep formation comes from Delaney, who singlehandedly if perhaps inadvertently orchestrated a future universal stage move for guitarists all over heavy metal in the years to come (think KK Downing and Glenn Tipton). Kiss is not just the four guys in makeup. There are indeed other masterminds at work.

Regarding the critics, the snobbery of elitist rock journalism has been in full effect since the decade began and it continues to get worse as the class of the *Jann Wenner School of Catering and Pandering to Celebrities to Gain Acceptance and Respectability in Highbrow Society* has grown and given birth to this widespread mentality all over rock music and not just *Rolling Stone*. The *New York Times* runs an article on June 27 about the recent explosion of live albums, questioning just how *live* some of them are, though acknowledging the new viability in their existence while listing and reviewing recent live albums as well as past live albums that went unnoticed until the new trend that began last year with Kiss *Alive! Frampton Comes Alive* is the obvious one as it has already sold several million copies and has turned Peter Frampton from a cult figure into an instant headline act, just as *Alive* did for Kiss earlier this year. Kiss, however, is systematically left out and not even mentioned even though they started this trend. Older live albums by the J Geils Band

and Bob Seger are given nods though...two names that just happen to currently be opening acts for Kiss, and Kiss has clearly surpassed both in popularity. It's not just that the most "important" critics hate Kiss. Many don't even acknowledge them. Yet, the *Times* certainly takes the advertising dollars which allows the band to get some exposure in the venerated Arts and Leisure section right next to more respectable acts like the American Ballet Theater, Judy Collins, Pete Seeger, Loggins and Messina and the Stills Young Band. The Spirit of '76 photo shoot has become the ad for the new Kiss show coming to Roosevelt Stadium on July 10.

Here's the problem though...

A widespread community reaction is going on in the wake of a kid's stabbing last week outside a Yes concert. The victim, Guy Porzelt has since died, putting a stamp of public concern around future events. There's a growing push to cancel the entire summer concert schedule, though promoter John Scher is in talks with the city to not let that happen. Now, Jersey City seems to have taken issue with the upcoming Grateful Dead show for July 2 which is quickly cancelled. The reason offered is the lack of law enforcement due to the need for police in other areas over the Bicentennial weekend. Though this looks and sounds noble on the surface, it's bullshit. While the Dead reveals a new makeup date that will make the cancellation merely a postponement, the city cannot and will not confirm. In the coming days, Scher will get the city to agree to a rescheduled date in August for the Dead show, but Arthur Delo, press secretary to Mayor Paul T. Jordan quickly announces that 1976 will be the last summer for concerts at Roosevelt Stadium.

5

THE PARTY

Sex.

When encountering the crossroads where Seventh Avenue and Broadway meet, it's sex you see everywhere you look. You see it to the north, and you see it to the south. You see it to the east and west and all along a span of blocks in between the intersections where the streets meet the avenues. Seedy is the word they use. Always seedy. When it comes to the description of the Deuce, that stretch of Forty-Second Street between Seventh and Eighth Avenues, seedy is inevitably the common adjective. Times Square is testament to the entrepreneurial idea that sex sells. And it's not just the Deuce decorated and ornamented by big marquis highlighted in erotic language in big block letters that you don't want your kids to read while passing by in the car. It's not just the Deuce that's permeated with the flashing light bulbs and neon arrows pointing to neon lips and big red Xs illuminating the pulsing rhythm of New York's Midtown. It's not just the Deuce...it's all of Times Square that's lined with gay bathhouses, parlors, peepshows, avant-garde performances and hookers. Prostitution is often left alone by law enforcement where many of these establishments are owned or infiltrated by the mafia which offers protection. Police are known to take a cut of the profits while partaking in the services provided along the Deuce in exchange for looking the other way in most cases. Whores and pimps alike rarely get arrested, nor do the sex workers in the many theaters that offer live humans fucking on a stage in front of an audience and other deviant acts that most of mainstream society would consider abhorrent from what the normal people do.

Times Square...bookended by the Sony and Canadian Club face on the north and the Times building on the south...sits nestled comfortably for the long haul...shamelessly indifferent to how it's viewed and portrayed around the rest of the civilized world. To some, it is the nerve center of the city. To others, it is a gaping wound, not to mention a dangerous and embarrassing eyesore, although the city is pock-marked with quite a few of these depraved sections that most of the sane and fearful general public knows to stay away from. Most people only go through these parts of town when they God-forbid have to drive through them. And unless you're packed uncomfortably into the annual New Years Eve crowd, the only reason you'd willingly go into Times Square on foot is if you're up to no good. And that's precisely what the degenerates of the suburbs have made their way out to the city for on this humid and clammy midweek afternoon while the rat race limps along in desperate chugs...trying to make it from point A to point B while the hot dogs, smoking pretzels, raw sewage and piss of midtown boil to a steamy aroma that captures and raptures the soul in a perverse nostalgia for those experiencing their first impressions of summer in the city.

On West Forty-Second just off Eighth Avenue, a young Latina named Fancy who's made her way over here from Vine Street in Callowhill, marks her territory while she can...bedecked in platform pumps, some vintage 1960s homemade denim shorts, candy-striped halter crop top and her big fat ass sticking out the passenger window of a beat up blue Maverick that she's leaning into while she negotiates a blowjob with the driver. The beat up blue Maverick with the mildew stench that won't go away and the gas station maps with the soda cup rings and ketchup stains and cigarette holes and the overflowing ashtray that lightly dusts the transmission hump in between the seats...the beat up blue Maverick with the holes rotting and rusting into the floor so badly that you can see the ground underneath you while you're riding over it. Fancy with her fat ass in the quick of a few playful trafficking words knows these guys are deadbeats and that this exchange is going nowhere. Pulling herself out of the car where she was literally hanging over the passenger seat and some kid named Zoltan, she straightens up, fixes her crumpled top and trots back over to her friend Carmen who's looking a little worse for wear in her high waste hot pants and silk bell sleeve tie-up wrap top that isn't doing her any favors when the weather is this scorching.

One block over to the east, a rush of southbound cabs of assorted taxonomy darts toward the diverging break of Times Square where they can either continue on Seventh Avenue or veer off down Broadway. Some are independent livery cabs while the majority is made up of older Checkers of gigunda size and more compact Dodge models.

The crosswalks of every avenue/street intersection are faded and chipped, badly in need of repainting, although it blends in with the rest of the street surface...the dirty festering rot that cooks on the hot surface of the New York City streets. You can literally see the heat...the waves that deceive the eye into thinking the air is being squeezed, massaged and caressed by some perverted invisible presence in the earth's atmosphere. The kind of heat you can see is the kind of heat you can move with your hand. It's the kind of heat you can breathe in...the kind of heat that once the temperatures crack 90, goes to work on the molecules in the air and converts it all to ozone. But there is no public conscience about that yet...and so the collective elements create their poisonous landscape. Garbage...crushed cardboard Coca Cola cups so matted down into the street that they've actually become part of the pavement...painted into it, unable to be picked up with the human hand... crushed cans, Burger King bags with tossed away wilted lettuce, ketch-up-smeared used napkins and straw wrappers...empty Marlboro boxes and soft pack Winstons that only old men over 60 smoke, stomped into the gutters...white paper plates piled in twos and threes on any given corner, stained with pizza grease and remnants of crusted cheese. Ever since the strike last summer when garbage became so plentiful on the streets that people started to stack it neatly like Christmas gifts, this seems to have started a new trend. Even on days when garbage is picked up, the garbage never really seems to go away in some parts of town. And the sanitation workers themselves are shit scared to even pick up the garbage cans before they kick them over first for fear that rats will emerge and run up their arms. It happens in New York.

Then there's the occasional dog shit. In the America of 1976, we don't pick up after our dogs...we let them shit wherever they stop and then we walk onward. And the suburbs are not exempt. There's more dog shit in the suburbs than anywhere...especially those homes with lawns. Nobody is exempt! Every lawn has dog shit somewhere...dog shit spread out and sometimes hidden amongst the dandelions. Dandelions are plentiful. Dandelions are of near- epidemic proportions in the mid-1970s. And dandelions are one of the key physical characteristics of the suburbs, where the bigger the lawn, the more vast the field of dandelions to radiate and sparkle like mosaics surrounding split-level, ranch and Cape Cod homes.

We are approximately twenty years into the suburbs, where most of these developments were built in the mid to late Fifties...which means that most of the baby trees and bushes planted when the neighborhoods were new, have now grown into fully-realized adult trees. The sky over each street in these developments is lined with endless chains of telephone wires connecting houses to poles and poles to more wires. The wires are occasionally obscured by the trees, which sometimes cause problems after a storm. Sometimes if a tree grows too high or a branch creeps along a wire in such a way that compromises safety or power, the electric company shows up to cut that piece away, leaving the tree ridiculously shaped. But in the modern world, it's not the hideous wires that throw a monkey wrench into an otherwise picturesque vista of trees and sky. It's the trees that rudely interrupt the stretch of power line highways imposed on the landscape sometime during the middle decades of the century...and certainly by the time the houses were built, and these power lines connected it all. Trees freshly planted back then have now accumulated some twenty years' worth of growth in an all-out race for the heavens...only to be rudely cockblocked by these manmade formations of cables connected to telephone poles sticking out of the ground like middle fingers. Perhaps these wooden phalluses are necessary in modern suburbia or anywhere else for that matter, but they sure are a fucking drag to look at.

And the dog shit.

Dog shit is a fact of civic structure. It's as common as the architecture, street signs, park benches and parking meters. And no...as you may have guessed, people don't dispose of their garbage properly when they're in transit either. If you're eating while driving and you happen to be finished with your McDonald's meal, the whole fucking thing gets tossed out the window of your moving vehicle. To be fair though, this is not exclusive to city life. This too is a commonality in the suburbs...places like Central Jersey where you can find just as much garbage along Route 1 and its adjoining back roads. The irresponsible spillage of unruly kids along those vast stretches between strip malls and shopping malls...the crushed Slurpee cups of 7-Elevens, the White Castle rat burger boxes, cigarette butts by the ton, lollipop sticks, candy wrappers, dried and flaky used condoms embedded in the cracks between the asphalt and the curb, and spit galore...because everybody spits...it's a teenage thing, more so with the boys...they spit. This is not just exclusive to baseball players with big wads of Red Man stuffed in their chaw-jawed cheeks...these are teenagers in 1976 who have to spit onto the ground outside for no other reason than just a macho posturing behavior fad. Our walking feet have to dodge the white bubbly gobs as much as they have to dodge the dog shit. America, even as it prepares for its biggest birthday party, is a filthy fucking place in 1976.

Squalid as it is, America is also in the hopeful convention stretch of a presidential election year going into the Bicentennial summer. Former Georgia governor, Jimmy Carter, an outsider to Washington who has refused to be a cog in the political wheel is running a Democratic ticket with Walter Mondale against Gerald Ford, Nelson Rockefeller and the remnants of the Nixonian afterbirth. It is now July, and the convention will be happening here in New York City in less than two weeks. The American summer is filled to capacity. A political convention alone is enough logistical nightmares for any major city, let alone the Bicentennial. Then there is the Summer Olympics that also begin in mid-July, but that's Montreal's problem to deal with. Any other year would see such a sporting event saturate the news media, though in the States, especially in New York, it is a non-event or at best, takes a backseat to the spirit of 76 and the election. The terrorism of the last Summer Olympics is still fresh in collective memory, with several previously selected cities bowing out before Montreal became the host. The recent Winter Olympics passed successfully without incident and has already influenced pop culture in the months since. You can see it in the ocean of wedge haircuts along any given stretch of the avenues and beyond...increasing numbers of young women cutting their hair to look like figure skater Dorothy Hamill, who just won the Gold for America. Now she's just as much a young celebrity as John Travolta and probably more famous worldwide.

On Thursday, July 1, a Pointillist-like appearance of dotted markings make up the whole of Narragansett Bay at Newport, Rhode Island. Hundreds of private boats containing spectators offer water-level views as a parade of tall ships and small ships sail by before departing for New York City. Hundreds of thousands of people watch from the shores as multifarious vessels make their way into line throughout the afternoon, firing salutes from their cannons and answered by salutes from nearby Fort Adams.

In the New York suburbs surrounding the urban nerve center where the party's ground zero will be, kids have declared that Independence Day has already begun. They mark their territory in every neighborhood, reminding the adults of the party. But the grand visual extravaganza the nation has planned on a scale that only millions of dollars could provide is not the same party these kids are attending, nor do they really feel invited. Still, the startling *pat pat pat...paa...paa...pats* of random loose firecrackers going off amateurishly around the city lift the tension in good yet neurotic ways. It gives you the exhilarating rush of summer...magnified to infinity with the knowledge that the bash of a lifetime is just days away, though it doesn't appeal to the side of you that only has a limited threshold for noise and mayhem...that feeling you get late during the Fourth of July when things have detonated out your window long enough to drive you to mutter to yourself in *motherfuckers* and *little fuckin' assholes* under your breath every time something outside explodes because you just want quiet although you know the Fourth will echo on for the next few days. That's on a normal year. But this is no normal year. That sense of not being able to put your foot on the brake is already there because the cables have already been cut. But this is New York City and you know there's nobody really engineering this train anyway. Those random rounds of pat pat pats pattering away in intervals long enough to make you flinch because you forget about them until the next ones go off. It's still the work week though the celebratory feelings even in the work place is one of *anything goes*. That means don't get carried away with the party atmosphere building and mounting both outside and inside. It's not like you can just leave the party for a remote safe haven room that exists outside the party. You can't leave the party for another room where the party doesn't exist. The party is everywhere and when you leave work today where the party is, you'll be joining the same party in the street. When you go home tonight, the party will be on the TV news and when you go to bed you'll be hearing those random rehearsal bursts that nobody asked someone's kids to set off, but they're out there anyway having their little sub-party...one of many offshoots of the big party. They're out there in the streets...setting off their random rehearsal bursts...those random rehearsal bursts that scare the living shit out of you and your grandmother who had just gotten to sleep but is now sitting up and saying the rosary. Those random rehearsal bursts that are not really rehearsals at all because these are kids with little to no supervision who live the party every day. There's no separation between the Bicentennial and what their everyday normal lives are. They're street kids doing street things like drugs and stealing shit from innocent people who play the game the right way...the people who do everything they're supposed to do and still have to hope for the best and pray to God that things go right in their lives. These are the kids who have fallen through the cracks who are so low they can look up and see bottom...these kids without a shred of hope...not even so much as a prayer. But they've been to Canal Street by God, and they've got their fireworks. If nothing else, they've got their fireworks.

The Bicentennial is a celebration for all of America, they say, and the festivities are nationwide. The mother of all parties, however, at least on the level of spectacle is taking place in New York Harbor where you could just see with your own eyes the intersecting lines and crossties from forced marriages of bumbling bureaucracies at both federal and local levels. In

Lower Manhattan, the Mormon Tabernacle Choir is singing on the steps of Federal Hall on Wall Street while the Fulton Fish Market Band plays outside the Stock Exchange. At City Hall, trumpeter Clark Terry begins the twelfth season of a free concert program known as Jazzmobile. Though it is only Thursday, the rumblings around the city are already lifting the mood and spirit to that of a collective and heightened awareness of what has become very apparent...the party is beginning.

By Saturday, watercraft by the thousands have sailed into New York Harbor meeting the weekend to display themselves. Shipping consists of two major fleets...the one coming from Newport is Operation Sail, a windblown fleet of sailing ships consisting of square riggers, barques, barquentines, schooners, topsail schooners, ketches...a vast collection of vessels representing 30 different flags. This includes 16 of the 20 largest sailing vessels in the world that are currently active.

52 military ships from 32 nations make up the Fourth International Naval Review, the other fleet. Tiny tugs, cruisers, guided missile ships, destroyers and frigates are the stars in this convoy of gray hulls that includes the 79,000-ton aircraft carrier Forrestal. The International Naval Review is over 20 miles long and led by the U.SS Wainwright, a guided missile cruiser with 400 crewmen dressed in tropical white uniforms. As the long column of vessels enter the Port of New York, a 21-gun salute is fired from Fort Hamilton at the Brooklyn approach to the Verrazzano Bridge.

The entire gathering is a logistical mindfuck for New York City and New Jersey police as well as the Coast Guard who have all worked together to arrange designated areas to place the ships so they can be viewed from the shore. In the coming days, some will grant access to the public to come aboard. Op Sail's biggest ships will be docked along the West Side at Piers 92, 90, 88, 86 and 84. Three of the tall ships will be housed on the East River at the South Street Seaport. The smaller vessels will be tied along Piers 97, 76, 59 and 40. Most Naval units will remain along the Hudson River piers at West Houston and between West 46th and West 57th. Brooklyn, Staten Island and New Jersey will also host additional ships for public access.

On Saturday, a nighttime parade takes place in midtown. Parades are plentiful and occur throughout the city. The night parade is staged by the Nichiren Shoshu Academy, a Buddhist organization with its origins in Japan. The organization of the night parade is on a level of precision and planning on par with the best and biggest parades in New York. Over 3000 participants from all over the United States, Canada and South America, wearing lights of various assortments march up Sixth Avenue, covering a 33-block stretch spanning Thirty-Sixth to Fifty-Ninth streets. Colossal floats that depict the Golden Gate Bridge, Philadelphia's Independence Hall and the Boston Tea Party share space with an enormous telephone and a sweaty team of white-wigged musicians. The Academy is no stranger to New York, as this summer marks their twelfth annual convention in the city. They will also appear at Shea Stadium between games of a Mets Fourth of July doubleheader. The night parade along the Avenue of the Americas is bathed in light and illuminated in international cheer long after dark. Along the lower tip of Manhattan however, and all along the seaport and the piers that trail the west side of the island all the way up to the George Washington Bridge is an infinite multitude of rigging...the Tall Ships...the dark haunting outlines of sails, yards and masts against the backdrop of the skyline...some subtly lit while others remain docked in darkness into the wee hours imposing a macabre canvas and an intimidating presence along the Hudson overnight. This is the collective calm in the final hours before America's biggest day.

SUNDAY

On the Fourth of July 1976, perhaps the most memorably extravagant Sunday in American history, the rock band Kiss has a full-page ad in the *New York Times* advertising what is billed as the New Kiss Show, a rock and roll spectacle to be held at Roosevelt Stadium just across the Hudson in Jersey City in one week. These little details are important in painting a picture of as much visual stimuli by way of the arts and culture as possible in recreating Bicentennial America in our imaginations. For context, the following is also going on in and around New York City on this day. Jethro Tull is promoting a major upcoming concert at Shea Stadium to be held on July 23 with special guest, Robin Trower. James Taylor, Loggins and Messina and John Sebastian advertise concerts to be held at Long Island's Nassau Coliseum later in the summer. Shows at the legendary Bottom Line club this week consist of Pat Martino, Kenny Rankin, Eric Anderson, Livingston Taylor, Mary Travers, Tom Paxton, and Novella Nelson. The nearby Westchester Premier Theatre has concerts booked for this week with the Band, Judy Collins, Kris Kristofferson and Rita Coolidge. The three week-run of the Russian Festival, a production of Hurok concerts is still in residency at the Metropolitan Opera House until mid-month. *The Wiz,* the winner of seven Tony Awards last year, is enjoying a successful run on Broadway at the Majestic Theatre. *Doug Henning's Magic Show* adorns the Cort Theatre. Jules Feiffer's *Knock*

Knock with Lynn Redgrave and Charles Durning is in the last weeks of its engagement at the Biltmore. *Something's Afoot*, the musical who-dunnit for the entire family dubbed the funniest show in town runs at the Lyceum. Anthony Perkins in *Equus*, the Tony winner for Best Play of 1975, occupies the Plymouth Theatre. At the Delacorte in Central Park, New York Shakespeare Festival Productions twentieth anniversary of Shakespeare in the Park is running a production of *Henry V*. 1976 Tony winner *A Chorus Line* continues at the Schubert Theatre. Other Broadway titles include, Neil Simon's *California Suite, The Runner Stumbles, Very Good Eddie, The Belle of Amherst, Pal Joey, Who's Afraid of Virginia Woolf, Same Time Next Year*, the longest running musical, *Grease*, and the return of *Guys and Dolls*. Movie theaters run *The Omen, Midway, Silent Movie, Buffalo Bill and the Indians, Benji's Life Story, Murder By Death, The Tenant, That's Entertainment Part 2, Logan's Run, Hawmps*, and *All the President's Men*.

The major retailers are all having red, white and blue sales, although Macy's, Gimbels and Bloomingdales are having white sales...the latter with 200-thread no-iron supercale irregulars from Wamsutta now 60 percent off! Abraham & Straus...suspendered jeans, Stetsons, trail bags, rancho pants, buckle-up belts all by American West...mink coats 63 percent off at Alexander's where they're having a *Buycentennial Sellabration* ...and goddamn it, Polaroid has just announced a brand new SX-70 color film that'll make your pictures shine with sparkling radiance and sheen! If you need a new rug, the entire stock is priced to go at Allen Carpet.

On Fifty-Sixth and Fifth Avenue, Bonwit Teller displays futuristic themes in its windows addressing not only the holiday occasion, but some fun trivial speculation about the coming century. What better way to mark the Bicentennial than to take a crack at the Tricentennial? Bonwit Teller has asked twenty of America's most prophetic designers to help transform the Fifth Avenue façade into a window of the future where everyone involved gives us glimpses of what the fashion world might look like in 2076. They call it the outer limits of imagination, and they've recruited Scott Barrie, Alice Blaine, Bill Blass, Stephen Burrows, Patti Cappalli, Oscar de la Renta, Cathy Hardwick, Carol Horn, Victor Joris, Bill Kaiserman, Calvin Klein, Anthony

Muto, Rena Rowan, Fernando Sanchez, Morty Sussman, Giorgio Sant'Angelo, Koos Van Den Akker and Diane Von Furstenberg. Everyone involved offers something to showcase in the realm of futuristic fashion...a tantalizing glimpse of what they could imagine as shocking new ideas such as plastics molded to the human form, or clothing that contains its own self-contained climate-controlled environment providing heat in the winter and cooling mechanisms in the summer. Imagine a jacket you put on in July that comes equipped with its own built-in air conditioner! Bonwit Teller asks the intriguing question of what shape, form and scope we will reach by the Tricentennial and invites its customers and passers-by to come and take that first bold look.

The grid system is now labyrinthian as streets normally passable are closed for the multitude of simultaneous heritage festivals randomly spread throughout the island...Norwegian, Swedish, Slovak, Polish, Greek, Italian, Ukrainian, Irish, Turkish, Korean, Puerto Rican, Filipino, Indian, Chinese, Japanese, Cuban, West Indian, Haitian, Hungarian, Armenian, Lithuanian and Finnish festivals all sharing the same 10 AM to 6 PM window of space with an Ecumenical Service, Mayor's Civic Ceremony, Roll of the 50 States, Cannon Salute, United States Navy Band concert, 1776-1976 Revolution in Fashion stage show, children's entertainment, readings of the *Declaration of Independence*, band concerts, historic reenactments, nautical crafts and displays, maritime exhibitions, George Washington exhibition, religious services, raising of the Colonial flag and the beheading of the statue of George III...all throughout the day within the same timeframe so as to all be done before nightfall and the greatest fireworks display the world has ever seen.

Between Mayor Abraham Beame and New Jersey Governor Brendan Byrne, the ships go through several greeting ceremonies. On the west side of the Hudson, the crowds from Jersey City all the way up to Weehawken and beyond gather and watch in the same numbers as what's amassed along the Manhattan side. On July 4, 1976, cars are strewn along the West Side Highway and Belt Parkway trying to get anywhere near the waterfront for the fireworks ...many of those who can't are simply stopped and unintentionally parked....trails of traffic much like that of Woodstock or Altamont.

Among the Tall Ships, the first vessel, the three-masted Coast Guard Barque Eagle passes beneath the Verrazzano-Narrows Bridge while plumes of red, white, and blue water are sprayed through the air by fireboats. An entire armada including the Denmark, Gorch Fock (Germany), Dar Pomorza (Poland), and the Nippon Maru (Japan) move north up the Hudson along the West Side skyline while the winds gust downstream. Speaking of the Dar Pomorza, the vessel subsequently sailed to Savannah, Georgia just to deliver an urn filled with soil from the birthplace of Count Casimir Pulaski. Pulaski was a Polish hero of the Revolutionary War who is simultaneously being honored at the Parliament in Poland on this very same day, along with General Tadeusz Kosciuszko. Polish leader, Edward Gierek presents the U.S. Ambassador with models of statues commemorating both war heroes. The statues, a gift to the United States from Poland will be erected upon arrival.

Mayor Beame watches from the 90-foot-high flight deck of the host ship, the aircraft carrier U.S.S. Forrestal, President Ford standing next to him after changing his mind just a few days ago after telling the city to go fuck itself last year. The nice president has also decided to loan the city 500 million dollars, temporarily holding off bankruptcy.

Each little town elsewhere is a microcosm of the big picture of America, and the party on a grand scale is really what is happening all over the country...the Pacific Northwest, the Southwest, the Midwest, the Southeast, Northeast and both coasts. Families in urban, rural and cookie cutter suburban developments are watching fireworks somewhere or setting them off to backgrounds of barbecues, beers, laughing kids, music cranked at top volume as background to their own Bicentennial bashes on their own properties which serve as their own little piece of the American Dream... these Boomers with their World War II Generation parents and Generation X children are living the dream. In their driveways are Chevy Malibus and Impalas and Caprices and Oldsmobile Cutlesses and Ford LTDs and Pontiac Catalinas and Dodge Aspens. The cooler youth have Chevelles and Dusters and Challengers and Chargers with big apunna-punna wheels. Some people drive Datsuns and AMC Gremlins and Ford Explodemobiles, AKA Pintos. Cars come in various colors like yellow and red and blue and brown and black and cream and gold. Their starters all have distinctive voices when you turn the key in the ignition. For instance, when the Catalina turns over upon starting, it says...

Sawa-wa-wa-nee-nee-nee-nee-nee-nee-nee-nee-nee-nee-nee-nee-nee-nee-nee-nee-nee-nee-nee...

Whereas the more restless Impala says...

Tantada dida-da-vvvroooooommmmmmmmmmmmmmmm!!!

And the imposing Charger goes...

Pabubba-bubvvrrrrrooooom-bubububububububububub...

The post-war boom of the 1950s and 1960s has produced a unique situation in the United States where most Baby Boomers who are now into adulthood will enjoy the stability of a job they'll keep for the duration of their working life. After 50 years, they'll get a watch and the security of a retirement plan and something called a pension because their jobs have been protected by strong unions. The much historically celebrated post-war boom allowed Americans a much higher standard of living as the economy assured U.S. dominance for nearly three decades. People spend more money these days money on their kids and on themselves clothes, appliances and home décor. Even women have more money to spend on themselves than they did a decade or two ago.

Suburban homes are muddled with the clutter of material possessions... the collecting of things and more things. Every possible inch of space is taken up by something. If there's a sofa, the sofa is speckled with newspapers and books. If there's a table, the table is filled with picture frames, pretzel bowls, ashtrays, cigarette packs, piles of Polaroids, calculators, writing utensils, notepads, half-filled glasses of watered-down 7-Up with half-melted ice cubes and beads of sweat coating the exterior. Zigzag patterns clash with vertical and horizontal lines as everything from the floor to the ceiling and the furniture to the wallpaper merge in psychedelic pop complexity surrounding puffy leather chairs and various degrees of shag. Dough boxes meant to serve as a place for rising dough serve more as side tables to store magazines next to sofas. The more conservative households are all in on the Bicentennial trend of Colonial motifs embedded in everything...wallpaper, table cloths, upholstery, bed spreads, pillows and carpeting, the latter decorated by liberty bells amongst backgrounds of Red Current, Colonial Gold and Georgian Blue in patterns so intricate they resemble lysergic acid diethylamide-influenced mandalas, not to mention the spinning wheels absorbed into furniture, cast iron eagles....all of it in its tackiness, front and center in splendid unapologetic Bicentennial chic. Children's bedrooms are wallpapered with wooden soldiers, fifes and drums. Bedrooms and dining rooms are often Spanish Colonial in the wood carving, but even this traditional style is side by side with modernity in the multi-color landscapes of clashing entities...brown, yellow and blue in one...or green, orange and yellow in another. Even the floor-to-ceiling curtains that often appear made of solid colors are really at close inspection a series of multiple textures and exhaustive ornamentation. Mirrored adhesive tiles that stick to your wall like Ronald and Louise DeFeo had behind their headboard when they were murdered in their bed in Amityville...they're all the rage...and even those mirrors are touched with a smokiness that curls and trails along, rendering the mirrors not completely see-through. Kitchens are filled with Faux brick and avocado stoves and fridges, Floral Bouquet and Blue Heather Corningware pots, floral placemats, Merry Mushroom ceramic napkin holders and wallpaper full of fruit and copper kettles, some of it old Sanitas from previous owners in decades passed. Family photos taken at Sears and school pictures of the kids, always one of the kids wearing headgear braces...school pictures always serving as preservers of the most fucked up awkwardness of childhood adorning the paneled walls of living rooms. The main focal point of every living room is a 60 x 40 oil painting of mountains, trees and a stream. It's usually surrounded by smaller kitschy art or still lifes. The center pieces are often sizable wall units showcasing stereo systems made by Fisher, Kenwood and Sansui while the more experimental cutting-edge homes have quadrophonic sound models by Pioneer and Marantz...big, beautiful silver face heads on their receivers with neon blue that completely lights up a room at night.

It's been three years since Peter Tompkins and Christopher Bird's best seller, *The Secret Life of Plants* revealed the spiritual and scientific benefits of talking to plants, and so 1976 is also a time when Americans hold regular conversations with their houseplants. There is no overstating the influence of green and its domination in the aesthetics of home and design. Ivy trailing up and around entire houses has become a common visual in the suburbs while foliage has seeped into interior decorating as it never has before. The green revolution has reached dentist offices, hotel lobbies and shopping malls where colossal potted plants are plentiful. The occasional asshole uses the pots as ashtrays...especially in the malls where cigarette butts protrude from the dirt of plants that otherwise adorn the scenery next to benches and fountains where kids toss coins and catch fish swimming mercilessly in filthy water littered with even more cigarette butts. Smoking is permitted everywhere...not just the malls, grocery stores, doctor's and dental offices, but in restaurants, movie theaters and hospitals. High schools however have rules, and most schools only allow smoking in the smoking lounge. With respect to the plant revolution, the more conservative households have artificial plants instead of real ones, usually made of polypropylene or polyethene with silk or polyester leaves.

One of the reasons people get sick far more in 1976 than in modern twenty-first century America, is because there are simply more germs...or more accurately, there are far more conditions for germs to thrive. Take carpeting for instance. Decades before hardwood floors were back in vogue, wall to wall carpeting served as shaggy Petrie dishes, holding all of the nasty collections that we bring into the house from the bottom of our shoes...things we step on in parking lots, grocery stores, schools, hospitals...things we can't just sweep or wipe away the way we do on our hardwood floors or linoleum kitchens. Sure, we can vacuum and even shampoo the rug, but there are reasons that dentist offices and movie theaters smell the way they do. It's the carpeting, stupid! Carpets are what give each home their unique smell. It's all what's embedded and entrapped in your carpet. Carpets not only contain the viral and bacterial elements of what you stepped on, but they exist as innocent vessels for carrying things through no fault of their own... things like hair and the particles of every sneeze and cough...stray ashes of cigarettes and cigars...the countless crumbs of myriads of meals and snacks eaten where they should never have been eaten and left to fall, forever entrenched in cavernous shafts of shag...flaked-off dead skin, crusty pieces of dead lip you bit off and spit out...the boogers and drool of ill children and the stanky stench of dirty butts planted there day after day after day after day. Carpeting, especially long wavy locks have also become popular in the bathrooms of many households. That's even more fibers to hold the remnants of germs and vomit spray and urine droplets and toenail clippings and the absorbed odor of every bowel movement that's ever taken place in these cramped 5x10 spaces, and we're not talking just one of those Flokatis that sit there unassumingly in rectangular cuts, but wall to wall carpeting that even wraps around and behind the toilet.

And let's go back to the hair. Hair is everywhere. It's a much hairier world, this 1976 is. Long hair on males is a norm, and short hair is still pretty fucking long. Foreheads and ears are not something commonly visible on men and boys. Permed hair makes it all wider. Hair on humans is usually bulky and shapely...occupying space off each human head that most twenty-first century heads don't occupy. And more importantly, in 1976, it's not common to shave your head regularly. If you're losing your hair with a receding hairline, you try to hide it as best you can in a stylish combover. You achieve this by combing every strand of hair you have left to one side of your head, or you sweep it to the other side. You push it forward with a brush or you wrap it around your head like a turban. You do whatever you need to do to give yourself a full head of hair, but you don't shave your remaining hair off, for Godsakes.

There is no such thing as grooming in 1976. And when it comes to pubic hair in 1976, women are just as unkempt. Humans are just hairy in 1976. In fact, the 1970s mark what is perhaps the hairiest decade in modern history.

If we consider today's times, it seems it's been forever since humans have been shaving off pubic hair and chest hair, and men and boys have been routinely shaving their heads or keeping minimalist hair styles. Some men even shave their legs and groom their eyebrows. Not in 1976. So, it becomes obvious that hair growth peaked in the Bicentennial era and has gotten less and less with each passing decade since, as we've transitioned inevitably into a hairless society...though right now there is lots and lots and lots and lots of hair at the party.

By dark in New York Harbor, explosions in the sky are visible from 15 miles all around in what is deliberately planned and carried out as the biggest fireworks display in the history of the world. It coincides with the other thousands upon thousands of fireworks presentations big and small in America that in no way are any less significant than the one in New York City, though the ones in the small towns where explosives are set off by the regular people are the ones where the amateur fanatics are more likely to get their fingers blown off

The Bicentennial in the suburbs where vast stretches of the American population reside rings to the strains of pop music and Paul McCartney's latest smash hit, "Silly Love Songs." The song reeks of heat and sunscreen and the scorched leather of the backseat on the way toward the shore with the wind through an open car window blowing in your face. It's the sound of skyrockets in flight and the afternoon delight of the Starland Vocal Band and the sexy tease of Andrea True Connection's "More, More, More." It's the rhythmic beat of "Boogie Fever" and "Turn the Beat Around" and even last year's "Love Will Keep Us Together." But with regard to the Starland Vocal Band, it's "Afternoon Delight" that is the true star of the Bicentennial. Network television and every other piece of unassuming media too clueless to realize the sexual connotations in the number two song of the week. For those who watch the Bicentennial on television, the day's entire programming no matter where you look is using "Afternoon Delight" as their theme.

You hear it in the Bicentennial program advertisements...you hear it every time they're about to cut away to a commercial...you hear it in montage clips of people celebrating around the nation. This inappropriately nondescript horny gentleman with an appetite, looking for his baby because he wants to hold her tight and get himself some afternoon delight...talking about things like rubbing sticks and stones together and making the sparks ignite...it's all the background soundtrack to the media collective's day and night coverage of America's birthday party.

The Bicentennial in the suburbs stretching the length of the nation smells distinctly like two things...first and foremost, the smoky traveling plumes of collective cooking in backyards, front yards and driveways that number in such frequency that you can form a chain link of Kamp-Kap Kook-Out, Caloric and Weber charcoal grills from ocean to ocean and the national incense of chicken, Armour beef franks and canned hams and Krakus hams and Cure 81 hams and shoulder clod and whole pork loin and shells of beef and shell steaks and spare ribs and ground chuck and charred burgers among all the barbecue favorites that were ripe for wholesale savings this week at your local Grand Union, Path Mark, A&P or Shop Rite. And then of course, there's the hovering marriage of sulfur dioxide, hydrogen sulfide, carbon disulfide, and ammonia, making up similar smoky traveling plumes in the gunpowder realm of the aftermath where the sky was lit up for hours and now there is only the day after.

7

KISS AND MAKE UP

Though they've only come into financial success over the past few months, Kiss doesn't have much to show for yet in terms of the excesses of the rock and roll lifestyle. While Paul Stanley and Gene Simmons are usually in lock-step with the rhythmic heartbeat and calculated mechanics of the band's upward climb, only Peter Criss and Ace Frehley have jumped into the deep end of the threshing machine where they've already upped their drug and alcohol intake to addictive levels. Granted, Ace has somewhat been an alcoholic since he was a teenager, but the mass quantities of cocaine consumed in recent months is already cause for alarm with parental units, Paul and Gene. But even from the earliest days, where the four-way stakes in Kiss have always been equal among members, personalities have long dictated the family-like social hierarchy within the band, where Paul and Gene are the parents and Peter and Ace are the irresponsible kids who need supervision due to their complete lack of trustworthiness. There is no known number for how many temper tantrums Peter has exhibited that has led him to "quit" the band. Just a month ago while in Europe, Peter was so out of control that his wife Lydia had to be called at home and asked to get on a plane to be with her husband in the hopes that he calmed down. Ace doesn't have much of a temper, but he's proven unquestionably unreliable. The first major red flag was in not showing up to the studio during key sessions for

Destroyer. One of his no-shows happened to be on a day when he was supposed to record a guitar solo. Ace was busy with a card game and couldn't be bothered, forcing Bob Ezrin to recruit Michael Wagner of Alice Cooper's band to play the solo. Needless to say, at the outset of fame, the cracks are already showing...and kids who have bought the new *Destroyer* album have no idea the solo in "Sweet Pain" is not Ace.

Ace is the nickname of Paul Daniel Frehley, born in the Bronx borough of New York City on April 27, 1951. His father is of Dutch descent, his mother of German. He has a sister and a brother. Growing up, there was always music in Ace's house. His siblings both play piano and guitar. Both parents also play the piano. Ace received his first guitar in 1964 for his thirteenth Christmas. But unlike most of the household where classical was the preferred choice of music, Ace was influenced by rock and roll. Still carrying the name Paul when he joined Kiss, it was a no-brainer when he opted for Ace as his stage name in avoiding a situation of two Pauls being in Kiss. Paul and Ace were both working as cab drivers at the time of the band's signing in 1973...both with their cabbie licenses expiring in 1974. Neither of them had to worry about renewing them.

The other Paul was born Stanley Bert Eisen on January 20, 1952, making him the youngest in Kiss. He was raised on the upper northernmost tip of Manhattan in the Inwood section, at least for the first eight years of his life until his family moved to the Kew Gardens section of Queens. Stan struggled through early childhood after a birth defect left his right ear profoundly misshaped, a condition known as microtia. He withstood the jokes and ridicule of classmates and neighborhood bullies, turning inward and living a largely introverted existence. Music made him extroverted though and his talent for writing songs was recognized by Gene when the two met in 1970. Gene wasn't doing much by way of being musically productive nor did he have much to show for by way of talent when he met Stan...and Stan could hardly have been impressed when Gene played him an original named "My Uncle is a Raft." Gene, however, knew he'd met his musical partner when Stan played him his own original, "Sunday Driver," though his arrogant indifference toward Stan may have veiled his enthusiasm on the surface. Gene could play bass, and as Stan would later come to find out, he could write some halfway decent songs. It was the unflinching and uncompromising work ethic the two shared along with a common vision...and though their personalities couldn't have been more different, their drive to make it assured them both that they were going to see that vision out together. Wherever the dream led, they were going to ride it to the very fucking end.

Gene Simmons was born, Chaim Witz in Halifa, Israel on August 25, 1949. Years later, he'd Americanize his name by changing it to Gene Klein and eventually to his stage name, Simmons. He was raised by his mother, Flora, who emigrated with her son to America in 1957 following a divorce from Chaim's father who stayed behind in Israel. Flora, a Jewish refugee from Hungary was one of only two members of her family who survived the Holocaust. Both of his parents for that matter were refugees from Hungary, though we don't hear much at all about Chaim's father during his formative years before Kiss or during Kiss.

While the format of this book deliberately stays in present tense to convey the chronology of 1976 and 1977 as much as possible, we'll briefly break form at this juncture to stress that the personal factoids we later learn about the members of Kiss are hardly known in 1976. In 1976, the members of Kiss are otherworldly and mysterious. Nobody has a single inkling of what they look like under the face paint, nor are they much even thought of as people with real and normal everyday lives, let alone a past entailing family histories and childhoods. But as the multi-generation appeal of Kiss has allowed decades of uncovering information, one of the common threads to Gene's story is the fact that Flora was a holocaust survivor and raised Gene as a single mom. Flora and Gene relocate to America, and this is important in understanding the events that Gene himself has often marked as crucial in his development. His mother's strength and determination for a decent life of dignity and accomplishment was his main inspiration as was the immediate sense of opportunity America offered. The influence of his mother has much to do with Gene's decisions not to do drugs, alcohol or anything she deems destructive or harmful. This is hardly consistent with the hellish image of the demon, but respecting his mother is at the foundation of the demon's personal choices in life. As for the groupies, we can consider that one of the few mother-free vices Gene allows himself. At this rare instance that we break the fourth wall, it's important to note that Paul's childhood is also a factor in his adult personality. As we mention, the microtia that leaves him with a deformed ear as a child and all the scarring ridicule he endures plays a significant part in Paul's insecurities and defensive arrogant stance on many things. His standoffish attitude in real life is undoubtedly a defense mechanism in a world where he's unable to trust many people. To America in 1976 however, he is merely the Starchild...the lover with the puckered lips... the guy with one star on his eye who's New Yawka accent screams its way through the four sides of the blockbuster *Kiss Alive* album. Nobody knows about the underdeveloped ear under his long black hair. Under his long black hair is the source of many of his insecurities that he manages to keep hidden for decades...that he manages to mask under the face paint...that he manages to disguise as a charismatic frontman who is the object of desire to thousands of horny teenage girls. Under his long black hair remains the scattered and tattered remnants of Stanley Eisen who upon forming Wicked Lester with Gene Klein in 1971, legally became Paul Stanley.

Peter is the streetwise Italian kid from Brooklyn. Born George Peter John Criscuola on December 20, 1945, the future Kiss drummer grew up in the Williamsburg section surrounded by like-minded musicians. Childhood friend, Jerry Nolan followed a similar path and briefly tasted success for a few years with the New York Dolls. Being the oldest member of Kiss, Peter had a head start on his bandmates and was playing in clubs when the others were still in high school. By the time Paul and Gene had formed Wicked Lester, Peter had already been through numerous bands like the Barracudas and Chelsea. The latter had a short-lived record deal with Decca that never went past their first album...very much like Wicked Lester, though Peter to this day has always charged Paul and Gene with not having paid their dues. Paying their dues is something he brings up frequently in reference to their recent and ongoing rise to fame. That rise is happening right now as we speak. It's not something that's already happened and now we're looking back on it. Kiss is in the process of that rise. But the "paying your dues" thing is Peter's own defense mechanism against the constant ridicule of Paul and Gene who through their own insecurities feel it necessary to constantly beat up on Peter, especially Gene, who belittles him every chance he gets. Gene is the only one in the band with a college education, having attended Richmond College in Staten Island before moving on to teach elementary school for a short period of time. Gene flaunts his education and uses it often against Peter, taunting him as inferior and illiterate. Peter can't relate to Gene's snobbery, though the real cultural elites and intellectuals of the music world probably look down on Gene the same way Gene looks down on Peter. Gene is in Kiss after all, and Kiss is not taken seriously by the elite. Peter is also streetwise in a way that Gene can't relate to, and if it ever came down to it, Peter could kick the shit out of Gene if he wanted to. Gene openly mocks Peter for what he sees as a lack of education and an inability to speak correctly.

"Yeah, and I'm in the same band as you," he tells Gene in response, demonstrating in a display of wit that Gene could never conjure no matter how much education or class he thinks he has. Peter is just cooler...even with the hot temper. Ace is cooler too. But they both seem along for the ride while Paul and Gene are the only two of the group who take an interest in the business end and quality control. Paul and Gene are not without their vices though. While Gene doesn't partake in the drugs and alcohol of the rock and roll lifestyle, he carries a photo album of all the women he's taken back to his hotel room over the past two years. This ritual started instantaneously once their commercial flight landed in Edmonton in February 1974, and two guys who could barely get the attention of women on their own were suddenly fucking their way through Canada on a short tour just prior to the release of their first album. Why do we say two guys? Because as we just made the point of explaining, the social dynamic of Kiss informs us that there are two responsible adult members of the band and two irresponsible kids who can't be trusted. But surprisingly, Paul and Gene remain single and addicted to their groupies while Peter and Ace are both married. Peter and Lydia have been married since 1970, and Ace just recently married girlfriend, Jeanette back in May. Titles aside, nobody is innocent.

But onstage it all comes together and the four distinctive temperaments function as a single unit. Together, they're Kiss...and for as toxic as the dynamic becomes in later years, this is when it's untouchable. On the occasional night when one or more of them are not cued in or just off, then the wheels fall off. And they're all guilty of it because there are times when each one of them just outright sucks. But when they're on, they're on. And when they're locked in on some nights, they're the best band on the planet. On some nights. Still, as much as the hardcore fans love the music, it's the stage show that garners most of the attention bad and good. But until 1976, what did that entail? Aside from a drum riser in the middle of a backline of amplifiers and a candelabra, the live setup was rather unremarkable and not unlike your average stage from any number of early Seventies hard rock acts. The letters K-I-S-S distinguished their stage, however. The lighted Kiss logo that hung suspended behind and above the drums was an intimidating reminder to any band on a bill with them that you can't compete with a Kiss concert...even though, again...there wasn't much to the stage, as the theatrics saw their focal point in the stage antics of the individual members...Gene spitting blood and breathing fire...Ace's smoking guitar...Peter's levitating drum riser...Paul's prancing demeanor and increasingly hilarious but effective banter between and during songs...so many delicious flavors to a Kiss concert. Add in the smoke bombs, flash pots and explosions and you had your basic Kiss experience...even if the stage was rather no frills.

But money changes everything...including the stage set.

Until now, it was a tight-knit group in and around the band, most of all with the same loyal road crew that had been with them from the early days. They roomed together, drove together, ate together, drank together and partied together. Road manager, Rick Stuart even saved Paul's life when the Kiss front man almost drowned in Hawaii...this just a few months ago.

Since the earliest dates in 1974 that accompanied the release of the debut album, they'd all been on the road consistently...going home very rarely and only for short spurts of time between three studio albums and nonstop touring. They all remained in their modest residences because the future was looking more uncertain as they'd gone further into 1975 with no commercial success. Before *Alive*, Kiss was ready to fold. It was their last effort before Neil Bogart's brand-new Casablanca label would drop them. But none of that was to be. When *Alive* went gold, manager Bill Aucoin told each member of Kiss to find new places to live...in Manhattan. No more of this Bronx, Queens and Brooklyn stuff. Gold meant success. Success meant money. Money meant big leagues. The roller coaster was about to begin, and they'd barely had time to let that sink in. They'd played the small clubs for a year or two and paid their dues, though Peter might argue with that. But when success came, it came fast...literally overnight...because one night was just like any other...a show in support of their live album with the guys feeling uncertain about the future...and then the next day they were informed that they were about to be very rich. The next day it was *pack your things and go find a place in the city.*

Success and fame would come with a strict relentless schedule of album, tour, album, tour and the band members needed to be accessible, and their whereabouts easy to track. And so Aucoin insisted they all be in Manhattan on the same island and in close proximity to the recording studios and Casablanca office.

When you manage a small rock band that hasn't had much success, you operate on a small budget with the minimal amount of heads possible. You might hire a road manager to look after the crew that deals with staging, instruments, lights and hotel rooms. Bookings come and go, expenses are paid...or not...but everything is self-contained and exists on a relatively small scale. From day one, it was Aucoin paying for all aspects of the road. It was Aucoin who as early as September 1973 put each band member on a 75 dollar a week salary. This was two months before the first album was even recorded and five months before they played their first show on the road. By that time in February 1974, the band pulled in approximately 750 dollars a night to divide amongst its members and large crew. As that 1974 tour got off the ground, it cost 7000 dollars a week to stay on the road while the band wasn't taking in anywhere near that amount. That's close to 19 months of touring over budget and digging the financial hole deeper. These problems were not for Paul, Gene, Peter and Ace to deal with. Bill Aucoin picked up the tab gleefully and got in over his head, financing everything on his American Express card until the fall of 1975. The band members in their relationship to their record deal and chances at rock stardom weren't the only ones with their backs to the wall. The release of the live album in September 1975 was not only a last ditch effort by Kiss as a band, but a last desperate move by Aucoin, who owed astronomical amounts of money.

Everything changed for Kiss on November 7, 1975, when Aucoin first learned of *Alive*'s gold status...the marker of selling 500,000 units of an album. Aucoin called Lydia Criss at home that day. The guys had been on the road and Lydia wasn't doing that stretch of the tour. She was one of the first to know. In fact, she knew before Peter, and she knew before anyone in the band. They'd hit the big time and were about to come into a lot of money. For Aucoin, managing a band then became considerably more complicated because now come the accountants and lawyers, and in the case of Kiss, a whole new business management team, which makes it all the more peculiar when he quickly takes on the responsibility of an additional band...this one called Starz and eventually another called Piper.

May and June are pivotal months...the operations of Kiss are now divided into two fronts...Aucoin Management and Rock Steady Productions, In. Bill moves the entire entity to 645 Madison Ave where the sprawling Kiss offices will now be located, and two major figures in the Kiss universe now enter the picture to change everything. Now that Aucoin Management has hired business managers Carl Glickman and Howard Marks, a new era of Kiss is beginning. The very presence of Glickman and Marks in the band's orbit is to remind them, and everyone involved that Kiss, like it or not, is now a business.

Aucoin is determined to protect the mystique of the band to such a degree that one of the reasons he fires the original crew at the end of May, is because he believes them to be far too close to the band for comfort...his comfort.

The changes that have occurred amongst Kiss personnel in such a short period of time cannot be overstated, nor can the degree of how swiftly people were extracted, amounting to that of betrayal. The Kiss road crew was a loyal bunch. A small, modest but effective unit that kept the stage show up and running since the early club days when the guys in the band were travelling in a station wagon. Unfortunately, loyalty doesn't hold much influence in what is cost-effective because they've all been swiftly scrapped.

Fired.

Fineeto.

Adios.

Goodbye.

New faces...new chapter.

Fuck You.

The End.

Glickman and Marks is the big leagues and they've brought their own people in to oversee the big picture and the bottom line, including a young financial wiz kid of sorts to serve as a liaison between the band and management named C.K. Lendt, an accountant fresh out of business school and roughly around the same age as a few of the band members. The new additions include a fresh stage production that will be bigger in scale, scope and ambition. But again, professional show business outweighs the loyalty of friends who thought they'd always have a job. However, multiple technical mishaps involving pyro and explosives along with hospital stays and damn near blown off hands were enough to inform Aucoin's decision to hire a professional crew at the urging of his new management team.

Rick Stuart, who handled every aspect of the band's touring is given the boot...as is JR Smalling, the voice that opens *Alive*...the album that is now headed toward platinum status and opens with what will become the immortal battle cry introduction...*you wanted the best and you got it...the hottest band in the laaaand...Kiiiiiiiiiisssssss!*

In pop culture, it's an introduction topped in fame only by "Here's Johnny" and "Ladies and gentlemen, the Beatles." And it's JR Smalling's voice that opens one of the hottest albums of the year...and now he's out of a job...

cut by the new team that will oversee Kiss's millions. But it's not just in the original road crew where outrage and unrest are seeping in.

Down south while on tour with Starz a few weeks earlier, Sean Delaney had gotten an urgent call from Bill Aucoin who insisted he get on a plane back to New York immediately. What it amounted to was the entire Kiss entourage ending up in a monstrous airplane hangar at Stewart International Airport in Newburgh where a group called Theatre Techniques worked out of. They'd been there for some time already and Aucoin was beside himself as the entire band and new crew of several hundred seemed to have all but declared mutiny.

It seems that upon returning from some brief European dates, Paul Gene, Peter and Ace have been shown the new stage set for the upcoming summer tour and they're not happy about it. Apparently, Glickman and Marks hired stage designer Mark Ravitz to come up with something bold and ambitious to take on the road for Kiss's *Destroyer* show. It's not that the band hates every aspect of the stage design, but the fact that they weren't consulted or told about any of it pissed them off enough to be sent into screaming tantrum mode before accepting the new details and settling into them. The new live production resembles the set of a Broadway musical much more than a rock and roll stage and portrays that of an annihilated burnt-out city.

Despite the inner turmoil the first few shows of the tour are mostly without a hitch and it's been raved about in the Virginia press as the most extravagant rock and roll show one can witness. Kiss are the gods of glitter and gimmickry and make artists like David Bowie seem tame in comparison. Still, while certain mega success is already in motion, they're not as big yet as we think they are in certain places. The run of *Destroyer* on the pop charts has stalled and the singles haven't lived up to the promise of last year's "Rock and Roll All Nite." The only real mishap during the first week is in Richmond on the third night when Peter narrowly avoids injury when a fan throws an M-80 toward the stage and it lands on the drum riser before detonating just inches from him. The real issues related to the *Destroyer* tour take hold when most of the stadium shows are scratched with some cities to be rescheduled for later dates in smaller venues, as Aucoin Management seems to have bitten off more than it can chew in some places, overestimating the band's popularity. When it comes to stadiums and multiple-night stands in one venue, underwhelming ticket sales will be a factor time and again resulting in periodic wake-up calls. Roosevelt Stadium stays, however, even as local politics meddles with it. While Jersey City tries to halt the remainder of scheduled performances, the Kiss concert is given the green light as John Scher slowly pieces back together the summer concert series, though he prepares reluctantly to take a huge financial loss on the Kiss show, which has only sold 7000 of 40,000 tickets. Regarding that massive full-page ad in the Sunday Times, Scher asks Aucoin and Kiss to pay for half of it.

It's a glorious weekend sun that beams over Hudson County where a New Jersey and New York gathering of wasted teens collects on Droyer's Point in Jersey City on this, the first Saturday after the Sunday. The Bicentennial summer has reached its zenith...and now, one week past the Fourth of July celebrations, nothing has changed. At the very least, the pat pat pats of the most basic firecracker packets remain a constant, though every once in a while, you get the random blockbuster or M-80 that rattles the nerves.

Hazy, hot and humid is the common description that every weatherman from the television networks and radio stations always come up with for days like today. In the mid-afternoon stench lingering above and beyond the Newark Bay Extension that feeds into New York City and downtown Jersey City straight from the New Jersey Turnpike, the sweaty mass of humanity collects across the dank soiled green of Roosevelt Stadium's trampled baseball field...stoner teens and twenty-somethings...guys in wavy shoulder-length hair that droops over naked sunburned shoulders...shirtless youth wearing only cutoff denim shorts and sneakers. It's more common in Bicentennial-era America than at any other time in the nation's history to see teenage boys and young men all shirtless. The sea of bare skin in the concert crowds of the 1970s is a visual phenomenon in and of itself. The kids who do wear clothes dress in primary and secondary colors...the customary dungarees on almost everyone as raucous riffraff engages in the throwing of objects...an onslaught of cardboard orange juice containers, glass bottles and just general garbage...flying and floating about the crowd.

While acts like Bob Seger and the J. Geils Band get a lot more respectable attention from the local New York music rags, both are the opening acts before Kiss takes the stage just after nightfall. The show begins erratically as the guitars jump ahead of the band introduction.

Danna-nanna-nanna-nanna-nanna-nanna-
nanna-nanna-nanna-nanna-nanna-nanna-
dugga-da-dugga-da-dunt...
dannaaaaaa....
dannaaaaaa...

As Peter steers a shaky ship behind the kit, Paul and Gene descend from the staircases on either side of the stage. Paul is cued in, engaged and always on point. Gene, however, is selling us some bullshit, as he demonstrates that he has not yet learned how to play "Detroit Rock City," the show opener and opening song on *Destroyer*. He doesn't miss a step though...confident and bold in his delivery of the painfully wrong bassline...acting like this is how the song goes...perhaps counting on the fact that maybe not everyone in the crowd has purchased *Destroyer* yet and maybe won't notice. Performances are loose and unstable at best. Kiss is not particularly noted for their musicianship even by the critics who are on their side. Even those who champion the band are fully aware that the live delivery rarely goes more than a few minutes without a wrong chord, note or out-of-time fuckup. Whereas the powerhouse live acts like Zeppelin and Floyd on a musical level become a conduit to something on a cosmic plane for many people, Kiss merely shocks and titillates visually with the music playing a secondary role. Kids walking out of a Kiss concert express their delight in the theatrics. We'll be repetitive to stress that the theatrics are what have people talking...Ace, blowing up his guitar...the levitating drums...Gene vomiting blood...Gene spitting fire... oh, the fire...the fire...the fire...man, all the fire. And the explosions!

In Jersey City, a sort of homecoming, tables backstage are covered with countless tubes of face paint, powder, brushes, silver and black eyeliner, lipstick...each member with their own personal makeup box. This is one of the first things indelibly etched in the memory of C.K. Lendt who is introduced to the Kiss live experience tonight at Roosevelt Stadium. He sees the members of Kiss in all their outrageous rock and roll glory for the first time at this performance. The personas are striking, and they embody perfectly the wide spectrum across good and evil and power. Backstage is a compound of tents made up of food and game stands that resemble an Italian feast... something akin to St. Rocco's or San Gennaro's. In fact, the clams are from Umberto's and the pastries are from Ferrara's. The aroma of zeppole, calzone, sausage and peppers is the furthest experience of the senses as one can expect in a rock concert environment. Even the Perugina candies that are plentiful throughout the backstage area remind one much more of every Italian grandmother's living room than a sex, drugs and rock and roll adventure. There is seemingly just as many people backstage as there is in the audience...friends, family, record execs, industry insiders, other musicians and their families and friends, and of course, the hangers on who wouldn't have given any of these guys the time of day just two short years ago. The band has rented something like five sightseeing buses...the kind that take tourists around New York City. These vehicles provide transportation to the numerous friends, family and VIPs coming into Jersey from the city.

For C.K. Lendt, it's quite an initiation into the nightly life of a successful rock band, and Roosevelt Stadium is his breaking-in. At 24, he's a babe in the woods by his own admission...a brand-new MBA graduate one year out of business school in a recession economy where jobs aren't falling into people's laps. There is no recession in rock and roll though. While popular music and the bad karma of the hedonistic lifestyle of excess on every possible level eventually comes round in later decades to humble most rock stars while decimating others, rock and roll knows no limitations in 1976. And so C.K. Lendt observes the money. He sees it all around him in every bit of hospitality offered to Kiss and the hundreds, maybe thousands backstage and the party atmosphere that will no doubt spill out of Jersey City and back into Manhattan before the night is over. It's clear that Bill Aucoin spares no expense from the band's costumes to the light show to the drum rise to the pyrotechnics to the backstage catering that feeds the band, crew, families, friends and groupies...and even further once they return to the road...the hotels and transportation. And then there's the bill for Ace Frehley's champagne, which is its own separate expense. Money is no object here, and it will be Lendt's job to be a part of the machine that guards and handles the very finances that he is so thoroughly observing at Roosevelt Stadium.

Glickman and Marks could potentially have extended their own responsibilities and handled Lendt's role themselves. Both are adept in financial matters. Glickman is known as a financial genius with a knack for taking bankrupt companies and turning them into millions of dollars for himself. Marks has already intervened in a brief three-way royalty dispute between Aucoin, Casablanca and the band earlier in the year when the success of *Alive* was bearing its first fruits. Truth is Marks could probably have handled the job. But the point is, he didn't have to. So, he hired C.K. Lendt because with the job came the responsibility of traveling with the band and maintaining communication with them every day...a liaison of sorts to bridge the band with management and the label. The guys in the band seem indifferent to Lendt's role, though they mostly know he's one of the important guys doing important things with the money and the business and that's all they really know or even want to know or care about. Ace and Peter, especially. Paul falls somewhere in between, though he is just as serious as Gene as being the ones responsible for maintaining the vision of the band, and they take their success seriously. Paul likes to have a good time like everyone else and will occasionally drink alcohol and take a hit off a joint, but he makes sure to not fall into dependency or addiction. His vice is women...not quite to the extent of Gene, but while drugs and alcohol are Peter and Ace's pastime, it's the groupies who take priority for Paul and Gene's entertainment. Again, Paul is steering the ship with Gene, though Paul remains as clueless about the money and business end as Peter and Ace even a little naïve. Gene is the only one in the band with dollar signs in his eyes and he is always paying attention.

The day after Roosevelt, Paul and Gene are in Cape Cod doing a radio interview when he casually mentions *Destroyer* not being very popular among the band members and that they'll be working again with Eddie Kramer on the next album.

On Sunday afternoon, July 11, 22-year-old Fancy approaches several men along the stretch of Eighth Avenue between Fortieth and Forty-First. She's a few blocks out of her usual territory and one of the men reports her to an Officer Seckler of Manhattan's South Precinct. He tells Seckler that she had offered him a "good time" for 20 dollars. The only difference on this day from any other day was that until this day, offering a good time for 20 dollars was still legal in relation to "loitering." In other words, had Fancy tried to sell her ass on Saturday just 24 hours earlier, she wouldn't have had the cuffs slapped on her wrists. But she tried selling her ass on Sunday instead, and so she gets taken away and held under New York State's new law that makes loitering "for the purpose of engaging in prostitution," a crime.

The anti-loitering law is going into effect literally hours before the start of the Democratic Convention, and any prostitute tramping the streets anywhere near Madison Square Garden will be rounded up into overcrowded holding cells, leaving the streets of midtown with a slightly less number of whores. The convention runs from July 12-15. Though it takes Democratic nominee Jimmy Carter until the final day to announce Walter Mondale as his running mate, party unity is nearly unanimous as far as the clear message within the Democratic Party. There is no division, no strife and no contesting pushback in the candidacy of Jimmy Carter, and unlike the tumult of the previous two conventions, this one goes off without incident.

Following opening night, *Rolling Stone* magazine throws a party for Carter's campaign staff at Automation House on the Upper East Side. Several staff members considered "young and hip," Hamilton Jordan, Jody Powell and Pat Caddell are in attendance as well as a who's who among celebrities. Having gone from small hippie enterprise in San Francisco to schmoozing with the cultural elite, *Rolling Stone* is aiming at respectability and now the establishment is mingling with the anti-establishment...an eclectic assortment of politicians, journalists, authors, actors, comedians and rock stars... names like John Belushi, Jane Fonda, Ben Bradley, Carl Bernstein, Warren Beaty and Gary Hart.

It's not surprising that Abe Beame was the first mayor of a major city to get behind Carter given the poisonous attitude of the Republican opponent Gerald Ford toward New York City. As far as the mayor is concerned, it's been the city's misfortune along with the misfortune of America that the people who should have been healing the country have been further dividing it, thus revealing that these few Ford years have merely amounted to an extension of Nixon. This is the Nixonian Experience incarnating in the form of a division problem with Ford as the remainder. Beame himself is not very popular among New Yorkers. As comptroller for former mayor John Lindsay, he foresaw the fiscal crisis years earlier. Beame entered the mayoral race in early 1974 resentful of the New York columnists claiming that Lindsay left the city in good fiscal condition. He'd contest that the city was left with a 1.5-billion-dollar budget deficit. By late '74, Beame slapped a freeze on all municipal hiring. A few months later he eliminated public employees. This hadn't happened in New York City since the Great Depression, angering the unions until the backlash was so great it prompted him to partially reverse his decision, hiring back a limited percentage of the workers. Many of Beame's critics were put off by the mayor, painting him as weak and lacking in confidence in times of crisis. For the pip squeak mayor, it wasn't a good look to go before the President of the United States and ask for a bailout or as the more vicious bootstrap Republicans would say, a handout.

"We are not asking for a handout," Beame would argue. "We are asking for equal treatment in times of extraordinary economic and social pressures."

Ford saw it as a temporary fix before someone had to ultimately deal with the problem or go into Chapter 11. And so, Ford said fuck you. Beame saw it as a betrayal, not just to New York, but to the rest of the country, as New York is the nerve center and heart of the country. It wasn't lost on Beame that foreign correspondents covering City Hall were incredulous over how the richest country in the world would abandon its preeminent city.

"Would the French disown Paris?" he'd challenge. "Would the British allow London to become insolvent? Would the Soviets abandon Moscow?"

That was nearly a year ago.

But with Ford brushing shoulders with Beame aboard the Forrestal last week leaving the impression that the two have kissed and made up even if it's obvious political theater, and an energetic convention with the brightest of hopes for the future being hosted by the city, things seem to be looking up in the peak weeks of this most patriotic of American summers.

8

KISS AND SAY GOODBYE

As if the gimmicks of Kiss aren't enough, word of mouth has it that the local girls of the nearby Patricia Stevens modeling school will be giving away kisses in the lobby of the Baltimore Civic Center before the band's show on July 13...not that any of this has anything to do with the band. These types of distractions exist all around the main attraction on these tours...groupies, radio stations doing promotional stunts that entail competitions and contest winners and numerous outside entities that attach themselves to the event. The band members see and hear nothing of this. But distractions also penetrate the band itself. By mid-month, Peter is playing with a fractured thumb, courtesy of his fragile temper. He plays the July 17 West Virginia show with his hand wrapped in tape. Physical mishaps aside, it is always concert attendance numbers that show up to remind the powers that be that their venture is not yet as big as they would like it to be. It's another baseball stadium, this time in Birmingham, Alabama where they only sell some 12,600 tickets among the 20,000 capacity.

As the tour gets into full swing and moves through the remainder of July in the Midwest, Aucoin Management is faced with more harsh realities that they've overestimated the popularity of Kiss in some markets. Consequently, more dates are cancelled, including the Comiskey Park gig in Chicago which is given a different reason other than ticket sales. The July 31 show is supposed to have been the second in a series of concerts dubbed the World Series of Rock. Comiskey has a curfew though that prohibits concerts from going past 8 PM. For Kiss to finish their headlining set in time for curfew, they would have to go on in broad daylight which defeats the purpose of the Kiss stage show. Tampa Stadium is also cancelled. That show would have presented problems even had they sold the place out, due to the Tampa Bay Buccaneers organization. The expansion football team is set to play their inaugural season in the stadium in early September. Given the damage to the turf already done at a recent Jethro Tull concert, there's a lot of logistical pushback against rock concerts these days, and it's all over America and not just places like Florida and New Jersey.

Without a studio providing financing yet, Robert Stigwood is putting up the three and a half million dollars that will be necessary to film his movie based on Nik Cohn's *New York* article. At the outset, director John Avildsen meets with screenwriter Norman Wexler whom he wants to hire to write a script. He's worked with Wexler in the past on *Joe* and trusts him. Wexler most recently received some accolades for the *Serpico* screenplay. The problem with Wexler though is that he is known to be somewhat unstable and suffers from manic depression. He also spent some time in jail for threatening to kill President Nixon in 1972, which merely amounted to some flippant comments he made on a flight from New York to San Francisco. Stigwood is a bit unnerved in their first meeting when he notices a gun in the bag next to Wexler's feet. Reluctantly, they hire him to write the screenplay.

John Travolta is spending the summer researching the disco scene in preparation for his role in Stigwood's film. He prepares on two fronts, the first of which is to attend outer borough dance clubs to get a feel of the crowd and the people who frequent these establishments. The other front he's working on is the dancing itself. John is quite aware of his celebrity status upon entering places like 2001 Odyssey in the Bay Ridge section of Brooklyn. He frequents these clubs not only as a means to understanding the club scene, but as research into the role. He knows what he's going for in terms of playing the Vinnie character, the head Face of Cohn's article, but he wants to do it by way of observing the behavior of the real people who go to these clubs...getting to know their nuances and characteristics...how they walk, talk and interact with each other...what their view points and values are... even how they view him as John Travolta, a celebrity wandering into a local place filled with regular people and how they react to something like that. It's all a means to adding depth to his role...or as he puts it, *character coloration*. Bay Ridge is predominantly Italian as are most of the kids inside 2001. Most are heterosexual as well. The local discotheques seem at least on the surface more mainstream friendly and don't resemble what the judgmental mind might refer to as the deviant world of the city's underground. Disco now seems universal in race and sexual preference, though some might argue that this belief depends on location. And though Manhattan caters to money, disco isn't preferential to class. The outer boroughs that house the suburbs are just as hopping with the current trends of the dance craze, and it extends far out of Brooklyn and Queens and even the Bronx. Mamaroneck and New Rochelle are hotspots for discos...Zazous in the former...Peachtrees and the Second Floor in the latter. These clubs are all characterized by their own flavors informed by fashion and age. Some places attract crowds over 30 while others cater to teenagers and younger adults in their twenties. The crowds that attend are usually made up of regulars and even the regulars are compartmentalized. There are the weekend people, the weeknight people and the people who show up for specific occasions. Special events like Barbecue Night at Peachtrees which happen on Wednesdays draw an enormous crowd during the summer, mostly kids in their late teens and twenties. Donna Lauria and Jody Valenti of the Pelham Bay section of the Bronx frequent Peachtrees. The girls are on hand for the final Barbecue Night of July. Lauria, 18, and Valenti, 19, both nursing students, are typical examples of the patrons of this establishment who come into New Rochelle to dance. Nobody famous...nothing pretentious...no old money or new money...none of the plastic superficiality of Manhattan's socialite scene...just real people living real everyday lives. The regular people.

The freshly-painted Bicentennial flag mural on the brick wall of the building at 2874 Buhre Avenue in the Bronx represents an era gone by when kids play out in the street and ride their bikes throughout the neighborhood...a relatively safe period when everybody is outside at the same time, everybody knows each other, and you talk to your neighbors whose names you also know along with the rest of their personal business and gossip. Yes, there are places even in the Bronx where you don't have to worry about being robbed, hit over the head, stabbed or raped. There are parts of town where you have the luxury of hearing about these things happening only in other places. The Bicentennial mural sits half a block from the elevated subway platform that hovers over the Buhre/Westchester Avenue intersection, slicing through Pelham Bay from the Hutchinson River Parkway to the Bruckner Expressway. Across the street from the mural is the neighborhood candy store, owned by a friendly fella named Tom who welcomes daily all the kids who normally flock there after school with pockets full of quarters. Kids get lost in the pinball machine while buying up the Bit-O-Honey, Pop Rocks and Bazooka Joe bubble gum. Outside, the Evel Knievel kids jump homemade ramps on Ross bikes with banana seats. School has been out for summer, and so the store is active all hours of the day. Except for the dead of night when the rest of the world has gone to sleep and only the residual glow of dimly lit streetlights bathe the ground below and the store front that wraps around the corner of Buhre and Pilgram Avenues comprised of multiple signs reading Candy, Cigars, 7-Up and Breyers. It is 1 AM, and just diagonally across the street from the friendly candy store a blue Oldsmobile pulls up in front of the Buhre Arms apartment building. Jody Valenti is dropping off her friend Donna Lauria in front of her home after a night at Peachtrees. Weekend DJ, Tony Amato was part of the scene tonight in a rare Wednesday night appearance. Amato normally doesn't work Barbecue Nights, but on this occasion, he must have been filling in, so the dynamic was a little extra special on the dance floor.

As the girls sit double parked, Donna's parents stroll up to the car after having just arrived home themselves. They peek into Jody's car playfully enquiring about why they are outside this late, Donna's mother a lot less dramatic than her father.

"What are you doing here at one AM, you gotta work tomorrow," Mike Lauria says to Donna.

"What is she doing that's wrong?" Rose Lauria says in defense of their daughter before going up to the window, sensing some pressing conversation taking place. Jody is usually talkative with Rose, often telling her about her boyfriends. Rose asks her if anything happened.

"It's a long story tonight. Donna will tell you when she gets upstairs."

Mike and Rose say goodnight to the girls and head upstairs into their sixth-floor apartment. The girls continue discussing and recapping the evening.

The calm and quiet of the later hours of early morning are a soothing audible elixir after some of these disco nights when all you can hear is the ringing of your ears in a hiss that underlies and overrides everything else including the rumbling of the car engine. As Donna is getting out of the car, she turns to see a man approaching the passenger side door from about eight feet away. She turns to Jody, with slight annoyance in her voice.

"Who is this guy now?"

The man pulls a handgun out of a paper bag and fires three shots into the Oldsmobile, striking Donna and killing her instantly. Jody is hit in the thigh, though not enough to cause serious injury. The screaming and incessant blowing of the car horn can be heard by Rose from all the way upstairs in the Lauria's apartment. Mike is on his way to the elevator to go back down to walk the dog. He too can hear the commotion below, yelling for Rose to see what's going on outside. She goes over to the window, and from the street, Jody screams that Donna has been shot, sending Mike scrambling to get downstairs. In the car Donna Lauria slumps over dead into the street... and just as quickly before anyone in the area could know what's just happened, the man with the gun has disappeared back into the shadows along Buhre Avenue and its surrounding streets.

Kiss settles into August in Indianapolis for a show at Market Square Arena. During their stay at the Hilton, Gene runs into Karen Carpenter who is also in town for a concert. He goes to her room where they spend three hours talking, Carpenter grilling him on his debaucherous choice of lifestyle. In Little Rock on the fourth, the band is prohibited from using their pyro theatrics when the fire marshal withholds his blessing. Logistical setbacks are nothing new though and have been going on since the very beginning of the band when some shitholes had ceilings so low that they couldn't even hang the Kiss logo and had to place it on the floor. Despite cancelations in some of the bigger shows on the tour, Kiss concerts at Anaheim Stadium and Atlanta's Fulton County Stadium remain.

Kiss's summer of growing pains is offering them a buffet of the ups and downs of major rock stardom. Are they really major though? There are mega acts that routinely sell out stadiums and multiple arena dates per city. Kiss is not one of them, though not many bands achieved the success of Kiss in such a short period of time in terms of selling out sizable venues. It's only been a little over two years since Kiss appeared on the scene. Granted, Led Zeppelin played Madison Square Garden by their third album, less than two years on the scene. This would probably be the pinnacle for Kiss, and that certainly seems on the horizon, though now it's still an upward climb. In June of 1972, Paul Stanley, then a cab driver still in the process of putting Kiss together, dropped off some people in front of the Garden who were there to see Elvis Presley. He swore one day it would be his name in front of the Garden and the fans on line outside would be waiting to see him. Well, now his band is certainly on the arena circuit, and that will inevitably include the Garden when the time comes. But when it comes to selling arenas with capacities between 13,000 and 20,000 seats, some bands have been able to do it on multiple nights, so it only makes sense as to why the stadium circuit has become commonplace and necessary for some of these acts by 1976. While the Rolling Stones get the credit for the first arena tour in 1969, only the Beatles were stadium-big ten years ago. Nobody came close to that level of popularity. Now bands like the Stones, Led Zeppelin, Pink Floyd, and Yes who are filling arenas for four, five and six nights at 17,000 seats per night, can easily fill a 60,000-seat stadium for a night or two. In the case of Anaheim Stadium, the home of the baseball California Angels, rock concerts have bailed the stadium out of being dangerously in the red and the venue is now run in the black after a handful of shows.

Outdoor gigs of mammoth proportions are no stranger to rock and roll audiences, though most have taken place as festivals, uniting a number of acts on the same bill. This still happens at most non-festival shows, where more acts than usual are on the bill...more acts than the headliner normally carries with them on any given tour, though most of this tour has one or two opening acts...usually Bob Seger and Artful Dodger or Ted Nugent. The stadium gigs, however, are higher profile events with far more promotion behind them. The Anaheim show gets the most hype with multiple opening acts...among them Bob Seger, Ted Nugent and Uriah Heap. A mammoth yellow billboard with colossal Kiss logo in fiery red, orange and yellow hovers over Sunset Boulevard...the four recognizable figures in makeup and costume stand against the display as cutouts of the *Destroyer* album cover. This is Kiss's second billboard in Southern California...the first one back in early 1975 advertising their *Hotter Than Hell* shows at the Sports Arena.

It's no easy task to find an adult who won't completely trash Kiss just for existing let alone take them seriously. Every grownup lets you know whether by media or as responsible adults, that Kiss appeals to young teenagers who are attracted to the antics of fire, blood and bad music. Most concert reviews are scathing, as if the writers are personally offended by the shows they are paid to attend. The *Evansville Courier* of Fort Worth, *Technique* of Atlanta and the *Flagstaff Lumberjack* all within a week of each other offer vicious diatribes while the *Arkansas Democrat* singlehandedly starts the rumor that Kiss stomps a live chicken to death onstage to the beat of the music. It is said that if a Cool-o-meter existed to gauge the hipness and squareness of parents, it would be measured in how well they handle the realities of Kiss in the lives of their kids.

Between Houston and El Paso, the band flies into Atlanta and settles at a Holiday Inn before quickly getting into full costume and makeup for a plug of their upcoming show at Fulton County Stadium. They do it Kiss style in the form of a fundraiser for muscular dystrophy. In the parking garage, the band is confronted by reporters.

"We're talking to some strange people here."

"Not so strange," Paul objects. "We're on our way to Peaches to sell some kisses for muscular dystrophy. It's 93 cents a kiss and it's for a good cause. The more money for muscular dystrophy the better, so come down and we'll give you kisses!"

"And you're just gonna be in Atlanta just to do this thing?"

"We're flying out, but we'll be back towards the end of the month for a concert."

"You got a big thing coming up at the stadium, right?"

Right.

On this tour there is a press kit going around recounting the band's history...all three years of it, but to illustrate their rapidly growing fanbase, one of the stories told repeatedly is of Kiss's very first major concert which was held at New York's Academy of Music on the final night of 1973, just six weeks before their debut album was released. That night, they opened for Blue Oyster Cult and Iggy and the Stooges. The band likes to remind everyone that just a few years later on New Years Eve, it was Blue Oyster Cult that opened for Kiss, but this time the show was held at Long Island's Nassau Coliseum. This little factoid will be beaten to death for the next fifty years. Sure, it's part of their history and they certainly have the right to include it in their timeline...hell, it was a big deal. But even decades after the band no longer needs to boast, Gene Simmons will recount the Blue Oyster Cult/Kiss history every little chance he gets. The band is no doubt on their way to stardom, even the haters know that.

Kiss appears outside Peaches discreetly, being dropped off some yards away and led through a wooded area surrounding Peachtree Creek and finally into the parking lot outside the establishment where swarms of local Georgian fans await to catch a glimpse of their new, and in many cases, first rock and roll heroes. Inside, Peaches is a sauna...the collective body heat of a few hundred people all pressed into the enclosed space along with the overall humidity of summer in the South make it an oppressive environment. Paul and Peter are seemingly the most relaxed under these conditions while Gene is noticeably uncomfortable, continually dabbing beads of sweat from his painted face with a tissue. Ace, who shows up swigging a bottle of champagne, reclines on the counter, comfortably spread out horizontally while signing autographs and telling fans he didn't get much sleep.

As Ace and Peter become more erratic in their behavior and substance use this summer, it becomes a focus of Aucoin's to make sure they don't become a liability while there are millions of dollars at stake...especially on tour. One of the priorities of Glickman and Marks is to keep Ace and Peter happy and keep them provided with whatever they need to make it to every city and every show. For Ace, a weekly supply of the finest Don Perignon is loaded onto one of the band's eight 45-foot trailers and travels with the stage equipment to the next city. From there, the champagne is transferred to a van and brought to the hotel where it is kept in a steel traveling case that was custom built for this purpose. Ace's weekly champagne bill is roughly 1000 dollars.

But that's pocket change!

The guys don't even see the money...at least not yet. They're given wads of cash when they ask for it, but they have no clue how much they're really making...or spending. That childlike naivete and overall sense of being along for the ride is not just exclusive to the band members who are starting to get a false sense that this money is going to be infinite and that every care and worry in the world is gone now. That stuff is for the managers to worry about...those guys in the suits, they've got it figured out and they're taking care of it, and they know what they're doing.

Right?

Those are legitimate questions, especially since the money hasn't quite come rolling in yet.

Or has it?

In El Paso, they wait for the latest incarnation of the theater of the absurd, and that's spoken lovingly by critics who praise the show even if slightly tongue-in-cheek. What's referred to as thunderous acid rock by someone who says the only greater stage show is the giant hydra animal spewing lasers for Yes's current tour...those same lasers that raised a ruckus in Jersey City after the broken mirror blood massacre. Critic Grace Hartger calls for Elvis to eat his heart out.

August 20, 1976...Anaheim Stadium.

Promoter David Foster spares no expense for extravagance in a backstage display that makes the backstage at Roosevelt Stadium seem like an elementary school classroom birthday party. Aside from the celebrities and groupies among the hundreds and hundreds of guests and buffet tables and champagne bars under circus tents are waiters and waitresses walking around tending to your every need, masseuses, arcade games, ice cream stands and a swimming pool. Long into their history, it will become the biggest show Kiss has ever played in America...with all the trimmings of those legendary and even mythic days on the green that sees bands dwarfed on a stage on the opposite end of a sports stadium before a sprawling sea of shirtless fans, arms upward reaching toward the sky in exaltation while a summer sun beats down on the whole scene...the type of picture we'd see on the front or back of many album covers during the Seventies and early Eighties. Though they don't play until well after dark, Anaheim is their day in the sun. The gates open on this Friday afternoon at one with a four o'clock showtime. Legendary Turtles voices Flo and Eddie host the festival-like bill that also features Bob Seger, Ted Nugent and Montrose who replaced Uriah Heap after their cancellation due to lineup problems.

The band takes full advantage of the extra space a stadium provides. An illuminated neon cityscape lights up the space well above the stage It is the *Destroyer* stage show fully realized to its maximum potential, containing every component designed for the tour all at once, including an electrical Tesla coil-type device that will become known in Kiss lore as the God of Thunder machine. The effect which seems to produce lightning is well-intentioned on the surface, but it will ultimately prove too dangerous and inconvenient to drag around on tour and it will not last much longer than Anaheim. The neon city that hovers far above the stage is only revealed in the final seconds of "Black Diamond" when the ritual of the main set's closing song sees Peter's drum riser levitating while flash pots scorch and sear the senses and bombs detonate at deafening levels. The illusion of the skyline floating atop the skeleton of the stage's lighting rig is a dazzling display of illumination and flash in conjunction with the ginormous lightning bolts that shimmer and flicker in red white and blue as a nod and wink to America's summer of patriotic spirit...even if it's Kiss blowing shit up and destroying said city and completely annihilating everything in its path. That is the concept of *Destroyer* with respect to the album's artwork and the comic-like characters inhabiting the rocks on which they hop, skip and jump in exhilarating victorious defiance while the charred remains of the city's outskirts leave nothing aside from the few scattered pieces left to burn. *Destroyer* is a work of bold ambitious vision, though that vision belongs much more to Bob Ezrin than to Kiss. But even as the band continues to grow in popularity, the core fanbase has not been very pleased with the direction Kiss has gone.

In the summer of 1976, Kiss is in the middle of its third full year as a recording entity. The fans from the beginning...the earliest ones that go straight back to that brief Canadian tour just prior to the release of the debut album were initially attracted by the dark nature of the band's appearance, and of course the music had to be good for them to pursue any further interest following their first encounters with Kiss. Many of those first fans who attended those early 1974 shows had no idea who they were, and most were taken aback by the face paint and stage theatrics. They then went out and bought the album, followed by *Hotter Than Hell* later in the year and then *Dressed to Kill* in early 1975. While those albums didn't sell enough to make a commercial impact, it was the live shows that created the word-of-mouth. But it was the raw energy of the music that worked in concert with the provocative nature of the live performances those first fans were seeing. Kiss had seemingly arrived fully formed with a dark and abrasive visual of black and silver to match the power of the music. And those first fans of Kiss for the most part were in their early twenties or at the absolute youngest, late teens. For a band to suddenly appear on the scene playing clubs and colleges, the audience simply had to be older...at least drinking age to catch Kiss's first live performances. Bob Ezrin's entrance into the orbit of the band came on the heels of their live album which unexpectedly catapulted them into the next level with "Rock and Roll All Nite"...a tier of success that makes you visible to the names in the industry that matter. Eddie Kramer, legendary for his work with Jimi Hendrix and Led Zeppelin, recorded and produced *Alive*. As he was not available in late 1975 going into '76, the prospect of Ezrin's involvement was predicated on the question concerning whether the guys wanted the next studio album to be cursed by the same formula only to sound mediocre, not deliver on the success of *Alive* and quickly risk disappearing into obscurity as a one-hit wonder...or if they wanted to take the next step and create a masterpiece. Ezrin is in the business of masterpieces and has forged his name into the rock and roll world with production credits on Alice Cooper's *Love it to Death*, *Killer*, *Billion Dollar Babies* and *Welcome to My Nightmare* and Lou Reed's horrific showpiece, *Berlin*. Ezrin has established a signature sound and when he produced *Destroyer*, he clearly had a vision for what Kiss could sound like. That sound...the subtle and vague voices in the background of random places...car keys, car engines and car crashes... the children's choir and grandiose choruses, lush guitar harmonies, a piano ballad with sweeping strings and orchestration...an emphasis on melody and the total grandeur of it all in conjunction with the visual presentation of Kiss in cartoon superhero form has not aligned with the purists.

Now let that assessment sink in.

Think about it for a moment.

Kiss is evolving at such a high rate that their audience already contains older purists who sit in judgment of the new material and the fact that public awareness of them is beginning to reach young children. Regarding the overproduction of *Destroyer*, it stands to reason that the tepid response to the album has much to do with the band's decision to work with Eddie Kramer on the next album.

So, while most of the stadium gigs have been cancelled or rescheduled in smaller venues, Anaheim is an event which allows the expanding fanbase of kids to witness for themselves just what they've been hearing about for the past year. For the band, the Bicentennial summer has been one of trial and error. Paul and Gene have already second-guessed the *Destroyer* material and are increasingly too self-aware of how older fans are receiving the newly doctored sound. There are also elements of the *Destroyer* stage show that are being reconsidered as the final weeks of the summer tour wind down. More dates are planned for late fall and winter, but as the band will move into re-thinking their direction in the coming month, it remains questionable at this point whether they will continue supporting *Destroyer* or record the follow up album sooner than expected.

If You Leave Me Now

Eight weeks have passed. Autumn has settled in. There hasn't been much of a playoff race in the American League East this year since the Yankees have safely held a lead over the division, which is why there is merely a nonchalant underwhelming enthusiasm in response to the team's first post-season in a decade...at least until the final moments of the final game of the American League Championship Series.

The best of five series against the Kansas City Royals goes the distance... both teams taking two games each. With the series tied, the Yankees come home to the Bronx where they are slightly concerned about Dock Ellis starting. Dock doesn't have a good history with keeping runners close to the base and the concern is whether he'll be able to keep the Royals from running. This puts a great deal of pressure on Thurman Munson behind the plate. This season, Munson became the first Yankees captain since Lou Gehrig. He knows this is how Kansas City maneuvers their way into scoring runs as they're not very endowed when it comes to power, so they need to move runners. Munson committed several errors in Game Two, allowing the Royals to do some running on him. For Kansas City, their only true power hitter, Amos Otis is missing the entire series with an injured ankle, so they need their tactics to be on the ground. They bring Game Five into the bottom of the ninth tied. Two significant things happen in the next moments. One, the first post-season walk off homerun is hit...the collective reaction from the crowd signifies and initiates the unruly New York City bedlam that becomes the backdrop of this Yankees era and puts a reaffirming visual on the city's image as projected to the rest of the country.

And two...Chris Chambliss, 27, first baseman who conveniently came to New York from Cleveland soon after the arrival of Steinbrenner, Paul and Nettles in one swat delivers Mark Littell's pitch clear into the right field stands to send the Yankees into the World Series for the first time since 1964.

Just before Chambliss's at bat, groundskeepers combed through the field, picking up scattered remnants of broken glass from bottles that had been thrown out of the stands and onto the field. New York, even in sports... even in its team's most crucial moments of a do-or-die game, has become a dangerous place...not just on the outside of the stadium...but now on their own ball field where flying beer bottles could assure that nobody...not even the players are safe.

As Chambliss attempts to circle the bases, he instantly goes from a jovial trot to a frantic and desperate maneuvering, tripping over a charging fan on the way to third base while hordes of others surround him by the time he gets there. The base line is no longer visible or possible to navigate as the swarm begins to consume the entire infield while Chambliss is forced to run into foul territory against the obstacle course of fans who mob his every step. In the booth Phil Rizzuto laments on how the new old stadium will never be the same. This surge of New York humanity ready to tear up the playing field hasn't happened since the Mets won at Shea in '69. But the way this frenzy occurs is more symptomatic and symbolic of destitute, depraved and debaucherous New York City than it is an innocent celebration of winning the pennant. It is blatant lawlessness where there's no respect offered toward players from fans as they block, charge into and fall over Chambliss as he tries to cross home plate, which he never manages to do. Once Nettles reminds him that he didn't touch home, he runs back only to discover that home plate has already been ripped out of the ground by fans and replaced with an empty bottle of Hiram Walker peach-flavored brandy.

The merger bringing together the two leagues of professional basketball promises the most exciting and successful year in the history of the National Basketball Association as the new season approaches. With the American Basketball Association out of the picture, it is the NBA with the clear path to thrive in a new era of unlimited possibility...only it doesn't know enough to appreciate it yet. Between the World Series and the addition of the New York Nets into the NBA, it's been half a decade since anything remotely exciting has happened in city sports. Though to be clear, it's not so much the Nets that anybody gives a shit about...it's Julius Erving. The NBA at the time of this merger is without a star of Erving's caliper and it's been a while since New York has had an effective star in basketball since the Knicks last won anything meaningful. What we know is that the Knicks organization is not happy about the very existence of the Nets. Not everyone across the board is all that ecstatic about these ABA teams coming in with their unorthodox three-point shots and slam dunking, though the NBA will not adopt the three-pointer for another three seasons. *That modern nonsense won't go over in our league*, say the stick-up-the-ass traditionalists from their protective stances behind the old guard. *And the Knicks are New York's team! There's no room in New York City for two basketball teams! We have the Garden! The Garden is New York! The Nets are Long Island. Long Island is like being out in New Jersey! They might as well play in New Jersey, it's closer!*

The Nets in New Jersey?

As if that would ever happen.

Behind the new guard, Roy Boe and the New York Nets are in financial trouble that seems to be spreading outward exponentially as the weeks go by into autumn 1976. The owner has reportedly borrowed heavily to pay the 3.8-million-dollar extortion that the Knicks have demanded. There is also the million-dollar loan given to Boe from Home Box Office, an up-and-coming cable company that provides pay TV services in 36 states. In Mineola, a state Supreme Court case is pending against Boe whereby one Charles F. Dolan of Long Island Cable Communications Development Company is claiming that Boe's agreements with Home Box Office, Viacom, Home Entertainment and UA Columbia violate a prior agreement. Boe's agreement with the four cable companies are currently allowed to stand until the pending case is presided over later in the fall. If Dolan wins, Boe will have to return the money he obtained from said cable companies as the agreements will be voided. Boe's biggest problem, however, comes in the form of his biggest asset.

As training has turned into pre-season and the Nets prepare for a gala entrance into the NBA, Julius Erving is refusing to report. Going into the fourth year of a seven-year deal, the Doctor is insisting he will not report to his team until his 1.9-million-dollar contract is renegotiated. Erving symbolizes the Nets franchise as well as the excitement in the merger...he is clearly the hottest player in all of basketball, and the NBA knows it. Boe has other ideas though, disputing Erving's claims that verbal promises concerning bonuses have not been kept. Boe contends that Erving simply wants the remaining years on his contract renegotiated. Talk in early October within the sports world is already putting out the possibility that Boe in the midst of his financial troubles, sees Erving as part of some sort of merger indemnity. Fans speculate on this hypothetical idea. It's being reported that Boe is considering selling Erving to cover what he owes. By mid-month the specifics are that he has allowed the Los Angeles Lakers, Milwaukee Bucks and the Philadelphia 76ers to negotiate with the Doctor. Lakers owner, Jack Kent Cooke is on hand with his lawyer Alan Rothenberg. There's Pat Williams and Wayne Embry, the respective general managers of the Sixers and the Bucks who have also been in contact with Erving's business agent, Irwin Weiner. They're feeling him out to see what his demands are. Owners... general managers...lawyers...the whole deal.

Fans aren't buying it though.

Trading or selling Dr. J for the sake of covering debts would amount to the biggest betrayal in New York sports history and go against everything the team and its fan base had worked for in its nine seasons...world championship notwithstanding. The commercial profit in merchandise alone is testament to the value of Erving. Souvenirs like t-shirts run a spectrum of prices...though a regular Nets team logo shirt is $3.75 each while Erving-inspired shirts reading *Is There a Doctor in the House* go for a whopping $4.50. Despite talk of Erving's future on the team being questionable, nobody takes it too seriously. It's the Nets. They're the champions. They're entering the NBA on primetime national television in just a few weeks. Eventually, there will be a ring presentation. The biggest star in basketball...*their* star...will be there. That's the way we'll logic this out. He hasn't shown up at training camp and he's skipping the exhibition games. But not to worry! He'll return and play, just wait! All of this contract stuff and talk of money will fall away.

It'll all work out in the end.

Won't it?

At Yankee Stadium in the final hours of Thursday, October 14, 1976, the site of the former home plate that is now filled with some peach brandy is not the only location on the field tying one on. Just across the diamond an empty bottle of blackberry brandy protrudes from the hole where second base used to be. Third base is a bottle of Dewars. These are not the remnants of the Yankees celebrating their first pennant in twelve years. That celebration has just happened in the locker room. What the groundskeepers face on the field, however, is the pigsty of unrelenting unrepentant mayhem where trash is the dominant prop. It's not just the brandy bottles making up the bases, but there are hundreds of additional glass bottles scattered throughout the otherwise carefully manicured lawn that now serves as a trampled and worn-out shithole, ornamented by tens of thousands of pieces of shredded paper. This is New York as victor for the time being. They still have to play here in a few more days when it's a whole new ballgame.

The five game layover that the Big Red Machine has had this week is grounds for the naïve to imagine that this period of rest might cool off the hot hitters and it just might give the Yankees an advantage. The Yankees may have finished with the best record in the American League, but they finished third in the majors and won five less than the Machine's 102 for the season.

Still, the Yankees 97 wins is nothing to sneer at. For Billy Martin, it's his first pennant as a manager. He's been to the post-season three different times now with three different teams, so it's rather fitting that he's able to do this in New York where he built his name. He has so far delivered on his statement to Steinbrenner, and although he doesn't have all the pieces that he needs in terms of building the ideal roster, he's found his current team in the World Series against the defending champion Cincinnati Reds.

While the Yankees bicker with the Reds and the Nets bicker with Dr. J's agent and lawyers, the two gentlemen running for President of the United States bicker with each other. President Ford on the campaign trail and trying to legitimately win the election so he can say he won the presidency rather than inherited it, begins to sling mud on Jimmy Carter, claiming to the American people that Carter will say anything to get elected, depending on where in the country he happens to be. In Pontiac, Michigan he tells an audience, "He'll say anything anywhere to be President of the United States. He shouldn't be president." In 1976, this statement is controversial, and reporters are chalking it up to one of the harshest statements ever made by an incumbent president toward an opponent. When asked if he feels his comments were too much, he tells reporters that his comments were well directed. He proceeds to compare Carter's personality to liberal activist Bela Abzug whenever he's in New York City, but when he travels to America's rural areas, he conveniently becomes a peanut farmer. He warns America that Carter is a reformer and America doesn't want reformers. Carter will increase spending and raise your taxes and the tired mantra of irresponsibility that Boomers and Gen Xers will hear from Republicans about Democrats for the next half century until they are either too old to comprehend or they're lying in a box. Carter calls him out on it in a telegram the very next day, and on October 16, releases the telegram to the public.

The absence of Julius Erving from Nets training has become a soap opera in the sports press and the situation even has the Knicks concerned insofar as their advertising in the New York newspapers promoting their pre-season games against the Nets at Madison Square Garden. For the first game, an ad that reads *The Battle of New York: The Knicks with "Clyde" Frazier and "Earl the Pearl" Monroe take on the New York Nets with "Dr. J," Julius Erving* is changed for the second game whereby Erving's name is removed along with any pretense that he'll be playing. Since the Doctor has refused to join his team, attendance has been significantly down for the Nets. This not only affects the Nets, but a chunk of the NBA is feeling it as well...the teams that play pre-season home games against the Nets also experience low crowd turnouts once it becomes known that Erving isn't playing. Promoters who gave the Nets big cash advances to play are regretting their attempts to capitalize on Erving's popularity. In New York, fans are granted refunds after $65,000 in advance Garden sales give way to angry buyers once it becomes known that they won't get to see Dr. J. With growing concern, even CBS gets cold feet. The network that has signed on to show the Nets season opener against the Golden State Warriors on primetime television has now backed out of the deal, cancelling the broadcast amidst the uncertainty of Erving's status.

Historically, the Reds lost the World Series twice to the Yankees in 1939 and 1961. The era of the Big Red Machine began in 1970 with the advent of Sparky Anderson as manager and the move into a new stadium. This is really the only thing the current Reds have in common with the current Yankees who ushered in their new era with Billy Martin and their refurbished stadium. It ends there. After losing several years in the post-season, the Reds are finally the defending champions. Charles Finnley's A's dominated most of the early Seventies, winning three consecutive World Series. But the Reds are now the powerhouse of Major League Baseball, winning the championship in 1975 against the Boston Red Sox in what has become one of, if not the most memorable World Series in history. The roster is impeccable. Joe Morgan and George Foster are sluggers. Johnny Bench and Tony Perez have respectable homerun power as well, as does Pete Rose, the actual hottest hitter in baseball. Of the regular lineup's eight hitters, five of them have finished the season with batting averages over 300. The Red's top pitcher Don Gullet starts his second World Series in a row, defeating the Yankees in the first game on October 16. George Steinbrenner and Gabe Paul have their eyes on Gullet and are determined to make him a Yankee by the end of the year. It's hitting that gets most of their victories and it's hitting that demolishes the Yankees in the first three games, giving the Reds a swift three games-to-none lead in the series.

With the recording of the next Kiss album completed, the band spends the remainder of October on the West Coast. The latest round of photo sessions is mostly for the upcoming winter tour along with some seasonal promotional shots. October 19 is a full day as the guys begin in a Hollywood studio and a blustery set of fake snow with photographer Neal Preston who shoots the band holding Christmas candles and playing in their white surroundings. It's over the period of the next three days when photographer Barry Levine accompanies Kiss to ABC Studios in Hollywood for one of his very first on-location shoots where he'll photograph non-rock celebrities in addition to Kiss while they're in town to film their spot as the music guest on the *Paul Lynde Halloween Special.* Lynde is a comedian known for his quirky quick-witted one-liners. In recent years, he's gained mainstream fame as the middle square on TV's *Hollywood Squares.* Television is the number one source for promotion and visibility, and tacky as the Halloween special seems, Bill Aucoin sees the advantage and possibilities that could result from Kiss doing such a program. On the surface, the content seems quite juvenile and aimed at kids, though there is enough entertainment for older audiences who can appreciate guests like Margaret Hamilton who 37 years ago played the Wicked Witch of the West in *The Wizard of Oz.* Hamilton is on set revising her role and dressed uncannily like her younger self in the MGM classic. Kiss also shares the set with Florence Henderson of *The Brady Bunch*, Roz Kelly of *Happy Days*, comedian Tim Conway, and Donny and Marie Osmond...wholesome family entertainment at its Bicentennial-era finest.

And here comes Kiss...

...arriving onstage via the transport of a fragile looking wrought iron elevator to a nightmarish soundscape of wailing sirens. The band steps off looking serious and determined...especially Paul whose facial expression upon exiting the elevator is one of a fighter stepping into the ring with something to prove. Host, Paul Lynde usually full of his own unique brand of quirky comedy and never lacking in smiles looks genuinely horrified, even if it's an act. The band members take their spots on an abbreviated version of their stage, complete with a smaller and more compromised version of the Kiss logo behind Peter's drums. The macabre ambiance of hovering chandeliers and torches over the band suits the music and fits the dark nature of the performance. Without wasting any time, Kiss takes the stage as the sirens are eclipsed by a raucous explosion, and the first chord of the music literally segues out of that explosion in this lip-synched and edited version of "Detroit Rock City." Technically, "Detroit Rock City" is the latest Kiss single, though some wiseass DJ flipped the record over and decided the B-side, a ballad sung by Peter called "Beth" is better. In the weeks since, "Beth" has gotten the airplay over "Detroit Rock City" and seems to be a minor hit going into this TV performance. This takes nothing away from the furious attack of "Detroit Rock City." The fury and bombast of "Detroit Rock City" and the corresponding prancing of Paul Stanley will be a moment in television history that redefines glamour, glitter and sex appeal in rock music while defining cool for the younger generation of kids who have no fucking clue what he's singing about but are transformed and transfixed by how smooth and awe-inspiring he looks doing it. Gene just outright looks possessed... jumping, leaping and leering out demonically at the TV audience...reinforcing everything we've heard about how creepy and ghoulish he is.

The demon.

The bat lizard.

To little kids, the scary guy or quite simply the mean guy, depending on how young you are. Whether or not Kiss intends to appeal to the very young is beside the point...it's already happening. This whole shock rock thing that we can also attach to people like Alice Cooper only goes so far down the age spectrum. Teenagers are one thing, which Alice mostly appeals to...but Kiss, upon taping this performance for television will inevitably end up down the rabbit hole of notoriety, greeted first and foremost by children.

"Detroit Rock City" serves as a welcoming call to arms on the surface. Though, beneath the surface the tension-filled narrative recreates a reimagined account inspired by the true story of a fan who was killed in a car accident on the way to a Kiss concert. For "Beth," the setting is much more wholesome as the spotlight is on Peter who performs seated at a piano while the other band members stand around him, not very visible on camera. Originally called "Beck," and penned with Stan Penridge, his friend and former bandmate in Chelsea, the sentiment expressed by Peter in the song is dedicated to Lydia, though I defy you the reader, or anyone on God's earth to make the name Lydia fit into the melody.

From the moment Paul Lynde tries to talk to Kiss following "Beth," the comedian cracks unfunny jokes that to an audience of squares would seem hilarious, though Paul, Gene, Peter and Ace aren't amused as the scripted scene reveals the guys to be standoffish and dismissive toward their host. The six-year-olds who will watch at Halloween time won't know it's all an act.

"Your makeup is something else," Lynde tells them. "How long does it take to put it on?"

"We don't *wear* makeup," Gene says coldly.

"King of the Nighttime World" is the third and final song that Kiss performs, clumsily edited for television, not for content but for length. The band ends abruptly following Paul's bold disclaimer, chanting "I'm the king...I'm the king...I'm the king...I'm the king...I'm the king..." But whereas this would normally lead back into the chorus to ride out the song, the band ends on the final "king," coinciding with one last simultaneous chord and explosion, and capped off by the demon walking toward centerstage to breathe fire for all of America to see right in the comfort of their living rooms. As for the naysayers caught in their self-righteous religiosity, their misreading of the lyrics will empower them in time when they launch a campaign of moral judgement and contempt against the band, fueled by the rumors of grafted cow tongues, dead chickens, Satan-worshipping and the Starchild proclaiming himself king.

Wednesday, October 20, 1976 is a wet day in New York City, forcing a rain-out for Game Four of the World Series. The Yankees have an extra day to regroup and assess the obvious...that they were proving no match for the defending world champions. The Big Red Machine is aligned, well-oiled and shredding thinly any hopes New York has of reclaiming its past glory.

What glory? some ask.

This is Ford-era Metropolis, albeit a wasteland. Sure, it's suggested Carter will probably win the election in two weeks...but none of that takes away New York City's reputation as the armpit of the East Coast...or even perhaps America. You don't just win that away.

Well, a win could help the morale.

Sure, it could!

A win would boost the morale and give the city something to smile and cheer about. But it's three games down now. That's four games in a row that they have to win. Nobody takes four in a row from the Cincinnati Reds. Out of 162 games in 1976, the biggest losing streak they had was four games and that was a combined four losses to two different teams. But there's a philosophy that stands in the face of the "we have to win four games" mentality that says..."No, we don't have to win *four games*. We have to win *one* game. Tomorrow, we play just *one game,* and we have to win that *one game*. If we win that *one game*, we get to play one more game the *next* day. When that day comes, we'll have to *win* that one game. It's one game a day...not four."

As the sky rains down on New York on this very same day, the sudden question over the status of Julius Erving is being watched closely and inquired about periodically throughout the day by the sports media. This wasn't even a concern just a few days ago, as unsuspecting Nets fans awaiting the start of a new season as champions in a new league, now have this new thing thrust upon them and hanging over their heads.

It really does happen this quickly...the impact of which, as one might imagine, renders an entire organization and its fan base thrown off and speechless...running the gamut between shock, denial and back again. It's a magnitude proportional to the world ending...a sense of finality...the wind going out of the sails...the portcullis crashing down...the bitter, instant, unjustifiable difference between the championship and last place...all in the stroke of a pen.

It's over Johnny.

Julius.

Erving.

Is.

No.

Longer.

a.

Net.

You heard that right.

Although F. Eugene Dixon, owner of the Philadelphia 76ers, makes the announcement that his team has reached an agreement with Nets owner Roy Boe, it is said that Boe hasn't yet put his seal of approval on it. This only prolongs the sense of false hope registered in the hearts of every Nets fan until the eleventh hour when Boe and Nets lawyer, Bob Carlson make it official with their signatures...signing away their star and any remote possibility of being contenders in the NBA.

Simultaneously, the Doctor, meeting with another group of lawyers has signed a six-year 3.5 million dollar contract with the Sixers. Just hours before the start of the season, New York's homegrown hero and future NBA revolutionary now belongs to Philadelphia. Whether it's in the stars under the orchestration of some unseen greater power or force...or just by total coincidence, the backdrop of the lingering Bicentennial and spirit of '76 is not lost on anyone on either side of this event that sees Erving ending up in the city where the Declaration of Independence was signed and the Sixers have their namesake in that history of 1776...adding a symbolic significance of the Bicentennial that is perfect synchronicity for Philly, and insult to injury for New York...a city that within a few more hours will also lose the World Series.

In the Flushing section of New York City's Queens borough where Yankees fans aren't very plentiful, the World Series passes without much interest, as Flushing is home to the New York Mets, and let's face it...the Mets suck. For this reason, baseball in Flushing usually ends in May. In their fourteen-year history, the Mets have only made the post-season twice and the last time was three years ago. Between the Mets and the football Jets, Shea Stadium has grown accustomed to a great deal of losing. The Beatles are probably the best thing that's ever happened there. Add to this the season-long annoyance of the Big Red Machine's domination of the National League for two consecutive years, and it's not difficult to understand why most people in Queens couldn't give two shits about the World Series in 1976.

Peck's Depot Grill sits on 164th Street just off Depot Road in North Flushing. It's an old man's bar that often gets frequented by local kids in their late teens and early twenties as it is on the night of Friday, October 22. Twenty-year old Queens resident, Carl Denaro is three days from departing for the United States Air Force and has met some friends for a last hurrah of drinks and partying. He arrives at Peck's around 11:30 and for the next two and a half hours gets reacquainted with a girl he knows named Rosemary Keenan. Rosemary arrives with a group of her friends from her part of Queens, though she and Carl spend most of their time in the bar talking and playing pool and foosball away from everyone else. Enough drinks in to be feeling no pain, he and Rosemary split to go off somewhere a little more private. They leave Peck's in her blue Volkswagen Beetle. With Rosemary driving and not knowing the neighborhood, Carl directs her a few blocks north where they pull over and park on the Northeast corner of the 159th Street and 33rd Avenue intersection. The two have been making out for a few minutes when the car seemingly explodes, at least in Denaro's mind. In an unknown blast of force that sends a raining deluge of shattered glass descending downward and outward over the front seat in numberless miniscule fragments cascading onto the floor of the car and over Denaro himself. Whatever has just occurred, he knows they're in trouble. He instructs Keenan to floor it out of there and then loses consciousness.

Carl Denaro wakes up after having been passed out for some ten to fifteen seconds...long enough to freak out Rosemary Keenan who has pulled away from the location where they were parked and is driving aimlessly because she has no clue where she is. He directs her back to Peck's. On arrival, a dazed Denaro walks back into the establishment he left just fifteen minutes ago and is greeted by his friend Vinnie.

"Carl, you don't look so good."

Denaro stumbles in looking for a place to land.

"I don't feel so good. The car just exploded."

Vinnie sits him down.

On observing Denaro his friends are shocked to see his t-shirt turn blood red in a matter of seconds. Whatever has happened, his dirty blonde shoulder-length hair has been holding a torrent of flowing blood back until he tilts his head forward and it all rushes out to drench his shirt. Whatever has happened isn't clear, as his brief utterance of the car exploding is vague.

What car?

Whose car?

But the second he sits down, and his friends see the blood running rapidly over his shoulder and down his body they're mortified. His friend, Vinnie promptly helps him up and gets him to the ER.

This was supposed to have been a jubilant evening. After bouncing off various jobs and community college for a few years, Carl Denaro had made a decision to visit a military recruiter some months back. When asked why he wanted to join the Air Force he told the recruiter that he wanted to follow in the footsteps of his uncle which wasn't entirely true. The truth is that he needs some sort of direction in life and some sort of career, though he feels bad about not being honest with the recruiter. Denaro has a passion for photography and has photographed a number of rock concerts in the area. The idea was to complete his Air Force training and then specialize in one area of focus in aerial photography. The weekend of October 22-24 was intended to have been his last free one before embarking on this major life decision.

But Denaro will not be making his departure in the coming week. Nor will he be going into the Air Force. Instead, he'll be issued an honorable discharge.

In the hospital, and in and out of consciousness for several hours already, Denaro is only somewhat aware of what doctors have been doing as they remove shards of broken glass from the back of his head and unbeknownst to him, skull fragments. His arms are also pretty nicked and cut up as well. He also notices a presence of police officers in and out of the room... one of which approaches him. He asks Denaro if they should contact his parents. His dad lives upstate, so he's of no concern to the dazed and confused young man.

"No," Denaro tells the officer. "As long as I'm home by seven my mom will never know I was out."

Denaro obviously has no idea what's going on. The officer takes the initiative to wake him up to the harsh reality.

"Son, you're not going home, you've been shot in the head."

10

ROCK AND ROLL OVER

The rustic landscape of the Palisades Interstate in its twisting northward spread of autumnal colors veers off toward 59 West at Exit 8 and continues in local familiarity that could pass for any random stretch of highway in the suburbs of New Jersey, though we've crossed the state line some time ago where we are well into New York State...a small location known as Nanuet where the only actual remainders of Jersey is situated further west on 59 where the New York Thruway intersects with the Garden State Parkway. This little hamlet of Rockland County exists a few minutes out of Nyack and just six miles across from where Tarrytown and Sleepy Hollow hover above the banks of the Hudson. The Star Theater is a three-million-dollar theater-in-the- round that sits comfortably in a spacious lot just off 59 East in Nanuet. The place is now defunct, having closed its doors in 1975 after just a few years of existence as a concert venue. The building is not without purpose however as the acoustics of the unique architectural layout and its remote location lent themselves to the recording of the next Kiss album when the band rented out the theater with Eddie Kramer for several weeks throughout September and October.

Kramer, already legendary for his work engineering Jimi Hendrix, Led Zeppelin, Traffic and enough others to merit his status was the mastermind behind turning *Alive* into a listenable cohesive experience. He recorded the four source concerts that went into the live Kiss album and then did all the post-production, though at this time in 1976, it is perceived that the album was recorded at Cobo Hall in one night. The guys have put all their faith into Kramer, and they go back with him all the way to 1973 when he did their demo in Studio B at Electric Lady Studios. One of the problems with the first few studio albums as discussed by fans and even the band members themselves is that they never captured the raw power of Kiss as heard on the concert stage, which is why *Alive* was so crucial in translating that energy. Fans who would later get their hands on that 1973 demo would lament those first few albums ever further in comparison with the sound captured by Kramer on songs they already knew so well. Among the variety of producers that slip in and out of the Kiss orbit, it is obvious that Eddie Kramer understands the band better than anyone and is the only one to capture the closest thing to a definitive sound for Kiss.

Against the backdrop of the Ford/Carter presidential debates, October 1976 continues to be not just a time of bitter consequence in New York, but also one of insult to injury as the month comes to an end. Out on the Island, the Nassau Coliseum plays host to one of the more humiliating nights in the history of the venue. What should be a homecoming celebration is a non-event. The Nets give out their championship rings in Uniondale while the man who helped them get there is 120 miles away in Philly. The embarrassing crowd size of 4,239 with most of the arena empty is a clear indicator that nobody cares. The Nets lose to the Indiana Pacers 90-89. Nate Archibald leads the Nets with 27 points and 8 assists and keeps them in the game enough to contain the Pacers, but it's not enough. John Williamson is the leading scorer at this point six games into the season and he's on the bench during the final minutes of the game. He scores 16 of his 20 points during a hot first half, but Kevin Loughery believes the team to be doing well enough during the final minutes and doesn't think of putting Williamson back in. Of course,

Williamson is going to defend his coach when asked about the decision after the game.

"The team was doing well. Kevin made the best decision. He knows we have a tough game tomorrow night in Philadelphia."

In Philly, the Sixers route the Nets 104-80. The press is much more ruthless toward the Nets than sympathetic, portraying the Nets as the former New York Ervings that are now the New York Used-to-Bes.

Erving is still presented with his championship ring in a rather tiny makeshift presentation out in the hallway of the Spectrum where Nets trainer Fritz Massman game him his diamond ring. The Doctor shows off his ring to his new teammates. Joe Bryant is particularly impressed.

"That's a bad ring," he tells Erving. "People around my way would shoot your hand off for it."

In Philly, the Nets could make anybody look good. The morale is at an all-time low...as low as any sports team could go. In a specifically devised defensive strategy, Loughery puts Jan van Breda Kolff on Erving, who shadows him through the first half, allowing the Doctor to score only four points. Erving doesn't break open until the third when he scores ten straight Sixers points in a row within a two-minute period. He puts up 18 points total...not his best game and he certainly isn't in mode to be his usual self...no slam dunks, nothing fancy.

At the end of the night, Erving is not gleeful or celebratory in the victory.

"In a lot of ways, it's kind of sad. You enjoy it when you win, but you enjoy it with reservations."

Though he will transform the game and the league with his revolutionary stamp on the slam dunk, time will be unkind to Julius Erving's career statistics as five of his 16 years as a professional basketball player are spent in the ABA which will result in difficulty in assessing an accurate or even fair reading of his accomplishments through a system that will not allow those ABA stats to be absorbed into his NBA career. While the story of Dr. J in New York ends in October of 1976, Julius Erving remains a universal symbol of the merger's profound impact on the NBA and how the game of basketball will be played long into the twenty-first century.

In the first days following the World Series, the entire city and their unruly sports fans are all but put on trial by the rest of the nation. The talk of many towns and their media have turned to the dangerous environment of Yankee Stadium and the hostile nature of the fans and their outrageous behavior, occasionally captured on live television. It's not just the constant verbal obscenities often hurled at players of opposing teams, but fans who feel compelled to jump out of the stands and onto the field as if it's a birthright... fans who throw glass bottles and other objects at the other team, and what a disgrace and an atrocity it is to put themselves on display in this manner on the most hallowed ground of all sports fields. They're still talking in Kansas City over two weeks later about the debris falling all over the field as players from the Royals had to pave their own path in order to retrieve the ball in the hazardous outfield of Yankee Stadium. *These are adults we're talking about, not children and they act like animals that need to be caged! How dare they throw bottles at the Royals!*

And Reds fans...you'd think they'd just appreciate that their team won the world championship, but noooooooooo...

Reds fans have to complain about the vulgar unruliness of New York's citizenry, dropping straight from the arrogance of the rural heartland the clever analogy that there's a worm in the Big Apple.

There are two major incremental changes that elevate Kiss's popularity and success between fall 1975 and fall 1976. The first, as we have already surveyed, is the success of the *Alive* album. The second takes place 11 months later when the *Paul Lynde Halloween Special* airs on ABC. This is where all of mainstream America gets to see Kiss at the same time...and some for the first time. If there's a Beatles/Ed Sullivan moment for Kiss, this is it. There are parts of the country that had either heard of the band and never saw them or had seen their pictures in magazines and heard the urban legends that were already circulating. The TV special coincides with the rapid climb of "Beth" on the pop charts, and while lots of people had already been hearing it for a few weeks on the radio, not many knew it was Kiss. The Peter Criss ballad is turning out to be an unexpected hit for two reasons. One, because of its B-side status, and two, it's a ballad, hardly representative of Kiss. But in its own brush with phenomenon, it's found a life of its own...especially in the weeks since the Halloween Special. By early December, the unlikely smash will peak at number 7. Paul Lynde is where most of America actually sees Kiss perform for the first time...seeing that they are indeed 3D figures who move like real people and not just flat pictures on pages and posters. Sure, some of the older teens scraping their twenties had already seen the *Midnight Special* last year or perhaps Mike Douglass two years ago...but let's face it...that show's demographic is housewives. Paul Lynde is the point where teenagers and small children alike are met with a common interest, and kids of all ages in school are talking about Kiss...the youngest ones already begging mom and dad to buy them *Destroyer*...or *Alive*...or anything that says Kiss on it!

If you're a child out shopping in a store with your parents...let's say Two Guys or Korvettes for instance...and you sneak off to the record department, you can't miss the Kiss bin because their new album *Rock and Roll Over* is front and center. You peel back the records one and at a time. *Woah! What's this? This is Alive? It's so fat! It has two records in it? Holy crap! What's up with their costumes? Why are they different on Alive than they are on Destroyer? And this one over here...Hotter Than Hell! The costumes are different again! What kind of a band IS this???*

Then you pick up this other record where you see the Kiss guys dressed in suits looking all proper. This one is called *Dressed to Kill*. This entire experience captures your imagination unlike anything you've ever seen before. You have to have these records. You have to have all of these records! Imagine what these records must sound like! You hold them all in front of you. You want them all. You're going to ask mom and dad for one...or two...but you really want them all! You want to put them in your mouth and suck on them like candy. That's how intensely these little square works of art appeal to your senses! You want to be it! You want to consume it! And instead, it's consuming you!

The visuals and image of Kiss is now driving the music. There's a reason that although Paul's name is credited with writing "God of Thunder," it is Gene who sings it and uses it as his showcase song for vomiting blood onstage. The songs are tailored to their personalities and there is just no way Paul could be convincing in the role of such a song. He and Ezrin knew enough to pass it to Gene just as he knows Peter's raspy voice is more suited to "Hard Luck Woman," a brand-new ballad penned with Rod Stewart in mind. More suited to Gene's temperament is a new mid-tempo rocker, "Calling Dr. Love." The egotistical male confidence brought about by sudden fame is evident in the newer songs where Paul and Gene now have the dominant upper hand over the females they address...whereas early songs like "Parasite," "Two Timer," "Hotter than Hell" and "Strutter" all see the women having the upper hand. All that has changed in less than one year, and in two particular songs, Gene in his domineering vocal presence adopts what become trademark works. In "God of Thunder" he belches angrily and authoritatively like something only half human...

IIIIIII am the looorrrd of the waasste...laaaaaannnnd...
and IIIIIII com-maaaaannnnd youuuu tooooo kneeeeeel...

In "Calling Dr. Love," like a demented vampiric lothario, he warns...

In the ennnnd youuu'll lehht meee ee-inn...
youuu'll let meh thru, there's nuthin' you can do-oo-oh...

Kiss makes it clear from here on in. Females will submit. Females will bow down. Females will obey.

The funny part about Kiss and its growing audience is half of the fan base is much too young to detect the chauvinism in songs like "Love 'em and Leave em" and "Mr. Speed." When a first grader prances the playground at school singing *Put yaw haaaand in ma pah-keht...grab onto ma rah-keehhht*, it's unlikely that said first grader is aware that the rocket he's singing about is a penis. The content in new songs like "Take Me" and "Ladies Room" is lost on most kids who have no true understanding of the rock star life, while a frightening number of parents have no fucking clue of what their kids are listening to.

Rock and Roll Over, Kiss's fifth studio album is released on November 10 to an unsuspecting public that was just becoming aware of *Destroyer* with "Beth" in the collective conscience. But this is the way new albums happen in 1976. There is no big three-month promotional lead-up to the release. Most new albums just suddenly appear in the store, often very quietly...and then the promotion starts which is nothing more than newspaper and magazine ads...maybe the occasional billboard if you're on the West Coast, but nothing more by way of visual reminders. In representing *Rock and Roll Over*, Kiss pushes a promotional single that quickly follows on the heels of "Beth." As much as the new album captures the raw rock intensity of the band, it is "Hard Luck Woman" that gets released to the radio and all within the space of a month or two, Peter Criss has seemingly become the public voice of Kiss. This probably doesn't sit very well with Paul who craves attention. Realistically, if Kiss has a leader, it's Paul. He's the one who addresses the concert audiences, though we'd never know it if we only heard Kiss on the radio. But Paul is the one. The starchild. The star. But in the very first year or two of his increasing stardom, he complained to Aucoin and Delaney about Gene getting all the magazine photos and the photographers down front paying much more attention to Gene. Delaney schooled him in the art of getting attention and woke him up to a few hard facts. Gene was getting all the attention because Gene was more interesting. Gene breathes fire. Gene spits blood. Try prancing around a little more, he told Paul. Slide on your knees. Command that attention. If you're the starchild, then be the fucking starchild.

It worked.

With respect to the misconception that the raspiness of Peter was the main voice of Kiss, that may have been true for a few months on the radio, but visually, people were starting to know better. Plus, if you had *Alive* which preceded "Beth" and "Hard Luck Woman" by a full year, you knew. It is Paul's unparalleled stage raps that are an attraction alongside the gimmicks of Gene and Ace. If you've heard *Alive* and haven't yet been to a Kiss show, you go to that show not only expecting to see smoke, fire and blood, but you also look forward to Paul's open canvas of verbal banter. You go to hear him say *People...I know! I know-oo-oh! I just....know-oo-oh-oo-oh-oo-oh! We gonna get this place so hot..."*

What makes this all the more peculiar is what most people don't know... that Peter Criss was at one time the onstage MC who addressed the audience. His rough-around-the-edges but from-the-heart personality clashed with Paul's vision of Kiss from the earliest shows in 1973. No matter how unknown Kiss was at the time, the idea was to create the illusion that the band was bigger than it was. Who are these guys with these big amps? Who are they that they have their own crew setting up equipment for them? Who do they think they are? To Paul, even tiny suburban dives like the Daisy in Amityville were Madison Square Garden to him. In his mind, Kiss was always playing the Garden. So when Peter would thank groups of friends by name for coming out all the way from Sheepshead Bay or Canarsie, it just sounded smalltime to Paul. Sean Delaney agreed and suggested very early on that Paul be the one to address the crowd, and if possible, be the only one to speak onstage.

Aside from Jimmy Carter winning the presidency on Election Day and the press giving rightly deserved attention to it, November is all about John Travolta, at least in the media. Even with the heavily advertised excitement of *Gone With the Wind* finally making its television premiere on November 7 as part of NBC's fiftieth anniversary year, Travolta stays in the spotlight during these weeks. With two films released during the same week, the *Welcome Back Kotter* star is on the lips of families and film critics alike. Reviews of Brian DePalma's *Carrie* are not very kind, although the harshest criticism is reserved for DePalma and not his actors. Sissy Spacek's lead performance is viewed favorably even if slightly over the top. Travolta's character, Billy Nolan is minor but effective, sleazy and brutal. At first, he seems a carefree caricature of Vinnie Barbarino until the fucks start flying out of his mouth and in his limited time onscreen, he proves to be far more sadistic and violent than Barbarino could ever be.

The Boy in the Plastic Bubble, a made-for-TV movie is a far different world for Travolta, though not unlike the surroundings of either Billy Nolan or Vinnie Barbarino. The film is loosely based on and inspired by the story of a young boy named David who was born in 1971 with a hereditary disease known as Severe Combined Immunodeficiency. This condition of a depleted and virtually non-existent immune system renders his body completely susceptible to infections that most people's immune system would naturally heal from. In the case of David, he could easily die. Consequently, he lives his life in a bubble-like containment system, breathing air separate from the outside world, cut off from physical contact with other people, including his own family. David's full name in 1976 has not been released to the public out of concern for the privacy of him and his family, though the media has made a spectacle of his condition in recent years, referring to him as Bubble Boy. The film imagines a teenager who has lived his entire life so far with this condition. Travolta plays Todd Lubitch, a boy born without an immune system and forced to live germ-free in the forced environment built specifically for him...a makeshift containment bubble compartmentalized into little rooms where he lives out his entire existence like a hamster in a Habitrail. This kid who looks like Barbarino gets into his teen years where his conflict begins leading us into the film. His only real friend from childhood has been his neighbor, Gina Biggs. Until now, he seems to have gotten through early childhood pretty smoothly considering...and for as trying as his unique life-threatening condition is, he seems happy and trouble-free except for his dwindling patience with doctors telling him he might be able to live outside his bubble one day. Eventually Todd is integrated into society with the use of a containment suit which allows him to go to school and be outside amongst other people, though he is still restrained and cutoff physically. When the outside influence of teenage life begins to grab hold of him, the restraints of his condition begin to tear at him. His lifelong friend Gina introduces him to her circle of friends. On the surface they seem rather cliquey but display compassion for Todd and treat him to the best of their efforts like one of the crew. They include him in their gatherings and outings but only at the insistence of Gina. To the viewer's eye, however, it seems as though under any other circumstances without Gina in the equation, these kids might not be all that different than the troublemakers and jealous pranksters in *Carrie*.

By now, enough press has reported that Travolta will belong to RSO for the next several years through which he will star in three major motion pictures...pictures that don't completely exist yet, although Robert Stigwood has had him in mind for *Grease* for several years and so far we know that *Grease* will most likely be the second of three films. The first, we know is an adaptation of Nick Cohn's *New York* Magazine article. This does not in any way alter John's involvement with *Welcome Back Kotter*. There is not much said publicly about this film that now has a working title of *Saturday Night*, except that Travolta will be dancing in it. And then there is the fact that most young Travolta fans aren't even aware of the article let alone *New York* Magazine, so their knowledge of whatever the actor is working on is a complete mystery. At the most, they hear it's "some disco movie." On the level of gossip, the actor's personal life becomes a brief tabloid focus when his relationship with *Boy in the Plastic Bubble* co-star Diana Hyland first becomes news. Hyland, at 40, is 18 years older than John. The veteran actress who has an illustrious history in TV, film and theater plays Mickey Lubitch, Todds mother, and the two met and fell in love during production over the past spring. While Travolta is preparing for his starring role, Hyland has a co-starring role in a brand-new series for ABC called *Eight is Enough*, premiering early in 1977. With both actors well entrenched in multiple simultaneous projects, it is their relationship the tabloids remain focused on, though they do their best to keep their private lives private.

Speaking of tabloids, Rupert Murdoch, an aspiring newspaper mogul in Australia has been bent on spreading his grasp on the public in both the UK and now the United States in recent years. Murdoch is of that cheap sensationalist brand of journalism aimed at grabbing readers and gawkers with sex, violence and phony outlandish stories, though there's always a sucker to fall for it when it's passed off as news. When Murdoch moved to the States in 1974, there was no indication whatsoever that he would later metastasize into the nasty, dirty and fraudulent old man who'd routinely deceive and brainwash entire portions of the populace. No siree Bob! Even the respectable Dorothy Schiff believes Murdoch is just a normal and dignified businessman. Schiff is the longtime owner of the *New York Post*...for better or worse, a New York institution, being one of the city's three major newspaper publications over the decades. Schiff, at 73, is in the process of selling her paper to Murdoch, allowing him to establish a foothold in the New York press. Murdoch runs 83 newspapers and 11 magazines, all of which are the type of tabloid rags that specialize in headlines about the 117-year old grandma who fits an entire hubcap into her mouth, the Queens woman who gave birth to an Ethiopian Leopard Tortoise at her own birthday party, and very often some otherwise vital, fit and perfectly healthy celebrity who is reported to be living out their sad final days in some beach house in Malibu, while said rag lures gullible readers with headlines about said healthy celebrity's last dying words and wishes. The *Post* is the kind of newspaper you're likely to find sitting disheveled on an empty subway seat, coming in handy as bed sheets for homeless people. The tabloids always seem to be focused on Travolta these days, either on his relationship with Hyland or his whereabouts...the candid reports that he's been seen visiting the local discos both in New York and out on the West Coast, but now it's quite clear that he's doing some disco movie.

As Stigwood and McCormick go through casting auditions, the producer is more than pleased with the screenplay he receives from Norman Wexler. There are subtle changes from the article, such as the Vinnie character being changed to Tony. Still, Stigwood can envision everything, and he knows exactly the movie he wants his director, actors and crew to make. While John Avildsen is preoccupied with the release of *Rocky*, he's not very responsive to the tasks needed to lay the foundation of pre-production and completely unsure of how to approach the needs of preparing Travolta. As of yet, he hasn't even chosen a choreographer, though John has already been working with a dance instructor named Deney Terrio. Terrio has studied the original moves of Don Campbell of the Lockers and the cast of *Soul Train*. He knows those moves fluently and confidently...the knee drops, the clock splits...and his goal is to make Travolta fluent in the same manner, but also to make him come off as a believable street dancer...everything that aligns with John's own vision for the role. John is also working with Jimmy Gambina, an actor who is probably more useful as a boxing trainer. Gambina has just worked with Sylvester Stallone in *Rocky* and has recently been putting John through a ruthless regiment of cardio, helping him trim 20 pounds off his frame, which was getting a little heavy from the waste down.

In the baseball offseason, the unfolding drama, if you follow it, is almost as juicy as the tabloid world of gossip. After Charles Finley's controversial moves in disassembling his Oakland A's team part by part, trading his star, Reggie Jackson to Baltimore in the process, the advent of free agency has become a reality, and now Jackson after only one season with the Orioles has declared himself a free agent.

Major League Baseball has long been protected since the 1890s by the reserve clause which bound a player to a team permanently unless traded or sold like property. If you were a player, the owner of your contract controlled you for the entirety of your baseball career. Even if your contract expired, the team owner still had the rights to the player. For years, players tried to no avail to unionize until the formation of the Major League Baseball Players Association (MLBPA) in 1966. That was ten years ago, and although the conditions had only slightly improved in the years since with the players union inching toward free agency, it's only become a reality in the past year and a half. The owners have fought back through every step...not just toward free agency, but toward the very act of arbitration, more pension money and salary increase. With MLB raking in more money than ever in attendance and television revenue, most baseball players were still making under $50,000 a year. The owners had always been successful against any challenge to the reserve clause. Player/activist Curt Flood proved more successful than anyone before him in getting the issue all the way up to the Supreme Court...but it wasn't until one year ago when independent arbitrator, Peter Seitz ruled that the expired contract of Andy Messersmith and Dave McNally rendered the players as free agents. Messersmith and McNally became eligible to sign with whatever team they wanted. As usual, the league fought against it, but this time, the owners lost. While McNally transitioned into retirement, Messersmith was able to sign a three-year one-million-dollar contract with the Atlanta Braves. That was the catapult the players needed to make it real for the owners and everyone involved. It put them on notice while everything else regarding the terms of free agency were ironed out in hearings over the past summer.

Only a few weeks into the off-season, there is reason to believe that Reggie Jackson is going to follow Dick Williams who has just been named manager of the Montreal Expos. Williams became manager of the A's just at the beginning of their dynasty and shared in the glory with Jackson... three American League titles and two World Series championships. Jackson sealed his star status under the leadership of Williams, winning the American League and World Series MVPs in 1973.

Now, Jackson is in a much stronger position than he was when the year began. In the post-'75 off-season, he'd been in arbitration with Finley and lost after seeking a meager $28, 500 salary hike. The argument in arbitration against a raise for Jackson was that he struck out too much. The A's organization was also displeased that they'd only last won a division title and not a fourth World Series title. Jackson protested by showing up for camp a week later, to which Finley's response was to approach him on arrival with a check for $2500...a single stand-alone payment that Finley didn't want attached to Reggie's salary in the event they ended up in arbitration again the following year, and he didn't want his star hitter starting arbitration at $142, 500 instead of the $140,000 that he was already making. A few weeks later, just prior to the start of the 1976 season, Jackson was traded to Baltimore.

In mid-November, Thurman Munson flies into New York after it's announced that he's been named the American League's Most Valuable Player of 1976. Munson feels he deserved the award due to his achievements on the field, but wasn't sure if he'd get it, due to his notorious personality. Ever since winning the 1970 Rookie of the Year, Munson has been known to be rather discourteous and downright nasty to the media, though the beat reporters are somewhat used to him, as he is to them...and it must be said, he really came in to his own this past year, finding a new maturity and diplomatic approach to handling interviews. After being the most productive Yankee player in recent memory and leading his team to its first pennant in 12 years, Munson has also become the first Yankee in 13 years to win the league's MVP award.

Now if they could only win a World Series!

With the inevitable subject of Don Gullet coming up to the surface, the fruits of free agency are drawing closer to reality for the 25-year-old pitcher from Lynn, Kentucky. Gullet has spent the first six years of his career in Cincinnati and has become one of the Big Red Machine's more reliable pitchers, and he seemed to have found a home there until the talk of recent months. There is no measure for how free agency has profoundly shaken up the sense of stability and control that owners have always had over their rosters afforded them by that dreaded reserve clause, but no more. Aside from the technicality of the Catfish Hunter situation two years earlier, Gullet becomes the Yankees first free agent, signing a six-year deal for a reported two million dollars.

Munson is still in town from the MVP announcement, so he attends the press conference to welcome Gullet. Elsewhere in the league, the noteworthy acquisitions are roughly from the same pool that Reggie swam in while building his name, as the Oakland A's continue to lose any semblance of a winning team by losing Joe Rudi and Don Baylor to the California Angles. Baylor, for one season, came to Oakland from Baltimore in the trade for Reggie. He filled the gap where Reggie used to be by bringing not only power to Oakland, but speed. Bobby Grich, also from Baltimore, signs with the Angles as well. Grich has been on the minds of Yankees fans, as he is versatile as a second baseman and a shortstop and has homerun potential... though word on the street is that Gabe Paul and George Steinbrenner want a left-handed power hitter and Grich bats right-handed. George wants Reggie and is determined to get Reggie. Billy doesn't want Reggie. Billy wants the opposite since Rivers, Chambliss, Nettles and Gamble are already lefty batters and Billy wants a powerful righty hitter. Joe Rudi is his answer. *Joe Rudi has power, and he doesn't have a bad attitude* is Billy's pitch to George. George, who's just spent millions renovating the stadium with redesigned field dimensions, sees plenty of opportunity in the short porch that lends itself to homeruns behind right field. Why would he want more righties when lefty hitters tend to hit to right field?

Billy should know these things.

Billy does know these things.

Billy does not want Reggie.

George sees Reggie as the missing piece...the juggernaut to base his masterpiece of a team around...the featured name that puts more people in the seats...the show stopper. Billy disagrees with the PT Barnum approach. It's a baseball team, not a circus.

Several players on the Yankees want no part of Reggie as the news begins to focus on the possibility of Reggie landing in New York. The common complaints and consensus is that Reggie's ego is far too big for what the Yankees are prepared to deal with. They say he's not a team player and the entire picture will inevitably become all about him. *We don't need a star of that caliper. Stars are bad news and the Yankees don't need the kind of distraction that a star would bring to New York.*

Yeah, go tell that to the Nets.

Team captain, Munson, who is one of the players who are not very fond of Reggie has pushed for him to be on the team and has advised Steinbrenner to go get the Big Man.

While owners check out players, be sure under no uncertain terms that players also check out owners...and what impresses Jackson the most about

Steinbrenner is his commitment...not just to bringing the championship back to New York, but his commitment to his team and the affection with which he speaks of a number of his players...Munson, Chambliss, Piniella, Lyle, the new second basemen, Willie Randolph...

Steinbrenner flies Jackson into New York during the last full week of November. They meet in the Yankees owner's apartment in the Carlyle Hotel. Steinbrenner cuts right to the chase by asking what it would take to get him to sign with the Yankees. Jackson laughs and tells him that he only wanted to meet up with him and find out how much money he was prepared to spend. Steinbrenner, without missing a beat tells the slugger that the Yankees don't want to spend more than two million dollars, so he was sure they couldn't do business. They both laugh and the ice is broken. From there, Steinbrenner takes Jackson to the 21 Club for lunch, the common establishment for all of the businesspeople and Wolfean Masters of the Universe who run New York. After lunch, the boss sends away his driver, opting to walk with Jackson back to the Carlyle. Whether or not this is a strategic move is always questionable, but in the streets, New Yorkers spot the pair and immediately begin showing love to Jackson...imploring Steinbrenner to get him to sign a contract...bring him to New York...telling Reggie how badly they want him in New York. This is the guy who recently remarked about the hypothetical situation of playing ball in the city, and if such a transaction occurred, the city would name a candy bar after him. Walking around toward Central Park South, the star is quite taken aback by the adoration...yet, again...he has his suspicions that the boss knows undoubtedly what he was doing by walking him through the New York City streets, but it sure helps him in reaching his ultimate decision.

Jackson has considered the Dodgers. He had played there in the 1974 World Series and was familiar with Dodger Stadium, a ballpark that he considers nice and small, and he knows he's already hit very well there. He likes the energy of manager, Tommy Lasorda, and admires their farm club as well as the O'Malley's who own the team. Los Angeles picked him in the free agent draft, but they didn't make an offer. Montreal made an offer. The Expos have offered him five million dollars for five years. The Bronfmans, owners of the Expos, also own Seagram and so would like Jackson to wear a number 7 uniform. He is also fond of Dick Williams and would have no problem playing for him again. Reggie has a thing about America though. It's where he most associates Major League Baseball. As generous as the Montreal offer is, Jackson has a need to play in the States.

With time winding down, Jackson is anxious to get a deal done for the peace of mind of knowing where he'll be playing in 1977, and doesn't want to spend much more of the off-season worrying about it. On the night before Thanksgiving, he and his team of advisors are camped out at the Hyatt right outside of the Chicago airport. Anyone with last minute offers are invited. Steinbrenner has already been in town and then back and forth again between Chicago and Culver, Indiana twice today and has returned with his final offer. Most of the deal is agreed upon while they sleep on a few minor details overnight.

On Thanksgiving morning over breakfast, Steinbrenner writes out his final version on a table napkin and is able to close the deal. The final offer is 2.6 million dollars. The boss makes it clear to Jackson that he promised Munson a long time ago that he'd always remain the highest-paid player on the team...which means that he'd now give Munson a raise...but Jackson is not to be paid more than $200,000 a year in up-front salary. The remainder of Jackson's pay will be deferred or in bonuses. Jackson agrees and the two shake hands. Just after the meeting, the Dodgers get in touch with a three million dollar offer, to which Jackson declines as too late...he's already promised George, and he intends to honor that promise. He signs a five-year contract on the morning of November 29, 1976. The press conference, held in the Americana's Versailles Terrace, the same room where Munson's MVP announcement happened is a news event that grabs the sports world front and center. Munson flies in from Canton to attend. Yankee veteran and senior, Roy White is in attendance, as is Elston Howard, the Yankees first African American player, Yankee legend and coach, Yogi Berra, Jackson's father, Martinez Jackson as well as his mother, Clara. Munson also sees Jackson's signing as a salary boost for himself. The agreement with Steinbrenner is that he will always remain the highest-paid player on the team.

In the Versailles Terrace Room, Reggie is asked if he's worried his star will get lost somewhere else. His swift response rubs them the wrong way.

"I didn't come to New York to become a star. I brought my star with me."

They persist.

"But wouldn't your star have got lost if you'd gone to Montreal or San Diego?"

"Fort Knox is in Kentucky. But Fort Knox isn't lost. Everybody knows where Fort Knox is."

They've already gotten into his head.

11

TONIGHT'S THE NIGHT

With John Travolta as Robert Stigwood's new star under contract, the prospect of success for RSO in the film industry seems promising. The mogul's other key component in the ingredients for his disco film besides Travolta is the music he envisions for the soundtrack for which he intends to look no further than his own clients and source of mounting prosperity. The success of the Bee Gee's *Children of the World* album has assured the completion of the group's comeback, with its first single reaching the number one Billboard spot soon after its release back in September. "You Should Be Dancing" is the hottest song at the moment, and along with "Jive Talkin" and "Nights on Broadway," the group has been re-invented and has now established itself as a major force in the world of dance music...a world they really had no part of just three years ago. The evolution really begins with Barry Gibb, who was coaxed into recording some of the background vocals of "Nights on Broadway" in falsetto. The Bee Gees did not invent or bring about the advent of the falsetto as a lead vocal in modern pop music...that credit goes to Frankie Valli who took a popular technique used in the background harmonies of vocal groups and brought it up front to the lead vocal. Gibb was in fact influenced by Valli's style but had no idea of his own strengths in using it. His falsetto voice has now become the primary recognizable sound of the Bee Gees, and it's Barry, Robin and Maurice who have been recruited by Stigwood to provide the main body of music for *Saturday Night*, which will also feature music from Tavares, a group that will be opening for the Bee Gees at Madison Square Garden in early December.

John Avildsen's *Rocky* is released just before Thanksgiving, and it quickly begins drawing attention to the real star and the proper name behind the film...Sylvester Stallone. Stallone, a relatively unknown actor who wrote the film, fought relentlessly to have this picture made the way he envisioned and just the fact that he got the studio to take on the project and allow him to star in it is a miracle. This is one of those word-of-mouth underdog films that will see large crowds over the next few months.

In the decades before global warming really begins to take hold of the planet, November is still a cold month, which means that the Thanksgiving Day Parade is lined on both sides of the streets with people huddled together for warmth under layers of sweaters and parkas and big blankets. Thanksgiving morning of the Bicentennial year is a harsh 32 degrees with a high of 44 for the day. Macy's puts on its fiftieth annual parade while blocks and blocks of its audience watch from the sidewalks, cheering...much of the sea of bodies made up of outer borough and tri-state area suburbanites who only flock to the city to do things like this with their families and kids...otherwise, the city is known as an unsafe hell where crime happens on all levels, and there are many situations to be avoided...namely the subways. So families choose the safe broad daylight and the false security of live national television for their rare excursion into Fear City, which has no doubt lived up to its name. But it's not just the shadowy element of bad guys committing bad things in questionable places and people dying for being in the wrong place at the wrong time in the concrete jungle of Manhattan. People are tweaking out at home in the suburbs as well. For instance, a 16-year old Levittown kid named George Foder is stabbed by another 16-year old kid right on his front porch before stumbling into his house, instantaneously dying right there in front of his horrified family on Thanksgiving night. In Montvale, New Jersey an 18-year-old, Harry De La Roche Jr. is charged with murdering his parents and two brothers while home from college for Thanksgiving weekend. Much like the DeFeo's in Amityville two years earlier, they were killed in their beds. In Floral Park, two girls Joanne Lomino, 18, and Donna Demassi, 16, are shot on the porch of Lomino's home by some random guy walking up the street asking for directions. Demasi sustains neck injuries but is expected to make a full recovery. Lomino, however, is in guarded condition in the intensive care unit of Long Island Jewish Hospital with serious damage to her spinal cord. At the Wollman Skating Rink in Prospect Park, two teenagers and a ten-year old were shot in what police believe to be related to Chinese youth gangs. Cypress Hills in Brooklyn has seen several days of protests after 15-year-old Randolph Evans was shot and killed by a police officer on Thanksgiving night.

Et cette nuit, oh...
Ah, cette nuit, oh...

On the latest leg of Kiss's trek through the States, this one in support of *Rock and Roll Over*, December 12 in Lakeland, Florida's Civic Center is a rescheduled show from the canceled Tampa Stadium date during the summer. Early in "Detroit Rock City," Paul Stanley and Gene Simmons have already descended the staircases and have assumed their positions on either side of the stage, Paul at the microphone. Ace Frehley remains above his band mates, still atop the landing where he begins his walk down the eight stairs by instinctively grabbing onto the metal rail for support...a move he does every night. The security of habit however is met with narrowly avoided tragedy when the guitarist, already notorious for his bad balance and increasing drunkenness, touches the rail, not knowing in this particular occasion that it is unearthed, creating a connection with his electric guitar. Ace visibly frozen in place is unable to move or let go of the railing as it jolts him for a few seconds until somehow, he breaks free and falls to the platform floor. The poorly recounted story over the decades has often suggested that Ace plunged several meters to the stage, which in itself is a bad enough fall...if it happened. It did not. He does not fall down the stairs, and he does not fall to the stage. He simply falls to the floor at the top of the stairs. What is remarkable here is not just the obvious...that he got lucky in that he could have seriously been electrocuted and possibly killed...but what is also worthy of wonder, is how Paul and Gene themselves don't fall and break their necks running down those stairs the way they do on a nightly basis...especially Gene in those gargoyle boots. Yes, Ace is known for falling on his ass during shows, so this is nothing new given the fact that he took a spill. But this puts Ace's caution into a category of common sense...grabbing a railing to hold on while stomping his way down a staircase in monstrous moonboots. Any sensible person might look for the help of a handrail. So, it is a wonder that more accidents don't occur on those stairs.

Around the holidays nearing the end of 1976, Diana Hyland, who has struggled with her health the past few years, learns that she has terminal breast cancer. She had been diagnosed with cancer in 1975 and went through a mastectomy and chemotherapy successfully before going into remission and returning to work. That's when she began filming *Boy in the Plastic Bubble*, meeting John Travolta. Now almost two years later, the cancer has returned aggressively, and she is told she only has a short time to live. Being out on the West Coast training with Terrio makes it slightly easier for John to spend as much time with her as possible before having to return to New York in a few months to shoot *Saturday Night*. To the best of their ability as two stars in the tabloid spotlight, they manage to keep Diana's diagnosis as well as their private lives completely off the radar, as nobody knows anything of the actress's sickness.

On Sunday the nineteenth of December, what has become known as New York's art-punk rock scene is welcoming John Cale in his debut at CBGB, a club downtown on the Bowery where an entire phenomenon exists. Regardless of and despite whatever the mainstream popular culture has drifted toward in recent years, the CBGB scene plays out around its own orbit. The Ramones, Patti Smith, Television and Blondie, all regulars on the Bowery have all been signed by record labels in the past year and a half with the Ramones being perhaps the biggest at the moment, though they've probably put the most time in, having first appeared at the club in the summer of 1974 and playing there through the entirety of the summer of 1975. If there's one band though, that is responsible for the art rock scene in the city, we don't find them in CBGB, which incidentally stands for Country, Bluegrass and Blues if one could believe that. These origins that have unfolded like an avantgarde urban mosaic are traced back to the Velvet Underground, which owes more to the Warhol scene at Union Square. As a founding member of the Velvet Underground, John Cale already has a built-in audience that packs the house into a tight uncomfortably crowded night as the artist premiers his new band at the club. Cale is also slated to be on the bill for Patti Smith and Television's New Years Eve show.

The members of Kiss are home for the Christmas holiday after a December 21 show at the Spectrum in Philadelphia. The concert serves as a fundraiser with all proceeds going to the Children's Hospital of Philadelphia. The sold-out crowd of 19,500 along with the sold-out crowd of 19,000 in Landover a few days earlier are clear indicators that at least regionally, Kiss are officially in the big leagues in the major cities. After a few days off, the tour will resume in Fayetteville on December 27. The late-year success of "Beth" and last year's "Rock and Roll All Nite" has assured a longer lifeline for Kiss and Aucoin while the uncertainty has dissipated with the year ahead looking to be the busiest yet. But it's not just the homecoming of Madison Square Garden that lies ahead...there's talk of Japan.

Another recent pop chart success out of the city is Barry Manilow. Manilow is a hometown Brooklyn boy who's made his mama proud. He's an ex-jingle writer for television commercials who also served as a musical director for Bette Midler. He's turned out four records in the past three years and has made a name around the New York club scene, especially places like the Bottom Line where he's been a regular since 1974. He's got long blonde shoulder length hair, a big nose and a friendly smile...not particularly hip-looking and certainly not rock and roll but not disco either. The young Manilow, a pianist, offers an adult-friendly contemporary sound of romantic ballads and shmaltz in the dramatic grandeur of minor chords and a seemingly endless series of climactic ascending key changes in almost every song. He appeals mostly to women over 30. Husbands hate him, but he's harmless. As a future artist of relevance named Darius Rucker would later say about him, it takes a real man to admit they love Barry Manilow.

1976 in New York City ends with *King Kong*, Patti Smith at CBGB and two weeks of Barry Manilow at the Uris Theatre. These shows, announced two months earlier and billed as *Manilow on Broadway*, are monumental in his career and serve as the marker acknowledging his true arrival as a major New York City artist and a superstar on the national stage. While he could easily play the Garden for a night or two, Manilow's two-week run at the Uris is more conducive to his sound and the dynamics of his show, and not just a total muscle flex and statement of his popularity. These shows will result in a TV special and a major double live album in 1977.

At 5:30 PM on Christmas Eve of the Bicentennial year, the observation deck of the World Trade Center, which is normally open from 9:30 to 9:30 closes early to observe the Christmas holiday. It will reopen at noon on Christmas Day. The Trade Center's twin towers have become a major tourist attraction in the past year. While most New York City architectural purists loath the existence of the towers and regard them as an eyesore against the integrity of the skyline, the casual majority of everybody else is quite fascinated by the new buildings, especially the ones just out of the city who can view them from across the Hudson or East rivers. That's one advantage that New Jersey, Brooklyn and Queens have over Manhattan...the skyline. Manhattanites exist in Manhattan and are surrounded by Manhattan. The buildings are above and all around them. They can't view it from a distance because they're always inside it. New Jerseans, however, always have the New York skyline to marvel at...something that's always in their view and something Manhattanites for the most part are unable to see in the same way.

The towers in recent weeks have been getting some extra attention in the wide variety of ads that arrive in the form of magazine and newspaper pages, posters, billboards and in some cases, building-size murals showcasing the horrific sight of an enormous ape atop the World Trade Center...one foot on the north tower and the other foot on the south tower...straddling both buildings...a screaming girl in one hand and a crumbled subway car in the other hand. In the earlier ads, it was a crumbled fighter jet. It's been only six months since Dino DeLaurentis put the finishing touches on his ambitious and monumental remake when he filmed the dead ape at the bottom of the towers. Post-production in record time has assured the Christmas release of one of the most highly anticipated films in recent memory. It was one year ago on Christmas when these promotional ads put New Yorkers and the rest of America on notice...*King Kong* is coming. One year later in the last remaining days characterized by the Spirit of '76, *King Kong* has arrived.

The frigid waters surrounding the downtown area and flowing through the city's boroughs during the holiday season are not without their own excitement as the NYPD and Coast Guard are met one morning with a two-hour pursuit of a hot air balloon. The 58-foot red, white and blue balloon floats, skips, jounces and even bumps its way through an expedition turned nerve-wracking chance event...sailing the skies from Staten Island and over New York Harbor as high as 1700 feet down to daunting dangerous dips that nearly brush the tops of some skyscrapers over Wall Street. The vessel now at the mercy of treacherous winds is carried northward. It travels over the Williamsburg and Queensboro bridges and across the East River into Astoria until it's met with dangerous gusts that blow it downward into a miraculous safe landing in a field across from Con Ed's Ravenswood power plant... just 200 feet from a 138,000-volt transmission line.

And finally, as we wrap up '76, those bitter waters of the city aren't the only to see seasonal drama, though the drama that follows is much more theatrical and deliberate. Along the banks of the Delaware River on both the New Jersey and Pennsylvania sides, crowds of thousands line up to witness a visual commemoration of history on Christmas Day. In the continuing spirit of '76, an historical reenactment of George Washington's crossing of the Delaware marks the event's two hundredth anniversary. Actors playing the roles of the general's troops are dressed in full Continental Army garb as they fill four Durham boats for the trek across the icy water. St. John Terrel, the longtime theatrical producer of the event, who has been playing the role of Washington in these annual reenactments since 1953 has returned for this major milestone and celebration. Terrell, at 60, is revered in the local acting community and is known for founding the Buck's County Playhouse in New Hope. The word among insiders of this event is that Terrell will be stepping down from playing Washington in the next year or two. As of now, nothing of substance that can be seen as confirmation of this rumor has been offered by anyone, but the feeling this year is that this extra special anniversary in light of the Bicentennial could be his last one in the role of General Washington. The reenactment begins just after one on Christmas afternoon... out of convenience much earlier than the actual crossing that occurred on Christmas night and well into the morning hours of December 26, 1776. As a northeast wind blew on Washington and his troops imposing one of many dreadful obstacles 200 years ago, the perilous conditions of freezing rain and a dangerous body of water made up largely of unforgiving sheets of ice certainly didn't help as they crossed under cover of darkness to sneak up on their Hessian enemies as they slept through the silent night.

While the festivities in New York Harbor last summer dwarfed anything in history involving boats, ships and fireworks, the celebrations in places like Lexington, Concord and Philadelphia were equally significant, though New Jersey Governor Byrne declares upon Terrel's arrival onto the eastern side of the river that this is a great day for New Jersey, reinforcing that the revolution wasn't just a part of said towns and cities, but that the Garden State too was critical in the outcome of the war with the mother country.

"Certainly," he said to the crowd in the bitter and raw Christmas afternoon following the reenactment... "the paperwork was done in Philadelphia on the Fourth of July, but the war had to be fought and won in New Jersey."

Of course, no New Jersey battle ended the war, though Byrne's lazy non-specific assessment is likely suggesting that the war could not have been won without crucial victories in Trenton and Princeton following Washington's crossing of the Delaware into New Jersey. But that's neither here nor there. That said, the naivete is telling in that these microcosmic reenactments go a long way in reflecting just how out of touch America really is with itself. Take the yearlong Wagon Train Pilgrimage...the eastward caravan of covered wagons, one from each state that travelled across the country in celebration of westward expansion and all the rape, pillage, bloodshed and relocation it entailed. But those aren't the parts being celebrated...not because sanitized history hasn't regarded it all as little American victories, but because we're pretending it isn't part of our history, and we're doing that in 1976 simply by ignoring it. It's been 200 years since the colonies declared their independence from England. That, on the surface, seems to merely mark the Bicentennial solely as the Fourth of July, though we know the war comes next, and the war, also spawned straight from that spirit of '76, is filled with a chronology that spills into '77 and beyond...each significant moment also meeting their two hundredth anniversary. With that, New Jersey begins a 10-day festival on the heels of the Christmas reenactment that eventually leads to Washington's march toward Trenton. The spirit of '76 is winding down, at least on the calendar. But it's 200 years later and the birth of America is still fresh in the collective memories of the millions who weren't even there...the people of 1976. Two hundred years of independence from England. Two hundred years of separation, pride and celebration over the fact that America became its own country...while the most bigoted of today's modern population beats their chests every Fourth of July over how we're American, *not* English...all the while chastising the brown ones who come here for a better life, just like they did.

"You're in America," they tell them. "Speak English!"

Mon Dieu, qu'est-ce qu'il va devenir?

PART TWO

“The weather’s turned and all the lines are down
The things we do for love”

– 10CC

12

AT THE CARWASH

1976, the year of America's Bicentennial, ends with the legendary Guy Lombardo hosting his last New Years Eve over Times Square. What we don't know at this time is that Lombardo will not live through the next year. Lombardo has been the television tradition for families ringing in the New Year for decades and until recently he seemed to have a monopoly on the holiday event. That is until 1974 when Dick Clark, host of *American Bandstand* and a legend himself with younger audiences began his own institution over Times Square called *New Years Rockin' Eve*. So, for the brief period of time comprised of three consecutive years, Lombardo and Clark co-exist peacefully as New Years Eve fixtures.

If you are in Loews State on Forty-Fifth watching the 10:15 showing of *King Kong* or the 10:20 *Rocky*, the movies end shortly after midnight and you walk out to the maelstrom of an electrically charged crowd that seemingly has no beginning and no end. In the decades before crowd control becomes regulated by police barricades and gates separating spectators into organized sections with walking space in between, there is no order to the Times Square assembly. There are no markers of reference. The entire crowd is all stuffed into one collective space for blocks without any breaks or dividers. Once you're in, you're in...you ain't getting out. There is no distinction between the sidewalks and the streets. Both are filled with bodies from Forty-Third Street to Forty-Eighth Street. Lombardo estimates between 50 to 75 thousand people all saying goodbye to 1976 and hello to '77...waiting for the ball to drop down at the top of what used to be called the Times Building, now Number One, Times Square. He reminisces and contemplates 1977 as a year that will bring us a new president and a year of expectancy, curiosity and hope and another adventure of its own time.

1977 begins with the Ice Capades and Alex Haley's *Roots*.

The Ice Capades have been a winter institution since the 1940s. In past decades, the focus has been on Disney-related themes. In recent years, the biggest notables of Olympic figure skating have joined the ranks of star attractions. This year's Ice Capades stars Dorothy Hamill, upping the popularity of the event and causing the demand for tickets to surge. Madison Square Garden is home to the Ice Capades from January 11-27. Hamill, despite being a seasoned and confident Olympic and world champion, is racked with nervousness and falls twice during her debut.

Slated for late January is the highly-hyped television adaptation of *Roots: The Saga of an American Family*, the 1976 best-selling novel by Alex Haley. The 12-hour miniseries will take place on ABC over eight consecutive nights from January 23-30. The tailoring for television came rather quickly for Haley who released the novel just last summer, and the much-anticipated presentation is suddenly thrust into the public eye weeks before the series airs. Much is being said about *Roots*, both good and bad. Though Haley's book has been criticized as not being completely truthful in the events portrayed, the TV series swiftly attracts a consensus that reveals itself to be a major leap forward for television. Unprecedented in its content and deliberate and unapologetic portrayal of slavery and of the horrid and inhumane conditions African Americans faced upon arrival into the so-called New World, *Roots* is the subject of many a conversation in the coming weeks of early '77.

The early days of '77 are glacial, wet, and uncomfortable...at best an uncompromising drenching drivel of driving snow in the forecast of forlorn freezing and fettering frostbitten extremities. The city has seen snow frequently and now a January thaw of 41 degrees has turned everything into a slushy calamity. Yet, if you're in the great metropolis, the act of scurrying along in squishy shoes trying to step somewhere that isn't a puddle, much less a lake, isn't even an issue compared to what the people upstate and west of New York are dealing with. Take a place like Buffalo for instance, where they seem to get a foot of snow dumped on them by default every two or three days...and those are just the days in between snowstorms. On the days of the storms, the real snow happens. It's a real symbolic marker of background presence to the early part of 1977, the weather is. And whether we like to talk about the weather, and whether the weather is a worthy subject of discussion on any other plane is not pertinent when examining what historians will inevitably refer to as the coldest year in hell. The weather is a factor here. The weather is everything here. The weather is whether or not we understand the full capacity of just how 1977 1977 really is. And whether the weather is part of our story is just how vital and accurate our telling of our story is.

The weather is indeed part of our story.

Be it Rocky, Reggie, Kiss or King Kong, none are as dominantly present, nor do any cast a shadow remotely impressive enough in comparison to the elements shaping the winter...for it is the weather that informs, defines, alters and preserves the first few months of 1977. It is the weather that ravages the northern states and spills its wrath across the Great Lakes and into the Northeast. It is the weather that encroaches southerly into states unfamiliar with states of emergency due to weather. It is the weather acting as immediate culprit to a natural gas shortage that is testing the will, patience and adversity endurance of Americans. It is the weather that occupies the headlines, and not by any means is talking about the weather a cliché form of conversation just to break the ice, pun intended. Not this winter. This winter, it is the weather that people are talking about and for good reason, it is the weather. It is the weather that will ensure that you recall this winter. It is the weather that will be remembered years and decades from now. It is the weather that will be marked in 10 and 20 and 30 and 40 and 50-year anniversaries every time another ten years passes from this winter. It is the weather, by God, and the weather is cold.

Ohio gets it first. Michigan too...Wisconsin, Minnesota...anywhere near the Great Lakes. The snow is one thing...and there is snow...lots of snow. But there are other conditions going on around the water that the bone-chilling numbers help to create. December causes January, and by mid-January the snow is repetitious. As one would expect, accumulating incidents of utility disasters and stalled public transportation are the norm as with any major storm. The weight of snow and ice on utility poles cause short circuits, power outages and fires. Rapid transit lines are crippled. Flights are delayed and then cancelled at Hopkins International Airport.

CEI Cleveland and Cleveland Municipal Light are working to restore power. Residential customers going into the weekend on January 21 are promised there will be enough natural gas to heat their homes, though industrial and commercial customers have been cut off, leading to mass layoffs. Residential customers are still being asked to cut their usage by lowering thermostats to uncomfortable levels. Though these blizzard conditions are on the surface reminiscent of any major snowstorm Ohio has seen, the freak and unique combination for disaster that Cleveland escapes is waiting for Buffalo one week later. The single digit and below zero temperatures prolonged for over a month is what everyone is talking about in Western New York, but what happens next in Buffalo is something new in the dynamics of any snowstorm in recorded history.

Although part of the eastern states, Buffalo is inland enough to not be able to claim the ocean as part of its geography, which makes its proximity to Lake Erie even more unique as its unobstructed view gives the city a chance to experience sunsets over water the same way the West Coast does...something not possible in any other major city in the eastern part of the United States. The exceptional physical layout of Buffalo is one of a radial system superimposed on an old-fashioned metropolitan grid system. One fun way to think of Buffalo's idiosyncratic street situation is to imagine Washington DC superimposed on midtown Manhattan, but with grass and trees.

AT THE CARWASH

What has happened in Buffalo since early December is a magnifying of the worst winter conditions to the utmost exponential extremes. Buffalo, notorious for unforgiving amounts of snow gains much of its reputation, at least with respect to modern recorded history, during this winter of 1976-77. Buffalonians are a hearty, rugged people, as are most anyone in Western New York who has endured the winter months. Record snowfall and prolonged temperatures below zero have ensured that they've already seen the worst winter of their lives by mid-December 1976, days before winter began on the calendar. In fact, December began with three feet of snow, and it's multiplied from there. Within days a natural gas shortage has added to the national story alongside the cold that is not just sweeping the Great Lakes and the Northeast, but the entire country.

But Buffalo is different.

Various states of emergency were declared in New York in the last weeks of the Bicentennial year, and Buffalo...especially Buffalo has become synonymous with snow. With regard to the Christmas season beginning with three feet of snow, that first week of December also saw four-foot drifts which only compounded everything. See, it's the drifts off the lake that make Western New York different, and it's the drifts that can bury housing developments and swallow entire towns. The news media often highlights Buffalo's snow problem and they are often slammed by the Buffalo Chamber of Commerce for doing so. And as Buffalo was under siege from the weather all through December, the Chamber of Commerce, like so many small businesses around town, have been closed too. It has become common to see cars strewn about randomly on the side of roads, abandoned. Grocery stores have run out of food and other necessities. Some have signs on the doors apologizing for the absence of milk and bread, promising replenishment as soon as the trucks can get into town. The Red Cross declares a blood emergency after storms have halted blood donations. They're asking hospitals to postpone elective surgery where blood transfusions may be needed. Shoveling heart attacks became common in early December along with downed power lines, stalled vehicles, accidents and jackknifed tractor trailers. On Thursday, December 2 though, the snow had moved out eastward and by late afternoon, the sun came out over downtown Buffalo. With a sense of false hope and a glimmer of bullshit, a weatherman declared that the worst was over. But that was before Lake Erie froze on the fourteenth, creating the conditions for a cataclysm of lake effect snow.

And that is a problem.

Normally, the lake freezes by February, but on this particular occasion, Lake Erie has indeed been frozen since mid-December, and the bitter cold of autumn saw to that. Now in late January, the temperature has not risen above freezing for the past 34 days. Western New York has been pummeled with snow for 28 straight days with a total of 93 inches accumulating since December 14...37 inches of which are sitting on top of Lake Erie. Since the prolonged subzero temperatures have prevented thawing and re-freezing, it's a fine powdery snow that sits inconsequentially on the solid lake until 69-mile an hour winds begin to blow that snow in the direction of Western New York. What nobody knows at this point in the early morning hours of Friday, January 28, 1977, is that the low-pressure system over nearby Ontario will stall for the next three days, creating one enormous clusterfuck of unfuckable proportions and leaving snow drifts of up to 30 feet to do the most damage on top of whatever the blizzard dumps on Buffalo.

Blizzard?

What blizzard?

Buffalo mayor Stanley Makowski declares a State of Emergency at 6:30 AM. Other than emergency vehicles, police and plows, people must be off the city streets. In the early morning hours, there are only eleven classifications that permit driving on the streets of Buffalo. Among those classifications are fuel supply, health and hospital service, food distribution and public transportation. The peculiar thing here is nobody sees anything coming. The weather forecast this Friday morning mentions snow flurries, so everyone leaves home for work and school as if it were a usual day. By ten AM there is still nothing happening outside in the already-white city. Why is there a State of Emergency called? What snow is there on top of the mountains that have already fallen? It's already been snowing for eight weeks... how much worse can it get? But then there is the lake effect and the increasing winds blowing those mounds and mountains of powdery snow straight into Buffalo...sideways snow not falling out of the sky but soaring in from Lake Erie, very quickly creating white out conditions. This isn't even part of the weather forecast. That snow hasn't started yet, though this phenomenon of high winds ferociously gusting and moving snow off a frozen lake and into a city is catching an entire mass of humanity off guard. Everyday people at work or traveling on the roads are now thrust into a new reality rapidly taking shape outside their windows. It almost doesn't even seem real, what's taking place. This monster squall...prolonged and dragging on into the afternoon until everything is just an eternal mass of white on white.

It starts at around 11 AM with those winds that seem to have come out of nowhere and increased into 69-mile per hour gales of high intensity, sweeping and pulling the snow eastward along Lake Erie into Buffalo...that powdery snow that sits for 37 inches on the lake has now developed into a gliding wall of white and dark grey. At first it looks like smoke rising off the ice, moving cyclically upwards in Van Gogh *Starry Night* paisley motion...heightening...hovering...extending outward and finally rolling in toward Buffalo. By 11:30 AM, panic is setting in.

The disaster that ensues is trying on two major fronts...one, the unprecedented amount of snow that is going to cover Western New York...and two, the below zero temperatures at a time when New York State Electric and Gas is asking customers to make sacrifices by setting thermostats at 65 during the day and 55 at night, while gas usage needs to be reduced by fifty percent by commercial customers for the next week. With the storm already settled in, residents are also being asked not to use their telephones for "chit chat" ...in fact, stay off the phone if you don't need to be on it. The lines need to be kept open for emergencies. Phone calls of a social nature will only jam up the lines. If by God you need to make a call, then by all means, call....but keep it short. If for whatever reason you don't get a dial tone, wait it out....the dial tone will magically appear. Don't hang up in frustration because you'll never get the dial tone and you'll only end up trying again just to not get a dial tone and you'll end up repeating the same grueling tortuous cycle. Again, to stress the obvious...this is not just Buffalo, it's all Western New York. In some places it's already snowing for two days. West Seneca, Hamburg, Eden, Amherst and Lancaster have gotten slammed two days in a row...Niagara, Cattaraugus and Chautauqua counties are also getting pounded with plowing operations suspended.

Lackawanna Mayor Edward Kuwik has announced that streets in the city are closed along with the additional advice telling anyone who is stranded on the street, to go to the nearest home and call the Lackawanna Police and they'll come out and take them to a place to stay for the remainder of the day and night. Thousands take shelter wherever they can find it...public buildings, police stations, supermarkets, hotels...any place that still happens to be open. By mid-afternoon, the temperature has warmed to one below zero, with the wind chill factor minus 54. AccuWeather is saying the blizzard will continue through Saturday with the overnight low of ten below zero. In other news, reports have come in from Los Angeles regarding 22-year-old actor and *Chico and the Man* star, Freddie Prinz who is in critical condition at UCLA Medical Center. Prinz shot himself in the head early this morning. Along the compromised reception of the radio dial, WKBW retains a somewhat strong signal as the station continues to go about its playlist of current pop music with occasional reports about the weather. As the afternoon gives way to darkness and the snow accumulation on major arteries such as the Thruway reaches critical mass, KBW's Friday drive home becomes a plead to get drivers off the road as safely as possible. Disco jockey Jim Quin cuts in repeatedly between songs.

"This is Quinn. Listen carefully to me if you are in your car right now." There is a pressing urgency in his voice. "First of all, the New York State Thruway is closed from Syracuse to the Pennsylvania state line... which means any attempt to get on the Niagara section of the Thruway will meet with complete futility. You will be stuck for the night if you try to get on the Niagara section of the Thruway. If you are already on the Niagara section of the Thruway, stay in your car. There are people trying to reach you. Police are trying to reach you with snow mobiles and with cars and with whatever if they can move. But don't panic. If you're afraid, it's okay...listen, if I was out there, I'd be afraid too. Being afraid is a normal human emotion. Being panicky is not a normal human emotion and it's something that you can control. And if everybody panics, there's going to be some serious problems... and maybe some people aren't going to come back. So the best thing to do is just sit there, compose yourself and relax. If you're going to leave your motor running, make sure you watch out for carbon monoxide poisoning. Leave your window open a crack so you can get some fresh air if you feel tired or nauseous or you smell exhaust gases, open your window. But just relax. There are people whose job it is to get to you, but it's gonna take a while... you're gonna be out there for a while. It's gonna be a story you're gonna tell your grandchildren...but you're gonna make it."

Quinn at 5PM on Fri, Jan 28:

"The New York State Thruway between Amsterdam and the Pennsylvania state line....everybody who can hear my voice right now...for all intents and purposes, the Thruway is closed. The New York State Thruway is closed." Quinn is not bullshitting, making the situation sound as dire as it really is. "Now here is the important part. The Niagara section is closed. The state police have reported that along the Niagara section, there may be entrances that look like you can get on it and get away with it. The fact is, you cannot. If you get on the Niagara section of the Thruway...pal, you're on it for the duration...because you are not gonna get off. Now those of you who are on the Niagara section of the Thruway, state troopers and other law officers are attempting to rescue you...and they will. There are some injured motorists... they're gonna help them first. All I can tell you is, if you are stranded in your car, remain calm. If you let yourself panic, there is a chance you could get killed out there....If you start smelling fumes, open your window...get some fresh air in there. Watch out for that. Watch out for frostbite. Keep your radio on KB and relax because we're gonna get you out of there."

Roads are jammed like clogged arteries, impassable...immovable. Air traffic is called off. Even the snowplows are halted as they prove no match. Buffalo is paralyzed. East of Buffalo, the entire town of Cheektowaga is shut down, although the running joke is that the entire town of Cheektowaga has already been shut down for years. All residents of the entirety of Western New York must stay indoors. Nobody is allowed out unless there is an emergency. A list of school closings for Monday is already made public by 6PM Friday night.

In New York City, Con Ed orders supplies cut off to all of its 475 commercial and industrial customers. In addition, the Public Service Commission announces 200,000 layoffs, but that pales in comparison to the immediate danger upstate. There is no relief in sight to ease the fallout from the arctic cold. Life is disrupted across the board as primitive and abrasive conditions impose themselves on the unsuspecting modern age where none of this was in the cards. Taken-for-granted conveniences are rendered useless and unapproachable...a life thought to be real and untouchable without any concrete consequence of infrastructure or man's vulnerability to nature now seems to be memories from another lifetime. The spirit of age, though festive on the surface, is suddenly one of widespread panic and emergency beneath. The vehicles on the Thruway that stall and won't start back up or have run out of gas are now death traps. Without the necessity of heat, it's only a matter of minutes. Those who find themselves in such a situation scuttle about the limited physical space they have left in the universe in desperate attempts to find warmth. Some have gone as far as to slice open their car seats to stuff their coats with the foam cushioning for further insulation.

For those who managed to tune in from their stranded cars, "The Things We Do For Love" by 10CC, "I Will" by Stevie Wonder, the Eagles' "New Kid in Town" and ABBA's "Dancing Queen" among other hits of the day is the soundtrack that accompanies the inevitable transition from the earthly plain into the spirit world for those whose fate it is to freeze to death...those with nothing left on the planet...nothing left in life aside from a faltering dashboard playing the radio and local DJs pleading with them not to panic... people who were told they'd make it through...and now hours into their ordeal, some are already dead while others take a little longer to run out of gas. As the five o'clock hour pushes into Friday evening, death is certain for many on the Thruway whose cars are now buried. The lucky ones die quickly of carbon monoxide poisoning. Quinn cuts back in to those who can still hear the radio.

"Well, again, if you're in your car on the Niagara section of the Thruway or you're stranded wherever you are, don't be afraid...relax, this is a great adventure. A miserable adventure, but you can tell your grandchildren about it. And you'll survive it if you just relax. There are state police and law enforcement officials whose job it is to get to you, and they're working on that right now..."

The DJ launches into ABBA's new song that will stick around the charts for several months...climbing...inching...stretching itself out slowly but inevitably toward that Top 10 of the Billboard Hot 100 where it will go through week after week in a shit-or-get-off-the-pot dilemma for itself until it finally reaches the number one spot for one measly week in April when the weather is a lot warmer. But now in subzero January, you hear it as a brand-new song as you fidget in the car watching the gas gauge, estimating in panic how much time you may have left before your vehicle is completely engulfed in white, thus covering you in total darkness. If you've run out of gas and are in the process of freezing to death, you are now cut off from Quinn and whoever else is out there back in the civilized world trying to assure you that you're going to live...you're cut off and the time estimation of gas preservation no longer matters as you begin to slow down.

Youuuuu can daaaannnce...you can jiii-hiiiive....
haaavin the time of your li-ii-iiife...
seeee that giirrrl...watch that sceeeene...
diggin the dancin' queeeeeennnn.

Hypothermia sets in after only a few minutes for those who no longer have a defense against the raging cold except to kick and writhe around the front seat shivering for warmth, moving as much as you can until you're too cold and rigid to continue. Your normal body temperature has dropped from 98.6 degrees to 95 and will soon slip even further into an inner arctic abyss of the bloodstream.

Friday night and the lights are looow...
looking out for a place to...goooo.

Six are found dead on the first day after...all stranded in their cars have either froze to death or have been poisoned by carbon monoxide. Some people think they have it worse like the ones who couldn't make it home but still managed to find shelter somewhere, or the dude in Rochester pushing a piece of shit orange Fiat with his father on Portland Avenue and Clifford where the car ran out of gas. They think they had a bad day, not even realizing that lots of people died in their cars.

Government helicopters are briefly considered an option to search for lost and stranded vehicles but are grounded due to the overbearing winds. A city fire truck tending to a three-alarm blaze on Virginia and Whitney Place freezes and gets locked into the solid snow leaving it to remain in place, disabled for a few days until the Niagara Mohawk Power Company arrive to pry and free the engine from the ice it is encased in. In the time in between, vandals find the time during the storm to strip the radio and the bell from the truck. Squad 8 on Hamburg and Miami is also vandalized with unruly kids stealing the radio and first aid equipment and throwing it all over the street. Arrests have been made.

While upstate is submerged in the White Death, life goes on in the metropolis. For the five boroughs of New York City, the horrific turn of events is merely a news story a day later. Outside, the ground remains a raw topography of ice patches and occasional snowbanks from storms of past weeks. Still, the single digit temperatures on this clear icy Saturday night are enough to keep most sane people home. But not the young. The young have to get their fill of the weekend and all of the partying and good times they feel they are entitled to. But for some entrenched in the nightlife, it's not all just about sex, drugs and disco. Some people go to the movies.

Shortly before eight, 26-year-old Christine Freund gets out of her fiancé's Pontiac Firebird to stand on a line outside the Forest Hills Theater. It is a lengthy line as Freund secures her spot to purchase two tickets to see *Rocky*. In the meantime, her fiancé, John Diel, 30, chugs along Continental Avenue in search of a parking space. He circles the block to no avail. The streets are quite lively for such a dangerously cold night as Diel makes his way through the intersection of Continental and Austin, a commercial hub of this downtown area amidst the Forest Hills section of Queens. Just down Austin in the opposite direction, another theater is showing *Silver Streak*. There are many theaters per town as most of them only show one or two films. These godforsaken multiplexes of modern times don't exist yet, and so good old-fashioned movie theaters are plentiful in each town. Diel proceeds around another block, headed south and through the underpass where the Long Island Railroad tracks exist above, entering Station Square, now heading west on Burns. The series of grids making up numerous neighborhoods throughout the city is given a pleasant intermission right smack in the middle of Forest Hills where a train station co-exists within a garden community reminiscent of Elizabethan England. The street, made of an intricate-patterned red brick seems sprawling in what is really a confined space, absorbing those passing through into a brief and temporary excursion into another world. The Forest Hills Inn, a trilogy of connected buildings surrounding the square is the dominant presence, drawing the eyes upward where two of the buildings and their interconnecting footbridges culminate in that majestic tower along with the turrets that overlook a seemingly remote locale of gables, wrought iron, dormer windows, alcoves and impeccably landscaped greenery. This area...or more accurately by definition, square...or plaza... or oversized glorified courtyard or whatever you want to call it...all that is known as Station Square is the public face of Forest Hills where you'd never know the devil was right around the corner.

Diel parks on Burns, directly across from the Inn. He then proceeds on foot through the underpass leading back to Continental where he walks a block and a half back to the theater. He and Freund watch the 8:15 showing of *Rocky*. They stay until the end of the 119-minute film that lets out quarter past the ten o'clock hour. Diel and Freund leave the theater and walk to the end of the block, turning right on Austin where they continue another block and a half to the Wine Gallery restaurant. The conditions are brutal, so the Wine Gallery offers warmth and some good food. The couple is not content to end the night after their meal and discuss going dancing. At around 12:20 AM, on what is now January 30, they pay their bill and leave the Wine Gallery, once again taking to the blustery streets. They walk east on Austin and make a right on Continental, quickly crossing the street diagonally toward the underpass leading to Station Square where Diel's car is parked. As the couple are about to step onto the curb approaching the underpass, a man coming in the opposite direction and crossing the street bumps shoulders with Diel.

"Sorry, sorry," Diel says, looking back at the man.

"Okay, okay," he quickly mutters back at Diel and keeps walking.

Getting through the underpass, they turn left on Burns approximately 30 feet from the car. Inside the Firebird, Diel and Freund sit and wait while the engine warms up. In the meantime, Diel turns the radio on.

Youuuuu can daaaannnce...you can jiii-hiiiive....
haaavin the time of your li-ii-iiife...

As active as the surrounding streets may be at this hour, Station Square is more a thoroughfare than a hangout spot. The architecture is quite macabre bathed in the residual glow of the streetlights, and when the straying mind veers off into the sinister, it becomes apparent that this area with its many trees, columns and inconspicuous angles is a total ambush zone.

...seeee that giirrrl...watch that sceeeene...
diggin the dancin' queeeeeennnn...

Three bullets shatter any form of serene that may have existed in the frozen night, smashing through the Firebird's passenger window, hitting Freund in her head and shoulder. The third shot strikes the windshield. Diel is not hit.

While Freund is slumped over bleeding on the passenger seat, Diel jumps out of the car and runs across the street toward the Inn, screaming for help to no avail. He has not seen the shooter, nor are there any witnesses. Helpless and desperate, he gets back in the car and guns it half a block to the end where he stops and blocks the intersection of Continental and Burns, disrupting traffic until the police arrive. Christine Freund dies four hours later at St. John's.

13 MSG

For Kiss, 1977 looks to be a banner year ahead where the band will build on the success of the past twelve months. Already a 30-million-dollar entity, Casablanca Records has now merged with a small film company known as Filmworks Inc. to become Casablanca Records and Filmworks. The Press Office is yet another division of Aucoin Management that has just recently opened, serving as an in-house publicity entity that will also work with other artists, some involved with Aucoin Management, and some not. As the details of booking, promotion and travel are still being worked out, Australia and New Zealand are slated to be attached to the Japanese tour, but the logistics do not line up with the itinerary, leaving the tour to become a minimal two-week trip to Japan scheduled for late March into early April. Following the January 20 show in Lincoln, Nebraska, the band celebrates Paul Stanley's birthday with a drag theme by dressing up as women...each member wearing dresses and full makeup...this post-show after the removal of the Kiss face paint. Now deep into their winter tour, Kiss enters the Motor City for the upcoming last weekend of the month while the East Coast is getting pummeled with snow.

On Thursday, January 27, the band appears without makeup on a local TV news station with anchor Max Kinkel. They keep their back to the camera so as not to ruin the mystique. Though TV hosts and radio DJs and other professionals in the world of media get to see Kiss without their makeup, their identities are kept under tight security. That night they begin the first of three shows at Cobo Hall. The following afternoon, the band learns they've won a People's Choice Award for "Beth." The televised event will take place in a few weeks, but the band will still be on the road. With the weather as their brutal background, Kiss has built a momentum that they are nearing the top of. While the blizzard is pounding the Northeast, the band completes a three-night stand at Detroit's Cobo Hall, the same place they played one year ago while riding the success of *Alive*. It is also the venue pictured on the album's back cover. Though Kiss is a New York band, Detroit has become a second home. There is also a misconception among lots of people that the band is from Detroit, as they are clearly more popular there and they sell far more tickets there than in their hometown. Then there's this little song called "Detroit Rock City." Not "New York Rock City." Detroit gets three big arena shows while New York City will get one. The big news is that Kiss will finally be playing Madison Square Garden. It is not that they can't fill the Garden three nights...but within the short window of time that they'll be in the New York area, the Knicks and Rangers schedules do not allow for multiple concert dates. To satisfy some of the demand, a show at the nearby Nassau Coliseum is added.

Eight is Enough, the new ABC series starring Dick Van Patten and Diana Hyland has been filming throughout January. Van Patten and Hyland play a married couple with eight kids in this comedy-drama that is scheduled to start running in March. On the set, now in February, Hyland who is aware of her serious condition looks perfectly healthy to her co-stars and nobody suspects anything is wrong, though the actress is in severe pain. Quietly knowing her time is short, she manages to get through the first three episodes. Van Patten eventually notices her distress as do others on the set. Diana attributes it to a backache...at least to her co-stars. While shooting the fourth episode, she is unable to continue and calls John who comes to the set to pick her up and bring her to the hospital. In the seven months that they've been together, it's been their thing to take off when John shows up...usually every weekend to Big Bear, Palm Springs or New York. But now things have slowed down, and Diana's health will keep them rooted in California when they're together and at least until John must show up for his new role on the opposite side of the country. Diana has become close with her *Eight is Enough* co-stars, especially Van Patten...though she leaves the set for the hospital knowing what Van Patten and the others don't know...that it's unlikely she will be returning.

With filming of Robert Stigwood's disco film getting underway in one month, everything seems to be falling into place with the set locations and logistics in Brooklyn. However, Travolta's treacherous pace tending to Diana while working with Terrio is already taking a toll, though it's paying off in some brilliant dance moves that have helped boost the actor's confidence and help solidify his vision for the role. There are several layers of negativity hovering over this production, however, and they all point to John Avildsen. The director got along famously with his lead actor at the outset of the film announcements a few months back but is now said to be clashing with the actor's ideas of how he will dance and how some of the scenes will unfold on camera. The director who seems to be the only one not completely on board with Wexler's screenplay doesn't even think Travolta has the proper training for the role. Stigwood is fine with Travolta offering creative feedback and largely agrees with the actor's input. Word also gets back to Stigwood that Avildsen doesn't want the new Bee Gees tracks to represent the core of the soundtrack. The director envisions a gritty urban street film and isn't sure how to approach something that to him seems more akin to a musical.

Whatever the truth is regarding what happens next will never completely be known, as it resides solely with Stigwood. What some of the guys on the set seem to know is that Avildsen has been hooking up with Kevin McCormick's girlfriend while McCormick has been hooking up with Stigwood...a situation that Avildsen will later describe as a triangle to location scout Lloyd Kaufman. Even supposing this is the real reason Avildsen gets fired, there are enough issues with him regarding the production of the film that could easily justify his dismissal from the project...and that is exactly what happens. With McCormick as the middleman, Avildsen is summoned to Stigwood's home on February 10. The day has otherwise begun quite pleasantly for Avildsen who has just received an Academy Award nomination for *Rocky*. The announcements are made in the morning and by the afternoon, Stigwood confronts Avildsen.

"John, I have good news, and I have bad news. The good news is you've just been nominated for an Oscar. The bad news is you're fired."

Creative differences and not seeing eye-to-eye are cited on both sides to the press.

That same afternoon, George Steinbrenner brings three more players to the Yankees...a reserve catcher named Elrod Hendricks at 36 years of age, a 26-year-old first baseman, outfielder and 295 Triple-A hitter named Dave Bergman, and a young left-handed relief pitcher named Ron Guidry who has been around on and off for the past few seasons. Between 1975 and 1976, Guidry has pitched in a total of 17 games for the Yankees. Seven of those games took place last year when he finished with a 5.63 ERA (earned run average) though at Syracuse he finished with a 5-1 record, nine saves and a 0.68 ERA. Not much fanfare surrounds Guidry, though Billy Martin believes probably more than anybody with the team that the 25-year old pitcher holds a remarkable amount of promise.

That night, the third annual *People's Choice Awards* are presented on live television from the West Coast. With Kiss performing in Iowa and unable to attend, Lydia Criss flies out to accept the award on behalf of the band. The award is presented by Goldie Hawn who uncannily wears the same exact dress as Lydia. A performance of "Beth," taped a few weeks earlier in Detroit is shown with a piped-in acceptance from the Kiss stage.

In the hospital, Dick Van Patten and some cast members of *Eight is Enough* visit Diana soon after she arrives. The actress is up front with her co-stars.

"Look," she tells them. "The backache I've been complaining about is much more serious. They say I have terminal cancer. They say I only have a few weeks to live."

Everyone is flabbergasted, as one minute she seemed completely fine and the next she tells them this news. In the conversations that follow between Diana and Van Patten in the ensuing days, she keeps him posted as she begins chemotherapy. Whether or not she believes it herself, she informs Van Patten that she plans on staying in the show.

"Maybe I'll beat this thing," she tells him.

John Badham seems an unlikely candidate for the director's role in Stigwood's production. He's been the director of a handful of made-for TV movies, and his name isn't well known around Hollywood. Born in England, Badham grew up in the fire of the American South in Birmingham, Alabama, has barely set foot in Brooklyn and has zero interest in disco music or dancing. He's just been fired from Universal's production of *The Wiz*, a musical take on *The Wizard of Oz* based on the Broadway musical of 1974. It would have been the biggest project he's ever been involved in, but much like Avildsen, he had objections to some of the logistics, namely not wanting Diana Ross in the role of Dorothy. So, he's just become available, and he loves the screenplay which makes him perfectly qualified to direct Stigwood's picture.

When Badham meets with Stigwood, he's played a tape of two new demo recordings... "Night Fever" and "Staying Alive." These are the first two tracks presented to RSO for the soundtrack and Stigwood bluntly declares to Badham that the songs will go to number one. Unlike Avildsen who took issue with the idea of the Bee Gees providing the primary music, Badham is fine with the music, though he quietly feels that Stigwood is unwarranted in his bold prediction which has an heir of arrogance and a tone of certainty as if to suggest he's already been to the future and back. Travolta and Terrio have already been training and practicing to the existing recent Bee Gees material, so he sees no reason to break the cohesive sound of the film he has in mind. Whatever heights the Bee Gees have attained in the past year through their new sound, it's apparent to Stigwood that they're still climbing and are about to peak. The only thing he isn't crazy about is the title of "Night Fever," which he feels sounds like the title of a porn film and tries to convince the group to change the name of the song. Aside from this tiny gripe, Stigwood does see the future, and he senses that the key to the film's real success will be in the music. He also knows he has the double opportunity to succeed on two fronts by selling a movie and not just a soundtrack, but a standalone album that he envisions as a blockbuster.

Rock and Roll Over is holding up well on the radio with "Hard Luck Woman" climbing the charts, coming in at number 16 on the Billboard Hot 100 when Kiss returns to New York City for their big homecoming show at Madison Square Garden, though lots of the little kids just coming to Kiss who have never really seen them in action still think it's Paul with the raspy voice. On Friday, February 18, 1977, the tri-state area converges on the city. Again, they could have done better with the Garden in terms of meeting the demand for tickets as the show is completely sold out.

While this is indeed a landmark event in the history of the band, and let's face it, the pinnacle of everything they've strived for, it doesn't seem all that different from any other day. By the time of soundcheck, Ace is already plastered and unable to play. It's not the first time one of their friends or someone from the crew has to fill in...there are just days when one of them can't make it in time or in the case of Ace and Peter, are simply incapacitated. This is the least of the problems when the local union is making the day difficult for the crew in setting up the stage, lights and sound. The logistics are further complicated with the new wireless sound system in place to be tested. It is a new and improved means of performing live and frees the artist from dragging cables behind, often limiting movement onstage when holding a guitar or microphone. Ace's near electrocution in Lakeland is the main catalyst in the new technology. But this day is different in that it's New York City, and in New York City, there's extra everything, including photographers and obligations to them.

Late in the afternoon after the makeup and costumes are already done, the band has a photo session with Ken Regan for *Music Life* magazine followed by several other small sessions with photographers. The guys even pose for a picture with their parents who are all in attendance. Two years ago, the guys did a set of homecoming shows at the Beacon Theater which enabled their parents to see for the first time that the success of their kids was real. It was at a time when Casablanca Records was in financial trouble, as was Bill Aucoin, and the shows at the Beacon to anyone behind the scenes carried an underlying sense of fatalism that could extinguish Kiss within a matter of months if something big didn't happen soon. As we know, for the hundred forty billionth time, *Alive* happened. And *Alive* was the epiphany for the ones who have taken Kiss to the next level. Kids saw that album cover...the live shot...the costumes...the makeup. The album cover left them scratching their heads in wonder. *What is this? Who are these people? Why do they look like that? What does this record sound like?* Eventually they'd get *Alive* and play it until they could mimic every second and possible sound within those grooves from beginning to end. It's as familiar to them as the air going in and out of their lungs. It's that ingrained in their conscience, subconscious, mind's eye, memory and DNA. *Alive*, to them, is also the ultimate air guitar album, though in 1976 there's no such thing as the term "air guitar"...it's just something you instinctively do when the music is playing and the music is good. It's impossible not to get entranced in Ace's guitar solos, without which, Kiss's songs would be a fraction of what they are and it would never be the same. Ace is far from the greatest guitarist on Earth and is quite limited in his playing abilities and knowledge of the guitar neck as he rarely leaves the confines of the pentatonic scale. And yet, very few guitarists could craft solos as brilliantly as Ace. His solos are songs within the songs and you can hum them or sing them just as you can sing the vocals. Most fans at the Garden are of that percentage that has never seen Kiss in a state of movement aside from the Halloween special...the ones who have only seen them in magazine images. But *Alive* was the connecting tissue that along with those images...especially the live ones, completely captured your imagination if you are among a major chunk of this audience inside the Garden. You know Kiss concerts only from *Alive* and now you're going to see it for yourself. You're going to see what you've been listening to...the fire, the explosions, the blood, Ace's smoking guitar, Peter's drum solo, the levitating drum riser, the comical but loveable banter of Paul Stanley, and the episodic bombast of "Black Diamond." "Black Diamond" is the peak of the main concert before the encores. It starts off slow and pretty. And then it gets frantic and furious. The trajectory of the song and its recording on *Alive* is cinematic, and by the time it gets to the second guitar solo, the intensity of the explosive finale is enough to change a nine-year old's life forever. There is no Youtube. There is no MTV. So, when we think of why the experience of *Alive* is so powerful, we must remember that it's not just what we hear going on in those last moments of "Black Diamond"...it's what we can't see happening. And that right there is the magic of *Alive*. It completely captures the imagination and lends itself to the myth and majesty of rock and roll and all those elements that leave us wanting more...and until these moments of mass jubilation on the arena level, it's been all imagination for most fans who are now getting to see it for themselves. Until now, they could only imagine "Black Diamond" because they could only hear it and not see it.

Wow, what is going on in there?

What are those explosions?

What does this look like?

In the hazy marijuana fog of the smoke-filled Garden, the majority of the crowd is under the age of 20, though there is an alarming number of kids as young as eight being chaperoned by parents who observe in horror at the barbaric atmosphere.

Kiss...Kiss...Kiss...Kiss...Kiss...Kiss...Kiss...Kiss...

The chant breaks out on and off in little pockets around the venue. People keep coming in, finding their seats...the chanting fading in and out as different clusters of souls attempt to get the entire room going.

Solo artist Sammy Hagar is relentlessly booed as he tries to open the show. Some know him from Montrose while some have no idea who they are looking at, nor do many of them care. The Kiss audience is intolerant of anyone at the moment who is not Kiss. Disgusted and disillusioned, Hagar flashes his dick while enthusiastically telling the New York crowd to fuck off before making his exit. The behavior of the unforgiving Kiss fans comes as a shock to more or less everyone backstage.

As the Kiss chant now consumes the Garden, the crowd is startled into a singular collective gasp as all attention turns to the front row of the upper deck where some idiotic kid has just breathed fire in a risky imitation of his hero, Gene Simmons. As if it's not bad enough that the entire venue reeks of lighter fluid and lamp oil, the brainless nitwits of suburbia have brought along with their ignorance, an arsenal of flammable shit. These are the ones who fuck themselves up at home trying to stage their own Kiss concerts... suffering Kiss injuries when using their imaginations doesn't quite cut it... and so kids blow shit up at home. Not all, just the stupid ones.

At the Garden, the hometown audience takes it all in from the moment the four of them appear at the top of their platforms above the stage.

"Alright New York City," security guard Eddie Balandas begins. "You wanted the best and you got 'em...the hottest band in the land...Kiiiiissss!" Balandas, the new voice of Kiss introductions, has brought a new ferocity to commencement of the band's live performances.

Danna-nanna-nanna-nanna-nanna-nanna-
nanna-nanna-nanna-nanna-nanna-nanna-
dugga-da-dugga-da-dunt...
dannaaaaaa....dannaaaaaa...

If this has been the coldest winter in recent memory, you wouldn't know it inside the Garden. Twenty minutes in, just before "Firehouse," Paul addresses it all.

"Ya know," he says to the hometown crowd in the screaming sermon wail that has become his signature. "This has been a year where we been havin a lot of freaky weather. One day it gets really cold. Next day, it gets real hot. Don't mean shit. I don't care...cause ahh know...if everybody loosens up... gets down with a little rock and roll, we gonna get this place so hot...we gonna have to call out..."

The starchild struts to the drum riser to grab a fireman's hat, places it on his head and strolls back to the mic.

"...the firehouse!"

"Firehouse" used to arrive seamlessly straight out of "Hotter than Hell," while it was "Hotter than Hell" that received the "so hot" rap. "Hotter than Hell" has been dropped since the last time Kiss made the rounds. "Firehouse" is one of only four songs off the debut album that are still played, and one of only six that remain in the setlist from the first three. It was those first three albums...the originals that cut the world's teeth on Kiss and provided the material on *Alive*, which many new fans got first, straight off the heels of "Rock and Roll All Nite." Then they went back and bought the first three records. There are also many newer fans who bought *Destroyer* first and then backtracked through the others. This accounts mostly for the fans who were introduced to Kiss either through "Beth" or the *Paul Lynde Halloween Special.* But a lot of those newer fans, the much younger ones who even missed *Destroyer* on release, bought *Rock and Roll Over* first, as it happened to be the new album following the Paul Lynde special. In the vast immensity of the cavernous Garden, the younger fans share the space with the older ones...a crowd between 12-22, and it's the older ones, many of which on board from 1974 and 75, spoiled with the fruits of unyielding energy and the uncompromised power of a band still hungry...a band with something to prove. And those first three records...*Kiss*, *Hotter Than Hell* and *Dressed to Kill* provided the pallet for those entrancing and enticing first Kiss experiences...or as present-day Kiss fans like to put it more simply...magic. Now that Kiss has five studio albums to their catalog... now that much of the original material of that first wave culminating with *Alive* has been discarded for newer songs in the setlist, the older fans in the Garden as well as every venue in 1977 are sharing the inevitable experience of Kiss as a band evolving. But the younger fans aren't thinking along those lines, nor do they care. This is the only Kiss they know. And it's *all…every bit of it*, beautifully new. Kiss belongs to you…Kiss belongs to me…Kiss belongs to all of us…if you want it. And so four guys from New York City who painted their faces in the spirit of current glitter and glam trends but ended up with something much darker and original and played loud and heavy songs about girls, women, sex, having a good time and living for the joyous spirit of rock and roll have followed that dream to its triumphant realization. It's been slightly less than five years since 20-year-old Paul sat in his cab on Seventh Avenue looking at Elvis's name on that giant MSG marquee, the one that lines up so perfectly symmetrical to Thirty-Second Street. Now it's 25-year-old Paul with his band on the same marquee. The Garden afterparty at the Parc Swim and Health Club features dinner menus with the headline *The Triumphant Return of the Conquering Heroes*.

On the twenty-second following the Nassau show, moody Peter Criss slams his Camaro into a wall of his parking garage. While this is just one of many Kiss car crashes, Peter's anger is too unmanageable to contain, so this particular crash is deliberate, unlike Ace's accidents which usually occur while the Spaceman is intoxicated. After a visit to the hospital, Peter needs to rest for a few days, forcing the band to postpone the next show scheduled for Hampton, Virginia. The drummer is still feeling a little off by the time the tour picks up again in Johnson City, Tennessee on February 26 leaving the band to omit "Beth" from the setlist and Paul to take Peter's vocals on "Black Diamond." A small handful of shows in the American South with Legs Diamond and punk band Dictators opening rides out the month of February with crowds ranging from 7,600 to 16,500 in attendance with Kiss swinging back into Hampton on March 7 to close out the American leg of the *Rock and Roll Over* Tour.

14 Evergreen

On the first Saturday afternoon of March, 26 states participate in Jimmy Carter's Dial-a President call. A sizable selection of Americans from all walks of life shares a conversation with the new president and get to ask him questions on issues of tax reform, jobs, negotiations with Panama, state rights, women's rights, Medicare, coffee prices, costly housing and his commitment to public education along with the obvious elephant, the natural gas crisis. For Carter, largely an outsider to the DC political machine, it's been trial and error for the first six weeks. The new administration brings many young fresh faces to the Beltway who share the process of learning from mistakes when it comes to working and cooperating with the aging but established members of Congress who are there to reject the new president's proposals and provide political adversity at every possible turn. These venerable foils on Capitol Hill aren't the only twist in the road on which Carter must share his power, but also those at the Federal Reserve where the valve to the money supply is open and closed.

By Monday, March 7, the routine has been established in which the administration's key economic advisors meet to discuss the president's economic stimulus package and budget revisions. It's a meeting that happens every Monday at two o'clock at the big oak table in the White House conference room, recently renamed the Roosevelt Room by Richard Nixon. For years, it was simply known as the fish room where Franklin Delano Roosevelt kept his many fish tanks. And for years, the room was subject to the hostility of past Republican administrations and the infighting that often characterized their meetings in Kissingeresque fashion. The Carter presidency so far offers much more informal and laid-back forums, making for warmer surroundings for all involved as opposed to the cold unfriendly environment often created by the egos of the past clashing with each other, even when they were supposedly on the same side.

The coldness of impersonal formalities in civic leadership isn't the only realm where inhospitable context dissolves. In New York City, the deep freeze has thawed, allowing a mild Tuesday afternoon in Forest Hills with temperatures climbing into the fifties. With spring only a few weeks away, it's tempting to put away your winter clothes completely. Those freakish warm days that characterize March often fool people into thinking winter is over. They break out the T-shirts and booty shorts, and everyone takes to the streets for a few days.

But winter is not over, and March can never be trusted.

Just as fast as deceiving warm weather lures you out of your parkas and stringy yarn ball hats, the nipple temps return with angry vengeance. But let's put all that aside for now...for on this beautiful March 8, a random weekday, it's just as good as any other day to look at how cozy this Queens community of Forest Hills Gardens feels in welcoming this sunny touch of the spring to come. Joggers and walkers of this development are out in large numbers through the late afternoon and into the early part of the evening, though these deceptive temperatures have worked their way back toward winter, dropping nearly 20 degrees in the past few hours. Some walkers remain, moving through the quiet and private suburban streets, made uncomfortably public by the overshadowing presence of Forest Hills Stadium, which sits for better or worse in the center of this neighborhood like a lazy dog in the middle of the living room floor. The luxurious Tudor-style homes continue in the aesthetics of nearby Station Square.

As full darkness begins to settle in, assorted residents strolling the vicinity have already gone inside, while the urgency that the nighttime brings begins to inform those who remain on the street still chugging along toward their homes. The murder of Christine Freund just five weeks ago is still hovering over the Gardens for anyone who passes through Station Square or its surrounding streets.

20-year-old Virginia Voskerichian comes up from the Continental Avenue subway station at approximately 7:30 PM after attending class at Barnard College in the Morningside Heights section of Manhattan. Virginia and her family are of Armenian descent and moved to the United States from Bulgaria in 1968, residing on Exeter Street just a few blocks past Station Square. After waiting ten years for permission just to get here, the Voskerichian's are now thriving as proud Americans who have made the dream happen for themselves. Virginia's father is a watchmaker who works for Longines, as does her mother. At Barnard, Virginia is an honors student of Russian studies and a brilliant linguist who speaks five languages. Prospects are high for her to have a successful career as a translator if she chooses to follow that path. She currently has a job at JFK airport. Virginia, in a tan checkered jacket, black blouse, black skirt, brown gloves, brown and tan knee-high socks, tan boots and a yellow metal watch on her left wrist, is obviously dressed more for the deceiving cold.

In the now chilly early evening, Virginia moves through Continental Avenue, heading toward the south side of the tracks where the LIRR passes above the archway that serves as the entrance to Station Square. She proceeds through the underpass, where the concrete ground gives way to the red brick that makes up the Square. She crosses Burns and steps onto the curb that runs along the west side of this public hub. In the weeks since Christine Freund was killed here, the incident is never far from anyone's mind as they enter this area, often voluntarily glancing in the direction of where the murder took place. The whole thing has put the community on alert, though Freund's murder has only been the last straw in what residents have observed as an overall rise in crime through a series of vandalism and robberies around this Forest Hills enclave. In recent months, members of the community have tried organizing a private security force through the Forest Hills Garden Corporation which owns these streets. Residents contributed mostly fifty to a hundred dollars from each household but only 35,000 of the necessary 70,000 dollars was raised, which has only resulted in said residents receiving their money back. The somewhat busy Station Square disappears into the background as Virginia Voskerichian walks through the second underpass which leads to a fork in the road where you can either stay on Continental or veer off to the right which becomes Dartmouth Street. Either way, the activity of Station Square is instantly forgotten about once you move through the underpass where it seems as if the entire world you've just passed through has been muted. Though the interior walls of the underpass that connects with the Forest Hills Inn are lined with white graffiti, they serve as the entrance to the private streets of the affluent where it is noticeably and uncomfortably darker than the bustling opposite side of Station Square...especially moving from the underpass onto Dartmouth which is lit only by dim lamps reminiscent of England's gaslight era. Virginia trudges onward off the right-hand turn from the archway through a curve in the sidewalk that quickly straightens into the duration of Dartmouth. Her leather boots trot over a sidewalk covered in pine needles between grass and bushes, a street sign and a newly planted tree to her left. As the turn in the sidewalk straightens under her boots, Virginia is approached by someone who appears from between parked cars and raises a gun upward toward her head. Instinctively she holds up a textbook to hide her face as she recoils in fear. It happens in a split fraction of a second as the raised hand places the gun directly on the book, firing a bullet straight through it, hitting Virginia in the mouth, blowing out her teeth and lodging itself in the back of her skull, killing her before she even hits the ground.

Who does this sort of murder in such a heavily populated area? No, the streets on the south side of Station Square are nowhere near as active as on the north side, but the angular zigzag of how Dartmouth comes out of Continental is plentiful in numerous means of witnessing something on the street. Private houses and three and four-story apartment buildings surround the shooting location. Not to mention the active Station Square on the dying end of rush hour. What kind of demented soul just walks up and shoots a girl in plain sight?

Someone who probably wants to get caught, that's who.

When police arrive to find the body of a young girl lying across the sidewalk less than fifty yards from Station Square, the immediate thoughts are *another one. It's happened again*. In fact, from where Virginia's body lay, you can see straight through the underpass to the location of Christine Freund's murder. Several textbooks lay on the ground next to her. One third of her face is virtually taken out. Even the police are stunned and beside themselves in this shooting where the wholesome beautiful youth of Virginia Voskerichian hits home for many of them who are parents.

"They killed a girl again," a distraught elderly woman with an Eastern European accent sobs to a reporter on the street, struggling not to break down in front of the news camera. "All these years I never hear those things. What's happened now? What's changed? We need protection. We are paying taxes and plenty."

In 1977, there is a fine line between a time when humans could be shocked by certain events or behavior and a new desensitized reality where nothing is shocking and the depravity of the human mind and spirit has the potential for unspeakable acts. Perhaps location plays a part in the measure of shock one feels toward the news of the day. Perhaps location is key. Perhaps in some places the people are just different. But in New York City, all sorts of gruesome things happen. Just two days after Voskerichian is murdered, a 21-year-old woman named Rachel Brecher walks into Gabriel Coat and Suit Company on West Thirty-Ninth, presumably to shop, and she is dragged into the basement and forced into the oil-burning furnace where she dies of asphyxiation. An arrest has already been made as police are focusing on a part-time elevator operator in the building. This story, however, is largely overshadowed when Mayor Beame and Police Commissioner Michael J. Codd make a press announcement at the 109th Precinct related to the Voskerichian case. What police have determined in a quick investigation is a clear match in the bullets retrieved from Voskerichian and Christine Freund back in January, and it appears that both women were shot with the same .44 caliber bulldog revolver...the same gun also believed to have been used to kill Donna Lauria and injure Jodi Valenti in Pelham Bay last July. In addition to these three murders being linked to the same gun, police have concluded that the same gun was used in several other shootings in recent months... Carl Denaro in Flushing back in October, and Joanne Lomino and Donna Demasi over Thanksgiving weekend. Denaro, who lost a chunk of his skull has since had a steel plate put into his head and is still recovering from multiple surgeries for the past five months. Lomino hasn't been as lucky, having been shot through the spine and paralyzed from the waist down. Lomino has since been confined to a wheelchair. One interesting tidbit that the public as no real knowledge of at this point, is that Rosemary Keenan, the girl who was in the car with Carl Denaro when he was shot, just happens to be the daughter of John Keenan, the chief of detectives who is putting together a task force to deal with this newly-arisen panic. Out of the five shootings, three of which have resulted in the death of young women, two of them teenagers, one has taken place in the Bronx and three in Queens. These cases were not forgotten about and each have their own police report with witness sketches.

"We have determined that there has been a .44 caliber revolver used in every one of them, which is why it's important for anyone who has any information with respect to anyone who's in possession of a .44 caliber revolver, call us."

The general description that we have is of a male white...25 to 30 years of age. Five feet, ten inches to six feet in height...medium build...well-groomed with dark hair which is combed straight back. In the ensuing days, the media scrambles to get the word out on every possible level of appealing to people's fears while setting the public tone for better or worse. Police do not believe the killer selects victims in advance. They believe he operates by prowling the neighborhoods by car and when he sees a likely target, gets out of the car and stalks them on foot. So far, apart from Miss Voskerichian, Miss. Lomino and Miss. Demasi, he seems to be going after couples in parked cars. The joint press conference between the NYPD and City Hall puts the public on alert to be extra vigilant while navigating the streets throughout all of New York City. A simple yet stern warning...someone is out there with a .44 revolver shooting people late at night...mostly women.

There is very little shock value to crime these days. New York City is indefensible when it comes to people doing the wrong thing, and the notoriety is nationwide. When the city is dealing with at least four murders per day by default, media headlines of a serial killer create a few extra ripples, but most of the population goes on with life unaffected.

Sure, it's crazy...these shootings in Queens...two in Forest Hills in the past six weeks. But what can you do? This is New York City. What do you want?

Forest Hills is probably now on much higher alert than any other part of the city. The general dialogue however seems much more matter of fact.

But the same gun is tied to those girls in Floral Park...and some guy in Flushing. All Queens.

And that one in the Bronx.

The one in the Bronx? There's a million in the Bronx. Shithole is so bad they're burning it to the ground block by block.

That girl that got killed in the car last summer right in front of her building... that was a 44. All these Queens shootings were a 44.

A 44 magnum? That Dirty Harry gun?

No, those guns would blow your head clean off. They say it's smaller...a .44 caliber...a revolver...a bulldog...some kind of dog...I don't know...it's a fucking gun and girls are getting shot randomly out of nowhere! What a world boy, I tell ya!

Bold print warnings in tabloid papers begin resembling noir-like Gotham-esque headlines about the ".44 Killer."

15

BILLY AND REGGIE

The other 44 is Reggie Jackson. Aside from the few people associated with the Yankees who attended the press conference, nobody else greets Reggie... no formal welcomes...nothing. From the moment he arrives for spring training in Fort Lauderdale, he's made to feel awkward through the silence and indifference shown to him by his new teammates. The Yankees are a proud bunch. They see themselves as a team...not just in the rhetorical sense...but a real team...one collective group effort with significant contributions from several players. They've just been to the World Series and suddenly here is this star getting all the attention. Billy Martin's favorite thing about the 1976 team was that it was a team of effort...it didn't revolve around or depend on one or two players. Chambliss, May, White, Rivers, Munson, etc...had all come through at times when it was necessary to rise to the occasion.

Prior to Reggie signing with the Yankees, it was well-known around the baseball world that he occasionally did spots as a sportscaster sitting in the booth with the lead men, most recently the American League Division Series between the Yankees and the Royals. He also did a network TV show called *Battle of the Superstars*, a competition featuring stars from different sports all competing in events such as relay races, obstacle courses and tug of war...much like *Battle of the Network Stars* where sitcom celebrities from CBS, NBC and ABC all competed in the same kind of events. This year, the event which took place during the off-season, featured the two teams that just played the World Series, the Reds and the Yankees. Although Reggie is now a Yankee, he was not part of this particular World Series team, and so he retained his broadcasting position for this matchup. This was probably the first time he'd come into contact with a group of his new teammates all at once, and he saw it as a good occasion to break the ice with some of them... guys like Nettles, Chambliss, Lyle and White...none of which even acknowledged him. This was the first sure sign of trouble for Reggie and a clear indicator that things aren't going to go so well in New York.

Many players still don't understand how free agency is going to work. Most haven't and don't get involved in the politics and/or inner workings of the behind-the-scenes...and most don't fight for themselves, even though many have long been unhappy, while even more are content enough to be happy that they get to play professional baseball for a living and simply accept the old ways of the league as unchangeable gospel. Yet, many resent some of the bigger players who are coming away with bigger and better deals for themselves after having found themselves in control of their own destinies. Reggie is a symbol of this entire change in baseball, not through any fault of his own, but as the one who is getting the most media attention out of it...and the one who has brought saturation coverage to spring training. While a fresh and optimistic approach to Reggie could have been offered by his teammates, some of the things that come out of his mouth do not help him.

Upon arriving in Fort Lauderdale, Reggie speaks of himself in third person to reporters.

"Reggie Jackson on your ball club is part of a show of force. It's a show of power. I help to intimidate the opposition just because I'm here. That's part of my role."

Reggie has often spoken in recent weeks about how he prepared himself mentally for New York all through the winter, though as ready as he thinks he is, New York will probably show him otherwise.

About a week into spring training, Reggie walks into the Banana Boat Bar on the beach in Fort Lauderdale to meet a reporter for what he hopes will be an interview that will help him in New York. He sees Martin sitting at a table playing backgammon with Mickey Mantle and Whitey Ford, so he goes over to say hello.

"Man, oh, man...a superstar!" Mantle says in a sarcastic tone that hints at mocking, referring to Reggie's *Battle of the Superstars* t-shirt. Though the Yankee legend could easily suggest he's only playing, Reggie is livid by the time he gets to the bar where he orders and sends the guys drinks on him. Munson is also bitter for the way things have turned out. Although he got the raise he asked for after reminding the boss about their agreement, he's not happy about Reggie's deferment and bonus money. His salary was raised to match Reggie's, but without the deferment and bonus money. Reggie has also received a Rolls Royce and Munson has not. Steinbrenner refused Munson these extra incentives. The team captain begins venting about wanting to be traded or having his contract bought out. The media facilitates the situation as a permanent fixture in the daily headlines...always focusing on the relationship between Jackson and Munson...or Jackson and Martin...or Jackson and the team....or Jackson and somebody or something...but always Jackson. But then he makes this comment about being the straw that stirs the drink within the team, and whether written in or out of context, it will enrage his teammates when the interview is published.

Billy Martin is a different story in relation to Reggie. Reggie at the outset feels the frustration in Billy toward the acquisition...one that Billy is resentful for not being a part of. But, Billy should at this point know that while an owner might sporadically consult a manager in the process of choosing players or new prospects, the front office and general manager are responsible for the majority of decisions. Reggie also knows that Billy didn't want him on the team, and that the Yankees manager wanted Joe Rudi instead. They don't call it Billy Ball for nothing. Billy has clear and precise ideas of what a team is, what a team does and how a team works, and he wants people who will comply and fall in line and work for the overall good of the whole. Individualism has no place on the Yankees. To Billy, Reggie doesn't fit the mold, and maybe an even bigger problem is that Billy is just as outspoken as Reggie. There's also this thing about stars and veteran players getting days off during spring training, and Reggie has been playing every day. He's asked about it by reporter Phil Pepe and acknowledges frustration over it. When confronted with the subject by Pepe, Billy expresses surprise, insisting that Reggie requested to play a lot of innings during spring training.

The biggest obstacle in Reggie's path is his collective experiences with the Yankees regarding what he'd later refer to as racism and antisemitism, especially on the part of Billy. Beginning in spring training and throughout the season, Reggie repeatedly overhears if not completely within earshot, racist remarks made by the manager. His old friend and teammate from Oakland, Ken Holtzman is also subject to Jewish jokes, though they are mostly behind his back. It's evident that Billy isn't fond of Holtzman, though Reggie believes it's out of antisemitism that the manager harbors toward the veteran pitcher whose best days are obviously behind him. Reggie believes this type of bigotry is behind the manner in which Holtzman is treated and often ignored by the Yankees manager throughout the season, though it is difficult to accuse Billy of antisemitism since so many of his closest friends and business associates are of Jewish heritage. Reggie, who is one of six children of African American and Spanish descent, was raised in a Jewish community. He naturally gravitated toward the Jewish people of the community knowing that they too, like African Americans, had a history of experiencing social ostracism and bigotry.

Chambliss tells Reggie to be glad he's black and getting all the publicity and getting away with everything he gets away with because if he were white, he'd be just another white boy. In some ways, Reggie could be viewed as an extension of Satchell Paige and Jackie Robinson and Hank Aaron and Bob Gibson. Players who left an indelible mark on the game of baseball but were treated much differently in society.

Race will indeed come up, but not nearly as much as in the hindsight of later years. As a whole, the entire situation of the animosity and dysfunctionality that will surround this Yankees team can be summed up and reduced to that of childish squabbles. Billy is bitter because he wasn't part of the process in obtaining Reggie. Billy is baffled over why he didn't get his way with the players he wanted who George didn't get. Billy believes George is interfering with the team by injecting his authority into issues that should be left to the people implementing the strategies down on the baseball field. George rides Billy like a suffocating parent determined to have a hand in every move and establish control over it. George insists that Billy ride the Yankees bus with the team rather than drive himself to the games. He humiliates Billy, often in front of the team, though Billy shows a lack of respect for the chain of command by lashing out at George in verbal tirades. When Reggie feels unwelcomed by Billy's silence, indifference and refusal to even acknowledge him along with the fact that he never even offered so much as a handshake, it's Billy who believes Reggie should have been the one to call and reach out instead. And for the very fact that Reggie didn't initiate an introduction between the two of them, Billy is offended. This is nothing new, however, and in no way is it surprising. Billy is one of those people who can turn any situation into a moral issue and be insulted by it...the eternal victim...and Reggie will get the brunt of it.

Bay Ridge, Japan and the Voice of God

In the southwestern portion of Brooklyn just at the mouth of the Verrazzano Bridge is Bay Ridge. The mouth of the bridge exists before the length of the bridge which runs over a body of water known as the Narrows, all the way to the asshole of the bridge which discharges you straight into Staten Island. Bay Ridge was once known as Yellow Hook, established on December 16, 1853, and later changed by locals after voting to rename it. Native Americans had a village there when the Dutch arrived establishing their colony while driving the natives west. The farmland that existed there was eventually gutted during industrialization with the buildings and subways appearing near the turn of the century. In 1977 Bay Ridge is primarily Italian and Irish with the occasional Syrian and Lebanese families.

Lloyd Kaufman is the location guy on the *Saturday Night* project who goes back with John Avildsen's earlier works like *Joe*. After Avildsen's firing, Badham has kept him on the crew and he has produced splendidly in securing spots in Bay Ridge that will lend themselves to the visual permanence of the film...places like the house at 221 Seventy-Ninth Street, the 2001 Odyssey club and Lenny's Pizza. Technically, Lenny's is in Bensonhurst because it's over the line that divides Bensonhurst from Bay Ridge. Compared to many of the discos Badham and Kaufman look at, the interior of 2001 is an enclosed dark and dreary space that could use some window dressing and cosmetics to work. For $15,000 they purchase a multi-colored floor that will eventually become the color scheme of the film graphics. They tinfoil the walls, much like Andy Warhol's Factory, and string lights throughout the perimeter of the club, creating depth and a much more uplifting ambiance.

With respect to casting, the actors who make the cut in the roles of the Faces are relatively unknown and roughly around the same age. In the role of Joey is Joseph Cali, a New Yorker and the oldest of the bunch, turning 27 just a few weeks after filming begins. Double J is played by Paul Pape, 24 and born in Rochester. Gus is played by Bruce Ornstein, 20...and from Los Angeles is 19-year-old Bobby Miller to play Bobby C. In the role of Annette is Brooklyn girl Donna Pescow who turns 23 during the first week of shooting. The role of Travolta's dance partner, effectively the most important part of the film besides John remains empty through most of pre-production. It takes a while to come up with an actress who will play Stephanie Mangano and the role is left unfilled until very late in the schedule.

Karen Lynn Gorney is ultimately chosen as Travolta's dance partner rather late in the casting. Badham has the two actors rehearse by improvising in character with each other for two weeks...not reading the lines of the script but rather communicating in real life as Karen and John, but in their characters. Though Gorney was born in Los Angeles, she is a true easterner having grown up in New York City in and around the same locations that her character, Stephanie aspires to. After graduating from the High School of Performing Arts in Midtown, she attended Carnegie Mellon University in Pittsburgh where she earned her Bachelor of Fine Arts. She then earned her Master of Fine Arts degree in Waltham, Massachusetts where she attended Brandeis University. Gorney has had a few uncredited roles in some major films but has worked mostly on television for the past six years in the role of Tara Martin in the ABC soap opera *All My Children*.

Travolta, about to go into the biggest role of his life in a matter of weeks, is by necessity remaining on the East Coast as the preparation of pre-production demands he remain in New York as much as possible. He stays in constant contact with Diana by phone as she goes through treatment, talking for hours at a time. Somewhere in this pre-production phase, Stigwood's costume designer Patrizia Von Brandenstein takes John shopping to look at clothes and try on anything that might strike them in relation to the film. The trip doesn't last long, as within 45 minutes a massive crowd has assembled outside. Suddenly, the distance from the door to the limo seems non-negotiable. Von Brandenstein has to call for a police escort out of the store. As she takes this public experience with John back to the film production and to all involved, she does so with a sense of what to expect on and around the set in the New York City streets...a heightened awareness of something they had greatly underestimated. Travolta is much more popular than they thought he was...and they really have no idea what is coming.

Most of the production will be filmed in Bay Ridge, and though there is no real way to keep anything like this on the DL, Badham and his crew believe the outset and initial filming will run a little smoother. By mid-morning on the first day of production, March 14, word has spread that Travolta is shooting a film, and almost by the minute, the crowd begins to multiply and grow to the point where Badham realizes they're not equip to contain such a situation.

As the icy tundra of the grueling winter tour thaws, the Kiss *Rock and Roll Over* trek through America is over. As mid-March settles in, the boys are back in New York preparing for one last cap on the experience. With the kind of popularity they've cracked wide open in the States over the past year comes a sprawling recognition of the band in other places of the great big wide world...countries like Japan. Australia and New Zealand are originally slated to be attached to the Japanese tour, but the logistics do not line up with the itinerary, and so the tour becomes a two-week trip to Japan and back. Aucoin doesn't want to alter the constant press attention on the band. With the U.S. tour over and studio time booked after Japan, he's afraid of the band losing popularity in the States if they don't remain in the public eye.

For that reason, he invites a group of journalists to travel to Japan with the band to cover the tour.

Clipper Kiss, the name of the Pan-Am 747 taking off out of JFK, is carrying the band, crew, wives, girlfriends and the press. It's a two-level airplane that leaves New York City on the morning of March 17 headed for Tokyo. The upper level is reserved for the band to put on their makeup and get into their costumes, though much of the flight sees the entire entourage seated on the lower level. Lydia Criss, appreciative of the entire experience, approaches Gene and Paul to thank them for giving her the chance to travel and see Japan. Gene in response thanks her. Without Lydia Criss, there'd be no "Beth," and without "Beth," they probably wouldn't be riding this wave of popularity. Whether or not that's true, Aucoin has deliberately held off on bringing Kiss to Japan when he feels he easily could have done so a year ago. Now, only three months into '77, Casablanca is already seeing some 11 million dollars just in Kiss and Donna Summer revenue alone. Strategy has been his priority as he knew he was building demand and anticipation to such an overwhelming level that not even he nor the band understands what to expect once they get to Japan.

Back in Bay Ridge, actress Donna Pescow gets a taste of the Travolta madness when she enters a trailer on the set to do hair and makeup. John has already been in there for some time and when Donna enters, a large crowd of kids is surrounding the vehicle. Inside the trailer the actors can hear the screams of "John" and "John, come out" in multitudes. As much as the star would like to go outside...and let's face it...as much as he needs to go outside to shoot, he opts to stay put for fear of the mob that will ensue. The kids outside then begin shaking the trailer, much to the ire of a nervous and fidgety Pescow who has already had her jacket stolen off the wardrobe truck. The frenzy forces Badham to shut down production for the day and rethink security measures.

By day three, the small handful of police officers prove no match for the crowd of Travolta fans that easily numbers in the thousands. As the crew sets up to film John in a car with the rest of the Faces, Joe Cali, Paul Pape and Bobby Miller behind the wheel, the actors are concerned and almost frightened of the bulging crowd that could seemingly break through the barriers at any given moment.

And that's just what happens.

As the crowd of fans bursts through security lines and begins surrounding and shaking the car, Travolta screams to Miller to floor it the hell out of there. Miller drives away...off the set and into the surrounding streets of Bay Ridge, momentarily escaping the crowd. Travolta, with his hands full trying to balance his attention to the film with the weight of Diana's situation some 2800 miles away, is not adjusting very well in the first days of filming. The impact of celebrity has easily made its way into John's life, as well as the early production of this project, while Stigwood and Badham quickly realize they'll need additional security. What they have in mind however isn't what they receive after their filming location is firebombed while the set is closed down overnight. The producer is visited the next day on the set by some friendly but scary faces of the mob who just happened to have heard about the trouble they're having and of the danger that can accompany filming in such a hazardous environment. *After a firebombing, they'd clearly need protection or else these sorts of incidents could surely continue* is the way it's put to them. The bowling alley down the block also wants a few grand to string some set lights up on their establishment. The 300-pound man who gets out of the Cadillac to spell it out for the film crew gets back in and drives away with his mission of extortion accomplished. And so, Stigwood is strong armed into paying the mob for protection.

Those first days, for the most part, are shot in the house where the Tony Manero character resides. Manero lives with his father, mother, grandmother and sister in a house where enough turmoil exists to make one hungry to escape from. With respect to the hoods that have forced their way onto the set, the reports that later circulate about John Travolta being approached by the district attorney to wear a wire, even with the possibility of being true, have never had any basis in fact. If this did in fact occur, John wanted no part of a sting operation, though nobody has ever confirmed or denied any of this. By the end of the first week of production, John gets the phone call that forces him to leave New York and head to Los Angeles where Diana has taken a downhill slide and is said to be near the end of her life.

Van Patten and his wife, Pat, have frequently visited Diana Hyland through her treatment. The thing that strikes them the most is how beautiful and full of pep Diana still is despite the physical toll of what she's been through. She sports a headdress and a wig after having lost her hair from the chemo, but to the Van Patten's still seems radiant and full of life. That changes in an unexpected flash when they go to her house on Sunday, March 27. They've just attended a church service nearby and simply want to say hello. It wasn't initially in their plans because they know John is expected this weekend and they want to give them some time alone. Diana's parents happen to answer the door. The doctor has just left after telling everybody that Diana only has a few hours left. She is at the end. When the Van Patten's go inside, John is sitting beside Diana who is now wearing an oxygen mask and struggling to breathe. It is 1:30 PM.

Curious over the sudden tragic turn of events, Van Patten asks if Diana has received last rites and is told no. Feeling there's no time to waste he leaves the house and goes back to the church where he frantically beckons Father Curtis to go to Diana's home with him. By mid-afternoon, Van Patten returns with Father Curtis who recently performed last rites on Freddie Prinze. Father Curtis does the same for Hyland who is aware of everyone around her and what is happening. As the hours wane, Diana's parents are worried about what happens next, as their daughter's wishes are to be cremated. They're concerned over the terms which dictate that the next of kin must first approve cremation. Diana's next of kin is her son, Zac, who is only three years old. This means the next of kin's legal guardian has to approve, and that happens to be Diana's ex-husband who she divorced in 1974. This is nothing they should have to deal with in the wake of losing their daughter... nor should John be faced with contacting Diana's ex. These are the thoughts that plague Van Patten as he mulls over this awkwardness that they will be presented with in a matter of hours. As that time approaches, he volunteers to locate Joe Goodson to inform him of the unique circumstances.

Diana Hyland passes away in John Travolta's arms at 7 PM on Sunday, March 27, 1977. He feels her last breath leave her body as she transitions into eternal rest.

Upon arrival in Japan, when Clipper Kiss empties, the band exits in full costume and makeup, just as they had in Europe a year earlier. Customs, however, is not amused to see that their Starchild, Demon, Space Ace and Kitty Kat faces don't match the faces on their passports. While Aucoin's main priority is to avoid cameras at all costs, even before getting through customs, he knows the band has no choice but to get back on the plane and remove their makeup. Once they get through customs, they immediately duck out of sight and quickly get the makeup back on. After a few years of this process, almost daily, the guys are able to get it done in under a half hour.

The Kiss entourage has a few days off to recover from the long flight and the 13-hour time difference, exploring Osaka and reaping the rewards of the seemingly endless luxury that surrounds them in the form of the best of everything...food, clothes, hotels, women...lots of women and screaming girls...a lot more girls than they see in the States. It's been a constant bombardment of touring and supporting albums and going from here to there with very little time to enjoy what little they've seen of their newfound fortunes. They still haven't had much of a break in touring...not since they got on that first plane to Edmonton in early February 1974. It's been three solid years, with only brief intervals of time off to record new records or take a breather before the next five-month block of shows. Now, in Japan, it's finally starting to seep in...Kiss is huge.

Late in the morning on Tuesday, March 29, Travolta boards an American Airlines one o'clock flight back to New York. The flight is filled with celebrities returning from the Academy Awards and half the plane is taken up by First

Class. Artist, Andy Warhol, always with a keen observing eye notices John getting out of his seat to walk toward the restroom. He gives Warhol a slight nod of acknowledgment as he passes...his eyes red as if he's been crying. When John returns, he tries to stay occupied with a script as he pours orange juice into a paper cup and mixing it into some unidentified alcohol before eventually returning to the restroom several times. At one point, John becomes overwhelmed and buries his face, sobbing into a pillow. A concerned Warhol, afraid to approach John asks a stewardess why he's crying.

"Death in the family," he's told.

Unwarranted photographers are the enemy. Cameras are not your friends. The usual protocol for Kiss security is to grab the cameras out of a photographer's hands and confiscate the film if they manage to get within range of band members without their makeup. Perhaps in earlier years at the very beginning of the band they were a little more lax in their management of the entire presentation. But it cannot be overstated just how overprotective of the Kiss mystique Bill Aucoin has become. Kiss only exists from 15 minutes before they go onstage when the makeup is done until the end of the show. Once they come off stage and the makeup comes off, Kiss no longer exists. Much like Superman. Clark Kent goes into the phone booth and removes his glasses and suit. Superman emerges. Once he puts those glasses back on, Superman no longer exists. This becomes added pressure to the security team. The key is to not allow anybody to get a picture of the guys without the makeup. Nobody is to know what they look like. This becomes an even more overwhelming concern in Japan because everybody in Japan seems to love photography and cameras are everywhere. With ten journalists, a photographer, publicist, accountant, Sean, Bill, Jeanete, Lydia, security and the band in tow, the Kiss entourage, not counting the stage crew, totals around 30 people.

Between the band, the crew, security and the journalists, all western faces, there is a lot of long hair which makes it difficult for Japanese photographers to know who the members of Kiss are.

Music Life magazine is easily the most prestigious rock and roll rag in Japan and one of the biggest full color rock and roll publications in circulation around the world. In its large glossy paper, each issue feels more like a book. Prior to the tour of Japan, Kiss management made a deal with *Music Life* to do a special issue with the band. The only requirement is to show that Kiss is in Japan. The usual poses and live shots wouldn't cut it in the respect that *Music Life* is asking for. That said, the fact that Kiss only exists for concerts and public appearances and then the makeup comes off is not going to work with what *Music Life* wants. To fans, especially the younger ones, the evolving mythology of the band is that the Kiss characters are real. They're real and they all live together and do everything together, and the makeup is their actual faces. The idea is to put them in restaurants sipping drinks, sitting in chairs, visiting tourist spots in Japanese cities and generally making it appear as if Kiss lives in character and that they look like this all day. Very early in the trip, photographer Bob Gruen takes a cab around Kyoto with Mr. Udo, the tour promoter, and takes Polaroids of various locales. He returns to the hotel at night and asks the cab driver to meet him back there in the morning. Gruen shows the locations to the band, and they all agree on four places. In the morning, the driver meets Gruen who gets in the cab and shows him the pictures of the sites he wants to go back to. Behind Gruen and the cabbie is a bus with the entire Kiss entourage. Gruen takes them to the site of a giant Buddha. Upon arrival he sees Mr. Udo racing down a hill frantically and seemingly in a state of panic. The two of them miss each other as Gruen already has the entourage headed up toward the Buddha. What he quickly learns is that the statue is a sacred shrine to the dead, and Mr. Udo had gone up to warn the monks in charge that this band of outsiders from the West were about to descend on them. The monks of course object and are not happy. They see it as a disruption and a sign of disrespect. Gruen advises his translators to talk to the monks and keep them distracted while telling the band to pose in front of the statue as if they're tourists. They spend only a few minutes before dispersing, but in that short amount of time manage to inadvertently attract a group of fans who now attach themselves to the entourage, following the bus in their own vehicles to the next tourist site. Throughout the course of the photoshoots, they pick up more and more fans who end up following them with a convoy of some forty vehicles behind the Kiss bus by the time they arrive at the Golden Pagoda.

Kiss plays nine shows throughout Japan, hitting Osaka, Kyoto, Nagoya, Fukuoka and Tokyo. If Japan is an indication of anything, it's the new stage that gives it away...and that's that the machine that is Kiss is fully invested in the present with the big picture in mind...thinking long term with no end in sight...though Bill Aucoin halfheartedly speculates to journalist Elise Krentzel that Kiss has one more album and tour in them before it's all over. The question remains after the successful U.S. tour and a record-breaking romp through Japan...what comes next?

During a small break of a few weeks while the guys are not together, Gene bides his time by getting some local musicians to assist him with a demo. Some time ago, he'd seen a group he got excited about called Van Halen. He brought them to Bill Aucoin who ultimately passed on them. Gene brings the guitarist Eddie Van Halen into the studio to record a guitar track for a song called "Christine Sixteen." Originally intended to be a guide for Ace's eventual guitar parts, Gene insists that Ace learn and play the solo note for note the same way Eddie plays it. Paul also presents Ace with a fully fleshed out chord progression that he recorded on the airplane. The lyrics are a promising work of pure poetry about his penis, appropriately titled "Love Gun."

The working song on John Badham's set is "Staying Alive," and it's blasting 86th Street as John Travolta glides south toward 20th Avenue...strutting to the beat in a button-down red shirt under a black leather jacket. His Vinnie Barbarino hair has been perfectly coiffed and cropped up and he's fashionably and infinitely far beyond the look of the Sweathogs. He's swinging a can of paint as he strides towards Lenny's Pizza. The cameras follows...a close shot of his feet and patent leather shoes...a mid-shot staring up at him from below and no real inkling of just how revolutionary and earth-shaking these moments will become. It's their second attempt at getting this scene in the can. They tried it a few weeks back on the first day of shooting, but that was when the crowd was at peak intrusion, and they had to shut down by noon. That was before they were paying the mob. But now they're paying the mob.

The reconditioning of baseball contracts in and around the Yankees isn't exclusive to Reggie Jackson and Thurman Munson going into the new season. In the final days of spring training, the subject emerges with Graig Nettles and Chris Chambliss as a brief run of exhibition games gets underway. Chambliss's contract has been under negotiation for the past month, and on March 31, he signs for a reported one million over the next five years. He tells reporters he's happy with the deal, that he had not been under any pressure and that he had been confident everything would be settled. Nettles, however, is thinking and behaving differently. The 1976 American League homerun leader played the entire ten inning practice game against the Detroit Tigers a few days earlier. The Yankees lost the game 6-5 and then moved on to Dunedin to play the Toronto Blue Jays when Nettles left the team and didn't show up to play. Gabe Paul tells the press that the third baseman will be fined 500 dollars a day if he fails to show up without providing justifiable cause for his disappearance. The media can only speculate aside from the possibility of Nettles's departure being some personal emergency, whether it has something to do with the barrage of negotiations going on all through the off-season. The $400,000 contract he signed in 1976 has never been a point of contention for Nettles...no gripes, no demands...yet we must wonder as those in the know suggest Nettles had been hinting at wanting negotiations. The new deals with Jackson and Gullet have been a game changer with players suddenly complaining about their contracts and owners whining about expenses while the players-versus-owners dynamic has been the culprit for the most hostile and controversial off-season in baseball history. If ever there was an isolated cluster of months that profoundly reshaped this dynamic, it's located in the transition between 1976 and 1977. Nettles is gone for two days but returns by March 30 when the situation is addressed publicly by his financial advisor, LaRue Harcourt. Nettles indeed wants a revision and an extension of his contract, and the team has promised him these discussions.

"Graig feels the guys who have already made contributions to the team should get salaries similar to the new guys coming in," Harcourt tells reporters.

In the final move toward his 1977 Yankees team, Steinbrenner trades Oscar Gamble and two insignificant pitching prospects to the Chicago White Sox for the much-coveted Bucky Dent and solves the shortstop problem and more importantly fills in the final piece of the championship team he's been assembling bit by bit since 1973.

At the outset of Opening Day ceremonies, Reverend William Kalaidjian prays with the Yankee Stadium crowd of 43,785, asking God to give the Yankees a world championship. The chaplain raises eyebrows in the press booth after he suggests that God is in attendance in the Bronx. He thanks God for the 1976 pennant but doesn't give God any flak for letting them lose the World Series. Finally, the voice of God introducing the home team, addresses the crowd.

"Ladies and Gentlemen...in defense of the American League title, the New York Yankees..."

And so begins Bob Sheppard, who for the first time in 12 years can read such an introduction at Yankee Stadium...an acknowledgement of a Yankees post-season.

The game goes well and in the Yankees favor. Catfish pitches superbly for a guy who's been struggling with his arm. Before being beamed in the foot by a line drive, he pitches seven shutout innings. The spirit in the still newly refurbished ballpark is a continuation from last year's high without the hostility of the kind of raucousness New York is usually known for. Instead, there is something new going on in Yankee Stadium...the chant of

Reggie. It's a peculiar sound in the Bronx. The team and its fans have known Reggie for a long time, though he's played in New York on opposing teams. So, the sound is foreign and unfamiliar...and it irks Billy.

Reg-gie! Reg-gie!
Reg-gie! Reg-gie!

This is what George was going for, but certainly not what Billy wants. But regardless of all the quarreling at the top, the fans embrace their new right fielder who bats fifth in the lineup despite the question of why he's not batting cleanup at number four. Billy has insisted on batting Reggie fifth during the exhibition games and this will become the next problem for George who also insists that Reggie bat fourth.

Reg-gie! Reg-gie!
Reg-gie! Reg-gie!

In the meantime, Reggie turns in a modest performance with a walk and two singles as the Yankees win their '77 opener by a score of 3-0.

Let it be known that all this will be short-lived as the Reggie-ing will stop and be replaced by booing when the Yankees end up with a 2-8 record after their first ten games...Reggie with a series of mishaps like a dropped flyball and a pick-off at first base...now giving Billy some substantial ammunition to use against Reggie in his dislike of him. George promptly begins flying in for the away games and visiting the locker room, to impose epic-length rants with Billy sitting there taking it along with the team. Nobody is bothered by it though. No one is intimidated. It's quite comical and they're used to it, and the new guys like Reggie find this out rather quickly. Sparky Lyle and Ed Figueroa both get caught sleeping through one of George's rants and are both fined a hundred dollars. George is not beyond this sort of thing with his players and it's not the first time for Lyle, who along with Mickey Rivers was fined five hundred dollars each for not showing up to a game in Syracuse during the short exhibition season. One player tells beat reporter, Murray

Class, perhaps off the record, that there are far more players on Billy's side than George's, and if there's any upside to the Yankees losing...well, the more they lose, the more George will get up and fly out to the games...and the more he flies, the better the chances of his plane crashing.

It is important to note that despite Billy's reputation, he is usually in most cases diplomatic and avoids confrontation...or at least he genuinely tries to. These instances of rage are few and far between and often blown up and magnified by the press. His players defend him when needed, either by straight out coming to his defense, or simply by saying nothing or giving any credence to criticism. Beat writers who very often bring up the subject of race to black players on the Yankees are hard-pressed to come up with anybody who will criticize Billy or portray him as racist. Though Reggie claims Willie Randolph is the only black teammate who was welcoming and remains friendly, Randolph doesn't see much bad in Billy either. Everyone is aware of Billy's drinking and how it affects his mood and disposition. They know his temper and the triggers. Those older staff members who have known him far longer than the players are accustomed to his personality, and the players themselves, most of which have already spent a season with him, obviously know him better than Reggie does, and so they know what to expect, what to take to heart, and what not to.

It doesn't take long before the New York press begins a daily examination of the Yankees as a dysfunctional family...one that the Yankees themselves are making no effort to conceal. It starts from the top with the owner and manager, and proceeds downward through the staff, team captain and the new star. That's just on the surface. Early through mid-April is a portrait of a team struggling through the hype of expectations and the expectations of hype. On paper, the Yankees are already World Champions. On the field, they're pathetic losers who can't get out of their own way.

17

DON'T LEAVE ME THIS WAY

It's Sunday morning, April 17, 1977. The tri-state area is waking up to the S&L Entertainment Enterprises announcement of six Led Zeppelin concerts to be held at Madison Square Garden in June. The band has just gotten back on the road recently, but just a few days ago, had to cut their show in Chicago short when guitarist Jimmy Page got sick to his stomach and could barely stand up through his performance. The last time they played in New York was February 1975 with the process of getting tickets proving to be a debacle when unruly impatient fans stormed the Ticketrons in places like Bambergers department store, smashing through glass doors to get inside. The supply of tickets didn't meet the demand with only three concerts offered at the Garden, though a pair of shows was also scheduled at the Nassau Coliseum. The monumental six-night stand this time around should take care of the overwhelming demand as delinquent teens, burnouts and stoners all peaking in the sheer volume of their very existence should all be able to secure tickets with this many shows available.

In the Bronx where the Led Zeppelin announcement doesn't mean shit, the Pelham Bay section is waking up to the horrific discovery of two bodies in a 1969 maroon Mercury Montego parked on the service road alongside the

Hutchinson River Parkway, just a few blocks from where Donna Lauria was extinguished. Sometime around 3 AM, 18-year-old Valentina Suriani and her boyfriend Alexander Esau, 20, were shot as they sat in the car. Suriani was killed at the scene. Esau will die within a few more hours. This stretch of the Hutch is known as what they call a lover's lane. The shooting is not unlike previous incidents where victims, mostly female have been shot in cars. The couple knew about the heightened alert in recent weeks. They were aware of the 44 killer. They'd heard the warnings for the past month ever since the Voskerichian murder. For Val, as she was known to friends and family, the idea of a serial killer hit much closer to home since the killer's first victim lived only a few blocks away. Though public awareness of a serial killer has only been in recent weeks, the mysterious killing of Donna Lauria has haunted Pelham Bay for the past nine months and Val was very aware of the increasing danger out there. Still, they sat in the car at a very late/early hour for a prolonged period, which begs the question of why. Why the hell were they sitting in a car at three in the morning? *Oh come on! Why do people sit in parked cars at ungodly hours? They're either kissing, fucking or talking.* Both kids are found in the driver's seat.

This stretch known as the service road for the Hutch isn't exactly the Hutch, which sits just beyond the fence to the left of Esau's car. A wall of trees behind the fence separate the two roads, though the slow growth of springtime following the stubborn winter has kept the trees mostly bare, so it's easy to see straight down to the Hutch where rapid traffic passes in both directions, far removed and distant from the realities of the service road on Sunday morning where death lay at the doorstep of an unsuspecting neighborhood that went to bed not expecting the monster to return. It's mostly an Italian and Jewish neighborhood, and like most predominantly Italian neighborhoods, it has that Italian neighborhood look to the point where it's difficult to tell the difference between stretches of Pelham Bay and stretches of Elizabeth, New Jersey...that halcyon picturesque realistic neverland where everyone knew everyone...the flowerpot ladies always hanging out their windows talking about everyone as they watered their plants...they knew all the gossip...the best delis and the best bakeries...they knew when so and so left the house and when so and so got home and they knew the rhythm of the neighborhood in every shade, color and capacity. Val and her family had moved to 1950 Hutchinson River Parkway after residing in the Allerton Avenue section of the northeast Bronx during much of her childhood. The building at 1950 is much more affluent than the series of buildings making up the projects where they lived inside the square block between Mace and Waring Avenues one block down from St. Lucy's where Val went to elementary school.

St. Lucy's was in a vicinity that also had PS 89 and PS 135 and Columbus High School. Val was as popular as a student could get in elementary school all the way through high school and had a countless number of friends all through childhood. She was active in sports and played in various little league teams including a basketball team that her friend Gloria Calilli's mom coached. Val and Gloria were close friends since the first grade and held sports very much in common. Both girls were in love with Pete Maravich, though Val's real infatuation was with Major League baseball shortstop Tim Foley who played for the Mets during the 1971 and 1972 seasons before being traded to the Montreal Expos. Val was a diehard Mets fan and was lucky enough to see her team win the World Series in 1969. Foli came along a few years after that, and ever since his departure from New York, Val kept his baseball card stashed away in her wallet.

Across the street from St. Lucy's is a grotto named after Our Lady of Lourdes. The fenced-in enclosure served as a place of spiritual beauty and serenity but was also a hangout location for young couples making out...a sort of lover's lane for locals who weren't in parked cars. Perhaps that's where Val and Alex might have ended up had Val not moved to Pelham Bay when she did.

The random chance of Val and Alex meeting how and where they did in the first place comes to the forefront when we consider all these what-ifs. Growing up in the part of the Bronx that she did, Valentina Suriani, like so many neighborhood kids belonged to the Catholic Youth Organization, run by the beloved Father Oliverio. St. Lucy's parish served as the nucleus of the community. The teens indeed partied like normal kids everywhere else, but the community was filled with God and a backbone of morals and decency and that extended to the kids. When Father Oliverio came to the parish he arrived with the urgency of a social worker. He was the type of priest who made it okay to knock on the rectory door at three in the morning if you were feeling troubled enough to need someone to talk to at that very moment...Father Oliverio was there. Part of his legacy within St. Lucy's and the much larger whole of the Bronx was his organization of programs designed to get kids off the street and into more productive activities as well as being all about fun excursions for the kids. One day in early December a few years ago, he took about 70 kids into Manhattan to see the Christmas tree at Rockefeller Center. While Father Oliverio usually spared no expense for the CYO, there were certain decisions he made in the interest of being cost effective. In this case, that meant forgoing his initial plan of renting a bus and instead loading the kids into the back of a U-Haul truck. At the end of the day when the group was on their way back to the Bronx, the truck was sitting in stop-and-go traffic creeping along slowly from light to light. Though the weather was on the nippy side, Father Oliverio didn't want the kids crammed into the back of the truck to suffocate too much, so he occasionally opened the back door to get some fresh air. At one light, three male pedestrian teens walked up to the truck and began talking to the teens inside. Val was among the kids sitting in the back who began responding to the boys outside. It was a friendly exchange. Who are you guys? Where are you all going? What are you all doing? The type of curiosity that could only come from bored teenagers who would do any erratic thing for some kicks, and that's quite what they did when the three boys, Alex Esau being one of them, jumped onto the back of the truck and the rest is history. Alex lived nearby in Hell's Kitchen with his family and initially hit it off with Val's friend Maria who he ended up dating for a brief period. That was a few years ago. It was only more recently that Alex got together with Val and the two had been an item since.

In more recent weeks, Val, who always had a serious interest in acting, had mentioned potential plans for going out to the West Coast to check out some prospects she'd mentioned to friends. Gloria Calilli had run into her just a few weeks before the murder after not seeing her for a very long time.

In that short encounter, Val told Gloria her idea of going out to California. When Gloria asked her what her parents thought of the idea, Val shrugged it off. But next, she asked how Alex felt about it, and Val's only response was to tell Gloria they had to talk. This is ambiguous and vague at best, but that is how they left it. Read into it what you may. In the time that the two girls hadn't spoken, Val had gotten a new phone number, so she wrote it down on a piece of paper and gave it to Gloria. The plan was to meet for coffee and catch up on their lives and to talk a little more extensively on what Val's plans were. It's mere speculation on Val's response to Gloria's inquiry into Alex. How did he feel about Val's acting aspirations and going out west for whatever amount of time it might have been. Did he approve? Did he not approve? Would he have gone with her? Would it have eventually broken them up? That kind of speculation is warranted based on her response to Gloria. It is also known that some of Val's closest friends and family recently gathered for a dinner at Gino's Restaurant on Allerton to celebrate her decision to visit the West Coast in pursuit of acting, so we know her leaving New York was real and coming up soon. We will never know what kind of conversation Val and Alex may or may not have been having while sitting in the car in the moments before they were shot, or even the days before, but it is likely that the subject of Val's plans were a fresh and ongoing dialogue between the couple in those last days...which also brings about the possibility of that dialogue calling into question the future status of their relationship...and to reiterate, this is all mere speculation on the part of this publication, leaving us to make of it what we will.

The bullets are indeed from the same gun used by the 44 killer...though this time, it's not ballistics confirming it.

PART THREE

Make it move, set this place on fire

— *Heatwave*

18

44, 54 AND THE MORAL EQUIVALENT OF WAR

What they didn't expect at the scene of the crime was the rambling four-page letter left by the killer. In the week since the Suriani / Esau murders, the tabloid press is zooming in on a letter found by police under the tire of Alexader Esau's car. What police and media have dubbed the .44 caliber killer has now announced himself...or itself...as the letter addressed to NYPD Captain Joseph Borrelli is an unhinged and threatening rant of someone or something seemingly evil. He addresses himself as a monster...more specifically, the Son of Sam. Through cryptic language he has also acknowledged the other shootings he's connected to...thus verifying that New York City does indeed have a serial killer roaming the streets. At this point, the letter is being withheld from the public as is most of its contents, though the Son of Sam name is now being passed around in the news and even though the public has no idea of what's inside the letter, they know it's pretty bad.

While the main reason the police are keeping the letter private is potential use as evidence in a courtroom, they also don't want to cause mass panic. But then there's the tabloid media crowned by the *Daily News* and Murdoch's morally cheapened *Post* that tries to do just that when they begin running headlines designed to sell papers by scaring the shit out of the public. There are three main points repeatedly driven by the media...the three things we seem to know without question. One, that the .44 caliber killer operates at night, roaming the streets of so-far-Queens and the Bronx in search of his next victim. Two...that most of his victims are teenage girls or young women in their early twenties...and three...that his female victims are all brunettes with shoulder length hair.

On the Monday night following the weekend murders of Valentina Suriani and Alexander Esau, the big picture of the entire country takes priority over serial killers in New York when President Carter takes to live television to address the nation's energy crisis...something he believes to be the biggest challenge America will face in our lifetimes.

Carter is concerned about rapidly shrinking resources and the need to balance the demand for energy. In essence this is really the first collective consequence of the post-war modern age and all the mass consumption of American excess and excretia...a byproduct of the success of American life, which in Carter's mind is coming to a head and about to boil over. The earth's resources are finite. Energy is finite. Water is finite. Oil is finite. By his estimation, the world's oil supply will be gone by the end of the 1980s and he is preparing the American people that he's about to make some controversial and unpopular proposals to Congress. He spells it out in dire terms that the power of America as a nation is at stake, and failure to act would result in a national catastrophe. The use of the world's oil keeps doubling with every passing decade since the 1950s and the world is not prepared for the future's consumption as it continues to rise. He warns Americans that they'll have to put up with inconveniences and make sacrifices. The ability of the president and Congress to govern the nation will be tested by the decision they make on these proposals. Everyone remembers how cold winter was and the natural gas shortage during the incoming days of Carter's term in office. The winter is over and the warmth of spring is starting to settle in. People's homes are warm again and the long gas lines of 1973 are etched so deep into history that they no longer seem realistic. Well, here is the president to remind the American people that the energy crisis is far worse than it was back then. At the moment, the world is using 60 million barrels of oil a day with a five percent increase in demand each year. This pace can only continue until around 1985 and then the demand for oil will exceed the world's supply. Further plundering the environment in search of the earth's resources no longer seems a realistic long-term option, so Carter paints the picture this way...

"We'll have a crash program to build more nuclear plants, strip-mine and burn more coal, and drill more offshore wells than if we begin to conserve right now. Inflation will soar, production will go down, people will lose their jobs. Intense competition for oil will build up among nations and also among the different regions of our own country, which has already started. If we fail to act soon, we will face an economic, social and political crisis that will threaten our free institutions. But we still have another choice. We can begin to prepare right now. We can decide to act while there is still time." He spells out ten fundamental principles that his new energy plan is based on, including government responsibility toward the plan, healthy economic growth, protection of the environment, avoidance of embargoes, fairness, reduction of demand through conservation, prices reflecting true replacement costs of energy, government policies being predictable and certain, preserving the scarcest fuels while making the most of those that are plentiful...and finally, development of new and unconventional sources of energy that will be relied upon going into the next century.

Carter then lists the goals to reach by 1985..."to reduce the annual growth rate in our energy demand to less than two percent...to reduce gasoline consumption by ten percent below its current level...to cut in half the portion of United States oil which is imported, to a potential level of 16 million barrels to six million barrels a day...to establish a strategic petroleum reserve of one million barrels, more than six months' supply...to increase our coal production by about two thirds to more than one billion tons a year...to insulate 90 percent of American homes and all new buildings...to use solar energy in more than two and one half million houses."

Needless to say, Carter's appeal to the American people to conserve energy on multiple fronts is unpopular and met with the hostility of a populace advocating for the arrogance of a country that prides itself on excess.

Though Carter served as a governor, he remained on the outside of the Beltway in terms of being a politician...he was not one of them, and he acted as such straight into is presidency. Part of the challenges of his years in office would to a large degree run consistent with the karmic payoff of not being a politician and not playing their game. But at this stage in his tenure, this is where he stands in April 1977, and this is where we are as a country...festering in the shit of our own overindulgent extravagance.

The crowd along Allerton Avenue is made up of friends and family and strangers and media shoving cameras in people's faces as the line to go inside Ferenga Brothers Funeral Home is met with crowds in the street and crowds converging from around the corner, and there are so many people overall that it's hard to tell where the actual line is. The wake service for Valentina Suriani has attracted more attention than her loved ones could ever imagine. The press leeches swarm to the young females outside...anyone they could catch hold of to ask if they're scared or concerned about the killer as they wait to go inside to say goodbye to their deceased friend. The fucking bloodsuckers set alight from this newly-written reality that this situation, this monster, this thing is out there stalking girls in the nighttime, and this is their time to shine by sticking microphones in front of grieving teenagers. Though there have been other victims and survivors of these shootings, this is the first time the media is covering a murder story top to bottom, and the first funeral since this name Son of Sam has been in the headlines, though many still prefer to call him the 44 Killer. The funeral service itself attracts the same crowds at St. Teresa's Church just a few blocks from where Valentina lived and died.

On Tuesday of the last week of April, sensationalist media takes its focus off the 44 killer and transitions through the commencement of yet another discotheque. While the growing number of dance clubs in the city has become evident in the past year, this one commands attention in the metropolis for being the latest to attract and cater to celebrities. In the withering hours of daylight, last minute tensions of potential logistical fuckups threaten to alter the well-ordered grand opening. The old, converted theater at 254 West Fifty-fourth Street just off Eighth Avenue is the site of this new venture of one Stephen Rubell and two other young entrepreneurs who are in for over a million on the hitch that the celebrity elite and avant-garde will make this establishment a thriving success. It boasts a high-end light show made up of 400 different programmed settings and a waterfall. At press time, the waterfall is leaking, and electricians are warning Rubell not to add much more weight to overload the grid, which prompts him to deny an outlet to a Vogue photographer who simply needs to plug in a light. The Vogue guy pleads with Rubell who tells him one more light could be too many and then they'd have a blown fuse for the ages, though he ultimately gives in when confronted with the question of how they'll light all of the celebrities as they walk in.

People file in slowly. It's almost a deliberately measured amount of time that passes from the opening doors at 9PM before the substantial numbers start to swell. Celebs arrive fashionably late, and the big names don't stay that long past an hour, at least not on opening night. Still the club is filled to its 2500 capacity and in the coming weeks Studio 54 will swiftly become a pop cultural phenomenon...one of several that will happen by the time the summer passes. But here we are, in the mid-spring, and names like Halston, Andy Warhol, Liza Minelli, Truman Capote and Mick and Bianca Jagger become regulars associated with 54's early days. There will be no shortage of the rich and famous, but it's not just the rich and famous that lures the wealthy and middle class alike...it's the promise of total debauchery that seals itself into the bedrock of the club's reputation...a breeding ground for unrestrained hedonism, promiscuous sex, vast quantities of drugs and an unchecked feeling that anything can and will happen, and not only will it happen...it will happen big, limitless and then there will be even more. It doesn't matter if it's the week or the weekend. The club will go to the brink of excess every single night. It will be a place where even the regular people will be able to get in...the ones who aren't actually in the tabloids, but the ones who buy and read the tabloids. But just as quickly as word spreads of the club's eclectic possibilities, it will become nearly impossible for most people to get in as an elite exclusivity will inform Steve Rubell's vision for said eclecticism and his ego will often work against his better judgment.

Even as the next Kiss album which will be titled *Love Gun* hasn't been recorded yet, the band gathers with Barry Levine on April 28 to be photographed in new costumes. With the look of *Destroyer* and *Rock and Roll Over* behind them, these new outfits will represent the Kiss image for the new album and upcoming tour and will take the band into 1978. In May, the band is back in Electric Lady with Eddie Kramer recording *Love Gun*, which follows the same studio album formula they've been using since the 1974 debut...an alternating sequence balancing the songs sung by Paul with the songs sung by Gene and the obligatory song sung by Peter. There is one major difference this time around. This album will contain the first song sung by Ace. Until now, Ace has contributed to the band by way of writing...he's penned songs such as "Cold Gin" and "Parasite" sung by Gene, "Strange Ways" and "Getaway" sung by Peter and has a few co-writing credits. This time, Ace has written a song inspired partly by his near electrocution in Lakeland, aptly titled "Shock Me," which Paul and Gene have convinced him to sing. Until now, Ace has always remained shy when it comes to vocals and the confidence needed to get up in front of people and sing lead. The crazy boisterous type that the guys know is more a symptom of substance abuse than a facet of Ace's natural personality. When recording the vocals for "Shock Me," an overly anxious Ace lays down on the floor to get comfortable and conveniently stay out of everyone's sight. His vocal delivery is one of unique mannerisms, blending the sharp treble street staccato of a tough talking kid from the Bronx and his New Yawka accent. It's part Lou Reed and part Tucker Smith in full Daddy-O fashion singing "Cool" in *West Side Story*. It's that finger snapping thing...that hipster thing with the swing, and it don't mean a thing if it ain't got the swing. But this time, it's three-chords and a Les Paul and a timid New Yawka hiding from his own bandmates as he belches into the mic...

Yaw light-nins all I need...
mah satis-FAC-tion grow-woes...
Youuu make meh feel aaat ease...
you even make me glow-woah

John Travolta is livid when he catches an early glimpse of some edits John Badham has made of the solo dance sequence, which in effect is the centerpiece of the entire film. He's adamant about his entire body being framed in the scene, and Badham has cut it in closeups. The actor and the director clash over what could make or break the film and Travolta threatens to walk if it's not restored to full body shots. What is the point in all of the training and dance lessons if the dancing will not be prominently featured...especially in one of the key scenes of the storyline. Travolta knows this specific part is meant to showcase the talent of the Tony Manero character and highlight why he is the king of the dancefloor at 2001. It's the moment he clears the floor just by walking onto it as the other dancers recede back to the sidelines to observe as he burns through some of the most revolutionary moves of the day. Travolta has a sense of the visual impact in concert with the lighting and soundtrack. Though Stigwood is often teased around the industry about what's being called his "little disco film," Travolta feels this particular scene can be something spectacular...perhaps one of the great moments in the history of cinema. Stigwood trusts his actor's vision and judgment, and sides with him on the edit, prompting Badham to restore the print to the full body shots and angles from which they were filmed. With RSO acting as producers for the film, Stigwood has now secured Paramount as the distributor.

On May 16, Billy Martin turns 49, though his birthday is marred by an 8-4 routing by the A's. On an unusually cold night In Oakland, Billy starts Ken Holtzman on the mound against his former team. Holtzman, an ace on the A's pitching staff just a few years ago is one of the few players besides Fran Healy who can sympathize with Reggie, having played with him in years past and having been shuffled around with him. The A's gut Holtzman in the first inning, scoring five runs on him before Martin marches out to the mound to send him walking. As Martin already has a dislike for Holtzman, this outing for the veteran pitcher will be one of his last, as Martin will do everything in his power to see to it that he gets minimal playing time for the remainder of the season. Reggie attributes it to an anti-Semitism that he attaches to Billy's character, just as he associates Billy as a racist in general... something the other guys on the team are unable to agree with, as most of them favor Billy and just don't see it.

It's on Monday, May 23 when Reggie's interview for *Sport* hits the newsstands. The June 1977 edition quickly makes its way through Yankees universe and no one is happy.

On the subject of Martin, Reggie tells Robert Ward that Billy is no dummy. He's smart and knows Reggie can help him win. He then attests that Billy is a winner and that he'd make winning easier for him. That's not the part that gets him into trouble. The part that Reggie claims he is misquoted concerns mostly Thurman but is also a jab at the rest of the team. When he commented about having to take up the task of leading the Yankees while denying that Thurman is that leader (he's captain after all), it all but seals the tone for the remainder of the season. Referring to Thurman as jealous and insecure doesn't help. Then there's the comment about being the straw that stirs the drink...something Reggie swears is taken out of context. Something that will follow him for the rest of his career and beyond.

When Reggie arrives at the stadium for a home game against Boston that night, most of the players are thumbing through the magazine, reading the article and passing it around to each other. Other than stern and not-so-pleasant glances from his teammates, Reggie is completely ignored as the cold shoulder prevails. Nobody talks to him...not in the locker room...not during batting practice...and not even during the game...all except for Fran Healy, the Yankees third catcher who sees very little playing time if any but is probably the most likeable. Healy, from day one, has been Reggie's only ally and real friend since joining the team. He's known as the most level-headed presence on the roster and often serves as a buffer in team conflicts...the guy who steps in and tries to settle things or at least smooth things over...the guy who people might confide in or seek advice from. He's well-liked on the team, though he's playfully known as Henry Kissinger by his teammates for his diplomatic personality.

With the Yanks down 2-1 in the seventh that night, Reggie steps to the plate and whacks a solo homerun to tie the game. While the stadium quakes with awakened cheer and "Reggie" chants, the slugger rounds the bases and crosses home plate, walking straight past Lou Piniella who waits on deck with a hand extended. Reggie bypasses him, ignoring the gesture. The remainder of the team on their feet at the dugout entrance await with extended hands to Reggie...Billy too. Reggie circumvents the usual entrance to the dugout, venturing into foul territory and down the line to the far end of the dugout where he enters and sits down by himself after snubbing the entire team. Following the game, he's asked about why he wouldn't shake anyone's hand or high-five them and gives a half-hearted flippant answer about his sore right hand that he didn't want to aggravate.

"He's a fucking liar," Thurman says unabashedly, almost out of character for someone who often says very little to reporters.

"I didn't notice," Billy says to the same question.

In light of the recent developments in new hostility toward Reggie concerning the *Sport* article and dugout snub, Billy is saying very little...perhaps trying to keep a distance from further confrontation. So while the flames have been fanned to nearly irreversible conditions, Billy is keeping quiet... almost out of character himself, at least on this Reggie matter. He's obviously...at least for now, not out to make matters worse with further comment... not for Reggie and certainly not for himself. For now.

On Wednesday, May 25, Kiss shows up in full costume and makeup to the Borden Chemical Company in Buffalo where they are accompanied by Bob Gruen and comic book writer, Stan Lee. On hand in Buffalo is also a safely secured kit containing some blood the band members drew at Nassau Coliseum back in February. In one of the more dangerously gross promotional events in rock history, Paul, Gene, Peter and Ace pose for photos while pouring their own vials of blood into a 55-gallon vat.

Local news reporter, Mike Hegedus addresses the visit later in the day, citing Webster's Dictionary, reminding folks of the definition of a kiss "as defined by Dan Webster, which is something pleasing...a caress...a gentle touch," Hegedus explains. "But there's another kiss that isn't in Websters. Kiss, I'm told, is a big rock group on some level of music...appealing to that portion of the population that finds its collective voice changing and reads comic books. Speaking of which, Kiss is going to have its own comic book soon, featuring the four strangely attired and hairy fellows to be printed by Arcata Graphics and printed in, if you believe everything you're told...in real Kiss blood!"

Mr. Hegedus dismisses the Kiss event as a public relations stunt in bad taste. However the public looks on the band's visit, the report is correct. The blood is to be mixed with the ink that will print the first Marvel Kiss comic book. Arguably, this is the moment Kiss officially becomes comic book characters. Going into the next phase that will begin in a few weeks with a new tour, the release of the new album and a comic book, the band will cross the point of no return. If *Destroyer*'s artwork and supporting images of the band hinted at this, the coming *Love Gun* cycle and everything entailed in it will represent the peak of Kiss's place in popular culture. It will symbolize the brief time in their history when everyone in their audience was onboard...a period when those suspicious original fans with raised eyebrows hadn't all quite dropped off yet, and a period when a younger audience of children was assured and locked in.

In Manhattan on that same morning, the wholesale flower district of West Twenty-Eighth Street wakes up to the wailing of sirens and the furious dancing of flames flaring out the second-floor windows of the Everard Baths, a building that's become a raging inferno in a matter of minutes. What seems to have started with a burning mattress quickly engulfed an entire hallway and has sent occupants jumping out windows and dangling from ledges while the rest pour out into the street. The bathhouse is known on the West Side as a gay safe haven where hundreds of rented cubicles are occupied mostly by homosexual men. At 7AM, West Twenty-Eighth is filled with 200 firefighters and scores of men fleeing the building, some wearing only towels. The lucky ones have robes. The others have nothing but their penises and their hands to cover them. Nine men perish in the blaze.

On this otherwise unassuming Wednesday in late May, production wraps up on Stigwood's disco film in Brooklyn while a small Hollywood movie with big ambitions opens in a limited number of select theaters around the tri-state area. It's called *Star Wars*.

The next morning, Thursday, May 26 sees the big news story of the day situated downtown where thousands of New Yorkers on their way to work are all stopped on the streets, motioning in the same upward glance as they watch a random civilian scaling the south tower of the World Trade Center... somehow climbing toward the top. For three and a half hours, thousands watch in shock, horror and sheer excitement while the NYPD figure out how to deal with the situation, attempting repeatedly to communicate with the climber and even sending a window washer's cage down to him. The climber avoids all but often waves to the pedestrians below. Finally, at 10:05 AM, he makes it to the top of the tower where he is swiftly arrested. Still, he proudly waves to the crowd below, not that anyone can really see him or make out humans from that high up. The crowd shows its approval with enthusiastic cheers and applause. By the end of the morning, we know that this man, George Willig is a toymaker and mountain climber from Queens and has been plotting this event for some time now...similar to Philipe Petit who walked a highwire between the towers three years ago, and much like Petite, he constructed the equipment he used. Willig used a contraption he designed made of nylon rope and some metal clamps that locked into the tracks for the window washing cages that normally move up and down the buildings.

Also downtown this morning, a judge throws out the New York Mets attempt to stop the football Jets from playing at Shea Stadium until after the baseball season is over. The two teams have long shared Shea Stadium, but problems have arisen in recent years. Just a few months earlier, the Jets announced that they will play their September and October home games in New Jersey at the newly built Giants Stadium. In fact, Jets owner Leon Hess is threatening to move the Jets to New Jersey permanently. The Mets complain that the constant back and forth transitioning between football and baseball configurations on the seating layout and the playing field is extremely damaging to the grass...especially in September and early October when the early weeks of the NFL season overlap with the final weeks of the baseball season. Justice Harold Baer warns lawyers for the Mets of consequences if the team doesn't comply with his orders of permitting the Jets to play two home games at Shea during the month of September, including one of the first two weeks of the upcoming NFL season.

Now that *Saturday Night* has finished production, Travolta, with little room to breathe, spends the next few weeks preparing for *Grease* on the West Coast. The second of Stigwood's productions featuring John will begin filming on June 25. This is the much anticipated one that all involved are looking forward to, as it could possibly be the blockbuster needed for RSO, and its star...especially now that the little disco film is out of the way.

19

GONNA FLY NOW

During the last week of May 1977, the *Daily News* receives a letter addressed to columnist Jimmy Breslin. Jimmy Breslin is one of the definitive voices of New York City journalism in the way he captures the sentiment of the little guy...the downtrodden...the underdog...the poor slob walking away from the hotdog stand with mustard dripping down his shirt...the regular people. He champions the regular people, and he usually writes on behalf of them. He's built a stationary reputation over the past few decades, turning out daily articles for his *Daily News* column. His column is a New York City institution. He writes about crime, race, sports and daily life, often covering the not-so-glamorous aspects of city life. He's not just a fixture in the nerve center of Manhattan either...he's revered (though not so much by conservatives) in the outer boroughs as well. At this time in late May of 1977, Breslin is 48 years old.

When Breslin goes to work at the beginning of the week in those final few days of May, there are three things he doesn't see coming that will transpire by the end of the week. The first is the letter given to him by his employers. It's a letter sent to the *Daily News* but addressed to Breslin. The second is the visit he'll be paying to the parents of Donna Lauria, the first known victim of the .44 caliber killer. The third thing he doesn't see coming is himself entering the narrative as a major figure within the Son of Sam case...something that will send shock waves of panic and further fear throughout the city.

The letter is combed over in detail repeatedly by Breslin and his colleagues seated around a table in deep consultation of how to proceed with regards to its content, law enforcement...and the public.

By Saturday, June 4, Breslin is traveling to the Buher Arms building in Pelham Bay and knocking on the door of the Lauria's apartment. Inside he has coffee in the dining room with Mike and Rose Lauria while reading the letter to them, which specifically mentions their daughter by name and refers to her murder multiple times. This is significant because the letter is written by the killer and carries an ominous and prophetic tone that warns of more killings. It is handwritten on paper that's marked up by a unique penmanship, iterations of the male female symbolism, riddle-like comments, mysterious nicknames and a sarcastic tone of mockery, almost chastising the police for not having kept up with him and his works of murder. He promises more though.

The Lauria's share pictures and stories about Donna and seem to have processed her loss about as good as any parent could possibly process something as horrific as having your kid shot dead in the street. After reading the letter, Rose Lauria puts it down on the table.

"He's probably a brilliant man...boy...whatever he is," she says matter-of-factly to Breslin. "His brain functions the opposite way."

They can only speculate over the killer. They have no idea who or what it is. The Lauria's have had almost a year without their daughter and that much time to live with the agonizing why's and what's.

"She was a dancer and a half," she says while looking at recent photographs. "Every place she went, people used to praise her. Is it possible he saw her some place and she didn't speak to him or something?"

These questions will torment them for the rest of their lives.

"Who knows?" Mike Lauria replies. "How can you say anything about a guy you don't even know?"

For parents going through the grieving process, they are remarkably level-headed and approachable on the subject. If anything positive has come of these .44 killings, if such a word dare be used, it's that the Lauria's at least have an idea of the details behind Donna's killing ...even if it's just the words of a psychotic madman. They went through the first seven or eight months after Donna's murder without the faintest fucking idea of what happened to their daughter and who might have been behind it. These questions are still unanswered, but they now feel a part of something...this big, unexpected juggernaut of societal menace that they now know began with their daughter's murder, and that they can at least attach it to something much bigger that other parents can relate to. The same can be said of Carl Denaro who the cops believed was simply the victim of some drug deal gone wrong. Case closed. Even his own mother blamed him for the company he kept and that he was in the wrong place at the wrong time and that's what you get for being up to no good. Well now the locals in Flushing including Denaro's mom can rest easy knowing it was a serial killer who shot her kid and not a drug dealer. All the parents of those early victims up until Valentina Suriani now know that they're all part of something and connected in this tragic way... that their kids were shot by someone who calls himself the Son of Sam and takes orders from this Sam character who has a thirst for blood and tells him what to do...this unknown figure of the night that has now left two letters. The first one left at the scene of the Suriani shooting in April and addressed to the police has been kept from the public with only choice bits released to the media. But the decision that's about to be made by the *Daily News* will now raise the tension within the city and set in motion a collective fear when Jimmy Breslin publishes the second letter in his Sunday column on June 5.

> Hello from the gutters of N.Y.C. which are filled with dog manure, vomit, stale wine, urine and blood. Hello from the sewers of N.Y.C. which swallow up these delicacies when they are washed away by the sweeper trucks. Hello from the cracks in the sidewalks of N.Y.C. and from the ants that dwell in these cracks

and feed in the dried blood of the dead that has settled into the cracks. J.B., I'm just dropping you a line to let you know that I appreciate your interest in those recent and horrendous .44 killings. I also want to tell you that I read your column daily and I find it quite informative. Tell me Jim, what will you have for July twenty-ninth? You can forget about me if you like because I don't care for publicity. However you must not forget Donna Lauria and you cannot let the people forget her either. She was a very, very sweet girl but Sam's a thirsty lad and he won't let me stop killing until he gets his fill of blood. Mr. Breslin, sir, don't think that because you haven't heard from me for a while that I went to sleep. No, rather, I am still here. Like a spirit roaming the night. Thirsty, hungry, seldom stopping to rest; anxious to please Sam. I love my work. Now, the void has been filled. Perhaps we shall meet face to face someday or perhaps I will be blown away by cops with smoking .38's. Whatever, if I shall be fortunate enough to meet you I will tell you all about Sam if you like and I will introduce you to him. His name is "Sam the terrible." Not knowing what the future holds I shall say farewell and I will see you at the next job. Or should I say you will see my handiwork at the next job? Remember Ms. Lauria. Thank you. In their blood and from the gutter "Sam's creation" .44 Here are some names to help you along. Forward them to the inspector for use by N.C.I.C: "The Duke of Death" "The Wicked King Wicker" "The Twenty Two Disciples of Hell" "John 'Wheaties' – Rapist and Suffocator of Young Girls. PS: Please inform all the detectives working the slaying to remain. P.S: JB, Please inform all the detectives working the case that I wish them the best of luck. "Keep 'em digging, drive on, think positive, get off your butts, knock on coffins, etc." Upon my capture I promise to buy all the guys working the case a new pair of shoes if I can get up the money.

Son of Sam

In the days following Breslin's article, fear on the streets is ratcheted up several notches to an elevated mass concern, sending media out into the boroughs to gauge the concern of teenagers. News reports begin featuring random girls on the street being stopped by reporters and asked how it feels to be in the crosshairs of a serial killer. Several police sketches from witness and survivor descriptions are becoming familiar to the public as these sketches are seen on television and in the tabloids everyday now. None, however, seem to match the others and they all look quite different from each other.

On the seventh of June, Led Zeppelin moves into Madison Square Garden for a week. The Garden will have a busy few months in what will amount to New York City's biggest summer concert season in the history of rock music. Decades from now...let's say the 2020's when there will be zero rock bands popular enough to headline venues like the Garden, it will stand as testament to just how unpopular rock and roll will become when we look back at a year like 1977 fifty years later. The year 1977 will feature more bands headlining the Garden in any given month than in the entire twenty-first century combined...of course not counting the twentieth century bands and artists who continue to play there long into the next millennium. So far, 1977 has seen Kiss, Queen, Electric Light Orchestra, Genesis, Eagles, Boston and Chuck Berry all headline MSG. Even as disco erodes rock's influence on pop culture, rock is still very much present and dominant where radio doesn't necessarily play a part in success. Not only do some of these acts play the 20,000 seat venue, but they stay for multiple night runs. Just for MSG alone, the summer schedule looks something like this...

June 7,8,10,11,12, 14 – Led Zeppelin
June 21 – Crosby, Stills, Nash
June 29, 30 - Fleetwood Mac
July 1-4 – Pink Floyd
July 7-9 – Emerson, Lake & Palmer

July 31 – Bad Company
August 5-7 – Yes
August 22-24 – Peter Frampton
August 26 – The Isley Brothers
September 19 – Parliament- Funkadelic

It's also a time when rock albums are selling more than they've ever sold. Kiss's *Love Gun* ships platinum, making it one of the first albums to sell a million units before it's even released.

The album cover of *Love Gun*, painted by Ken Kelly who also painted *Destroyer*, has the band members standing together as a wall of brute force, much like the *Destroyer* cover. Worshipping girls sit obediently at their feet. Kiss appears in bold new outfits that suggest something royal and immortal...or, yes, we can say it...superheroes. They're surrounded by green marble pillars as they stand majestically in a palatial entrance...and just outside the archway, the fiery yellow landscape of *Destroyer*'s annihilated city burns behind them. At least that's what some kids who have taken acid are suggesting while nobody is paying any attention to them, completely missing the latest in a chain of secret message albums...much like the ones of the Beatles that told us Paul was dead...or the *play "Stairway to Heaven" backwards* craze...or the *Dark Side of the Moon/Wizard of Oz* hype. But this one with Kiss never catches on. So, when these suburban stoners stare at *Love Gun* for too long, it's the odd yellow slab in the color scheme behind the band members that bothers them, until they realize Kiss is standing at the entrance of a palace, and just outside the palace is...*Destroyer*.

"They knew what they were doing when they painted this, man. You see that yellow and orange? That's fire, man. You see that little sliver of dark purple? That's the *Destroyer* sky. That's *Destroyer* behind them, man!"

"Oh wow, man...they planted *Destroyer* right in the middle of *Love Gun*!"

Inside is a slipcover depicting a coarse green surface with Kiss spelled in blood. The package once again features a merchandise form offering belt buckles, embroidered patches and T-shirts. This time however is an ad for the Kiss comic book published by Marvel that will be released on June 30.

Kiss historians will later record June 30 as the release date of the *Love Gun* album itself, though there is plenty of evidence to the contrary in newspaper and magazine ads showing the album already on sale throughout June, and a June 1977 *New York Times Magazine* article that states the album was released in mid-June...probably around the fourteenth. If ever in the past year when the band being accused of turning themselves into superheroes seemed an overreaction, the packaging of *Love Gun* is the smoking gun, pun intended. The album even comes with a cardboard gun cutout. The new Kiss album in all its adult-themed imagery, double entendres and penis innuendos, the package, no pun intended, is marketed at kids, which has adults scratching their heads. In fact, the merchandise Aucoin Management offers is one of the bigger distractions that begin to highlight the various publications that have no choice but to start noticing Kiss...the ones that don't take them seriously but will inevitably cover them over the following year. While the fanzines aimed at kids put spotlights on the band members and the mythology of the characters, publications and TV news magazines start doing tongue-in-cheek spotlights on the unequaled merchandising and the millions they rake in. Millions is a word they always tie to these rock acts...they've got millions...they make millions...million-dollar stage show...million- dollar light show...million-dollar homes! In 1977 a million dollars is a lot of money and it's always helpful to say a million dollars when trying to convey the magnitude of someone's popularity or influence.

Because it is the younger children who are inevitably discovering the group, parents have no choice but to start taking note of this unfolding phenomenon luring their children into this God-forsaken world of hookers named Black Diamond, 93-year old creepy men in love with 16-year old girls, a doctor who cures ailing girls with sex, and creepy stalkers who watch sixteen-year old Christine coming out of school as depicted in the new single "Christine Sixteen," penned and sung by Gene. By 1977 standards nobody judges Gene over this...it is simply a sign of the times for lack of a better phrase. Sixteen is a popular number in modern music at least back to "Sweet Little Sixteen" or more recently Ringo Starr's "You're Sixteen." Not everyone sings proudly of their conquests though. At least Gary Puckett in his song "Young Girl" seems ashamed of his battles with pedophilic urges. The bottom line here is that with the release of *Love Gun*, Kiss enters a different level of popularity, and they are now 100 percent visible in the world of pop culture. In that world, that are primarily associated as something that young kids are going crazy over and the adults don't know what to do about it, so they either shrug it off or they're outraged. There are no in-betweens. For instance, one gleeful seven-year-old boy in a small suburb of New Jersey happily showed a relative his new copy of *Love Gun*. Glancing at the cover disapprovingly, the male relative of around 30 held the front photo up to the small boy's eyes.

"Do you see this? Do you see this guy with the star on his face?"

"Yeah," the boy said proudly. "That's Paul Stanley!"

"But do you see how he's dressed? Do you see his chest? Do you see how his shirt is wide open, and his entire upper body is sticking out? This is a grown man! Do you see him?"

"Yeah."

"How would you like it if your mother or father walked around like this? Is this normal? Do you think your mother or father should dress like this?"

The boy, growing ashamed as if he had done something wrong, only looked down and stayed silent. The relative continued to piss on his joy.

"How would you feel if your mother walked around with her shirt open like this? Do you see this guy with the chains on his chest? How would you like it if your father wore chains on his chest?"

No response.

"What about all the adults you know? Would you feel safe around them? What would you think of me if I showed up at your house dressed like this?"

The boy looked at the male relative who was dressed in red, white and blue checkered Tough Skin pants, but didn't say anything. The man continued to press.

"What about your teacher in school? Would you trust your teacher?"

He already didn't trust his teacher. His first-grade teacher was probably the most diabolical person on the planet. She was abusive and he was quietly tormented by her. Kiss was the only thing in the world that made him happy. Kiss was the only thing in this whole fucking universe that made him want to live.

With *Rocky* going on seven months since its premiere, the unlikely soundtrack comprised of brass pieces ranging from dark, moody and consequential to triumphant has made it into the Billboard Hot 100 with its theme song topping the charts at number one.

By Friday, June 17, the Yankees are in first place by a half game after rookie pitcher, Ron Guidry shuts out the Royals on a three hitter. The Yanks have a three-game weekend series in Boston to face the second place Red Sox. The Sox, in an explosive display of six homeruns, easily jump back into first after defeating the Yanks. Back in second place, the two historical rivals face off in a televised Saturday afternoon Game of the Week for NBC. From the beginning, the Sox begin dominating the Yanks again, maintaining a 7-4 lead going into the bottom of the sixth inning.

The sun over Fenway Park is brutal. It's suggested that the third base line, which sits on the western side of the park, is the best location if you want shade during a day game. The attendance of 34,602 is said to be the largest Saturday crowd in twenty years. The 90-degree heat only adds to the incoherence of beer-guzzling bare-chested men, sprawled out sporadically in prostration around Fenway. There is no love lost between these two contenders for first place, nor amongst the fans, but the oppressive heat has mellowed everyone in the stands.

After Fred Lynn gets on base with a single, Jim Rice hits a lowly blooper over Randolph toward right field where Reggie swears the blinding sun makes him assume Randolph is fielding the ball and probably caught it...all before it drops in front of him, prompting him to chug over and retrieve it. Billy doesn't see the sun from a right fielder's perspective as the obstructed view that assures that Reggie has no play on the ball. All Billy knows is that Reggie slacked off and took his time. He goes to the mound to pull Torrez out and bring Lyle in from the bullpen. By all accounts of anyone on or near the pitcher's mound, Martin begins walking back to the dugout, uttering "Watch this." Upon arriving back at the bench, he orders Paul Blair out to right field to replace Reggie. Blair grabs his glove and trots out into the yellow-orange glare of the Fenway hinterlands. An unassuming Reggie is standing at the fence as he often does between plays, chatting with the guys in the bullpen. He turns to see Blair headed straight at him. Blair knows what's about to happen, and he's glad he doesn't have to be in the dugout when it does. Reggie points at his own chest.

"You're in for me? What's going on?"

"You need to ask Billy...he told me I'm in for you."

Reggie jogs in, now painfully aware that this is a nationally televised game. He takes pride in his national television appearances and his track record on TV is impeccable. This year alone (and we're only two months into the season), Reggie has been in five nationally televised games and has hit home runs in four of them on top of a 360 batting average in those five games. He knows his TV appearances serve as a counterbalance to all the negative hit pieces that the press routinely does on him, especially in New York.

He comes in questioning Billy's motives and Billy is already in his face, shoving his finger hostilely toward him, barking like a dog that's just had his territory violated. Elston Howard gets between them, walking Reggie away from Billy. Yogi is also on high alert. These guys know Billy, and they sense when he's about to punch someone. It's not until Reggie spits out his disapproval of being shown up on television when Billy unleashes and charges at him only to be met by Yogi who swiftly holds him back with Elston. Torrez interjects on Reggie's side, standing in the star's way, motioning him...almost guiding him to the other side of the dugout. As the threats and the fucks are flying, it's loud enough for Red Sox fans to hear because the entire front row is climbing onto the top of the dugout, stretching their bodies, craning their necks as far as they'll go...attempting to hover over the team to peer into their business and see what's happening. This is what you get when you don't hustle on a play and Billy's the manager. Billy gives no fucks about who you are or what your star's expectations are of being served by national TV.

He sets out to embarrass the star and that's exactly what he accomplishes in Boston, though he orders a batboy to throw a towel over the NBC camera capturing the explosive moment. In plain clothes, Reggie leaves Fenway, walking the streets alone, back to the hotel.

After the dugout fight in Boston, George establishes the Seven Commandments...a set of guidelines to consider as a manager as well as any owner in evaluating a manager...

Do you win? Do you work hard enough? Are you emotionally equipped to lead men? Are you organized? Do you understand human nature? Are you prepared for each game? Are you honorable?

On June 23, there's a small break in the pressing flow of the season as the city's two teams meet in the fifteenth annual Mayor's Trophy game at Shea. Interleague play is non-existent in Major League Baseball, but the Mets and Yankees play each other once each season for bragging rights to at least Abe Beame's recognition of the winner. It's a game that's all in fun, and win or lose, doesn't count toward the season's standings. This year, in ten innings, the Mets on their home turf in Flushing defeat the Bronx Bombers by a score of 2-1. With the tension of the first three months of the season badly in need of dissipation, the dynamic will evolve in the coming weeks toward a more peaceful and cooperative effort through the summer.

In the basement of the Kenmore Hotel on East Twenty-Third Street, a forty-year-old entrepreneur named Larry Levensen runs a recently opened night-spot called Plato's Retreat. The idea of the club is to bring the same kind of total abandon and sexual adventure experienced in the gay discos, but rather offer that freedom to heterosexuals, whether single, couples or any imaginable configuration of human bodies. Levensen is in the process of moving his swingers club to a more respectable higher-end location in the basement of the Ansonia on the Upper West Side by the end of summer. The common thread here is the basement, and the idea of the underground.

In the same fashion as the word seedy is often attributed as an adjective for the Times Square vicinity, the concept of underground hedonism are the words journalists and culture critics are assigning to the ever-growing subcultures of New York City. But subcultures have always been underground, let that be understood as we acknowledge this.

The risqué intentions behind lots of party goers at Studio 54 are not unlike what we see in the swinger's clubs. The basement of 54 contains an ample number of mattresses laid out for those who exist in said underworld and haven't come there to dance. In the past two months since opening, the balcony of the old, converted theater has also become synonymous with promiscuous sex while the public shares the floorspace with celebrities below. But not everyone gets to have this experience or witness it.

Steve Rubell, the newly powerful owner gravitates toward the glamorous ones, male and female. The beautiful people...creatures who are undeniably gorgeous and attractive to swarms of hungry and horny individuals. That could also mean non-celebrities as people from all walks of life can often get into the club, depending on Rubell's mood on any given night. Rubell is in search of the perfect party from night to night. He mixes and matches and adheres to gut responses to his first impressions of people outside the club. It's a matter of who would be right for tonight. It could be anybody, rich or poor, famous or not. Which combination and collection of humanity would fit the party for tonight? Never mind last night and tomorrow. We're addressing the *now*. Consequently, celebrities have no protective gate or immunity from the regular people. What they do, can and will be seen, and will then become fodder for gossip. But that's mainly what attracts the regular people from the suburbs to the city in the hopes of getting in. It's the *getting in* that people hang onto. "Getting in" to Studio 54 becomes the basis for bragging rights among the regular people. The much sought-after quest for getting in becomes a social phenomenon that will spread itself out for the next few years among external wannabe socialites who now have more of a reason than ever to travel into the city.

The whining and wailing of women from the not-so-glamourous regular life calling out the name of Rubell, often in unison and always with voices overlapping sounds like a colony of feral cats as much as it resembles desperation to get into 54. The desperation of people to get past the velvet rope in recent weeks has no doubt been going to Rubell's head as he has even begun to reject some celebrities. Though 54 doesn't seem to be very inclusive, disco itself is inclusion long before inclusion. 54 aside, the scene as a whole includes under one tent, Civil Rights, women's lib and gay rights.

Then there are still those outer borough clubs that house the regular people. Back in the good ole world where they have jobs and work for a living, the outer borough clubs are where they spend their weekend nights. These are the places where the queers tend to stay away, opting for the more risqué side of pleasure-seeking indulgence that can only be found openly in Manhattan where they don't have to hide. It's the outer borough clubs where the straight people go...the couples and their friends...the ones who go to college or to jobs or to both. Or the losers who cling loosely to their dreams but see no real future like the guy John Travolta just played in that disco movie that's coming out soon. These guys are not guys who tolerate guys kissing guys or guys holding the hands of other guys or guys dancing with guys. These guys are guys who would probably kick the shit out of someone like that. And so the queers haven't come out in places like Queens the way they have in Manhattan. Manhattan remains the not-so-secret underworld.

Elephas is a disco located on the corner of Northern Boulevard and 211th Street in Bayside, Queens just three blocks from the 111th Precinct station house. The riffraff the club attracted just a few years earlier is gone...more like rock and rollers...kids causing unrelenting mayhem. The residents in the neighborhood don't miss that crowd, as disco in the suburbs brings a more affluent and well-dressed group...young adults in their twenties and early thirties. Still, there is never any peace along 211th during any given hour throughout the night and wee hours of the morning. The muffled thump of that four on the floor beat and the bass that chugs along nonstop, vibrating the block has become an imposing sound that neighbors have gotten used to, to the point where it just seeps into the background. The club's presence is something the residents have simply learned to live their lives around. The Dobrowski's of 45-39 211th Street are one of many families on the block who aren't happy about the noisy establishment down the corner, but they still manage to sleep through the night but are occasionally woken up by those pesky random bursts of firecrackers...especially lately with the Fourth of July once again approaching. Given the commonality of firecrackers in the area, it seems as if the Bicentennial never ended. And here we are, one year later, and sometime after 3 AM in the middle of a Saturday into Sunday, the Dobrowski's are awoken by successive firecracker bursts that sound as if they've been detonated directly under the giant oak tree on their front lawn. Numerous neighbors along the block hear it too.

Fucking asshole kids!

Fucking Elephas!

But Elephas has had a slow night with not many people coming out with the on and off thunderstorms of the past 24 hours. Still, there's enough for a ruckus. But firecrackers at this hour?

Firecrackers are plentiful enough to not warrant much concern, even in the wee hours as the Dobrowski's shrug it off and go back to sleep. A minute goes by and they're drawn out of bed by the continuing sounds of anguished cries for help, to which they run to the window to see a girl laying out in the intersection of 211th and 45th Road with a wall of people converging from the north, most of which coming from Elephas as a police car arrives with its circulating blue and red lights illuminating the block, all but verifying that it wasn't firecrackers the residents heard.

In the Sunday newspapers of June 26, 1977, a clueless Korvettes advertisement features the new Kiss album. The ad reads "Love Gun...Their sensational new release includes the hit single, "Calling Dr. Foster."

.44 Killer Hits Again, Wounds 2

He vowed to do it again, taunting the police and the public and it was only a matter of time before he made good on that...at least in his own mind. But on this particular shooting, the Son of Sam done fucked up. Both his victims are alive. 17-year old Judy Placido and 20-year old Salvatore Lupo, both shot as they sat in a parked car just in front of the big oak tree that occupied the lawn of 45-39 211th Street, just a block and a half from Elephas disco. Placido, who just graduated high school this past week, has been struck in the right temple, right shoulder and the back of her neck. Lupo was hit in the right forearm. Still, the headlines are striking in that they rattle the public into a renewed wave of further alarm.

As the Son of Sam hysteria is reaching fever pitch, the guys in Kiss are leaving New York City for the summer to embark on what will be billed as the Can-Am Tour, taking in cities around North America. As the drama heats up in the aftermath of the Placido/Lupo shooting, the band returns to their rehearsal facility in Newburgh where they'll spend the week running through a brand-new show. The *Love Gun* stage marks the visual pinnacle for Kiss. Some three quarters of the new set has already been seen in Japan, though there are a few new features to put the crowd in awe. The colors and overall brightness is probably the first thing the seasoned Kiss fan will notice as lighting rigs surround the top of the stage unlike the backlit *Destroyer* set which left a dark and dreary landscape for the band to play against. While the rigging above runs the spectrum of reds, whites, blues, purples and yellows, the dominant color to the *Love Gun* stage is always and forever a collective fiery orange glow that emanates against a black background that often appears brown around the orange radiance of the Kiss logo. The *Love Gun* stage is a fully realized version of the stage used in Japan, though now two major features have been added...a new lighted Kiss logo to hang above the drums, this one more proportional in dimension...especially the S's which were awkwardly thinner for the *Destroyer/RARO* stage. The other major addition are two hydraulic elevator lifts used for the beginning of the show to deliver the band members to the stage from above. Paul, Gene and Ace will no longer be descending long staircases, though the staircases remain as landmark visuals of the 1977 Kiss spectacle. The two new stairways on either side of the drums were premiered in Japan, and they are miles ahead of those dangerous decrepit black *Destroyer* stairs. These stairs have trailing lights inside them that move up and down.

Two more hydraulic lifts at the front of the stage raise Paul, Gene and Ace far above the audience, leaving the front rows of each venue's floor seats to stare upward in astonishment as they watch their heroes hover above them while bombs detonate and the stage erupts in smoke, fire and fury. Peter's drum riser performs another function this time around. In addition to levitating high in the air during "Black Diamond," the set now moves forward to the front of the stage during Peter's solo in the middle of "God of Thunder." There is also the signature confetti storm...nothing new to a Kiss concert, but still the exclamation point on the entire experience. The *Love Gun* stage is really quite something to behold. Edwin Newman of NBC visits the site to interview the band on the eve of their tour for a TV special called *Land of Hype and Glory*.

While the bulk of the summer dates are in Canada and the band scheduled to record some of the California shows in August, one of the places that keeps getting back to them is Billings, Montana where residents and law enforcement are on high alert because of this Satanic monstrosity known as Kiss that is coming to their pristine God-fearing town. To them, Kiss represents the worst of humanity, and they bring out the worst in their fans who are criminals, alcoholics, drug addicts and probably mass murderers. But ACI Corporation who booked the show for Kiss is suing Yellowstone County for discrimination and violating the Civil Rights of the fans with their selective practice of stop and frisk. Other cities like Rapid City, Sioux Falls, Seattle and St. Paul have all confirmed to local reporters following this quickly evolving story that their venues refrain from this unpopular practice as it is unlawful. The Billings venue in question, the Metra, has already seen a few concerts cancelled because security targets the fans of certain artists and certain types of music, but not others. Venues in other cities certainly inspect concert goers visually on the way into the show, but Metra security does the controversial pat down. ACI hopes to settle this matter without having to go into litigation and the only way to avoid litigation is for the Metra to agree on eliminating the frisk at the Kiss concert, which is scheduled for August 7.

The tour begins in Halifax, Nova Scotia on July 8 and moves through the most extensive trek around Canada that the band has ever done. Epic recording artists, Cheap Trick, a new band out of Rockford, Illinois will be the opening act. "Calling Dr. Love" will finally become a staple in the setlist as opposed to the last tour when it wasn't played even though it was a single. The *Love Gun* tour will also mark the first time Ace Frehley sings lead vocals onstage as he will tackle "Shock Me" mid-show every night before launching into his guitar solo. In his performances of "Shock Me," there is no hardcore evidence that Ace is shy behind the microphone, though he is plainly lax and as loose as a musician could possibly be onstage without throwing everything into disarray. His stumbling around is part alcohol-induced / part character-driven...the tripping around in rubbery motion is a controlled chaos on the part of the Ace Frehley stage persona. He remembers the words and appears relaxed while singing, though sometimes he seems too out of it with his eyelids hanging in his signature spaced out gaze. He often wanders away from the mic, not making it back in time for the next line. The first few words from each line that Ace sings are often inaudible. While Paul has always likened Ace's carefree approach to playing and performing as total shit, to Ace it's the very essence of rock and roll, and more rock artists would probably agree with him on that. It's difficult to imagine Keith Richards getting hung up on Ron Wood playing a little sloppy on any given night. But to that point, one thing Ace is always reliable on is remembering his own guitar solos. While he is always sure to hit a wrong note or two on occasion, his brain always knows where his fingers should go, even if his fingers don't always make it there. One area that Ace is disciplined as opposed to spontaneous is his solos. For as inebriated as he often is, he crafted those solos note for note. At one point in the Kiss story, he gave birth to them. He's committed them to memory and has played them so many times that they've become part of the air he breathes. He doesn't even have to play those notes because his presence exudes them.

Midway through "Shock Me" when the rest of the band exits the stage leaving Ace alone under a blue spotlight, it's just us and the two-octave pentatonic assault that he has perfected to the point where even the feedback and cacophony take on melody at points. He roams the stage from left to right and back aimlessly, almost desperately...swiveling, swaying, crouching down in guitar-shaking knee bends during which smoke begins to emerge from his top pickup. He shakes his guitar violently as the smoke pours out. He holds it out toward the crowd seemingly in an offering as his solo has now been reduced to single high-pitched squeals that echo endlessly before the next high pitch note overlaps, resembling a cross between an air raid siren and the shower murder in *Psycho*. Space Ace then lifts his Gibson over his head and places it down into a guitar stand at centerstage, still smoking. In the shadows beyond the spotlit guitar, Ace can be seen walking off the stage. The audience is now alone with the smoking Les Paul and an ear-shattering wall of rocket-fueled hiss that grows louder, faster and higher by the second until the guitar bursts into flames. From out of the shadows, Ace Frehley reappears on the opposite side of the burning guitar. He is now playing a different but similar Les Paul...hammering away on finger taps...something not widely done by rock guitarists. As the burning guitar disappears into the darkness and down into the floor, Ace flips the switch into a climaxing flurry of rapid notes that build into an explosive A chord that the band kicks back in on. They beat the chord to death, and this time it's Paul who approaches the microphone.

"EEEEE-YEAH-HAAAAAAAAAAAHH!
ACE FREHLEY, LEAD GUI-TAAWWH...
SHOCK MEEEE!!!!"

20

IT'S CHRISTMAS TIME

In the glistening New York City night where a serial killer lurks randomly and repeatedly as darkness falls on mid-July, the shimmering and flickering becomes more pronounced from the farther reaches of New Jersey and the outer boroughs...even from north of the city where mystical flashes light up the sky in the distance...mystical with a sense of mystery and danger. The light show cannot be viewed from inside the electric circus. In the glistening New York City night, as we've established, Manhattan is visible only from outside Manhattan. Manhattan has Manhattan, though Manhattan cannot see itself. Only New Jersey and the surrounding boroughs and counties have the Manhattan skyline to themselves. Manhattan cannot experience itself from a distance the same way that drivers can experience it from the New Jersey Turnpike or Queensboro Bridge or residents on a rooftop in Brooklyn. At night it's like a living organism, orchestrated only by the movement of light. The vertical lines of Downtown and Midtown like lofty ribbons of steel emit the light in up and down rows...the sections of town in between like little pockets of horizontal units in clusters...still providing a characteristic light in an unassertive proletarian dignity that carries its own weight. Each section of town like flavors rivaling and riling each other into a frenzy of fierce competition, bragging rights or claim to which New York, whose New York, their New York, my New York or your New York is preeminent in declaring exactly what New York is. It's all New York in the glistening New York City night.

The beauty and the wonder of those lights from afar to so many humans that view it from waterfronts, beaches, rooftops, faraway hills and peaks or just on television, is the pulsating be-all-end-all of civilization...the greatest city in the world, a sentiment often implied in the daily rumblings of radio stations like WABC where the morning drives and drive homes are accompanied by a comforting familiarity in the voices of Harry Harrison and Dan Ingram. The city is home to the homes of many, and mother of muses to those outside seeking inspiration, while to many who view it from afar, it's a fucking insane asylum.

WABC afternoon disc jockey, Dan Ingram at 42 is already somewhat a legend in New York. He just recently celebrated his sixteenth year on ABC, and his unmistakable voice has become engrained in the sound and template of New York City radio. While some find it quite annoying when DJs talk over the beginning of a song, especially in the age of taping music off the radio, there's no denying that Ingram is the master of the talk up and he's perfected it to an artform. The talk ups, one liners and jingles along with the reverb-saturated echo of every word he says creates the ambiance of the ride home for many a frustrated driver agonizing through rush hour traffic from Monday through Friday.

On the radio, the new 45-single cut of the theme from *Star Wars* has just begun to catch peoples' ears. It's from a guy called Meco who turns the John Williams score into a four-minute disco song, blending in the jazzier elements of a cantina club scene that exists right smack in the middle of the film. Instrumentals are drifting away from radio little by little, though they certainly still become hits when the right one catches. "Star Wars Theme / Cantina Band" is launched on radio this summer and it slowly becomes that one curious melody that seems to be everywhere, and people either must ask *what is this?*...or they already know that it's from this surprise hit movie that everyone is talking about.

Everyone is talking about *Star Wars*...this little film by a guy named George Lucas. If anyone knows his name, it's because he directed *Ameri-*

can Graffiti a few years ago. *Star Wars*, a story set in a galaxy far, far away, is a good versus evil arc that seems to be a metaphor for the 1960s culture wars of the old guard versus the hippie counterculture, except it takes place in space. Not since Stanley Kubrick's *2001: A Space Odyssey* from a decade ago has anything so visually spectacular been released on a movie screen. It stars a bunch of relatively new and unknown actors and obscure older names of the past...yet, for all the underdog specifics behind the logistics, word of mouth is causing sell outs and long lines to form outside of theaters. Kids are becoming obsessed with the characters, and some cutting-edge cats on the street somehow already have *Star Wars* t-shirts made by mid-July.

Early in the evening on July 13, Dan Ingram finishes his radio show, but before leaving the station for home, he goes back to his office to comb through his check book which has a discrepancy that he can't seem to figure out. Between the acts of going line by line, transaction by transaction and a few phone calls, Ingram learns that the bank has made an error and that he has an extra 2000 dollars in his account that he didn't know was there. This pleases him enormously, so he celebrates with a large martini and falls asleep at his desk. Down below on the street, two crotchety older gentlemen are complaining about the Yankees losing three in a row and those goddamn Orioles and that goddamn Eddie Murray and Dick Tidrow this and Dick Tidrow that, and now Sparky Lyle is injured, and Billy Martin should be fired. Then there's Jimmy Carter and his announcement that he wants to raise the minimum wage from $2.30 to $2.65. They've never heard of such fuckery. In their day, men made pennies compared to what kids are making today at their part time jobs.

Kids today, boy...these kids today.
When I was their age, I was...

Now they're having a go at Carter and his support for unions and how he's trying to stir the pot and change labor laws and make it easier for unions to organize and damn these liberals and these liberals and these liberals and these goddamn liberals and this fucking A.F.L.-C.I.O.

A third man cuts in to shake the moral fist. He illustrates that a minimum wage hike would not be anything unwelcome at all, and their disgust should be aimed at the fact that G. Gordon Liddy has been offered an early release from prison by the United States Parole Commission if the scumbag pays his 40,000 dollar fine and these bootstrap assholes are directing their rage in the wrong places and at the wrong people. The flashes in the sky from north of the city, probably over Yonkers hardly phase these men, now engaged in a passionate form of venting their frustrations at the new world at the expense of the good ole days. The heat lighting seen from Manhattan is subtle and so distant that the thunderstorm warnings don't seem to apply over the city. This is not the case in Westchester County where lightning has struck Indian Point 3, the third unit of the Indian Point Power Plant and one of the main generating stations on the electrical system. Indian 3 is knocked out, as is the major north-south feeder into the system which connects the city with the north. Ravenswood 3 is also lost to lightning. At Ravenswood, workers try to save the system with a five percent voltage reduction which in turn leads to an eight percent voltage reduction, shedding a great deal of load in Westchester. This is the fancy electrical terminology used by the utility spokespeople in their efforts to dress up the language of their explanation to the media. When accounting for the shit show you've just imposed on an entire population, you'd better be prepared to sound professional. Therefore, these guys don't simply turn off the power, nor do they shut down the system. They shed load. Shedding load refers to the indiscriminate selection of particular areas in an electrical grid system to be temporarily turned off or shut down in order to preserve the function of the grid is often a necessary means of coping with an overload and preventing a possible power outage.

When things stop, they often slow down first. Sometimes you can see it and sometimes you can hear it. Electricity is funny because you can always hear it whether you know it or not. You can hear the sound of the wheels turning like the sound of humanity itself, especially at night.

Even in the most desolate silences, you can hear the hum of humanity in the manmade sounds of the background...often miles away, but you can hear it. You can hear the grid and the machinery that keeps civilization moving.

When you hear that distant hum of humanity, it's actually the grid you hear. You hear the electricity. That's what it is. That's where the hum comes from.

But at 9:36 everything dies.

At 9:36 everything stops.

I'd like to say at 9:36 everything grinds to a halt, but to say that would be to imply that everything slows down before it stops, but there is no slowing process.

At 9:36 everything just cuts off in an instant.

Lights...televisions...radios...air conditioners...stereos...refrigerators... hair dryers

At 9:36 the lights go out. Everywhere. Even the distant hum of humanity cuts out for a fraction of an instance in a momentary breath of airtight silence, before it's followed by a quick collective gasp of surprise on every street. On every street, the human gasp sounds the same. On every street in the suburbs, residents in rows of houses that all look the same will scamper around darkened homes for candles and matches. On every street in the city, the only lights come from headlamps of cars in paralyzed traffic. On every street, civilians in plain clothes attempt to start directing some of that traffic. In the dark, the streets are wet from the unexpected thunderstorm that arrived around nine and quickly passed. The humidity is unrelenting and unforgiving as the rain wasn't enough to break the peak summer heat. If you have batteries, you probably have access to radio which is communicating back to you the city's appeal to residents to turn off all appliances and electronics so the surge doesn't cut everything off again when the power comes back. *This surely won't last long...the power will be back on by the end of the night.* Most people with radios are tuned to WABC, hoping to keep in the loop on what's happening. The station, one of the few with reception, continues on a backup generator allowing disc jockey, George Michael to keep the public informed. In his office, a groggy Dan Ingram wakes up to find himself in the dark with shouting going on in the hallway. He tries the lights to no avail and sees the streets below lit only by the headlights of cars and other vehicles.

Oh no, it's happened again!

Just three days ago the chairman of Con-Ed faced the House of Representatives subcommittee on Energy and Power and told them that there would never be a power outage like 1965 again. Ingram was on the air when the power went out in 1965 and when in mid-song the equipment started slowwwwiiinnnng dowwwnnn as if someone were dragging a finger along the record. New York City fell into total darkness for five hours in part of a much wider Northeast blackout.

'65 was different though. The world was different. People were different. This would become the narrative whenever the adults who live through 1977 will compare it with 1965. *The people were different.* When they say that, what they mean is *now they're animals.* It's not that people now don't have the same torsos, limbs, minds, hopes and dreams as they did in '65. It's not that the people now are made up of different biochemistry. What they mean is the demographic is different and consequently the socioeconomic balance is different and people who try to exist and survive in that environment are considered animals by the people who were there in '65. But what if what you do to survive is abhorrent from what is acceptable in society? At what point does morality enter into the equation in extreme situations? Is a blackout an extreme situation? Does it have to come down to violence and destruction and even the concern of life and death? Or could everyone just ride it out respectfully and help each other if need be? These were not questions people were asking in 1965 when power was knocked out in New York City, New England and parts of Pennsylvania. It was the Baby Boomers in their late teens and early twenties...just getting started in life...in their careers. They remember it fondly...one of those *never forget where you were* moments. Everything remained orderly while neighbors checked on each other and the worst thing that occurred was a lot of phone calls were made to the police and power companies. The whole thing was over in five hours in New York City. When they say the "good old days" now, they mean the blackout of 1965. It was something they could brag about. Dan Ingram was on the air when that blackout occurred...wandering around the same building.

Somewhere deep into the ten o'clock hour, Ingram manages to get down 23 flights of stairs before finding his car. A sea of vehicles along Fifty-Seventh Street just sitting there looking at each other keeps him from moving.

On the streets, more so the less busy streets where traffic is much more dominated by pedestrians on foot there aren't many cars to light the way, giving new meaning to the phrase pitch black. When you're in the trenches of those canyon-like streets where the tall buildings serve as fortress walls, the moonlight is very often blocked, so it's quite easy to take the little details of evening in civil society for granted...things like street lights that are so plentiful that we don't realize how visible life still is even after the sun goes down and darkness falls. That is until a full-scale blackout occurs, under which it's impossible to see who or even what's coming toward you as you navigate the sidewalks and streets. The mercury vapor lamps of the 1960s have since been replaced and changed to low-pressure sodium bulbs throughout the city. They create a pinkish orange tint to the New York City streets at night but do not in any manner provide even a fraction of the brightness of the LED bulbs we'd later see in the next century. New York is a shadowy city at night...not the reassuring shadows that come from the sun during the perceived safer daylight hours...but dreadful shadows that keep you looking over your shoulder while walking. But in the darkness of a blackout, even the shadows disappear, and all you see are the outlines of bodies walking either alongside you or in the opposite direction coming toward you. You can't see faces. All you see are various shades of black moving against black. Nobody can see who's coming so no one would know what hit them. You know there are people walking next to you on the street...you just can't see who they are. And there in turn is where your ears kick in, and senses that are usually not at the forefront in the same way that your vision is. Now you begin to notice things that you never would have noticed if you could see what was going on all around you. You begin to hear every noise that's never existed before, and it's the sound of footsteps that's front and center and creating the nerve-wracking canvas, adding to your vulnerability and paranoia. Then there's that part of the city that's probably more dependent on electricity than most places. There's something even ghostly about the unlit dingy palette of digital electrical materials against black silhouettes of buildings over Times Square and its surrounding vicinity...the place in all the city where we're used to the most light. All the colorful surrounding stimuli... the Canon sign above the Howard Johnson's...the trailing Burger King sign... the swirly Rollercoaster logo on the Forum marquee...the *It's the Real Thing* Coca Cola digital clock...Castro...Sony...Bonds and the mammoth Gordons gin bottle pouring itself into an awaiting glass. All of it has gone dark. None of it showing any life.

Those trying to direct traffic are often several deep in the streets and just adding to the confusion. Like on the Deuce where a local straggler named Orlando good-heartedly tries to help an officer who just randomly wandered over, not necessarily wanting to be there, but having to do something with himself on his shift parading through Midtown, and so he focuses on some barely dressed women walking frantically, carrying duffle bags, trying to cross Eighth Avenue. It doesn't matter if he's supposed to be there or not... every cop in the city has been called back out, even the ones who have just completed a shift. Even the ones who have just gotten home.

Along the Deuce the crowd of sex workers have poured into the streets, followed by the money takers and the jizz moppers...one of which is Jerome who because of his environment always wreaks of Pine Sol. So does Orlando who also mops the jerkoff stalls. Jerome, whose street name is Baby Alexander talks out loud to anyone within earshot whether they're listening or not. He moves among the shadow people of the black-on-black abyss, not seeing faces...not able to tell who he's walking next to. But he keeps moving toward his destination.

"Yup, I gotta get back and get that pickle. Miss Merriweather was nice enough to bring me back a pickle from the barrel over at the pork store, yup."

A police officer trying to direct traffic stops the human swarm at the corner.

"Hold up," the officer tells the crowd. "You can keep walking," he yells over to Orlando in the middle of the intersection waving hand signals to stationary drivers.

"I'm directing traffic officer," Orlando says, indifferent to the cop.

Jerome can tell it's Orlando from the sound of his voice.

"I don't need help, thank you," the officer tells Orlando.

"Man, git yo ass out the street!" Jerome scolds Orlando.

Orlando waves him off while walking toward the curb where the eclectic crowd awaits the officer's direction in the dark.

"Man, I'm headed home to feed the fish and then I got that nice pickle in the refridge, yup."

"Whatchoo talkin bout a pickle!"

"I gotta get that pickle out the refridge before it goes bad. I stop by Miss. Merriweather all the time, you know...she a nice lady, Miss Merriweather, yup!"

"She gave you a pickle?"

The ladies who can't mind their own fucking business ain't having it.

"Whatchoo all talkin bout yo pickle? Nobody want yo pickle!"

Orlando steps onto the curb where he knocks over a man holding a sign announcing the apocalypse.

"Man, what's wrowng witchoo?" Jerome chides.

Orlando is not even phased by the end-of-the-world preacher he just knocked down to the ground while Jerome chastises him.

"Man, git yo ass out!"

"All-a-yoos get ya ass out," the cop cuts in. "Let's go, let's cross the street!"

The cop waves a baton toward the east side of Eighth, motioning where he wants them.

"Man, I'm not gonna cross no street here," Orlando explains growing impatient, "I was just gonna help you!"

"And I said I don't need help, thank you. Now you gotta cross the street or get back inside."

"Back inside where?"

"You know where."

Jerome is already across the street. He looks back at Orlando sensing he's about to get his black ass beat by the white cop.

"Git yo ass!"

Orlando is more interested in the cop than being saved by Jerome.

"No, you get yo ass, you baum-boom-boom hat-wearin' muthafucker!"

"Man, I said git yo ass!"

"*You* get yo ass!" Orlando screeches back. "I'm talkin' to this T-shirt over here!"

"Who you callin' a T-shirt?" the cop says in Orlando's face.

"I'm callin' *you* a T-shirt...cause you a white T-shirt!"

"I'm tellin' you get goin'!"

"And I'm tellin' youuuu...I gots no place to go!"

The officer gives up and storms away, back to the traffic in the middle of a symphony of wailing car horns.

Orlando isn't finished with him.

"Yeah, dat's right! You keep goin'...you keep goin' with yo Lou Poopula mustache!"

"Excuse me?"

"You look like yo name Lou Poopla! Is yo name Lou Poopla? I think yo name Lou Poopla!"

The dozens of theaters and parlors offering live sex onstage and other illegal activities are out of commission in the dark. In this concrete den of ample sexual gratification, it's impossible to walk ten feet without seeing some variation of porn. But now all the *Live Sex Show* come hitherness in red or neon pink have too gone dark and faded into the backdrops of their respective buildings, no longer there to entice, disgust or lure the hungry into this area in and around the Deuce...the entire vicinity where some 40,000 hookers hover while rape and murder is a daily reality. If one of the girls is raped or killed, it's NHI. No Human Involved permits the police to quietly allow these crimes to get lost in the system. It's an unofficial code denying the humanity of black and brown individuals or anybody they deem unworthy or unsavory. Though cops are known to look the other way with prostitution, a rape case will often get the victim arrested. *Oh, you've been raped? Well, you're a whore anyway...you have the right to remain silent.* Yes, it's true...Forty-Second Street between Times Square and Port Authority is the sleaziest block in America. The con artists, hustlers, dealers, addicts and runaways prey on lost tourists just trying to find their way through. And that's both in broad daylight and at night when the lights are on. In other words, the police are useless here.

Cutting slowly across town, it takes Dan Ingram an hour just to reach the 59th Street Bridge, which sits unlit over the East River like a dead brontosaurus sprawled out between Manhattan and Long Island City as Ingram makes his way through the upper level under the skeletal steel, a light fog rising amidst total 360-degree blackness, even in the headlamps the fog marking a trail-like smoke spreading wide over the water below. Awaiting at the end of the bridge, lightning bolts touch down where the water meets land...a blitz of forked and jagged streaks falling like territorial gates crashing down to block all entrance. It's a much more surreal landscape this time, as Ingram moves through... remembering 1965...flashing on the past decade and a half believing it could never happen again...thinking we were seasoned vets on the experience of blackouts...and here, now twelve years later, in the midst of nature's fury unfolding all around him, the almighty God above reminding us that we're all just a bunch of amateurs.

Downtown in the Village, it's a celebration. Walk randomly through any stretch of the Village's labyrinthian twists and turns and you'll find townhouse after townhouse and stoop after stoop filled with residents in festive spirits...singing, dancing, and most importantly, drinking the night away... each block party adorned by hundreds of candles. The commercial blocks comprised of a plethora of bars and restaurants offer food and drink both to customers and passersby...many who wander aimlessly through the streets amongst myriads of candles in multitudes forming mosaics of fiery light throughout the Village.

At the top of the World Trade Center, they could see the lights go out in sections throughout the city. Management of Windows on the World, the prestigious restaurant that takes months to get a reservation for, digs into their champagne collection and offers free bottles to everyone stuck in the 107th floor establishment. Yes, the blackout is a major inconvenience if you're sitting in traffic trying to get somewhere, and it's indeed frightening for those on foot trudging through midtown...but in various stretches of Downtown through various stages of intoxication, New Yorkers are as WABC's George Michael puts it, feeling no pain.

In northern Westchester, the mood is anything but partylike. Buchanan and Peekskill residents, one hour into the blackout, are mystified by an encroaching electrical sound...a sizzling 60-cycle-type hum that seems to be vibrating from the ground only to reveal itself in the form of bursts of light to the sky...a blue glow followed by a quick flash and then two more flashes that last about thirty seconds each. The arcing in the sky causes an ominous blue illumination that lights entire neighborhoods up like daylight.

The focus has shifted. The power outages have momentarily dissolved into the background as suburbanites scurry out of their homes and into the streets. The streetlights remain out, though entire blocks are lit up from the sky, bathed in electric blue.

Oh, dear God!

What the hell is that?

What is that light?

What is going on?

We're being invaded!

It's aliens!

This has to be extraterrestrial!

It is obvious to these residents who regroup in their homes and grab what they can...only to re-emerge outside and into their vehicles to flee. It's most obvious that we're under attack. First, they hit the power grid...now the blue light of their arrival envelops the earth overhead. Those are the really dumb ones.

The somewhat more intelligent ones believe the nearby Indian Point nuclear power plant has exploded and the electrical arc in the sky is radioactivity wafting in to give them cancer. And so, *they* flee as well.

The brighter bulbs on the shelf know this occurrence has nothing to do with a nuclear accident at Indian Point, and in fact know that it's a blown transformer at Con Ed's Buchanan substation. Obviously, the Con Ed guys were working hard to restore power, and the transformer was overloaded until... *nnuuuuuuuurrrrrrrrrrrrrrrrrrrrrrrrrrrrrrrrrrrrrrrrrrrrrrrrrrrrrrrrrrr-rrrrrrrrrrrrrrrrrrrrrrrrrrrrrrrrrrrrrrrrrrrrrrrrrrrrrrrrrrrrrrrrrrrrrrrrrrrrrrrr-rrrrrrrrrrrrrrrrrrrrrrrrrrrrrrrrrrrrrrrrrrrrrrrrrrrrrrrrrrrrrrrrrrrrrrrrrrrrrr-rrrrrrrrrrrrrrrrrrrrrrrrrrrrrrrrrrrrrrrrrrrrrrrrrrrrrrrrrrrrrrrrrr.....*

The sound penetrates the suburban landscape, billowing across and throughout blocks and blocks. It's a multi-toned blare that combines the *nnuuuuuurrrrrrr* with a *ppippidiptpitup..pidtpitup...tfuuufffff...tfuuuffffff...*

Both tones resonate the surrounding communities....

nnuuuuuuuurrrrrrrrrrrrrrrrrrrrrrrrrrrrrrrrrrrrrrrrrrrrrrrrrrrrrrrrrrrrrrrrrrr-rrrrrrrrrrrrrrrrrrrrrrrrrrrrrrrrrrrrrrrrrrrrrrrrrrrrrrrrrrrrrrrrrrrrrrrrrrrrrr-rrrrrrrrrrrrrrrrrrrrrrrrrrrrrrrrrrrrrrrrrrrrrrrrrrrrrrrrrrrrrrrrrrrrrrrrrrrrrr-rrrrrrrrrrrrrrrrrrrrrrrrrrrrrrrrrrrrrrrrrrrrrrrrrrrrrrrrrrrrrrrrrrrrrrrrrrrrr.....
***nuuuuu**rrrrrrrrrrrrrrrrrrrrrrrrrrrrrrrrrrrrrrrrrrrrrrrrrrrrrrrrrrrrrrrrrrrrrrrrrrrrrrrrrrrrrrrrrrrr-rrrrrrrrrrrrrrrrrrrrrrrrrrrrrrrrrrrrrrrrrrrrrrrrrrrrrrrrrrrrrrrrrrrrrrrrrrrrrr-rrrrrrrrrrrrrrrrrrrrrrrrrrrrrrrrrrrrrrrrrrrrrrrrrrrrrrrrrrrrrrrrrrrrrrrrrrrrrr.....*
nnuuuuuuuurrrrrrrrrrrrrrrrrrrrrrrrrrrrrrrrrrrrrrrrrrrrrrrrrrrrrrrrrrrrrrrrrr-rrrrrrrrrrrrrrrrrrrrrrrrrrrrrrrrrrrrrrrrrrrrrrrrrrrrrrrrrrrrrrrrrrrrrrrrrrrrrr-rrrrrrrrrrrrrrrrrrrrrrrrrrrrrrrrrrrrrrrrrrrrrrrrrrrrrrrrrrrrrrrrrrrrrrrrrrrrrr-rrrrrrrrrrrrrrrrrrrrrrrrrrrrrrrrrrrrrrrrrrrrrrrrrrrrrrrrrrrr.....

ppippidiptpitup..pidtpitup...tfuuufffff...tfuuuffffff... ppippidiptpitup..pidtpitup...tfuuufffff...tfuuuffffff... ppippidiptpitup..pidtpitup...tfuuufffff...tfuuuffffff... ppippidiptpitup..pidtpitup...tfuuufffff...tfuuuffffff... ppippidiptpitup..pidtpitup...tfuuufffff...tfuuuffffff... ppippidiptpitup..pidt-

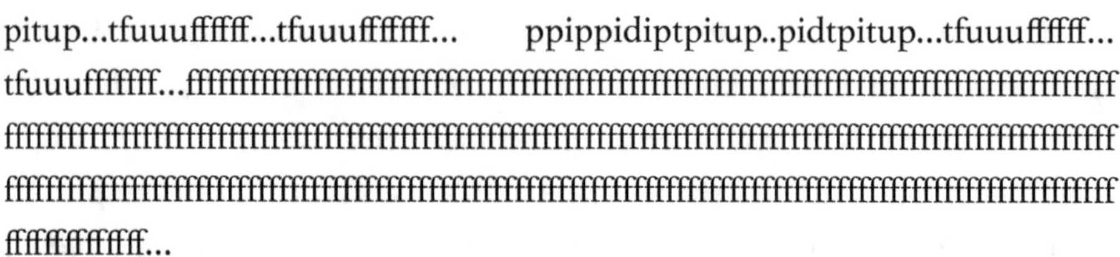
pitup...tfuuuffffff...tfuuuffffff... ppippidiptpitup..pidtpitup...tfuuuffffff...
tfuuuffffff...ffffffffffffffffffffffffffffffffffffffffffffffffffffffffffffffffffffffffffffffff
ffffffffffffffffffffffffffffffffffffffffffffffffffffffffffffffffffffffffffffffffffffffff
ffffffffffffffffffffffffffffffffffffffffffffffffffffffffffffffffffffffffffffffffffffffff
ffffffffffff...

nnuuuuuuuurrrrrrrrrrrrrrrrrrrrrrrrrrrrrrrrrrrrrrrrrrrrrrrrrrrrrrrrrrrrrrrr-
rrrrrrrrrrrrrrrrrrrrrrrrrrrrrrrrrrrrrrrrrrrrrrrrrrrrrrrrrrrrrrrrrrrrrrrrrrrrrrrr-
rrrrrrrrrrrrrrrrrrrrrrrrrrrrrrrrrrrrrrrrrrrrrrrrrrrrrrrrrrrrrrrrrrrrrrrrrrrrrrrr-
rrrrrrrrrrrrrrrrrrrrrrrrrrrrrrrrrrrrrrrrrrrrrrrrrrrrrrrrrrrrrrrrrrrrrrrrrrrr.....

tfuuuffffff...ffffffffffffffffffffffffffffffffffffffffffffffffffffffffffffffffffffffffffffff ffffffffffffffffffffffffffffffffffffffffffffffffffffffffffffffffffffffffffffffffffffffff ffffffffffffffffffffffffffffffffffffffffffffffffffffffffffffffffffffffffffff...

Kerk-erk-chiiiht...kerk-erk...chit-chit-chit...PLLUHHHFFFFFFFFFFffffffffff ffffffffffffffffffffffffffffffffffffffffffffffffffffffffffffffff......schkack-ack..kerk-erk...chi-chit....perrrffffffffffffffffffffffffffffffffffffffffffff.........

As the blackout crosses the other side of midnight, it's apparent that the power may not come back anytime soon. The Westchester explosion is now being reported on the radio when the real chaos begins elsewhere. Among all the seven million people left without power...among all the adversity and inconveniences imposed on the city's five boroughs and beyond...and all differing responses in the various sections in how people are coping with the blackout, most good, some not so good...nobody really knows where the first window was shattered. Nobody knows where the first match was struck. Nobody can pinpoint where the first fire was started or where exactly the rioting and looting began. But in the Bushwick section of Brooklyn, it began at 9:40, just minutes after the power died.

Hordes of them...

Barbarians...heathens...marauders...converging on Broadway. If you were already down there in Bushwick, your experiences of the blackout is bedlam at the outset...down here where the mostly white 83rd Precinct is usually overwhelmed by the predominantly black and Hispanic population of around 100,000. The 83rd Precinct, aka the Eighty-Three, is a station house that often gets called on to assist truck drivers with police escorts while making deliveries. It's a part of Bushwick where police send two cars by default to every call, no matter how small. If a matter calls for two or three cops to enter a building, one cop remains outside to guard the vehicles. Arresting minorities is the daily norm in Bushwick. No rookie wants to be assigned to the Eighty-Three, which houses some 130 officers doing at least 124 hours of overtime each month. They work with very little support staff due to budget cuts, thus stretching processing procedures of arrests to as long as 14 hours. But this is everywhere in the department, not just the Eighty-Three.

To add insult to injury in a city where the morale is already low and crime has skyrocketed, the physical plain is littered by garbage and graffiti, where law enforcement, fire departments, education, sanitation and social services have all been depleted, compromised and weakened by said layoffs...and here is the permanent underclass portion of the population completely losing its shit. If you're in the other boroughs, above Ninety-Sixth Street in Manhattan, say...there is an eerie calm before the looting starts, disturbingly cut short by the growing rumble of approaching footsteps. Dozens...hundreds...thousands running, sprinting, stomping. Residents living above streets where commercial businesses line the blocks begin to hear alarms, the smashing of windows, cheering, screaming...and the chilling declaration...

"It's Christmas time...it's Christmas time!"

And it quickly becomes clear what's happening.

They go for it all.

Everything.

It's all there to be taken.

And while places like the South Bronx are infested with an explosion of street gangs that routinely steal and kill, it is also the law-abiding citizens who have never committed a crime in their lives who take part in the desecration of property and the stealing of anything they can get their hands on...furniture, electronics, appliances, jewelry...even big ticket items such as washing machines and refrigerators...all being carried and even wheeled straight into people's apartments. Even cars are lifted by otherwise normal everyday people.

But what does that mean, exactly?

Everyday people. Trying to work hard enough so they can be accepted into the world of the regular people, even if the regular people don't accept them on any level.

These are the have-nots. The poor. The tired huddle masses who exist in this life as such.

Every day.

Not all of them are criminal minds who are going to sell this shit on Canal Street.

These are people who now have a chance to embellish their lives.

They've got no color TV.

And so, here's their chance at a color TV. Who cares if they didn't get an extended warranty or purchase a maintenance agreement on their brand new Frigidaire...they got that shit for free! Because it's Christmas time. The lights are out, and this is their blank check for lawlessness. If ever a chance in someone's life came about if only for a few minutes or a brief moment in time, this is it, motherfuckers.

These are the have-nots having a go at the haves.

"IT's CHRISTMAS TIME MUTHAFUCKAAAAAAASS!!!!"

Then the fires start.

On the Upper West Side, residents join hands and form a human chain around Tom's Restaurant which has been beloved for decades, and the people of Prospect Heights are saying hell no to looters. Manhattan is certainly not immune from the looting as various locations along stretches of the Upper East Side and Lower East Side are hit. One resident of Brooklyn Heights struggles to wheel his father to a hospital after carrying him down eight flights of stairs on Sixteenth Street. This gentleman trudged on foot all the way across the Brooklyn Bridge and up the Bowery. Once he got above Fourteenth Street, he walked right into a cluster of cats smashing windows and jumping through storefronts. His father who suffers Lou Gehrig's Disease is in critical danger after his respirator went out. This man, a hero by the name of Arthur Nersesian along with his brother, gets their dad to Mount Sinai where they have a working generator.

While New York is entrenched in a blackout and the city is coming apart at the seams, the Yankees are in Milwaukee recovering from a 9-8 loss against the Brewers. Downtown at the Phister Hotel, Thurman and Lou Piniella are a couple of drinks into an uninhibited conversation venting their frustrations over the state of the team. Questions over why Billy won't bat Reggie fourth...even bigger, why the hell is batting fourth so important to Reggie? Aside from the extension of a big ego, there is an unwritten custom that power hitters usually bat in the fourth spot...i.e. the cleanup spot...assuming the first three batters in the lineup will get on base and the fourth batter will clear the bases with a grand slam. In a perfect world in its purest form, that's what the idea behind the cleanup batter is. Thurman and Lou are also tired of George busting Billy's balls every chance he gets. It's not just Reggie pissing everybody off...it's the way their manager is being treated by the owner and the collective low morale on the team is not conducive to winning.

The more drinks they down, the bigger the cojones on Munson and his ability to talk a resistant Piniella into walking up to George's room in the hopes of...

In the hopes of what?

Talking to him?

Yelling at him?

Smoothing things over?

Pissing him off?

It's well after midnight when the drunken pair of Thurman Munson and Lou Piniella knock on George Steinbrenner's door. The team owner opens the door in silk pajamas. He lets them in, grabs a robe and makes drinks. The players proceed to tell him their gripes. They want Reggie to bat fourth. They want Reggie to keep his mouth shut with the controversial statements. And they also want George to leave Billy the fuck alone and let him manage the team. George has already been insisting on Reggie batting fourth all season, but he's been constantly met with Billy's noncompliance. As George pulls up the chalkboard and scrawls out various hypothetical versions of the lineup, the guys promise they'll back him in the push to get Reggie fourth... if he backs off Billy.

The walls at the Phister are thin...at least to Billy Martin's ears. When Billy returns from dinner at his favorite German restaurant in Milwaukee, it's 2 AM...which makes it all the more peculiar when he hears familiar voices coming from the room next door...George's suite. He recognizes those voices and his paranoia snaps into overdrive.

Billy pounds on the door, screaming about how George and whoever else is inside is plotting against him. The Yankees owner in a panic hides the two players in the bathroom like a cheating husband hiding his mistress. When Billy barges in, George can only stand helplessly in response to the hysterical manager's fit. The calls of *come on outta there, I know you're in there you sons-a-bitches* sound much worse on the surface, as Billy's bark is always much worse than his bite, though one gets the sense that anything could happen when he plows through the bathroom door to find his team captain and left fielder standing in the shower.

Back in New York, the city is ablaze.

Between the oppressive heat, incapacitated traffic, rioting, looting, helpless police and an overwhelmed fire department trying impossibly to respond to a mosaic of scattered fires, the power structure that represents New York

City can only sit back and watch while the great metropolis burns through its darkest of nights. In the morning and throughout the next day, the media is focused on the looting and the fires, even as the electricity is still down. The rape and pillage of the Bronx and Brooklyn becomes the story as the blackout becomes secondary. Early in the evening of Thursday, July 14, power begins returning slowly in sections. By 10:39 PM, twenty-five hours after the lights went out, the entire New York City grid is up and running again. The statistics will become give-or-take but the estimated totals on the result is some 1037 fires responded to, 3,700 arrests made, 1600 stores looted and destroyed, blocks and blocks of burned out stretches of decimated buildings and an estimated 300 million dollars in damages to the city.

With load-shedding devices for Con-Ed failing to shed the load of half of New York City's power last week leading to a total blackout, it's probably better that it happened on July 13 and not July 19 when there are over 56,000 people in Yankee Stadium for a high-profile national event such as the All-Star Game. In the hottest July since the Dust Bowl, the elite crème de le crème of Major League Baseball descends on the city on an afternoon that reaches 102 degrees by 2 PM. By game time, the temperature has cooled to 96. The Yankees are represented in the game by Reggie Jackson, Thurman Munson, Graig Nettles, Willie Randolph and Sparky Lyle. While there's much hostility in the New York crowd toward the Cincinnati Reds, their new pitcher Tom Seaver gets an ear-shattering standing ovation from lamenting Mets fans and just overall proud New Yorkers who all know Seaver's impeccable history here in the city. Suddenly here he is in a Reds uniform five weeks after the Mets traded him. '76 World Series managers Sparky Anderson and Bily Martin lead their respective leagues, as is the All-Star tradition. New York legends Willie Mays and Joe Dimagio are honorary co-captains. For the National League, Dodger Don Sutton stands on the mound as the starting pitcher...looking high up into the rafters and all around him...taking it all in. Yankee Stadium...where a much younger childhood version of himself as a

Yankee fan dreamed that he'd one day pitch. For Sutton it must feel bittersweet as he gets to stand on that Yankee Stadium mound where all his heroes stood, but only gets to do it as a Dodger, the poor guy. But still, he's living his dream now. Jim Palmer of the Orioles starting the game for the American League doesn't come without its controversy over the selection process since Nolan Ryan is the best pitcher in the American League and was not picked to start the game. The current status of the Yankees at the All-Star break has them in third place at a record of 50 wins and 42 losses, and just three games behind the first place Orioles. The National League wins it in the Bronx by a score of 7-5, marking the league's sixth consecutive All-Star victory, further enshrining National League near domination of the event over the course of several decades...doing it in the home of the Yankees on the national stage in a seemingly defeated city looked upon with great contempt across the rest of the nation...a city that as far as the nation is concerned is suffering its own karmic payback for being...

for being...

...well, for being New York City.

And while on that national stage in the wake of a blackout that's become a national headline...a city partially burned to the ground by its own inhabitants.

21

I JUST WANT TO BE YOUR EVERYTHING

In the pitch black depth of the Kiss stage, a single bass note seeps silently from out of the PA system, its volume slowly raising to a sustained drone in E. From out of the darkness a menacing figure appears leering down at the audience, its body bathed in an ominous green spotlight...the drone taking on other forms in its echoplex ether...twisting, turning on a dire canvas of electric distortion when the figure appears.

The Demon.

Or as some say, the bat lizard, which seems fairly accurate in the manner in which it stands in a vigilante pose...scanning everything left and right...its head jerking from side to side...eyes observing with its body ready to lurch forward at anything threatening or anything it sees as prey. The eyes are what carry the warning as smoke drifts upward into the green misty halo surrounding the Demon.

Gene Simmons.

The man behind the persona is often seen with the mischievous evil smile or the long tongue protruding from his mouth. But what is even more intimidating in the face of Gene is his closed mouth. It is when his mouth is closed that it works in co-ordination with his eyes to scare the living shit out of you. But at this stage in the Kiss show when we see those eyes looming out from the smoky green, and the foreboding swelling around the tightened lips, the crowd knows what comes next as the first traces of blood appear from the corners and begin to trickle down his chin. The imposing nature in his observance of those in the audience below takes a frantic turn as the reptilian mannerisms erupt into a shaking left-to-right tirade while the blood sprays and spills in all directions. In the wake of the blood trance, the Demon ascends far above stage level by way of his new hydraulic lift. With the entire crowd gazing upward, the Demon stays there just long enough to stamp out the final notes of the drone, establishing his command and dominance in reigning as the One. As the hydraulics carry him back to stage level, the drums kick in with the drone in E now morphing into a riff with Space Ace and the Starchild delivering "God of Thunder."

With the Breslin letter now public for the past five or six weeks, the most unsettling aspects have been the questions poised in its contents. What will they do for July 29? What will they have? What kind of remembrance? But the more chilling questions that inevitably come into the collective mind of the public...what is *he* preparing? Will he mark the anniversary of Donna Lauria with another shooting? Where will it be? Police patrol cars are concentrated mainly in the suburbs of Queens and the East Bronx with the entire city on heightened alert.

With everyone seemingly waiting distressfully for the next shooting, an Upper East Side girl has been missing for two weeks. She fits the physical profile attributed to Son of Sam victims, though there is no evidence connecting her to anything attributed to the 44 Killer. While the story takes a backseat to the Son of Sam, 23-year-old Ellen Jane Hover hasn't been seen since July 15. The anniversary of Donna Lauria's murder comes and goes, but it doesn't provide any relief or comfort. Just because he didn't strike on July 29 doesn't mean he won't strike again. Everyone is still in panic mode. You can feel it on the streets. Even in Brooklyn where life goes on in a borough untouched...even there where the shootings aren't causing much concern, the girls are cutting and dying their hair. In one example, 20-year-old Stacy Moskowitz has recently gone blonde, opting not to let the media frenzy stop her from going out at night, though her parents ask her to stay in Brooklyn, and Stacy complies with no hesitation. Of the seven known shootings attributed to the Son of Sam, two of them were in the Bronx while five were in Queens. Of the outer boroughs, Brooklyn and Staten Island are obviously the safest. Without a doubt, Stacy and her date, Robert Violante will remain in Brooklyn tonight where they'll see a movie. People are still out in droves this weekend in these boroughs, though the couple bypasses the more obvious films that are attracting younger crowds like *Star Wars*, *The Deep*, *Orca*, *Rollercoaster* and *Smokey and the Bandit* and instead opt for the musical, *New York, New York*, which is playing at the Kingsway at Coney Island Avenue just five blocks from where Stacy lives over on East Fifth. It's a quiet neighborhood, one without much of a reputation for disturbance let alone violent crime...though Stacy did ask a friend from a few blocks away to walk her home on the night of the blackout. This is Stacy and Robert's first date after meeting a week ago in Beefsteak Charlie's restaurant. With a high level of concern, especially this weekend, parents are warning their kids. On this particular Saturday night, there is a faint level of relief that July 29 went by without incident. And so tonight, the thirtieth, especially in Brooklyn, the kids feel some sort of safety in numbers and logistics. But still, Robert's parents issue a warning as he leaves the house just as Stacy's did. He assures his father that he has nothing to worry about because Stacy is a blonde and that he'll indeed be staying in Brooklyn where it's safe.

The service road that runs parallel to the Belt Parkway and hugs the curves of the Bath Beach section of Brooklyn is a quiet and unsuspecting spot where often the rumbling of passing vehicles along the Belt is the only sounds you'll hear in the middle of the night. It's a relatively dark road, considering the south side is inactive with nothing but the island of grass separating it from the much more active parkway. Though on the north side, residential buildings continue in the unbroken sequence of any other neighborhood... lit by streetlamps. The stretch between Bay 16th and 17th Avenue just north of the service road, however, is occupied by a park and a playground...a patchwork of land that subdivides walkways with benches, swings, basketball courts and a baseball field. The area is lit up more than the usual spot along the service road, which on the surface may seem like a safe location when Robert Violante parks his car there. Fully conscious of the Son of Sam, Robert and Stacy get out and take a walk along the footbridge that connects the service road with the Belt. They're determined to enjoy their evening and go about the night as normally as they can. After arriving back at the car, they head to King's Highway for the movie.

But after the movie, in one of those instances where you want to alter history and somehow redirect these kids to go home, they return to Bath Beach where they park in the same location as they were earlier in the evening. They get out of the car and walk across the street to the park where they spend about ten minutes on the swings, talking. Given the circumstances of the late evening/early morning setting and the high-level concerns as a collective society, the conversation inevitably turns to the Son of Sam, and Stacy abruptly decides she wants to leave. In the car, Violante wants to sit for a few minutes while Stacy expresses she's not comfortable in this location. It's not even a few seconds after Stacy asks to leave when the killer fires a bullet into her head from outside the passenger window. He shoots into the car four times and walks off calmly across the street, disappearing into the playground area of Bath Beach Park. The bullet that strikes Stacy in the head lodges itself in her neck. Another bullet passes clear through Robert's head. A third bullet misses both of them and gets stuck in the steering column. The fourth bullet hits nothing and goes missing. Stacy is quiet and slouched over in her seat. Robert, in a prolonged horrified scream, leans on the horn, letting it wail into the silent night. His left eye has been completely destroyed, and he has been blinded in his right eye. He feels for the door, opens it and manages to fall out of the car, grabbing on to the streetlight pole for support while straightening up to stand, clutching on to the pole.

He reaches into the car feeling his way around for the horn. Again, the loud shriek of the horn envelops the neighborhood as Robert's high-pitched cries begin to jolt the blocks of Bay 16 and nearby 14 awake...those who weren't already rocked by the gunshots.

"Help me!"

The horn continues to wail in long unbroken bursts. His cries are loud and desperate in the short intervals between.

"Help me! Don't let me die!"

He hits the horn again.

"Help meeee!! Don't let me die!"

A married couple named Dotti and David, both in their early thirties and living on Bay 16, sees Robert from the window. The sodium streetlamp directly over the car illuminates the scene immensely so they can see him clearly and that his blue shirt and blue pants have been stained with blood. Within a few minutes, they are down to the street with other assorted neighbors emerging and converging on the car. Dotti convinces Robert to lay down on the ground while they wait for an ambulance. The couple helps him down to the sidewalk where they place a towel under his head to shield him from the gritty, dirty concrete. He lays between the lamp post and the fence over the island of grass between the service road and the Belt Parkway.

A few other neighbors tend to Stacy, trying to comfort her as she remains slumped over on the front seat. She keeps slurring that she wants to go home.

"Where is the ambulance?" Robert cries from the other side of the car. "Where is it?"

It takes a good ten to fifteen minutes for an ambulance to arrive.

The task force heading the Son of Sam investigation has its headquarters at the 109th Precinct in Queens. In the past few days alone there have been at least 20 reports of shots fired in various localities, so inspectors don't think much of the report of shots fired in Bath Beach. The focus since July 29 has been mainly in Queens and the Bronx. Once the initial arrival on the scene unfolds and police see the setting and circumstances surrounding the shooting, it becomes obvious what they are dealing with. Within two hours of the shooting, a Code 44 is implemented. This is the strategic protocol the NYPD has put in place for dealing specifically with the .44 killer. From this point on, the area is roped off and heavily photographed. Hours after Stacy and Robert have been taken away by ambulance, local stragglers still hanging around watching in shock and curiosity are convinced to go home, as the area is now a crime scene. For at least a few hours, it will just be law enforcement. But that won't last long.

In the early dawn, the shifting atmospheric wanderings of an altered firmament illuminate the dark sky and transform the wee hours into faint gray morning light, even before the sun comes up. It's a gray pallet over Bath Beach, though still light enough to know the night is over. Facing northwest while standing right smack in the middle of the service road where just to the left, Robert Violante's car remains underneath a streetlight, one can stare straight down virtually to the end of where the road meets the horizon. And sticking out above the horizon, perfectly centered with the service road, one of the foreboding, portentous towers of the Verrazzano Bridge with its main cables travelling upward in their serpentine flow with their lights still faintly visible at sunrise. The lonely service road, otherwise known as the Shore Parkway has seen the night fade away...and the talking too has faded... the overlapping conversations of law enforcement and local onlookers by the dozen that cradled the scene in concern and vigilant solidarity...many silent...most knowing full well, even hours before the ballistics are confirmed that they are no longer safe...that Brooklyn too has now been hit. The lonely service road has seen that crowd disperse and only a few officers remain, mostly taking pictures and a few waiting for daylight to scan the area. The lonely car also remains. The other vehicles that lined the block throughout the evening are gone. Robert Violante's Buick sits by itself like an injured animal licking its wounds...a tainted and haunted remnant of the night before...still sitting there to remind the locals who have gone to bed that this isn't just a nightmare. When they look out their windows in the morning the car will still be there. And all of this before the media arrives and the further shitshow that awaits that will paralyze New York City.

Police Commissioner Michael J. Codd paints the grim portrait for the metropolitan collective of media that has sensationalized the murder spree for the better part of the spring and summer, greatly contributing to the fear and mass hysteria felt throughout Queens and the Bronx, though the picture he offers is one of concession that the police have their work cut out for them, and that this time, the Son of Sam has let them know in no uncertain terms that he can strike anywhere in the city. The reality is that police haven't a clue where to even begin, as none of the composites they have of the killer seem to resemble each other, though all surviving victims and witnesses agree that it's a white male, medium build and between 20 and 35 years of age. The special task force of some 70 detectives has barely made a dent and now Mayor Beame has ordered Dodd to assign another 100 police officers to the case.

In Kings County Hospital, Stacy Moscowitz remains in critical condition. She has undergone an eight-hour surgery where doctors removed skull fragments from her brain but now have revealed that she has irreversible brain damage with her chances of survival at a very generous 50 percent. Robert Violante tells police he saw the person who shot them, though it's now questionable whether he would be able to identify that person given the loss of his eyesight. In the past few hours, ophthalmologists have already removed Robert's left eye, while it is now uncertain how much if any of the vision will be regained in his right eye. Parents of both victims remain together in the waiting rooms while the cameras are kept at bay just outside while Jerome and Nessa Moskowitz and Pasquale and Teresa Violante occasionally talk to reporters who hover in search of anything they could tell the public.

The Yankees are in Oakland when Stacy Moskowitz and Robert Violante are shot. They have been aware of the shootings as well as the escalation of fear around their city, as it has now become a national story that the entire country is gawking at. Aside from having the Bronx as their home and having their season play out parallel to the unfolding Son of Sam story, everything for the Yankees has evolved rather peacefully since late June with everybody cooperating and co-existing for the overall good of the team. That is until the overgrowth of Thurman's beard begins to bother Billy. On the surface, there are certain no-no's that everyone involved with the Yankees abide by when it comes to Steinbrenner policy, and long hair and beards are at the top of that list. Though George seems to go out of his way to accommodate his most cherished players and even appease them, he doesn't want his players to have beards…yet he lets Billy deal with the situation, almost even avoiding it when asked about it. Thurman ignores Billy's orders to shave it off. The Yankees have been on a bombastic mission by the last day of July, accumulating 31 runs in their past four wins. In Oakland on this Sunday afternoon with the help of Cliff Johnson, Mickey Rivers and Ed Figueroa, the Yanks demolish Vida Blue and the A's 9-2, thus helping Charles Finley fulfill his ultimate legacy of turning his dynasty into a losing team as the A's now find themselves safely in last place. Of all the stupid owners Finley lambasted for not following in his footsteps, it seems he turned out to be the stupidest.

On Sunday night, neurosurgeons perform a second surgery in an attempt at reducing swelling on Stacy's brain stem, though nobody seems to feel good about Stacy surviving. At this stage, the only thing working is her heart, which stops on Monday morning just after 10 AM, prompting doctors to resuscitate Stacy. She now remains on a respirator while the media circus outside becomes relentless, in search of information, needling people's grief.

With the mounting pressure of the summer heat building to a combustible climax, the sky opens up at 3:30 PM on Monday, the first of August as the mid-80s of afternoon give way to a much cooler 70 degrees courtesy of an unforeseen downpour of heavy rains and violent winds that rock the city through nightfall. As New Yorkers dash to get off the streets while flooding plagues some parts of the outer boroughs, the Moskowitz's and Violante's keep vigil at Kings County while sporadic media linger in and around the hospital where a young girl of 20 is so far gone that she can't even fight for her own life. Her heart has stopped at least a half a dozen times and she's no longer breathing on her own...a girl who braved the tabloid warnings and refused to stop her life in the face of some unknown invisible coward who hides behind a gun. Fuck you, she said. The movies were more important. Robert was more important. The possibility of love was more important. Living was more important. And so, she never stopped living. But even in those last few moments in the car when she came to a realization that they were maybe pushing their luck by being out there...being a target at such a late hour...that moment when she realized she wanted to get out of there and go home, there just wasn't enough time. Amid a savage storm raging outside over New York City, Stacy Moscowitz is pronounced dead at 5:22 PM.

The kids on the street who are in their late teens and early twenties...the ones whose faces Geraldo Rivera is sticking a microphone in front of are so fed up that they now want to kill the killer. The adults want to kill the killer too. Anyone with a microphone talking to anyone in Brooklyn in the days after Stacy's death is told by someone that they'd kill the killer if they could get their hands on him. Or at the very least, the killer, when caught, should be handed over to the parents of the victims and handled how they see fit. But what does that mean? How would these law-abiding citizens handle the Son of Sam? Would they lecture him? Bring him to Jesus? Cut off his testicles? Slowly torture him? Kill him? The ones that use God in their expletives as well as their matter-of-fact comments...the dear Gods and the God forbids... the God knows to the Jesus H. Christs. Would they forgive him? There's vengeance on the streets.

Rivera, a young reporter for ABC with shoulder-length hair is popular among the youth and Latino communities who view him more as a hip and streetwise ally than a straight and square reporter of the old guard. He's far more associated with interviewing people like John Lennon and Mick

Jagger than foreign ministers and business tycoons. Rivera wanders through the grass median that separates the service road from the Belt Parkway. In the distance behind him, TV viewers can see the pedestrian bridge that has been there for a long, long time and will continue to be there for a long, long time, though to many, it will now serve as a location marker and a haunting reminder of what happened in its shadow.

While lawyers for Yellowstone County in Montana meet with lawyers for Kiss promoter ACI, it is decided that security for the upcoming Metra performance will not frisk fans entering the venue unless there's suspicion of contraband. In other words, don't walk in looking like you're carrying firecrackers and an ounce of weed, and if you're going to carry firecrackers and weed into the arena, at least have the decency to not look like you are. When the seventh of August arrives, it's much ado about nothing as merely a handful of marijuana arrests take place with not many other societal atrocities. One concert review defangs the threat of the band and the audience by equating the event to nothing more than a bunch of teeny boppers.

On the tenth of August, Billy Martin finally succeeds in getting Thurman Munson to shave his beard. Perhaps he's feeling in good spirits over this little victory, and in a sudden shift of character, he presents the batting lineup for the evening's game against the A's. After returning from the West Coast, the Yankees are back at the stadium for a seven-game home stand and manager Billy has plugged Reggie into the cleanup spot. Reggie bats fourth and the results are instantaneous in a first inning explosion that puts Vida Blue down five runs. Granted, Nettles is the only Yankee to hit a home run, but the lineup change adds a renewed sense of vigor and optimism to a team that's already been hot lately. The Yankees win the game 6-3, giving Ron Guidry his ninth win of the season.

About ten miles northwest of Yankee Stadium, a peculiar setup of police officers from multiple jurisdictions are gathered along a hilly section of Yonkers just a few blocks east of the Hudson. As the late innings of the game are wrapping up in the Bronx, police arrest a man as he walks out to his car in front of his apartment building on Pine Street. At the urging of a few residents and a police dispatcher, Yonkers police are helping to merge a Brooklyn parking ticket with past complaints from neighbors. The ticket in question is issued to one David Berkowitz, a postal worker whose 1970 cream-colored Ford Galaxie was parked in front of a fire hydrant just a few blocks from the Moskowitz shooting, and roughly around the same exact time of the shooting. By early morning, the Yankees game and all of sports and the election coverage and just about everything else of concern to New York City is secondary news.

When Abe Beame announces the capture of the Son of Sam, at 1:45 AM, the media blitz has begun again. Berkowitz, 24, is swiftly taken to New York City Police Headquarters where he's booked for the murder of Stacy Moskowitz. Police at first are unclear on the motive of the crimes, though they'll be flabbergasted, as will the press when Berkowitz gives his story upon admitting to all the known shootings. We say known shootings here because at this stage in 1977, it is unknown that the Son of Sam crimes extend much longer in time than we are aware of and they involve other guns, more victims and even a few dogs. Berkowitz is basking in his own glory...smiling at everyone...seemingly astonished that he's attracted such attention as he marvels at the crowds that have shown up and the flash bulbs that ricochet off the air. He doesn't look like a serial killer. He seems friendly...innocent...harmless and dopey. He's quite pleased with himself when he arrives at the Gold Street Station House in the morning accompanied by arresting detective Edward Zigo. The media mele approaches in one collective rush of reporters that moves together like a swarm of bees at the front door. The detectives avoid the cameras for the most part when they enter the Eighty-fourth Precinct and reporters are blocked at the door by a wall of officers. Within a minute or two, the flock of cameras and microphones convoy around the precinct through an alley leading to the Prince Street entrance at the back of the building. In this case, let's consider Tom Wolfe's description of one of the characteristics of being a reporter when he described it as someone who demands or at the very least requests information that they are not entitled to. With respect to information involving Berkowitz, it is the NYPD that made this situation the business of the public, which in turn created the immediate frenzy while the media ran with it. While the NYPD merely did what it was supposed to do in conjunction with the city's responsibility of alerting the public, it is the tabloid media that created the panic and set the tone for the past five months. With that, it is difficult to fathom Detective Frank McGlaughlin being anything but hostile in response to the aggressive mob of reporters that storm the precinct from the back entrance, shouting their disapproval of the manner in which Berkowitz was brought into the building and expressing their frustration of waiting for a statement and then having to relocate. McGlaughlin, who we've seen in other media reports of NYPD updates, often standing next to John Keenan in press conferences, gives the gathering of reporters the gist on what's happened so far in the hours since the arrest. As he attempts to give the details of the suspect's photographing, some antagonistic assholes are more interested in why Berkowitz was brought in through the front of the building when police procedure usually calls for a high-profile suspect to be brought in through a side or back entrance to avoid the press. The press knows this, and they were prepared and waited accordingly. Perhaps it's a legit question to ponder. Did they purposely try to avoid the cameras by thinking they could sneak in the front door after some press people waited for six hours? This is the bullshit that becomes the focus for a few minutes.

"We walked in that door," McGlaughlin tells a reporter, pointing toward the front of the building. "It's all over, it's done. Now are you interested in listening to me or do you wanna keep talking?"

"Okay, go," the reporter says smugly.

Behind McGlaughlin is Detective Joe Coffey whose entire presence marks a room with an intimidating cool. Coffey is perhaps the first person to conclude that the city had a psychopath on the loose. He was the first to connect the shootings as early as the Freund murder in January when he was placed on the case. The use of a .44 bulldog in two other Queens shootings was unusual, and it concerned him. His suspicions were confirmed when he went to the Bronx and talked with ballistics. But in January, he was told not to open his mouth for the panic it could cause. Coffey is one of those guys who come from that era, as they often say, when men were men. In a suit, he still looks like a badass who will swiftly knock the shit out of you as he nonchalantly lights a cigarette behind McGlaughlin. Together they look like a more menacing version of Starsky and Hutch.

As McGlaughlin begins again, he doesn't get far.

"Which idiot thought that up?" another asshole from the line of reporters spits out, still whining about Berkowitz entering through the front door.

The question sets McGlaughlin off.

"Fuck you!" he charges. "You wanna talk about idiots, I'll talk to you personally. We've had more opportunities tonight than you've had in a hundred years!"

Coffey slightly advances forward and lightly touches McGlaughlin on the arm, getting in his ear, subtly telling him to cool off. The expected shitshow has begun.

David Berkowitz was born Richard David Falco and was adopted by Nathan and Pearl Berkowitz. Pearl died a decade ago when David was 14. Four years later, David graduated from Columbus High School in the Bronx. He has a year of community college behind him and has also served in the United Staes Army, stationed in Korea. These facts are all part of the process in uncovering who this Son of Sam really is, and it all seems to hold no unusual threads as far as his history goes. What Berkowitz tells police takes the case into uncharted territory. He states that he hears voices in his head and that he committed the murders under the orders of a big bad talking satanic dog. It is unknown whether Sam is the dog or the owner of the dog. In the Borrelli letter left at the Suriani scene, Berkowitz warns that "Sam is a thirsty lad"... now seemingly filling in questions left by the letter. But as Berkowitz feeds them copious amounts of bullshit, there is some truth in that there is indeed a dog in this story. The dog's name is Harvey Carr. He lives at 316 Warburton Avenue in Yonkers. And then there is Sam Carr, the 65-year-old owner of Harvey Carr, also of 316 Warburton Avenue in Yonkers. The front of the Carr house on Warburton Avenue overlooks the Hudson River. The back of the Carr house faces upward toward an elevated area of woods with the Croton Aqueduct Trail slicing through it. Further above the woods forming the eastern horizon is Pine Street where David Berkowitz's apartment building sits like a sinister castle haunting this already macabre area. The Carr family that lives in the big, white-shingled house near the corner of Warburton and Wicker Street is made up of Sam, his two sons, Michael and John, and daughter, Wheat. Though Michael and John no longer reside there, Sam and Wheat remain with Harvey who often wanders the backyard barking. On many a day and night, David Berkowitz stared down from his window toward Warburton and Wicker Streets where he remained distracted and agitated, not only by Harvey's barking, but by Rocket's barking too. Rocket was a dog that lived in the Neto house on Wicker Street, and Berkowitz is likely to have shot and killed him on Christmas Eve, just as he is also likely to have shot and wounded Harvey back in April, probably from the Aqueduct Trail during the same week he killed Val and Alex in Pelham Bay. None of these crimes were ever solved. This however is not part of the news because they never made the news...though Wheat Carr has had her suspicions regarding who shot Harvey. Berkowitz also wrote an angry neighborly letter to Sam that further builds the evidence against him.

The Carr's run several businesses out of their house, one of which is a switchboard where Wheat works as a dispatcher for the Yonkers Police. It was by the slim chance of detectives working the Son of Sam case who began running checks on all the summonses issued on cars around the Bath Beach area on the night of the Moscowitz shooting. One of the tickets was issued to Berkowitz when his Galaxie was parked in front of a fire hydrant on Bay Seventeenth, just two blocks from the shooting site. When they called Yonkers Police, it was Wheat Carr who answered. When they inquired about Berkowitz, they could hardly have expected Wheat's response. She told them that she believes he's the Son of Sam and that they'd better check him out. Imagine their surprise when she turned out to be right.

Between the blackout, the looting and burning, the constant uneasiness of the Son of Sam delirium, the capture of Berkowitz...even the recreational hype of *Star Wars*...there is a living sense in real time on the ground that we're living through a different kind of summer...one that for better or worse will stand out by default for the rest of our lives.

While nobody is innocent on the groupie front, Ace Frehley at least tries to stay active in other ways aside from keeping score of sexual conquests through a photo album full of polaroids as souvenirs like Gene does. Whenever he's able to, he and Eddie Balandas will rent a boat and throw some fishing lines into a nearby lake...something they've made a ritual out of in places like Seatle where they stay at the Edgewater Inn on Lake Washington. In Seatle, Patrick MacDonald, a critic who trashed them the last time when they played the Paramount Northwest walks away slightly impressed before turning in a semi-favorable review for the Coliseum show, but making note that "Beth" is not played for some odd reason, though there were no real mishaps to make the band look as bad as he first made them out to be.

In concert, sometimes the mishaps don't always happen because of wrong chords or Ace falling or Gene setting his hair on fire. Sometimes they're just embarrassing technical errors on the part of the crew. As the first encore begins nightly, Peter usually takes center stage seated on a small round platform to sing "Beth" with recorded music piped in through the P.A. and the other band members off stage. The other nightly ritual happens when the houselights go on following a Kiss concert and the Beatles' "Magical Mystery Tour" is played while the crowd gathers themselves and begins to exit the venue. In Portland, Oregon, the sound crew prepares for "Beth" as they do on every other night, but little do they know the wrong tape has been cued. As Peter takes his seat in the spotlight awaiting those first notes of "Beth," the tape launches into "Magical Mystery Tour," much to the embarrassment of everyone involved.

The Golden State is next.

Earlier this year, 1976 was officially declared the fourth driest year in California's history, though 1977 has already surpassed that. Thanks to the stationary high pressure ridge existing in the Pacific that's been causing storms to be diverted toward Canada and Mexico, the rains have been bypassing the state of California with some extremely rare exceptions over the past year and a half, though for the most part, the ridge has been an impenetrable wall making the summer unpleasantly and often dangerously arid. With the drought as its consequential background, the Pacific Coast Highway rock and roll of the Seventies provides the soundtrack to that mythic romanticized view of California in much the same way as we romanticize the grit of New York City during this very same era. West Coast music tends to own the pop charts these days with "Hotel California" haunting the airwaves through springtime and "Go Your Own Way" and "Dreams" weaving themselves deep into the fabric of summer. The Eagles and Fleetwood Mac are prime examples of the new surge in album sales and a reminder that the age of the 45-rpm single as the dominant format of tangible music is long over. In the past year, the phenomenon of full LPs selling in unprecedented numbers was highlighted by *Frampton Comes Alive* and the debut album of a new band called Boston. With the summer of '77 close to winding down, Fleetwood Mac's *Rumours* has already established itself as the biggest selling album of all time.

Eddie Kramer is with Kiss on and off throughout the run of California shows. He's become the go-to guy for the quintessential Kiss sound and California is where they'll be capturing the sights and sounds of the second live album. With the recording set for Los Angeles and photo sessions set for San Diego, Kramer needs the intro for the album which usually doesn't translate well on actual live recordings in the same way pyro explosions often don't translate. As the crew is setting up the stage at San Francisco's Cow Palace, Kramer gets Eddie Balandas in the bathroom and asks him to scream his Kiss intro into a recorder. After he gets half a dozen takes, Kramer and Gene speculate over their concern that the intro sounds as if Balandas is saying "Piss" instead of "Kiss." The quick solution is for Gene to scream "Kiss" into the recorder with Kramer left to patch it all together in the studio.

It's been a week since the capture of Berkowitz and the media can't let go of it. He pleads guilty in a 19-minute arraignment, appearing in court in the same clothes he was wearing at the time of his arrest...a blue and white striped short sleeve button down shirt, blue jeans and a head of kinky Brillo hair with an easy-going, twinkly eyed, pursed lip smile. As if the story isn't enough for the swarms of reporters outside the court, the twisting turn of events just keeps going, and the national news is much different within a few minutes of the arraignment. By midafternoon the first breaking reports are coming in on radio and television announcing the death of Elvis Presley, America's most well-known rock star and one of the founding fathers of rock and roll music. The nation has had moments like this, though they don't happen that often. The last one was the death of John F. Kennedy...the ones that they say you remember where you were for the rest of your life. Those moments that stop time. For those who lived the 1950s onward, it's difficult to even fathom.

Elvis Presley is dead.

And this is one of those moments.

At Cow Palace...

Most fans in the building have learned of Elvis's death from radio reports on their way to the show. After a typical *Love Gun* set, Paul approaches the mic before the final encore. Given that Kiss plays a structured setlist and perfectly choreographed show from literally every step taken on the stage by the band members to every word spoken to the crowd, it's a break from tradition when Paul offers a rare spontaneous moment.

"We're gonna dedicate the last song...to the king of rock and roll...Elvis Presley, rock and roll all nite, an pawty ev'ry day!"

Rock and Roll All Nite will later become known in Kiss circles as the rock and roll national anthem. The symbolism in the moment is everywhere if you know where to look. Elvis Presley, known as the King of Rock and Roll at one time, let's say twenty years ago became a pop cultural phenomenon unlike anything ever seen in American history.

In the most recent issue of *Circus*, a cover story focusing on Kiss's success not only talks about the present success of *Love Gun* and the stage show across Canada and the United States...it highlights future plans as spoken about by Paul Stanley. Paul not only spills the beans on a second live album, but he tells Circus of the group's idea to record four solo albums...one from each member of Kiss...each with its own distinctive sound and style...and all to be released at the same time. Paul's time estimation on the Kiss solo albums forecasts a spring 1978 release.

On the nineteenth of August, the San Diego Sports Arena is the location for Kiss's photoshoot with Barry Levine where the band poses for live action photos onstage with full lighting and effects. For one of the shots, they recreate the end of the concert but incorporate both climaxes seen in 'Black Diamond" and "Rock and Roll All Nite." The first is Peter's drum riser extending as high as it goes, and the latter song sees Paul, Gene and Ace high above the audience on their hydraulic lifts...two moments that occur at separate times during the show, though Levine captures both simultaneously. They also decide to set off all the pyro effects at the same time. Though these effects are used at different times during the show, Levine's aim is sensory overload...everything great about the live Kiss show...all at once. Little do they know at the time is that the photo will do more for the band's myth and legend than any other photo they've ever taken or will ever take again. It doesn't capture what a Kiss concert is...it informs authoritatively what a Kiss concert is in our imaginations. It will take those luring bombastic last chords of "Black Diamond" on *Alive*, the ones that lead the imagination to wonder what the hell is going on during those explosive chords, and it will provide an answer by showing us.

The enormous billboard sitting atop the Sunset Strip displays the cover of *Love Gun* and the Kiss logo in dazzling enormity. From Monday through Sunday, it's all glitz, glitter, grime and grit. It's Kiss Week in Los Angeles where at the outset the band has a promotional interview for KMET radio... although it's the blue Ten Q billboards proclaiming 1020 KTNQ as L.A.'s only radio station. Billboards in L.A. are abundant for advertising for everything from whose radio station is better to new albums to films to fashion to Groman Mortuaries. The sacred strip is lined with the look and feel of money, but nonetheless subject to and highlighted by an undercurrent of intangible sleaze. The Daisy, Aquascutum, Jax, Matthews, the London Shop, Hermes, Gucci and all the elegant prestigious places that are all about location, location, location, and in some of these locations, people are sandwiches. You can eat them by name. It's a place where Allan Car is a chicken sandwich. Andy Gilmour is corned beef on rye. You can eat Buddy Hacket as a meat pattie and pastrami on a bagel. Bernie Kahn is a tuna and cheese sandwich. If you eat Katy Hepburn she comes as a meat pattie with fresh fruits. And if you've eaten Jack Nicholson by God, you've just had steak tartare.

On the streets people drive around in their convertibles with their 69 cents premium gasoline, surrounded by gas and wax and carwashes seemingly by the dozen offering hot carnauba wax and the service only of experts. Highways and strips are defined and accented by Chevron and Mobile stations and the towering height of those orange round 76 signs with their eye-popping dark blue numbers. These sights are not as visibly imperative in the places where Kiss comes from...those places where the critters rely more on mass transit and taxi cabs. In L.A. every motherfucker has a car.

The scheduled three-night stand at the Los Angeles Forum promises to be a highlight week of the tour. August 26, 27 and 28 are top priority dates in the itinerary. There is heavy promotion entailing a week of press events, radio interviews and non-stop parties every night, even on the nights off. This is all before and leading up to the shows that will make up the entire weekend. All involved believe Kiss to have surpassed the attendance they pulled in at Anaheim Stadium and so Aucoin and promoter David Forest estimate that they'd need at least three shows at the indoor venue to top Anaheim. At the Forum, Kiss would pull in 17,000 a night. At three shows, they'd need to sell at least 50,000 tickets, which Kiss can easily do. Or can they? The significant number of tickets still available is one of the reasons the band promotes the shows on KMET.

Coinciding with these West Coast dates in August 1977 is the addition of yet another division of Aucoin Management, this one called Aucoin Productions which will serve as a branch for TV and film production. While the entourage is situated in the L'Ermitage Hotel, another hub for the week is the new Casablanca office at 8255 Sunset Boulevard, their building basking in sunrays beaming from beyond the Hollywood Hills over Sunset. On the morning of the first Forum show, C.K. Lendt gets a call from Aucoin who has flown in for the weekend engagement. He makes a few playful jokes about how much money Lendt is spending on restaurants and orgies and casually mentions that the first night's show should do fine.

Then his tone shifts.

He reiterates what is already known...that all three shows are not sold out and that David Forest, the promoter is worried that he's about to take a financial bath. He instructs Lendt not to let Forest talk him into anything... and that should he call, there will be no last-minute changes to the contract, nor would Lendt be at liberty to make any decisions on a contract without the consent of Aucoin anyway. It is the first time that the carefree overboard splurging of extravagant spending has remotely seemed a concern for the upper echelon of the Kiss hierarchy. Just recently, a meeting was held between management and the members of Kiss. It has been almost two years since Alive went gold. It has since sold a lot more copies, and the money has been rolling in. In the time since, Aucoin has paid off debts and along with Neil Bogart, has helped expand Casablanca and the overall vision for Kiss. But the band members had questions. And so there was a meeting. The band members have lived luxuriously, but they've done it on the road because the road has been endless for the better part of the past three and a half years. They've all taken care of their parents and families in terms of financial security, and they've all taken up modest residency in Manhattan for the time being...but none of them have any money. The situation as it is, sees the band members asking Lendt for cash as needed, and he gives them cash and writes a receipt for how much they take. The band members indeed had questions in that meeting, and the number one question was when they will be millionaires. In their calculations, the conclusion management comes to in assuring Paul, Gene, Peter and Ace is that the real millions will start rolling in with the next royalty period. At the end of his call from Aucoin, Lendt hangs up the phone, suddenly remembering Ace taking several thousands of dollars just an hour earlier so he could go shopping for vintage guitars. No big deal. It's a multi-million-dollar operation with the money coming in. There's no cause for alarm.

The shows begin in L.A. with excitement at fever pitch when word cascades down to the ground that Kiss is recording for another live album. Special *I Was There* buttons have been made for fans upon entrance, most of those fans wearing Kiss shirts and a noticeable amount of people wearing *Star Wars* shirts...something fairly unusual for a movie, although we're also starting to see t-shirts out there of Rocky Balboa. There is something special in the making. There is a sense of a much higher profile focused on L.A. where Kiss Week climaxes in the thunderous realm of three ear-splitting, blood-spilling Kiss concerts. Kiss and Cheap Trick in the summer of 1977!

The Forum stand etches itself into the tapestry of legendary moments in Kisstory and everything about it is symbolic of the greatest yet most tumultuous summer of the decade...the absolute pinnacle to that laid back seismic circus of indulgence in the fast lane of rock and roll, slathered against the backdrop of the Pacific Coast's golden endless summer.

While Kiss fans are quite happy with the lore of the Forum shows in the vast canon of concert history, Aucoin, Lendt and some lawyers hold several post-Forum meetings with Fun Productions head David Foster when the promoter shortchanges the band on the remainder of the guarantee for the third night's show. Aucoin tells Foster a deal is a deal. Aucoin also reminds him that it wasn't he who pushed for a third night based on the success of the Anaheim show. Aucoin at first wasn't for a third show, and through the entire space of time since booking it, he requested more promotion from Foster, which he didn't feel Foster delivered on. Aucoin also spells out that it was he and Kiss who paid for extra last-minute promotion out of their own pockets once they got to L.A. earlier in the week. Foster reminds Aucoin that this third show has already amounted to a disastrous loss for him and Fun Productions, and for him to cover the remainder of the guarantee would mean financial ruin. After things verbally escalate to nearly ugly proportions, Aucoin and Foster quietly work out a deal, following which, the promoter acknowledges that his modus operandi has always been to run risks and take chances, and that was one of the things Aucoin liked about him in the first place. They've had a great working relationship until now. But in this case, Foster bit off far more than he could ever fit in his mouth. Kiss is Kiss big...rising star big...not Led Zeppelin big. Yes, he was delusional. He knew they were big, but now he admits that he was fucking crazy to think they were *that* big.

In the final weeks of summer, something changes within Robert Stigwood and RSO regarding their opinions of the song "Night Fever" sounding like the title of a porn film. With *Saturday Night* still being floated as the tentative title of their upcoming movie, it becomes time to begin the promotional campaign three months ahead of the December 16 release date. In that process of unforeseen evolution and mutation, something riveting happens to the title of *Saturday Night*. Throughout September beginning on the eleventh, full page ads begin to appear along with posters in movie theaters of a single image. The image is slick, fast, modern and attention-grabbing.

John Travolta.

In a white suit.

He's striking a pose on a dance floor, his body surrounded by flashing lights above and below...his left arm and hand extended outward but pointed down toward the earth with even more flare than Raphael's Aristotle... his right arm pointed upward with his hand reaching for the heavens. The tagline at the top of the ad reads

Where do you go when the record is over...

Near the bottom, the eye popping sleek and slanted lightning bolt font bearing the words...

SATURDAY NIGHT FEVER

"Christine Sixteen," the first single off *Love Gun* that has been hovering around the radio all summer falls off the Billboard charts during the week of September 11 after peaking at number 25. One week later, the album's title track enters the Hot 100 but will only stick around briefly to peak at 61. With *Love Gun*'s second single only making it to the charts a full three months after release, it's important to note that album releases and the trajectory of their singles are not the same in 1977 as they will later become in the next century. Singles rarely get released before an album is out. There is no big three-month leadup to an album with several singles issued before release. The new album usually just appears one day, and it often takes a month or two before most fans start catching on...only then does the first single begin to chart. There are obvious exceptions, though most bands that release a new album, still have a single from the previous album on the charts. Hence acts like the Steve Miller Band releasing *Book of Dreams* and its first single "Jet Airliner" when "Fly Like an Eagle" was still on the charts and promotion of its corresponding album still hadn't completely run its course. Simply put, album cycles overlap, especially on the pop charts.

By September 25, it's becoming clear in New York that this scrawny young pitcher, Ron Guidry is for real when he wins his eighth consecutive decision and his sixteenth for 1977. Billy and Gabe initially wanted to trade Guidry early in the season and had set up a deal with the White Sox, but George struck it down at the last minute. Guidry *is* for real, and the Boss knows he's now achieved his ultimate concoction of pitching, power and speed... the team he envisioned while assembling the pieces and the tools is now in place for another pennant.

At the outset of the playoffs, Billy has been talking freely to reporters about his strategy for a new contract in the event the Yankees win the American Leaue Championship Series and the World Series.

"If we win everything, I think it's a must for George to come up with a new contract. If he didn't, I'd have to seriously think about asking permission to talk to other clubs."

While the press is constantly speculating on the possibility of Billy being fired, they also make his three-year $100,000 contract part of the focus, which in turn probably helps him for the fact that George has no choice but to constantly hear about it. The results appear to be on Billy's side at the moment, having taken the Yankees to their first post-season in 12 years despite losing the World Series last year. This year the Yankees finish with 100 wins, up from last season's 97, and he made good on his promise to bring them back to October baseball, and now here are the Yankees once again... facing the Kansas City Royals for the second year in a row.

22

FEEL THE CITY BREAKING

On a cloudy, foggy and showery Tuesday afternoon in the last dying hours of summer, Wheat, Michael and Sam Carr granted an interview with the *New York Times* after avoiding the press for nearly six weeks. The association alone with David Berkowitz has been excruciating on the family as they've received death threats, hate mail and obscene phone calls in the time since the press outed Sam as the Sam in "Son of Sam." As if Berkowitz coming up with the Son of Sam moniker with Sam Carr in mind isn't bad enough for the innocent family, why the media would reveal their names and address is beyond comprehension. Although they have not granted any interviews nor taken any of the financial compensation offered to them, their lawyer has advised them to fend off the press with price tags of up to 20,000 dollars per interview. So, when they met with a reporter at Dino's Ground Round in Yonkers on that September day, they made it a point to stress that they were talking for free in the attempt at clearing their name and hopefully drawing attention to the fact that they're being targeted by people who believe that they're some sort of accomplices to the shootings. The biggest frustration of all however was vented by Wheat who revealed that the family has received a taunting letter from Berkowitz himself straight from the psyche ward of Kings County.

In Brooklyn, District Attorney Eugene Gold is challenging the findings of the two court-ordered psychiatrists who have found David Berkowitz mentally unfit to stand trial. Bronx District Attorney Mario Merola is also calling for a second round of psychiatric evaluations and wants to put the suspect in front of a panel of shrinks from Bellevue, while Queens D.A. John Santucci is preferring at this time to wait for the outcomes in Brooklyn and the Bronx. Gold has brought in a Dr. David Abrahamsen to conduct the evaluation. Abrahamsen, an expert in criminal behavior, has recently spent some time interviewing Nathan Berkowitz in a separate evaluation that he has yet to conclude. All D.A.s have waived court appearances for Berkowitz citing the same concerns, all wanting to avoid the media circus that would inevitably attach itself to said appearances.

As we get into autumn and election season, we will not concern ourselves with politics as 1977 has the luxury of not having politics at the forefront of a cultural divide...in fact there is no definitive cultural divide that we can name at this point in time...not in the manner of the divide that existed in the 1960s with age at its core. The divide that happened in the Sixties was generational in nature. Nor is there any divide like the one that will later emerge in the twenty-first century where the culture war is rooted in right vs. left politics. There is no Internet, and there is no cable news and Rupert Murdoch is still a benign blip on the media radar. With this in consideration, the mayoral race is without question woven into the fabric of this New York City backdrop, though it almost seems secondary to the societal calamities and revolutionary cultural miscellanea that have already defined the year. With some ten weeks left in 1977, the year is already being recollected and assessed in past tense as there is a collective desire sociologically, psychologically and anthropologically to be done with it. In other words, by October, the general attitude about 1977 is fuck 1977.

As the playoffs get underway in the Bronx, there's a search for five prisoners who escaped from Rikers Island overnight. Initially ten left the prison. One died while trying to swim across the East River while the remainder gave up because the water was too cold. Five inmates are still at large with two corrections officers suspended for dereliction of duty. This has been the second time inmates have escaped from Rikers in recent months since the blackout in July.

President Carter just passed through the South Bronx in what he is referring to as a sobering trip. As the six-car motorcade accompanied by police cars and three hovering helicopters made its way up the Grand Concourse, the president was treated to a firsthand view of the devastation of urban rot. But we the public are not concerned with urban rot anymore than we care about politics or energy conservation...though it's the oil companies that Carter rips for not being on board with his energy plan, but that's neither here nor there. We care about sports, recreation, gossip and excess while our government and media are attached to the same old tropes like our communism fetish or the obsession with Cuba that goes back at least for the past four administrations while we along with the United Nations completely ignore the genocide happening in Southeast Asia ever since the last chopper left Saigon and the Khmer Rouge slithered into Cambodia. Americans have no real interest in waterboarding, electrocution or having your fingernails pulled with pliers. Or having your skin sliced open followed by acid being poured in the wounds. There's no interest in any of this. We don't hear about live humans being hung on hooks through their mouths followed by the painful extractions of their gall bladders and then their hearts...or of something as simple as suffocation by way of a bag placed over a prisoner's head. Not even that. We're not even interested in an even more extreme form of suffocation by having prisoners hooked up to pumps and having the blood slowly drained from their bodies. None of that in America. Or to get as primitive as it gets, we don't even care to know about someone who's simply been slowly beaten to death with a stick. These are things virtually invisible in the American media while other conflicts like the never-ending feud between Israel and Palestine are treated as inconvenient background noise. It's baseball, dancing and cocaine that Americans want. In the Bronx two rivals can oblige at least one third of that as the opposition flies in from the Midwest for a rematch.

There is no overstating the hostility between the Yankees and Kansas City Royals. In the Seventies, the ALCS is a best-of-five series. Just hours after the President of the United States was rummaging through the rubble and dirt of dusty vacant lots surrounded by burned-out shells of buildings down the street, the Royals take the first game in the Bronx. Game Two is no shortage of drama when Hal McRae plows violently through Willie Randolph to break up a double play, knocking the second baseman onto the outfield grass. Do you know that philosophy we mentioned earlier that says a manager who once played the game of baseball will manage the same way he played? There's a lot of truth to that. The homerun hitters cultivate power and tend not to encourage small ball...i.e. singles, stealing, bunting, moving the runners along, etc...Pitchers create an environment where pitching thrives. Martin was a rugged and aggressive player in his day, so he knows quite a bit about sliding hard and knocking into unsuspecting infielders to fuck up their day and break up a double play. With this, he manages accordingly, telling reporters who no doubt will put Kansas City within earshot of the reminder that they have a second baseman named Frank White, who at some point will inevitably be in position for a double play. Martin minces no words. The incident lights a fire under the ass of the Yankees team, prodding them to explode into a 6-2 win, tying the series before taking it to Kansas City for the duration. In Game Three, the score is the same...6-2...though it's KC this time to pull ahead in the series as Dennis Leonard four-hits the Yanks in a masterful performance on the mound.

There is indeed a widespread dislike of the Yankees, and it's not just places like Kansas City and Boston. It's a nationwide dislike, and in some cases, straight-up hatred extends to New York itself...small markets resentful of the way big money has benefitted this team that couldn't reach anywhere near a post-season in over a decade...or large market major cities that are probably just contemptuous out of jealousy because they just can't put it together the same way as New York can. What does Boston have that the Yankees could possibly want? The last time Boston had something the Yankees wanted, the Yankees went out and got him, for Chris'sakes. In KC, the disdain is voiced by manager, Whitey Herzog who proclaims that everyone is rooting for the Royals and that nobody likes the Yankees. Martin threatens him when told of the comments. Herzog had better shut his mouth or someone will shut it for him, he says. Herzog isn't intimidated. He's ready anytime, anyplace.

Going into the final game of the ALCS, Martin feels he's against the wall and running a risk with an unproductive Reggie who is 1 for 15 in the series and has been unable to hit against Paul Splittorff.

Whether he's still trying to show him up or if he's acting in the best interest of the team or if he just has a bug up his ass, Billy's stubbornness takes no prisoners when he benches Reggie for game Five. Reggie against Splittorff is something he's seen enough of. If there's been any peace between Billy and Reggie, it's probably been cut short. Fortunately for all involved with the Bronx Bombers, the Yankees win.

And youuuu...light up myyy li-ii-iiife
Youuu give me ho-ohhp
To carry awwnn...

The New York Yankees.

The Los Angeles Dodgers.

The sense of history between these two teams is not lost on anyone as Game 1 festivities are underway for the 74th World Series. The legend in the post-season rivalry between these two neighboring New York institutions of the Bronx and Brooklyn is up front and center. The names and faces are different since the last time the Yankees and Dodgers met in 1963, and the Dodgers have now spent a decade and a half on the West Coast. In that '63 series, Walter Alston's Dodgers swept the Yanks, one of four world championships the team won during Alston's 23-year stretch with the team. The first one was in Brooklyn in 1955 and Alston accompanied the Dodgers through their geographical transition in the early Sixties and managed them straight up until his retirement last year, handing the keys to the kingdom to Tommy

Lasorda, completely unaware (because we can't really see the future) that Lasorda will manage the team for the next 20 years and take them through a few more world titles.

Gullet starts the first game. It's been a week since things fell to shit for him in the first game of the ALCS. He's had some great practices in the days since...yet he gets behind straightaway when he walks Davey Lopes and gives up a triple to Bill Russell in the first inning. He pitches splendidly throughout the game, however, that is through nine innings when Sparky Lyle comes in for him in relief after the Dodgers tie it up at three a piece. Game One goes 12 innings with Paul Blair lashing the winning hit to right field, driving in Randolph to put the Yankees up in the series.

Shortly before seven on Wednesday night, October 12, a fire breaks out at the abandoned Public School 3 in the Melrose section of the Bronx. By this time, Yankee Stadium is almost filled to capacity as fans make their way in for Game Two of the World Series. A westerly wind keeps the large plumes of smoke from blowing toward the stadium which sits east of the blaze. Television viewers, however, are filled in periodically by Howard Cosell and Keith Jackson as the ABC broadcast cuts back and forth to aerial shots of the fire as it stretches to five alarms and exceeds playing time, burning until it's finally under control just before midnight. As for the game, the Dodgers easily plow through the Yanks, taking advantage of a sore-shouldered Catfish Hunter whom Billy reluctantly goes with over Torrez and Guidry to give them both some adequate rest, having both pitched in game five of the Kansas City series. Burt Hooten puts in a masterful performance, pitching the full game and dominating with his signature hybrid knuckle-curve. The Dodgers tie the series with a 6-1 victory before taking it back home to L.A. Following the game, reporters ask Billy if he has any plans of pulling Reggie again, given his uneventful performance so far in the series.

"I'm not taking Reggie out. Reggie's in there. Splittorff isn't pitching for them."

Reggie is miffed when the comment gets back to him shortly after.

"I don't care what he says. I don't need to take that from nobody, especially from him. I know what I can do. If he did, we'd be a lot better off."

The death of legendary singer, Bing Crosby brings a moment of silence in the minutes leading up to the Game Three. Pop singer Linda Ronstadt, sporting a Dodgers jacket and jeans is on hand to sing the national anthem out in centerfield. Ronstadt is just on the cusp of her career peak. Her latest album is called *Simple Dreams*. Her current single, a cover of Roy Orbison's "Blue Bayou" is climbing up the charts. Ronstadt is primarily a covers artist, but unlike any other artist who performs covers today, she inhabits her versions with authority and makes them undoubtedly her own. As for the game...

Rivers goes into Game Three 0 for 10, unable to hit anything, but delivers early with a double. Through the swift bats and feet of Rivers, Munson, Piniella and Jackson, the pattern of the visiting team striking early continues at Dodger Stadium when the Yankees score three runs off Tommy John in the top of the first inning of game three. Dusty Baker, whose error in right field allows one of the Yankee runs, atones for his sins in the bottom of the third by smashing a three-run homer off Torrez. But Torres pitches superbly throughout the remainder of the game as the Yankees regain the lead and win 5-3, taking a 2-1 lead in the series.

Guidry starts the fourth game. Just ten months ago, this skinny 27-year-old Cajun kid from Lafayette, Louisiana wasn't sure what his role would be on this team that was expected to be back in the World Series, though it was originally intended that he would be the lefty pitcher that would either supplement or replace Sparky Lyle in the bullpen. Nothing and no one could have predicted the season he'd end up having as a starter. And for nine innings in Game Four of the World Series, Guidry puts on a master class in cool, calm and collected. With the exception of a two-run homer by Davey Lopes in the fourth inning, Guidry dominates the Dodgers, pitching a complete game, allowing just four hits and striking out seven batters, putting the Yankees ahead in the series three games to one. Reggie also breaks out of his homerun slump by blasting a shot to the opposite field to assure the victory with an insurance run in the sixth. With one game left in Los Angeles, the Yankees have a chance to win the championship in Game Five. In New York, that sounds bittersweet to the fans that would prefer their team to win it at home.

Game Five

Despite a few rallies in the later innings, the Dodgers dismantle Don Gullet and blow out the Yankees chances, at least for another day. While Sutton has clearly derailed the Yankees' chances of winning the series on Dodgers turf, Reggie smashes out a solo homerun in the top of the eighth on Sutton's first pitch. As he rounds the bases and crosses the plate, it's seems like a harmless homerun that couldn't touch the whopping lead the Dodgers still have...and that would be 100 percent true. What Sutton and even Lasorda don't know, however, is that they haven't seen anything yet. As Reggie exits this game with a quiet blast that seems innocent on the surface, he has just put the Dodgers on notice.

Dugga dugga dugga dugga
dugga dugga dugga dugga
dugga dugga dugga dugga
dugga dugga dugga dugga
dugga dugga dugga dugga
dugga dugga dugga dugga
dugga dugga dugga dugga
dugga dugga dugga dugga

Dugga dugga dugga dugga
dugga dugga dugga dugga
dugga dugga dugga dugga
dugga dugga dugga dugga
dugga dugga dugga dugga
dugga dugga dugga dugga

dugga dugga dugga dugga
dugga dugga dugga dugga
Dugga dugga dugga dugga
dugga dugga dugga dugga
dugga dugga dugga dugga
dugga dugga dugga dugga
dugga dugga dugga dugga
dugga dugga dugga dugga
dugga dugga dugga dugga
dugga dugga dugga dugga

The walls and pockets of mankind walking along various strips of bars and memorabilia shops outside Yankee Stadium's surrounding streets grow more immense in the three or four hours before gametime in the late afternoon of Tuesday, October 21. The surrounding streets drawing the eclectic mix of local fans, frightened fans from out of town and degenerate stragglers having nothing to do with baseball are mostly behind the building's bleacher section where the elevated rail provides a perforated cover over River Avenue. The roof-like structure above masks the block in darkness, even during the day when shafts of light beam down through the broken space between the tracks allowing daylight to seep in. Mass humanity trudges in both directions along River Avenue and on and off 161st Street.

Dugga dugga dugga dugga
dugga dugga dugga dugga
dugga dugga dugga dugga
dugga dugga dugga dugga
dugga dugga dugga dugga
dugga dugga dugga dugga
dugga dugga dugga dugga
dugga dugga dugga dugga

Tickets sold quick for this one and everyone who's anyone in the realm of New York City society is in attendance. Even Yankee legend Joe Dimaggio is here.

Dugga dugga dugga dugga
dugga dugga dugga dugga
dugga dugga dugga dugga
dugga dugga dugga dugga
dugga dugga dugga dugga
dugga dugga dugga dugga
dugga dugga dugga dugga
dugga dugga dugga dugga

The circular chug of Giorgio Moroder's signature beat pumps out of a car stereo in stop and go traffic along River, though it's not the red lights holding things up, it's the people...the disorderly heathens who tramp this sacred ground of warriors who have laid out the history over decades. And just inside is Reggie and Thurman and Billy and Guidry just waiting. Waiting for their shot...their crack at the Pantheon and their place inside it. But this pantheon seems more like the one in Rome where the lawless traffic has to clash and intermingle with pedestrians and there's no real set way in terms of direction on the streets other than survival even in your car. If it weren't for the painted lines in the road giving the illusion of car lanes, driving in this section of the Bronx might seem like dodging tourists in the Eternal City. Even Squeegee Man is out tonight somewhere closer to the outskirts with his bucket and bulging testicle, though the temperatures are down to the low 30s, so Squeegee Man is dressed for warmth.

Oooh, it's so goood, it's so goood, it's so goood, it's so goood, it's sooooo goooood.

Oooh, heaven knows, heaven knows, heaven knows, heaven knows, heh-eh-venn kno-ohs

I feel luuuuh-uuuuh-uuuuh-uv...I feel luuuuh-uuuuh-uuuuh-uv....

I feel luv.

As 1977 rots and festers into autumn, the continuous soundtrack loop in these last months of the year is marked with the voice of Donna Summer. "I Feel Love" haunts the nighttime. It blares from every bar and club that's not overrun with angry straight white guys with microscopic penises. But it's also the sound of a homogenized version of disco that will strip much of the soul and adventurous instrumentation out of the music and replace it with a constant four-on-the-floor beat. While that beat has always been part of the disco sound, it will now become its defining signature, though it probably owes much to some of the more progressive artists in trance music like Philip Glass, Kraftwerk and anything containing layered synthesizers. Historians will later describe this pulsing electronic mandala as the Moroder sound, though he becomes primarily associated with Donna Summer. Still, guitar-driven variations on that sound will influence rock artists in the coming years who all contribute their own version of disco to the pop music canon... artists like Rod Stewart, the Grateful Dead, the Rolling Stones, Pink Floyd, Heart...and of course, Kiss. "Boogie Nights" by Heatwave is also the sound of these first chilly evenings of 1977's final quarter when the putrid stench of the New York summer is dissipating in its last days, leaving the dislocated city desperate for the mercy of some sort of redemption arc.

So maan-eee nn-niiights
I'd sit by-ee mah win-doh-ooo
Waiting for sum-wwun...to sing me his saw-awnnng...

In the waning twilight of '77, one song comes seemingly out of nowhere and climbs swiftly up the pop charts in an immediacy that very few songs from the past could compare to.

So-oh maan-eee drr-eee-he-he-he-he-eems

I kept de-eep inside me-ee
Alone in the da-arrrrk...but now yooooou've come a-law-awnnng...

It's difficult to find a person alive who doesn't completely loathe the song and all its maudlin and saccharine sentimental agita. And it is also difficult to turn on your radio or go into a public place without hearing it.

And you-ooo light up mah-eye la-iiiife
You give me-ee ho-ope...to caa-ree ah-onnn
You light up mah-ah day-ee
And ffiiilll mah nah-eeeeets...with saw-awnnng ...

"You Light Up My Life" by Debbie Boone appeared with the summer-to-fall transition as the baseball season was winding down, and by the time of the World Series has become the number one song in the U.S. That means millions of people have bought the record, and so millions of people must like it. What we don't know at this time in mid-October is that the song is not going away any time soon. The song will be on in your mom's car when she drives you to school. It will be on in your friend's mom's car when it's her turn to carpool. It will be on in the restaurants. It will be on in the shopping malls. Never has a song topped the pop charts for such a prolonged period, nor has any song turned phenomenon so quickly. The song quite simply will be everywhere for the next three months and there isn't a Goddamn thing you can do about it.

Dimaggio throws out the first pitch. At the outset of Game 6, Steve Garvey triples two runs home in the first inning, leaving a deflated sense that this series will end up tied and come down to one last game. Up 2-0 in the bottom of the second inning, Burt Hooton walks Reggie before Chambliss comes up to the plate. Chambliss, who hasn't done much the entire series, smashes a low fastball 400 feet out into the bleachers in right-center field.

The problem with Hooton's knuckle-curve is when he struggles to throw it. Whereas most pitchers of knuckleballs hold the ball with their fingernails, Hooton grips it with two knuckles, pushing out with the fingers giving it the spin to where it usually breaks one of three ways...down and out, down and in, or straight down. When he's off, he's off. The Dodgers early lead is erased as the homerun ties the game. As this has largely been a series of homeruns, the Dodgers regain the lead in the top of the third inning on a solo blast from Reggie Smith.

After the next two half innings prove uneventful for both teams, a pensive Lasorda watches from the dugout with Munson and Jackson coming to the plate in the bottom of the fourth. He knows it was those two who did the damage in the second inning by evening the score. Hooten remains on the mound with the Dodgers leading 3-2. Up to this point, Thurman has hit safely in all nine World Series games he's played in during two consecutive Octobers. He cracks a shot to leftfield where Dusty Baker cuts it off at one bounce, quickly getting it back to the infield where Thurman holds at first base. The Yankee captain has just matched Garvey with eight hits in the series so far. The crowd is awakened into another level of volume, almost as if to insist on or even announce a rally. Jackson steps into the box, scraping his feet in the dirt and quickly settling into his stance. At 6 for 17 in the series, he's homered in the last two games and has an average of .353 going into this at-bat. Hooton pitches once to him. One throw, one swing.

Keith Jackson: Long drive, right field...
Howard Cosell: goodbye!

Yankee Stadium erupts

Howard Cosell: a big, big World Series for Reggie Jackson...despite all the talk about his discontent with Billy Martin...as he comes up with his third homerun of the series. Quickly, the Yankees go ahead.

The two run blast puts the Yankees up 4-3. They will not fall behind again.

Another run in the fourth...a sacrifice fly to leftfield by Lou Piniella drives home Chambliss from third base...the fans bursting in prolonged chants...

Louuuuuuuu...Louuuuuuuu...

...which sounds suspiciously like boos to the national TV audiences unfamiliar with Yankees crowds.

The damage to the Dodgers continues in the bottom of the fifth, picking up at the top of the order. Rivers in his first hit of the game drills a single to right-centerfield. Elias Sosa is already behind, facing Willie Randolph who can hit as well as run fast and Rivers with speed and notorious stealing potential already on base. Rivers takes quite a few lengthy leads off first base as Sosa and Garvey try to pick him off, while Steve Yeager prepares to try and nab him should he attempt to steal second. Rivers doesn't go, but Randolph bunts, leaving a play for Yeager who whips it down the line for Bill Russell to tag Rivers the speedster out on his way to second base. Next up, Munson pops it to center on a short fly ball, causing Randolph to hold up at first base. With two outs, Reggie is back at the plate. The audience mayhem of the fourth inning has died down into a comfortable hum of matter-of-factness... the crowd is relaxed in the game situation...up by two runs, a guy on first and Reggie coming to bat. They're settled into the turn of events these past few days with the Yankee slugger who has awoken to great effect hitting three homeruns in the series to show Billy and George and the rest of New York and the league and all of America and now the whole world that he's held up his end of the deal. It's 5-3 in the bottom of the fifth, and even though there's still a ways to go, the Yankees seem confident, and so do the unsuspecting fans who are now rather tame and quiet as Reggie approaches the batter's box...unsuspecting in a way that everyone is relaxed with what has already occurred last inning. And when Sosa delivers the ball to Reggie, it's one pitch and one swing, and nobody sees it coming.

Keith Jackson: Hard shot, right field, it's gone!

Howard Cosell: Ohhh, what a World Series for Reggie Jackson! Reggie Jackson now well on his way to becoming the most valuable player of the 1977 World Series...if the Yankees go on to win.

Reggie's second homerun of the game is met with ebullience in the Yankees dugout as the entire team gathers round the star in celebration, high-fiving, handshaking, back slapping, hugging their teammate who seemingly may no longer need to prove himself...this is why Reggie is Reggie...this is why George spent all that godforsaken money, and the investment has paid off... and this is why not all players are created equal...because some just know things that the others don't...and they know when it's time to deliver the goods that they've been hired for.

Reggie grabs a spot near the end of the bench, slightly away from the rest of the team and looks directly into the TV cameras.

"Hi mom, that's two!" he says joyfully, though on television we can only see his mouth moving as the roar of enraptured Yankees fans drowns everything else out, though it's clear what he's saying to the camera and his mother who is surely watching as her son cements his legend well into New York, baseball and sports history.

Going into the sixth and down 7-3, the Dodgers need to rethink their strategy of constant power and homeruns. Sure, it's worked for the Yanks in this game, but there have also been base runners, and the Dodgers need to put people on base. They need to start hitting to the opposite field in small ball fashion, put runners on base and drive them home. This is no time for solo homeruns and swinging for the fences.

But the Dodgers go down in the sixth. They also go down in the seventh. In the eighth they're hit with the final exclamation point.

Reggie has already tied a record with the handful of players who have hit four homeruns in one World Series. He is now joined with Babe Ruth, Lou Gehrig, Hank Bauer, Gene Tenace, and Duke Snider who did it twice. But now Reggie's name is on that list. These little statistics that pop up throughout the telecast as three guys in the booth need to fill nine innings and two and a half hours of talk on television, and so these little factoids always seem ready-made for any moment that the players want to throw at you. With that, Reggie throws us another... stepping into the batter's box for the final time in 1977. At this point in the game and what's left of it, it's all Reggie. It's hard for the Dodgers to even remember there's still the top of the ninth and that they're not completely out of it just yet. But now it's just Reggie.

This time, it's Charlie Hough on the mound...the fourth pitcher the Dodgers have used tonight. And like his predecessors, it's just one pitch and one swing. The shot rocks the south Bronx and reverberates throughout the five boroughs, beyond and well into Yankees history and baseball immortality. Reggie sends his third homerun of the game high into the crisp October air in a billowing burst of bombast and into the dark hinterlands beyond centerfield...that blacked-out unused empty area between the right and leftfield bleachers, which is now and forever associated with this magic moment in time.

The chants of Reggie go on as if they never ended during the season, and it now seems eternal. The sound is one with the metropolitan air as it dissipates but hovers amidst the New York City night.

Reggie Reggie
Reggie Reggie

It's a sound that is instrumental in the marketing campaign for what will be the Reggie bar...the candy bar he predicted would be named after him once he left his mark on New York City. And now here we are, as he steps out of the dugout to take a final bow...then sits back down, looking into the camera once again...this time flashing three fingers...and right before our very eyes, Reggie Jackson evolves and transforms mythically and mystically into Mr. October.

The teams transition between innings as the Dodgers come up and the Yanks take the field. Jackson's walk to right field is met with a standing ovation as he waves to the crowd, which is becoming rowdier by the minute, throwing garbage onto the field in Reggie's area. With the Dodgers down to their final three outs, Howard Cosell aptly offers the profound summation as the two teams enter the top of the ninth.

"Look at Reggie Jackson. The whole long season. The altercation in the dugout when his manager Billy Martin precipitously removed him from the game...later substitutions of him...and then swinging those mock swings and saying 'I can only answer one way. That's with my bat. I can come through with my bat.' And he has done just that. What a spectacular performance...and if they go on to win it, as it seems they will, maybe it's true that this was the best team money can buy...but victory hasn't come easy. The Yankees lived the soap opera on the precipice of peril."

Ron Cey, the first Dodger of the inning with his back to the wall, goes down on strikes for the first out.

It's Torrez who remains on the mound to pitch what will hopefully be the final inning and win his second complete game of the series. Steve Garvey fights through a routine ground ball and closely beats Bucky Dent's throw after the shortstop slips and loses his footing. Garvey is alive at first base. Baker comes to the plate with his team down to their final two outs. The last thing he'd want is to ground into a double play, so when he swings away on the first pitch, it clears Bucky Dent and drops into leftfield, leaving two men safely on base and suddenly the Dodgers have something going. In the dugout, Billy wastes no time getting Sparky Lyle up and running in the bullpen. Rick Monday is next and promptly gets behind in the count, 0 and 2 as the NYPD and stadium security begins assembling around the field, many coming out of the stands and jumping the wall. The extra 350 security guards line the perimeter of the field...in place to discourage unruly fans from rushing the field should the Yankees win...or more realistically, to attempt to contain them. The powers that be remember last year when Chambliss was rounding the bases. They remember Shea Stadium when the Mets won in '69, and then again in '73 when they won the pennant. It's become a New York thing to accent New York victories with your fans destroying the playing field and putting your players and each other in danger. Monday stays alive in a series of foul balls, dueling it out with Torres until he rips a high pop up to Reggie who returns it while Garvey advances to third. Vic Davalillo is now front and center. Davalillo played a big part in the Dodgers final win against the Phillies in the NLCS. He has the reputation of a venerable vet and had the good fortune to be called back to the majors from the Mexican league over the summer. He has a World Series ring from his stint with the Oakland A's. Straight away off Torrez's first pitch, he bunts, forcing Nettles to move in with a quick throw to Munson and a failed attempt at getting Garvey at home. The Dodgers are back on the board, and the score is now 8-4 with runners on first and second. The Dodgers are playing small ball, getting the singles and moving the runners along. Billy has gone out to the mound to see Torrez, and this is the part where many would expect him to turn to Sparky in the bullpen. Instead, Billy pats Torrez on the back and walks off the field, leaving his starter in with a vote of confidence.

Debris from the upper deck continues to rain down on the outfield. Reggie is in the line of fire. One fan jumps over the wall, running at him to shake his hand. Reggie obliges and walks the fan back to the stands before quickly trotting off the field at the sound of firecrackers. At first it appears as if he's leaving the game for his own safety, but he stops just short of entering the Yankees dugout, calling for a batting helmet. The team is initially taken aback at the site of Reggie approaching in the middle of play. The helmets are no longer within reach, as they've already been taken into the clubhouse. He waits as the crowd speculates on why he's just standing there in place facing the Yankees dugout. When he's handed a batting helmet, he places it firmly on his head and runs back out to his station where a sea of fans in the lower stands all sit on top of the short porch of the right field wall with their legs hanging over, just inches from the playing field where Reggie is posted just a few feet away. An announcement has been made advising fans to stay off the field, as if that will stop thousands of people. Law enforcement and the reinforced wall of security form a line around the entire stadium, in place and ready for the deluge. The deluge is unleashed by Lee Lacy and a miniscule pop up in the infield that is retrieved by Torrez for the final out. The extra security proves no match for the thousands of fans who storm the field as the Yankees celebrate briefly...jumping, hugging and collapsing just off the pitcher's mound as baseball teams often do when they win something big. Reggie wants no part of it as he runs haphazardly through the converging mob. He's not snubbing his team...he'll celebrate with them in the locker room. He's just running for his life to get there, charging through and around fans looking more like a running back than a right fielder. His teammates have to make it off the field as well, as the situation becomes more dangerous by the second. Reggie, darting forward and maneuvering around fans, knocking a few of them over, is only concerned with getting back to the dugout, which he barely does before he finally loses his balance, falling into the safety of his team who are already making their way to the locker room. The customary team celebration on the field is cut short and eclipsed by the explosive onslaught...the New York City populace...pent up screaming souls exuding years of frustration, rage, grief, fear, loss, budget cuts, garbage strikes, crime, vandalism, burning ghettos, serial killers, relentless media, political warfare, and a cumulative body of losing sports franchises... a synergic rush of humanity in the form of a mass exodus from out of the stands of Yankee Stadium...it all spills onto the ball field in one collective exhalation and all fucking hell breaking loose.

WE'RE THE FACES

And you-ooo light up mah-eye la-iiiife
You give me-ee ho-ope...to caa-ree ah-onnn
You light up mah-ah day-ee
And ffiiilll mah nah-eeeeets...with saw-awnnng...

The Sex Pistols are a foul-mouthed band out of the U.K. that has gotten in the news a lot over the past year after they managed to scare the shit out of the British media for about five minutes. From that five minutes sprang the foundation for what is being called the most revolutionary punk act of them all. Although in terms of authenticity, they've got nothing on the Ramones who predate them...though the first Sex Pistols album has finally been released and they're getting attention on both sides of the ocean, most of it stemming from controversy. In the UK, the lyrics of their song "God Save the Queen" are not greeted favorably as their takes on the monarchy equate it with a fascist regime, while on the other side of the Atlantic, it's their criminal records in the UK that have banned them in the United States. With an American tour set to start in Pittsburgh in late December, the Sex Pistols have been ruled ineligible for visas due to said criminal records which every band member has. Between lead singer Johnny Rotten, guitarist Steve Jones, bass player Syd Vicious and drummer Paul Cook, the charges have ranged from convictions of assault to fines for amphetamine busts and vandalism. Perhaps the assault conviction for Syd Vicious is the worst while the others amount to minor crimes. Still, it is enough for the U.S. government to attempt to stop these lawless anarchists from coming into the States! *Beware those godforsaken Sex Pistols! It is astounding how such youthful sneering snot-nosed little shits with their leather and ripped jeans and fishnet shirts and short spiky hair could have such a chaotic impact on the good of humanity! Stop these motherfuckers! Stop them!*

Youth is always key. The legends of fall spanning the vast spectrum of popular culture this year like any other year, or for that matter, all throughout history...are young. Granted, Thurman and Reggie are 30 and 31, though Guidry is 27 like most of his contemporaries in and outside of sports. Julius Erving, the pride of New York City a little over a year ago, who took his talent and headed for Philly where he is now revolutionizing the game of basketball, mostly from midair, is also 27. The average age of Kiss is 28. *Star Wars* hero, Luke Skywalker is 25 while George Lucas is still young at 32. Travolta in his white suit in a pose looking nothing like Barbarino but soon to be iconic is appearing on posters for this disco movie that's opening soon. These tantalizing ads are everywhere. He is now 23. It is an undisputed fact that much of the greatest and most influential creativity in every possible capacity has been made by kids in their twenties. But in our story, we also have the mentors, sages and overseers who play vital roles. The guys like Martin and Steinbrenner and Robert Stigwood, all in their esteemed and respected ancient forties serving as the elder statesmen who in their managerial, production, directorial, mythical or mystical roles preside over the actions, destruction and genius of the extravagant and brutal youth. Even Berkowitz at 24 is influential to someone...whoever they are, wherever they are....whether future serial killers who might seek their own notoriety or some conspiracy nuts spinning the entire Son of Sam story into a hoax containing decades of unsupported dribble about satanic cults. For better or worse, youth informs the culture.

In the Bronx, the turmoil is still oozing. One would think it would alleviate itself after a World Series Championship. But no. It oozes.

So here is Martin who was nearly fired two or three times this past year, at least within the speculation of the press, and now it's George who's telling the press that Billy is his number one priority for the future.

"The first thing I plan to do is sit down with Billy Martin and Gabe Paul and see what it will take to keep the Yankees on top. That's what we did last year after we lost to the Cincinnati Reds. We made up our minds it was not going to happen again."

Di Maggio has already referred to them as another dynasty.

The second free agent market is only a few weeks away.

The key players aren't as optimistic. Captain Thurm has no illusions about the *one-big-happy-family* façade that's been attached to the team in the last few weeks, as in a perfect world this might be the case as everything gets resolved with a happy ending. Bullshit.

"I can't go through another year like this, no way," he tells reporters following the game. "The series is going to hit me in a couple of days, but I was happier when we won the playoff just because of all the stuff we've been through and being under the gun all the time. I'm tired...I'm happy it's over."

Piniella is even more morose in his assessment.

"I don't think this club can take another year, another two weeks, another week of all this. You don't have to be one big happy family to concentrate on playing ball. But if everything isn't going to be tranquil, we might as well write off playing ball next year. I am emotionally drained from this season... all the questions about our internal problems. If things don't change from how they were this year, we'll be a good fourth place club next year."

George doesn't see it that way. He believes the adversity and inner turmoil made them even stronger and without it they may not have come this far. Critics still question whether the turmoil will ultimately sink them. Still, will it last that long? It's no secret that Munson would like to be traded...preferably somewhere closer to his home in Ohio. There is also speculation that Rivers would like to go back to the California Angels where he spent six seasons before coming to New York. Nettles, Figueroa and backup catcher Cliff Johnson are also not very happy and the rumors fly about their desire to be anywhere else. On the surface it's apparent that George has a lot more on his plate for next year than just making Billy Martin happy.

When Kiss gathered in Passaic, New Jersey in September to randomly record some unexpected tracks at the Capitol Theater, not everybody was privy to what was happening or what for. Even Ace wasn't there through most of it, though he probably should have been and was far too busy ingesting substances to show up. A studio musician and acquaintance of the band named Bob Kulick was then recruited to play lead guitar on the small handful of songs. Kulick had auditioned for Kiss in 1972, but his bald head and mustache weren't conducive to the rock and roll image that Paul and Gene were trying to convey. They had him sign a non-disclosure agreement and then they told him to play like Ace. The songs aren't unlike what we hear on the *Love Gun* album and are a natural extension and seem to be the logical progression toward the next studio album. Songs like "All American Man" and "Larger Than Life" could easily have come off *Love Gun*. "Larger Than Life" is yet another vehicle for Gene's demon and bears a twin brother resemblance to "Almost Human," while both are obvious distant cousins to "Watchin' You" from 1974's *Hotter Than Hell*. This is Kiss still sounding like Kiss. But the band only records five songs, and not a single person out there even remotely suspects that the last of this sound has already been permanently etched into history, and never to be heard again. With more tour dates coming up and concert advertisements still showcasing the *Love Gun* album cover, there is no evidence or even talk of a new studio album. By mid-October, however, the songs have already fulfilled their fate, as Kiss fans across the spectrum of six years old to 26 experience the same visual shock to the system and it arrives unexpectedly in the form of a fast-paced, quickly-cut TV commercial. It begins mid-scene...

...the KISS logo blinking letter by letter from left to right over the glaring and streaking stairways of the *Love Gun* stage while the members of Kiss sail through the air by way of the hydraulic lifts that carry them down to the floor. The ferocious roar of Eddie Balandas in mid-sentence...

"...THE HOTTEST BAND IN THE WORRRLD...KIIIISSS!!!!"

Then the quick flashes of rapidly moving scenes that last no longer than a second each...

Paul at the microphone greeting the crowd...

"I feel uptiiight on a Saturday na-ah-iiiite..."

Ace shaking a smoking guitar...

A seated Peter singing "Beth..."

Gene breathing a fireball, the camera placed below at an angle that makes the bat lizard stance all the more an iconic pose in its own time...

Gene shaking his head violently while a trail of blood dribbles out of his mouth and down his chest, breaking off into assorted pieces into the air...

A visual of the stage and it's concert-ending finale of full unrelenting pyrotechnic splendor...

And all the while, each scene is cut with the ultimate unexpected visual that blinks on and off the screen in split millisecond fashion as if subliminal...an unknown album cover...unseen by any fan until now, but now it's become quite clear of what is happening. The enormity of the letters on the album is shocking at first...for Kiss as an in-your-face band, this is as in-your-face as it gets. The expansive Kiss logo in red and blue takes up the top half of the cover while the bottom half is filled with colossal red letters and one tantalizing Roman numeral...

ALIVE II

Then the voiceover...

> *"You've waited two years to hear it! Kiss...Alive 2! The most spectacular performances in the history of rock and roll! Kiss...Alive 2! A special two-record set with five new songs...a full color Kiss history book...and a Kiss surprise! Kiss...Alive 2...from Casablanca Records and Filmworks!"*

Whoah!!!!

There's a Kiss Alive 2????

A Kiss surprise????

You mean like the surprise at the bottom of a cereal box????

No way!

Kiss Alive 2!!!!!

And you-ooo light up mah-eye la-iiiife
You give me-ee ho-ope...to caa-ree ah-onnn
You light up mah-ah day-ee
And ffiiilll mah nah-eeeeets...with saw-awnnng...

On Tuesday, November 1, President Carter signs a minimum wage increase designed to go from $2.30 to $3.25 an hour by 1981 much to the chagrin of the conservatives. On Friday, November 4, *Looking for Mr. Goodbar* opens in New York City. It's a lurid peak into the dark side of an alienation existing in the hidden cracks of the disco scene and singles bars, ultimately resulting in brutal murder. On Sunday, November 6, *I Claudius*, a brand-new landmark television event premieres on PBS's *Masterpiece Theater*. On the following day, the sky opens up, and the rain falls on the tri-state area with torrential downpours and hurricane-force winds pounding New York City. It continues into the second Tuesday of November...Election Day, as voters brave the treacherous conditions to make Ed Koch the new mayor of New York City.

On Saturday, November 11, NBC presents *The Godfather* "as you've never seen it before"...running a three-night edit of both films, parts one and two with the storyline cut into chronological order and glued back together into one long seamless mini-series. The start of the following week sees the premier of *Battle of the Network Stars* in which the most famous celebrity TV stars of CBS, NBC and ABC form teams to compete in sports events.

On the third Tuesday of November, another cultural moment when Hollywood's first answer in the post-*Star Wars* reaction is offered by Steven Spielberg. *Close Encounters of the Third Kind* has its premiere at the Ziegfeld. Spielberg for a short time sat atop the box office revolution that seemed to have begun with *Jaws*. The lines for *Star Wars*, however, eclipse even *The Exorcist*, which for better or worse brought us into a no-turning-back age of ruthless unrelenting shock value in Hollywood. In *Star Wars*, George Lucas took the mountain top for himself. He and Spielberg are film school contemporaries and remain friends, though they will both enter a back-and-forth dialogue and change the course of cinema and pop culture over the next few years. Like *Star Wars* and *Jaws*, *Close Encounters* will join the pop cultural fad of having its name slapped on bubblegum trading cards.

The bubblegum series will extend to Elvis in 1978, a Hollywood remake of *Sgt. Pepper's Lonely Hearts Club Band*, and the late 1977 masterpiece that nobody sees coming...*Saturday Night Fever*. On the last night of November, CBS runs a double shot of Christmas cheer, delivering the annual tradition of the animated *Rudolph the Red-Nosed Reindeer* first, but it's the second feature that becomes an historical pop cultural moment when audiences are invited to share one last Christmas with Bing Crosby. Just a month after his death, his television special *Bing Crosby's Merry Olde Christmas* airs posthumously with guests Twiggy, Ron Moody, Stanley Baxter, and the Trinity Boys Choir. However, it is the random meeting between Crosby and David Bowie that has people talking. This iconic respected legend of a bygone era wrapped in traditional values and perhaps the biggest star of a generation that looked down upon and cursed rock and roll...and a young rock star high on the chain of modern day popular culture, already a vital artist of the Seventies...and a beautifully arranged performance of "Little Drummer Boy" as two of the biggest artists of their respective eras join together in their mutual love of a song and in the common bond of the Christmas spirit.

While *Saturday Night Fever* will certainly appeal to disco culture, it is on the surface a dark gritty urban drama, not unlike New York City's portrayal in Seventies cinema up to this point in time. That is where it ends, however. In some ways, the film is even grittier in its depiction of racism and sexism. The language that the studio was concerned about is still very much intact as the dialogue is proportionately laced with racism and profanity. Perhaps with mainstream audiences in mind, the film depicts a homogenized disco crowd and doesn't touch anything taboo in terms of asking the audience to attach themselves to homosexual characters...the Faces are absolutely 100 percent heterosexual. Had Travolta's character been gay, the film would never have much of a chance in any capacity...not in 1977. Homosexuality is treated as an anathema. In the film's one subtle brush with it, a gay couple is met in the park with derogatory comments from the Faces as they pass each other. That is the extent of it. Still, there are the multiple camera pans on Travolta's body as he wears nothing but a small pair of briefs, and while that may titillate the women, it feeds the suggestion of Travolta and his character as something less than a man...perhaps something less than heterosexual that all the macho hotheads making fun of the film as something inherently gay attribute to both the Tony character and to Travolta himself.

Oh, he likes that gay disco music...look at that white suit...that's gay!

For the late Boomers and their Gen X kids, "gay" used outside its homosexual connotation goes from happy and joyous to illegit...stupid...lame... uncool...embarrassing...cringe...

GAY!

I have gay homework over the weekend!

I don't want to do math, math is GAY!

But it's Sunday...I want to sleep late...I don't wanna go to gay church! Church is GAY!

Jesus is GAY!

Dad, why can't we ride in your Mustang? Why do we have to go in mom's gay car?

That's GAY!
This is GAY!
They're GAY!
You're GAY!

GAY!!

For fans of *Welcome Back Kotter* and John Travolta, it will be a shock to the system to hear their heartthrob casually uttering racial slurs so loosely. The backseat rape that happens while the Faces nonchalantly cruise around in Bobby's car will also be an uncomfortable moment for the casual filmgoers and perhaps American cinema in general. Given the nature of the language and subject matter, the film ends up being closer than expected to the raw urban drama that Avildsen envisioned, even with such a strong focus on the music.

Saturday Night Fever opens with a wide shot of the World Trade Center, the Woolworth Building and the Brooklyn Bridge and pulls away to an aerial shot around the Verrazzano Bridge...the helicopter footage sweeping swiftly over Bay Ridge, reminiscent of the opening shots of *Dog Day Afternoon*. Only swooshing winds and distant traffic can be heard. The music announces itself as an unseen intangible star of the film right at the outset as we hear "Staying Alive" in the opening credits. When the camera follows Travolta's contemporary strut, the walk inevitably empties out onto Seventy-ninth Street where Tony Manero begins running toward home. From the first shot we see of him running down the street, we hear the Bee Gees singing the words, "I'm going nowhere..." and thus begins our entrance into Tony's life at the age of 19 where we've already seen the details of his dead-end job selling paint for Mr. Fusco at a local hardware store. Next, we see Tony in his bedroom preparing for the big Saturday night.

His room is a reminder that he's not unlike most other teens with modern and completely up-to-date pop cultural icons in the form of posters on his wall...one being the infamous 1976 Farrah Fawcett swimsuit poster...the other is a movie poster of *Rocky*, in a nod to Avildsen. He's fresh out of the shower and blow drying his hair into a perfectly coiffed thick and voluminous pile. When his father later slaps him upside the head, his hair is so high that his hand barely makes contact with Tony's head. Though his priorities may not be exactly where his parents might wish, Tony has his own priorities, and he takes pride in his meticulous appearance. He values clothes and much of his hard-earned pay goes to what he wears to the dance club. He's not totally useless as some in his family might believe.

At the outset of the film, Tony finds his mother in great distress as she waits impatiently for her other son, Frank Jr., to call her on the phone. Frank Jr., Tony's older brother is a priest and one of the only sources of parental pride in this family. While Mrs. Manero often turns to prayer for mundane things like hoping God will make Father Frank Jr. call her, it's simply a reflection of the typical Catholic guilt that Old World Italian and Spanish families had haunting them long into modern times. Upon returning home, Frank immediately reveals to Tony that he's leaving the church after a prolonged crisis of faith and an inner conflict that sees him trying to reconcile his own wants and needs with what his parents wished for him. Mrs. Manero is so proud of Frank as a priest that she crosses herself every time she speaks his name. But lately when Father Frank Jr. looks at his crucifix, all he sees is some guy dying on a cross.

Annette is Tony's dance partner early in the film, and from the outset, two things are clear. One, Annette loves Tony to the point of obsession and would probably do anything for him. And two, Tony doesn't give a shit about Annette, nor does he think she's all that good a dancer and only tolerates her because he hasn't stumbled on anyone special yet. Annette in a way is the lovable mascot of the Faces. She means well, doesn't do anybody any harm, and would probably make for a faithful girlfriend or even wife. Yet, the other guys want to get down her pants and often resent Tony for squandering and mistreating Annette the way he does. One senses that should they ever get down her pants, none of them would give a shit about her either once it happened. When Tony meets Stephanie Mangano, Annette has virtually no chance with him in any capacity...not even on the dance floor as Tony puts an end to their partnership to pursue the older and much more talented Stephanie. In this new dynamic for Tony, the dancing is undeniably flawless in both characters with mutual admiration and respect on both sides...but as a human being, Tony finds himself trying to measure up to Stephanie's expectations of what a worthy partner and friend should be. Stephanie boasts of her office job in Manhattan and of the celebrities who often pass through. She ridicules Tony for not being college educated and missing the cultural references she drops in conversation. She constantly puts him to the test, taunting him...reminding him how she's always trying to better herself which makes her, in plain English, better than him. It eventually becomes easy to see through her own insecurities as the front she puts up in front of Tony and everyone else begins to wear thin in sequences this book will not get into for the sake of not playing the role of spoiler to readers, who in the rare almost unheard of occasion may not have seen the film before picking up this book. But even as Tony assures Stephanie after all her chest-beating about betterment, he too would like to escape from the dead-end world he finds himself in amongst his family and friends, though he knows he hasn't yet found something that makes him feel alive, useful and productive the way dancing has made him feel. As we eventually begin to see the emperor's new clothes scenario revealed in the Stephanie Mangano arc, we realize that she's just as big a loser and cliché as she suggests Tony is, though Tony is real to the extent that he doesn't pretend to be anything he isn't, whereas Stephanie, a Brooklyn girl, tries desperately to fit into the elite world of Manhattan.

Bobby C. The Bobby arc is tragic in that the one Face in the group with a car and a girl is the one who is perceived as the weakest and most vulnerable, and probably the most disliked and abused. Like many, he idolizes Tony and hopes to be able to trust Tony when he confides in him as his life is spinning out of control. As Tony yesses Bobby to no end while borrowing his car and using him at times when it's convenient, he really has no time for Bobby's concerns and personal problems, as he is much too wrapped up in his own life. Bobby, seemingly with nowhere left to turn, ultimately sees this as a betrayal. And when our lovable Verrazzano Bridge reenters the picture, that betrayal plays a role in the film's tragic climax.

Youthful insecurities aside, Tony and Stephanie (or Travolta and Gorney) electrify the dance floor as well as the screen. But it is Tony...John Fucking Travolta who commands the screen and inhabits the public space turning it into his own domain...establishing his presence in the film as one of the most iconic roles in the history of Hollywood. He does this in a matter of three minutes during the solo dance scene that comes some 61 minutes into the film. As the Bee Gee's "You Should Be Dancing" is pumped loudly through the 2001 speakers, Tony clears the space with a few subtle moves that lets everyone know he's taking over, prompting the crowd to part down the middle and recede to the edges of the dancefloor. The dizzying sequence is hypnotic as the camera follows Travolta from the floor and through the air, floating under, above and all around him as he pioneers dance moves that the mainstream public has never seen before. The awe-inspiring language of his body and its marriage to the camera producing frame after iconic frame is not only the centerpiece of the film, but an achievement of modern cinema.

While *Fever* has its brutal moments of harsh racist and misogynist sentiment, it's important to note that the film is not unique in these characterizations. And because this is true of so many films of the day, this acknowledgment begs the question of why we need to point out the shock value of these moments...and that is because it holds a mirror to the culture in 1976 and 1977 and this is the way the youth of white lower to middle class America talks. There is also the shock of young Travolta fans who now get to see the actor in a much different light. Some are so young that the film's R rating will keep them from being able to view it, and so they'll still be immersed in the experience through the soundtrack album and bubblegum trading cards that will soon emerge on the market...that is until a censored PG version arrives in the distant future. Mainstream America is the primary audience for *Fever* and most are unaware of Cohn's article or of the film's origins. Those in the know among the elitist crowd who know the film's origins have some idea of what to expect in the storyline, but among both sides of Cohn's article, those who know and those who don't have no idea that they will be watching something that changes the cultural zeitgeist. You know you're in for something...you're just not sure what. That doesn't last long though...because upon first viewing, there's something exhilarating about watching in anticipation as the guys walk into 2001 Odyssey for the first time in the film and they're acting like typical wiseass knuckleheads and it's Travolta's character who asserts his authority over the group as well as his sense of class as he scolds them...

"Shape up you assholes...we're the Faces."

...and you know right then and there that nothing will ever be the same again.

December '77

In Madison, Wisconsin on December 3, the mishaps of the road continue when a beer bottle comes sailing through the air out of the audience and straight into Paul's head causing the show to come to an abrupt but brief stop. A few days later in St. Louis, Ace and Peter venture out into the Midwest nightlife with security guards Eddie Balandas and Rosie Licata and two local police officers. They pull up to a local hick bar in a limousine and once inside, immediately end up in the middle of a fight. Patrons inside the establishment already in fighting motion steal the batons and guns off the cops while Balandas and Licata scramble to get Ace and Peter outside to safety.

The absolute peak of Kisstory begins on Wednesday, December 14 and will play itself out over the next three nights. Unknown acts, Detective and Piper are picked to open these landmark Garden shows...the latter being one of Aucoin's latest ventures in expansion. Outside Madison Square Garden, the weather is mild but rainy and Kiss fans sprint in unity to get inside the venue. If New York City is the nerve center of the world, then tonight, Kiss finally rules the world.

By Friday, December 16, WNEW television has announced that the Sunday Morning staple *Wonderama* will be going off the air after 25 years. Metromedia so far has offered no explanation or information aside from the fact that it will no longer exist after next week, nor will Charlie Chaplin who will be dead in nine days. To borrow a word of the future, the pure fuckery of 1977 is offering no letup and seems poised to squanter around with its ass in your face right up until the New Year. But the sixteenth of December is both a peak and a crossroads of sorts

Hot off the sequencing of *Alive II* and their memories of the past tour, most kids are expecting the band to open with "Detroit Rock City," though many are taken aback when they come out to "I Stole Your Love," the opening track on *Love Gun* and the steady opener on the *Love Gun* tour...though the *Love Gun* trek didn't quite hit New York and you can't track setlists on the Internet so there is a true sense of surprise to kids who have no idea that "Detroit Rock City" hasn't been the opener on this tour. But even this tour is not the same tour. With this production at the Garden being in promotion of the new double live album now in stores, it is more or less the same setlist and stage show that have been presented in promotion of *Love Gun*. It's all there for the kids to witness in glorious real life when they come to Madison Square Garden to see the hottest band in the world. The hottest band in the world...the hottest band in the whole fucking world and it's been drilled into their heads for as many times as they've dropped the needle to hear the maniacal screams of Eddie Balandas telling them it's about to happen...rewarding them for wanting the best...and so they're going to get the best...the hottest band in the world. And when they see it come to life...what they've only known in pictures...those seven foot tall, larger than life superheroes that really fucking exist. They're not Superman and Batman...those fictional fucktoids that have absolutely nothing to do with real life, and if you hate science fiction and the promise of heroes that never quite jump off the pages of comic books, you're in for disappointment. But Kiss is real...and there they are in the flesh and in the silver and black and the fire and the flash.

The razzle and the dazzle and even the frazzle...sparks soaring as fountains ...the luminosity of the grand orange and yellow aura and emanation filling an atmosphere where everything is the color of fire.

Teetering on the brink of madness, the confetti storm rains down over the Kiss domain and well into the ecstatic crowd bathed in the purple blue and black that envelops the darkness of the audience while the residual orange and yellow spills in faint traces over the first few rows of a crowd populated by the youth of the 1970s...rock soldiers in unison with their jubilant arms reaching upward to the heavens in a spectacle of sensory overload with lights blaring...guitars braaaghhmming ...screaming voices shredding, throats tattering...the metabolic thermal energy of body heat high in the red...sweat spattering...the mass exaltation of the Garden, echoing like the collective exhalation of Yankee Stadium, but much louder with bombs blasting...rocking the fuck out of the foundation. New York City has been Kissed.

The guys meet up with friends and family after the first two shows, spending quality time catching up after nearly a full year on the road. These three nights at the Garden is their crowning achievement...the pinnacle acknowledging and recording for all of time and all of forever how big this thing called Kiss became. It has been their victory lap and the post-show celebrations are reserved for loved ones. It is the party planned for the final night at the Harkness Ballet School that will let the rest of the debaucherous world of fame and fortune inside where not only do they mingle with high society, but high society comes to them where people like Andy Warhol and George Plimpton are there more for the event. But for now, it's just friends and family. That's Gene, Peter and Ace...not Paul. Paul heads out of the Garden alone, escaping out of makeup into the New York City night, just a regular person blending in with the anonymous mass of unknown humanity...heading six blocks east and two blocks north to Sarge's Delicatessen. Just one-half hour ago, he was Paul Stanley, arguably the biggest rock vocalist in the world as of this December in late 1977, and no question the biggest in New York City. But walking into Sarge's he is just Stanley Eisen, his ever-present anonymous self who no matter how rich and famous he becomes, he'll never rid himself of. Though he gets to enjoy this anonymity in ways most famous people can't, he along with the other members of Kiss are beginning to feel the trappings of the makeup and the fact that Kiss only exists onstage, and not in the real world. Kiss completely disappears once the makeup is washed off and four regular unrecognizable people hit the streets. It becomes an issue at times for all four members, although it's Paul and Gene who need the constant attention and notoriety. In the Garden, he was adored by nearly 14,000 screaming fans tonight. Now in the late-night florescence of Sarge's, nobody knows who he is, and nobody has any idea that the lead singer of the biggest band in America is sitting there alone eating matzo ball soup. The ever-present dynamic of fans crowding celebrities in public places asking for autographs and pictures is something the guys in Kiss don't get to experience ...but sometimes egos need the notoriety and recognition. Paul enjoys the fact that he can go out in public and not have to deal with the rush of rabid sycophants, but it probably doesn't help when he's locked in his own mind...his troubles and insecurities that haunt him straight back to childhood always forcing their way front and center. He's Stanley Eisen...still the frightened child with one ear, afraid to make connections with people...afraid to trust...afraid to love...afraid of himself and of being alone...and without the Kiss face paint, nobody knows who he is and nobody really cares. He's invisible. As Kiss peaks, and everything Paul had hoped and wished for has come true, his inner world is just as unsettling as it was before the fame. No amount of money can fix what's broken inside. And that is the lesson we learn from the trials and tribulations of Paul's ride as a rock star. It isn't all glamorous and your sense of still being one of the regular people never fully goes away...especially when you can't get recognized as one of the regular people...nor as a rock star once the makeup comes off.

With the release of *Alive II* and the subsequent tour, Kiss will be at their absolute peak from the remainder of 1977 through the entirety of 1978. The *Alive II* tour is essentially an extension of the *Love Gun* tour. While our trip through Bicentennial era America ends at this moment in time, it's helpful to consider the idea that bands and artists survive and navigate the peak of success according to the decisions they make to follow up that success. With this in mind, it is significant to consider the decisions Kiss makes among the choices they will have from this moment on. Kiss will tour until April 1978 and then for the first time in four years, they'll get off the road and go home. It will mark their first extended break since they toured the debut album. In the time since, they've run eight consecutive tours almost seamlessly. They've released six studio albums, two live albums and a collection of the original three releases...essentially a box set without the box. They've won countless readers polls in musical fanzines, scored endorsements with premier names in rock and roll instrumentation, watched two major hit singles run up the pop charts and even won a People's Choice Award. Then there's that age old wisdom that says what goes up must come down...though none of that will happen until 1978 plays itself out. But how will 1978 play itself out? Going into the year, it seems as if Bill Aucoin and his highly successful venture can go anywhere they want. They can navigate this peak any way they see fit. Musically, they could go in any direction. Visually, they can do the same thing. Most bands of mega success in the 1970s quietly go away and spend a few years between albums (thinking Pink Floyd, Led Zeppelin, Yes). When Kiss enters 1978, they still have the ball in their hand. They still have the option to ride the success and proceed in a dignified manner...one that would not make a mockery of that success or their very existence. But instead of going away, they embark on a series of questionable decisions that will haunt them for all of Kisstory.

They begin in April with a self-congratulatory double album release called *Double Platinum*...a celebration and marker of the first collective era of Kiss that will also serve as a musical coffin preserving glimpses of a moment in time that came and went too soon, as many fans of the original lineup of Kiss would lament for the next fifty years. One month later, Aucoin has them at Magic Mountain in California...filming a Kiss movie...a celluloid spectacle pitched to them as *Hard Day's Night* meets *Star Wars*. By the end of summer, the commercialization of Kiss shoots the band into the stratosphere with a seemingly nonstop barrage of Kiss merchandise including a much-coveted set of Kiss figures (referred to as the "Kiss dolls"). If Kiss was not meant for children, you'd never know it. But while Christmas 1977 may mark the dignified peak of Kiss, Christmas 1978 marks the oversaturation peak of Kiss...an overwhelming period when it seems like Kiss could do no wrong...and a period when nobody knew that the damage had already been done. They say when you stand too close to something, you can no longer see it. On the surface, the last quarter of 1978 will see the release of the Kiss figures, Kiss bubblegum cards, Kiss Halloween costumes for children, the made-for-TV movie, *Kiss Meets the Phantom of the Park* and the simultaneous release of the Kiss solo albums...four individual records showcasing the talents of each of the band members serving as the exclamation point on the overexposure of Kiss, and one big financial debacle for Casablanca Records and Filmworks. Among the expanding ventures of Aucoin...Piper and Starz will no longer exist in a few short years as Bill's own excessive lifestyle and penchant for arrogantly biting off much more than he can chew assures that those acts under his leadership never have a chance. Of the four Kiss solo albums, the only one that gets any real radio airplay (remember, radio is still important!) is Ace's with his cover of Hello's "New York Groove" invading the airways all the way to number 13...one full year after the last Kiss single, Ace's "Rocket Ride" hit the Top 40.

For as much as Paul and Gene in later years will remain relentlessly persistent in downplaying the roles of Peter and Ace, it is ironic that in terms of accolades and achievements in the band's name, at least statistically, that among the nine Kiss and Kiss-related songs that make it into the Billboard Top 40 (for better or worse the gold standard metric of musical popularity in America), four of those nine ("Beth," "Hard Luck Woman," "Rocket Ride," "New York Groove") are sung by Peter and Ace, while three of the six highest-charting Kiss/Kiss-related songs ("Beth," "Hard Luck Woman," "New York Groove") are sung by Peter and Ace. Perhaps some fans may consider these unchangeable facts as nitpicking in defense of Peter and Ace. But when we consider the rise of Kiss and everything entailed in their inevitable climb to the top of the world of rock and roll and popular culture, we must remember that the four original members of Kiss share equally in that rise and peak, no matter how much Paul and Gene will continue to re-interpret the history in order to justify questionable decisions they'll go on to make years later under the banner of Kiss and in the name of the band's legacy... and the band's legacy is precisely the legend based entirely on that rise and peak...the period in which this book has been about.

Over the course of the excessive 1978, Ace and Peter's drug and alcohol abuse will continue and there will be more car crashes. Gene will become a tabloid fixture once he starts dating Cher while being caught mingling around high society without his Kiss makeup...forcing him to constantly walk around with one hand holding a dinner napkin in front of his face to conceal his identity when the cameras start flashing. Paul, ever lonely even in his intimate relationships will stay busy in the New York City nightlife... keeping his finger on the pulse of the trends...collaborating with a young writer named Desmond Child in an exercise in writing outside his comfort zone...in search of Kiss's next direction while they themselves in drips and drabs begin to experiment with disco. When the next Kiss album, *Dynasty* appears in May 1979, the tagline of the event will be dubbed "The Return of Kiss"...when in fact, Kiss never goes away. Historians of the band forever dissecting the ups and downs and what went wrong, always tend to blame *Dynasty* and the disco hit "I Was Made for Loving You" as the beginning of the decline in popularity, and there is indeed some truth to the idea that yes, some of the purists jumped ship. But the real beginning of the end of the original Kiss experience happens in the overexposure of 1978...something that Kiss never recovers from.

And yet...

Kiss becomes the band that most future bands cite as their first and biggest influence in the 1980s and 1990s. Though metal will come along to dominate the Eighties and grunge will define at least the early part of the Nineties, the common link will be Kiss. Kiss will be as much an influence to grunge as they are to metal and even country and pop, uniting acts like Motley Crue, Nirvana, Pearl Jam, Smashing Pumpkins, Garth Brooks, Lenny Kravitz, John 5, and Rage Against the Machine amidst dozens more under the same blanket of influence, while most influential hard rock guitarists over the next fifty years will cite Ace Frehley as their first guitar hero. With respect to the Kiss performance aesthetic, the *Love Gun* stage show becomes the template for stage designs and the gold standard by which future hard rock shows are measured.

But that's the future.

For now, we remain where this particular story and book ends...on the night of Friday, December 16, 1977 where Kiss has just celebrated a triumphant homecoming at Madison Square Garden during this holiday season of a banner year for rock performances inside this historic venue.

But even as Kiss rocked the Garden and rock and roll was still front and center, other parts of New York City were dancing tonight, while in the movie theaters it's Hollywood that's put the rest of America on notice that it'll be informing the trends for a while, thus marking those cultural crossroads that are imprinted as a result. *Saturday Night Fever* opened tonight in all its history-altering glory. Within one week, the soundtrack's first single, "How Deep is Your Love" goes to number one, finally knocking out "You Light Up My Life" after 11 smash weeks. Fever's release party is held at Tavern on the Green, followed seamlessly by a party at Studio 54 where celebrity tabloid civilization will for better or worse ring itself out through the remainder of the decade.

Saturday Night Fever will spill into 1978 as the hottest film in America and the soundtrack quickly becomes the biggest selling album of all time, eclipsing Fleetwood Mac's *Rumours* which had just set that record a few months earlier. The single "How Deep is Your Love" enters the year at number one with a second single for "Staying Alive" rapidly climbing the charts. Not only has disco officially entered mainstream America...it has become the zeitgeist. If there is one element of disco that could sum up the entire experience, that word is inclusion. Having come a long way on multiple aspects of sociological evolution if you were black, gay or female, the traction first gained in the 1960s all the way back to Civil Rights, the Stonewall and women's lib all blossomed under one blanket of inclusion. Whereas these one-time outcasts of society had to exist on the fringes where the club scene had to happen underground, everyone came together in the mid-late Seventies discotheques. They were festive happy gatherings where dancing was the common purpose and experience. On the surface, this seems a welcome change in America socially and overall, culturally. But the transatlantic interest in dismantling any remaining racial boundaries will be met with a backlash in the States more hostile than any backlash against one form of music has ever been seen. Things will get ugly as a war on disco perpetuated and facilitated by rock fans and disgruntled reactionaries more bent on traditional conservative values becomes its own short-lived subculture. The racially motivated segment of that backlash is already exemplified in *Saturday Night Fever*...not necessarily as reverberation against disco...these guys love disco...but in the racism and homophobia that feeds the backlash throughout the rest of the country. The characters of the film and the tiny world they inhabit are a microcosm of the larger picture and the bigotry that stretches end to end across America will to a significant degree be at the heart of the backlash against disco.

The Yanks in their post-championship glory make out famously from free agency when they sign relief pitcher, Rich Gossage to a six-year contract for three and a half million dollars on November 22. Between Gossage and Lyle, the Yankees have put together an impeccable bullpen. At 26, Gossage, whose nickname is "Goose," put together 11 wins, 26 saves with a 1.62 earned run average with the Pittsburgh Pirates in the past season. In terms of relievers, Goose Gossage is about the best there is. While the specifics of this monstrous contract have not been discussed with the public, Steinbrenner is optimistic in the face of critics and fans raising eyebrows at the amount of money to be paid to Gossage.

"I think I made a great business deal," George tells reporters. "Relate the cost to what the man can do for us, and I think it was a great deal for us."

Rightfully, the boss isn't content to rest with a championship, and neither is the team. They want a dynasty and the boss will move to right things with his disgruntled players and make whatever necessary moves to make that dynasty happen. In the following year, the team will indeed become that dynasty with a second World Series championship. The season will begin with the official release of the Reggie bar...that irresistible concoction of chocolate, peanuts and caramel...the candy bar that Reggie fearlessly predicted would be named after him, and the home opener crowd will flood the field with candy wrappers in appreciation of their star centerpiece. Guidry will also measure up to the hype, laying down a landmark 24-3 season, as well as a single game strikeout record, earning himself the nickname Louisianna Lightning. While the collective dysfunctional tumult doesn't end, it's best to repeat what is often said here...that's for another book.

Yet, there is nothing organic about the Steinbrenner-era Yankees. This team is the result of collecting a bunch of competing egos through a much-maligned new system of free agency where players could be bought for multi-million-dollar contracts...a time when the Yankees become notorious as baseballs tyrannical plutocrats. It was a time of shakeup to the business structure of baseball ...one in which the Yankees become longtime beneficiaries, and indeed the best team money could buy.

Following the Son of Sam case and the capture of David Berkowitz along with the death of Elvis, the sensationalist nature of tabloid media will escalate astronomically and ruthlessly over the decades and there will be no turning back as America inevitably abandons the occasional innocence of a Special Report and descends into the daily abyss of Breaking News. Rupert Murdoch will not stop with the tabloid world and will eventually take unapologetic advantage of the Reagan era overturning of the Fairness Doctrine, thus allowing him to lay the groundwork for FOX News and the politicization and blatant editorialization of TV news and media. These past 18 months that begin with the Bicentennial summer and end with the release of *Saturday Night Fever* cultivate what will profoundly alter and reshape the way sports, music, live entertainment, politics, film, television and news are presented long into the future. The plentiful visuals wrapped in Bicentennial chic that dominate the universality of style in America during the mid-1970s have run their course. The flag imagery has largely gone away or dissipated into the past. By 1978, it has been replaced by the imagery of a commercialized Hollywood that has quickly become the hub of pop culture...soundtracks...fashion trends...T-shirts, bed sheets, toys from *Jaws* to *Star Wars* to *Close Encounters of the Third Kind* to *Charlie's Angles* to nipple-popping Farrah Fawcett posters next to monster-sized Kiss posters alongside all the millions of dollars in Kiss merchandise that swallows 1978. It is the beginning of mass consumptive commercialism on a scale not seen before in popular culture where not only band names and sports teams occupy space on clothing and billboards, but big corporate logos and names occupying every possible free inch of space in the twenty-first century. Even professional basketball will never be the same once the merger revolutionizes the game and the way it's played with the advent of the slam dunk, and the holy three-point play while the league inevitably becomes a breeding ground for corporate endorsements. What may have inadvertently had its seeds planted in the 1976 merger will come to full fruition within a decade.

None of it is a planned conspiracy to sell sneakers and give Nike a lock on the NBA…but that's just the way it all unfolds.

And what about the Bicentennial itself? This was America in a time when for possibly the first time in its history, the nation simultaneously struggled with its past and future along with its very identity. Political tensions, social strife and environmental concerns were all glossed over and even masked by the façade of patriotism and unity. It was a time when the influence of the holy dollar began establishing a foothold in places once believed symbolically, morally or ethically sacred and no more fucks were given when it came to cashing in on anything and everything. So Bicentennial branding, though scoffed at, became inevitable, sparking revelations for the corporate-thinking mind about the possibilities of capitalism and commercialism in the face of major stories that need not always be hijacked in the name of making a buck. This, for better or worse, became the American Way and we've never looked back…and though many are naïve enough to believe the American Way is linked to the American Dream, some still believe in the American Dream. They believe in it because it shows us what we could be…when it's the American Way that shows us what we actually are. Still, we could wrack our brains trying to come up with some sort of legacy for the Bicentennial when the event came and went and all years of planning for things that never materialized went up in smoke. America during this period was as it always had been, with the latest generations of a white European lineage dominating the culture, just as it had from the moment they set foot to eliminate the natives from their home and forge their own bloodstained imprint. In 1976, politics, science, the medical profession, sports, music, film, television and fashion are still largely governed and managed by middle to upper class white Christian men who inform and control every aspect of the culture while minorities from every walk of life remain marginalized punchlines.

For Native Americans the abomination of those two hundred years is nothing to celebrate and merely amounts to a few centuries of oppression. What about African Americans? Frederic Douglass had already long made his views about America's so-called Independence Day in one of the more vital works of early American literature… Never mind the fact that the Declaration of Independence says nothing about women and slavery. The promise of life, liberty and the pursuit of happiness didn't hold true for so many, though it shamelessly was derived from John Locke's ideas that conveniently states life, liberty and property and so it's quite clear where blacks and women stood within what men were entitled to. Vietnam Vets who faced difficulties after coming home from the war felt largely betrayed by their government and by their country in general, also took issue with the celebrations and used many an occasion to talk about the war in relation to the false sense of patriotism that the Bicentennial seemed to be wrapped in. The official story of America was well-known, and it was a controlled and contrived story, though this period was a time when an unprecedented collectivity of downtrodden, oppressed, unrepresented and persecuted Americans began to tell their own story…and it reflected nothing of the myth of the American Dream.

But the American Bicentennial is merely the backdrop to our story here and only amounts to a single day in the life…and the heart of the 1970s, as we know them, exists within the space of 18 months from June 1976 to December 1977. Everything prior leads directly toward this period. Everything in the future flows directly from it. For the most part, it happens in New York City, though the ripple effects reverberate across America long into the twenty-first century.

It is the moment when subcultures merge into the establishment through mainstream acceptance, often to the chagrin of purists who watch these subcultures flourish on their own organically and now will either lament what they feel is the loss of something…or they'll keep on keeping on while continuing to dance and fuck their way through the remainder of the decade. So while everything crumbles to shit around us, maybe the quiet sentiment is really let's party while we pretend everything is okay and let's just indulge and define ourselves by our popular culture and let it consume us as we try to get our bearings, not even aware in the slightest that we're about to run ourselves off the road while we're busy watching ourselves in the mirror.

24

25, 35, Hello Baby (A Sort of Epilogue)

It's Christmas Eve, 1977 and the water drops on the windows in grandma's kitchen come from a combination of steam from the radiator, the heat of tonight's meal being cooked in the oven and the biting frost of a freezing winter's night outside. I'm seven years old and surrounded by the youth of all my cousins and all the adults comprised of my aunts and uncles and my parents and grandparents who seem old, but even they are still young and filled with promise and hopes and dreams for the future. Everyone is still alive and well. Sickness doesn't exist except for grandpa's asthma, but everyone else is largely healthy. This is the Baby Boomers thriving...the Baby Boomers in their early 30s and raising their kids.

On top of the obvious Kiss albums that the kids are asking for this Christmas, the hot attractions are AFX and Tyco slot car tracks. In much the same way as there are Coke people and Pepsi people, and Beatles people and Rolling Stones people, there are AFX kids and Tyco kids when it comes to the slot car craze. My cousin Pete is two years older than me and he's a Tyco kid. The family calls him Petey. Petey tells me all the time that Tyco is better than AFX, and although he's pretty pushy and always establishing his physical dominance over me, I stand firm and insist AFX is the better racetrack. One thing we do have in common on this Christmas Eve is our love for Kiss. While the adults gather in the dining room of our grandparents house in Elizabeth, New Jersey, it's that early part of the evening where everyone is saying hello and asking each other how everything is...how's work, how's school, what's new and all of the uncomfortable small talk that stains every family gathering well into adulthood until the ice is always broken by my aunt and uncle inevitably arguing about history and politics. During this time, Petey and me run out to the porch on the far end of the house...an addition that was built by my grandfather with his own bare hands and serves as the entrance. The porch is comfortable but cold in the winter. It's just me and Petey and he's trying to show me some karate moves that he learned. Every time I see him, he's always trying to demonstrate some physical feat that requires me to get into some awkward position and match what he's doing or simply be the recipient of some violent move that's going to leave me lying on the floor with the wind knocked out of me.

"Do you know it only takes fourteen pounds of pressure to break your arm?"

All I want to do is go inside and open presents.

"What?" I say from the floor, growing annoyed.

"I said it only takes fourteen pounds of pressure to break someone's arm."

"Oh," I said pretending to be mildly interested.

"So, if I lean on your arm with fourteen pounds of pressure or hit you with fourteen pounds of pressure or kick you with fourteen pounds of pressure or step on your arm with fourteen pounds of pressure, it'll break!"

The sound of steam from the radiator and the hiss and gurgle of water running through a pipe along a wall in the next room is a common and constant sound in this house during the winter months. The windows on the porch three floors over street level are filled with the same frost as the kitchen windows, though the courthouse jail tower is still visible on the horizon. The tower with its pointed crown and red flashing lights at the top is all I can see looming over the frosted portion of the window. Just below the pointed peak of the courthouse is a jail. At least that's what Petey tells me.

He says there's a jail at the top of the building just below the red lights and if I look close enough, I can see the bars on the windows. Up until the past summer, I thought the courthouse was the Empire State Building. Being a little kid, what did I know. I knew that King Kong climbed the Empire State Building, and I knew that the building was in New York. I also knew New York was across the water, but I didn't know that we couldn't see it from our grandparents' window in Elizabeth, New Jersey. But to me, every building with a point and an antenna was the Empire State Building. When we saw the remake of King Kong in the theater, my Empire State Building obsession became a World Trade Center obsession. Over the past year, everyone who has set foot in this house has told me that the building I see from the window is the courthouse and not the Empire State Building, and yet as I watch it from the window I somehow still have a need to believe it's the Empire State Building...so I continue to ask whoever is within earshot. Petey is the only one in the room with me.

"Is that the Empire State Building?" I ask him.

He pushes me aside and glances out into the ethereal night sky.

"Yeah. If you look close enough, you can see King Kong up there."

Footsteps approach from the long hallway connecting the kitchen to the porch. It's my Uncle Armand who walks into the room to say something, but Petey cuts him off, running up to him.

"Hey Uncle Armand, did you know it only takes fourteen pounds of pressure to break someone's arm?"

"Oh yeah?"

"Yeah. So, if I lean on your arm with fourteen pounds of pressure or hit you with fourteen pounds of pressure or kick you with fourteen pounds of pressure or step on your arm with fourteen pounds of pressure, it'll break!"

"That's nice. Do you guys wanna open presents?"

The clutter of the living room on Christmas Eve is one of the annual highlights of childhood. It's when the entire family...parents, grandparents, cousins, aunts, uncles and family friends are all together in an enclosed space at the same time and for one brief shining moment, everyone is happy. It's me, my brother Robert who's four, my mom and dad, my grandparents, my grandfather on my mom's side, my Aunts Teresa and Silvana, Uncles Armando and Bob, and cousins Petey, Angela, Mary and our latest edition, Baby Paul who was born back in February just days after the big blizzard sent its wrath far downstate and beyond while its residual effects were felt in our own lives here in New Jersey. Most of us are seated around the table, though the kids are speckled around the room, running and jumping in anticipation of the presents. The table is actually three tables lined up together and covered by concealing tablecloths that give the impression of one long unit. The dinner we ate earlier began with antipasto comprised of mortadella, salami, ham, provolone, black olives, Spanish olives, anchovies, artichoke hearts, mushrooms, and red peppers. This was followed by linguini with white clam sauce and the traditional seven-fishes comprised of flounder, shrimp, Baccala, eel, scallops, clams and whatever the seventh fish was that I can't remember. And then on every holiday one of the fixtures on the table is the inevitable Panettone cake in the irritating blue box that somebody always brings. Sometimes two people will bring one and then we have two irritating blue boxes on the table. The dreaded Panettone that somebody always brings but nobody ever wants. At least that's how it feels if you're a kid and all you want is chocolate. But the dry, coarse texture is boring, bland and uninspiring to a child, and attempting to eat the Panettone is like biting into fiberglass insulation. As we anxiously await the unwrapping of presents, the table is made up of the Panettone and other assorted cakes, pies, pastries, coffee cups, sugar bowls, and baskets of chestnuts, walnuts, grapes and tangerines.

The opening of the presents is a chaotic crisscrossing of wrapped boxes being handed to one another from all angles and all corners of the room... arms reaching in front of each other's faces in order to reach someone else while someone else is handing you a gift and vice versa. I watch my grandparents open three things...a toaster oven, a Luciano Pavarotti album, and a box set of *La Traviata*. My brother opens up an orange nerf car with big green wheels which he begins rolling up people's backs. My uncle hands me a fairly big box that peaks my curiosity. I carry the box through the crowd of my family out of the living/dining room area and into the kitchen where I find an empty spot on the floor to sit down. I position myself in a little corner between two doorways next to the counter and across from the kitchen table where I can see underneath and everyone's legs and feet walking by. The doorway behind me leads to a long stairway down to the ground level backdoor...a hallway we rarely ever use except to go down to the basement. The doorway to my left leads out onto the porch where the upper entrance to the house is...the room me and Petey were playing in. Sitting there I can feel the cold air coming from the porch where the cool blast clashes with the steam heat of the radiator next to me. I tear the wrapping paper off the box as my brother runs up to me and rolls his orange nerf car up my back, over my head and back down again. He then runs away to do the same to the next person. As my attention turns back to the box, I tear away the remaining paper, and I'm startled by what I see. It's an AFX track! To be precise, it's an AFX Daytona 500 race set featuring three magna traction cars. AFX is made by Aurora, and the brand is endorsed by famous racecar drivers Jackie Stewart, A.J. Foyt and Richard Petty. This particular set caters to Petty who is pictured on the box. What surprises me is that I've already asked Santa Claus for an AFX track. Does this mean I'll no longer get the track from Santa? Or will I end up with two tracks? How does this work? These are the things that are going through my head on Christmas Eve 1977. That is until someone (and I honest to God don't remember who) hands me an album. I immediately know it's an album by the shape. It also feels slightly heavier than an album so I have an idea of which album it is, and because of this, my heart begins to beat rapidly in a sudden surge of excitement that has me ripping the paper away in a mad dash to reveal the visuals that will blow my mind and capture my imagination for the rest of my life.

Kiss.

Alive II.

It is one of the earliest moments of my life where I can remember experiencing the jubilation of getting something in my hands that I've truly pined for and realizing it's all mine...my very own to keep.

I tear the last remnants of paper away and glance over at Petey, who is also sitting on the floor. He too has just unwrapped his own copy of Kiss

Alive II and has already taken off the plastic shrink wrap. I see him open the gatefold sleeve and then I watch his mouth drop wide open. It's the look of stunned disbelief.

"Woah, Michael did you see this?"

"What?"

"Open it, quick!"

Petey and I are in our glory!

I couldn't get the plastic off fast enough, nor was I sure how to. I gave the album to my dad who was passing through the kitchen. He reached into his pocket and pulled out his set of house keys and stuck the pointed end of a key into the opening of the sleeve and slid it to break the seal of the shrink wrap. He gave it back to me and I tore the plastic off. It is important to note at this time that I am only familiar with Kiss as far as the few records I have at home and my only knowledge pertaining to the visuals of the live show is the somewhat bare no-frills element of the stage we see on the cover of Kiss *Alive!* And although I've seen the split-second clips of the current stage show in the all-too-brief *Alive II* commercial, nothing can prepare me for what I see next as I sit cross-legged on my grandparent's linoleum floor, opening the gatefold sleeve of Kiss *Alive II* to reveal the most mind-blowing thing I've ever seen in my short seven-year old life.

I sit stunned, gazing down in wonder at the most captivating concert picture ever taken. Little do I know Kiss took the picture in a photoshoot and not during a concert. Little do I know the band decided to take all the pyro and theatrics used during the course of the entire show and shoot it all off at the same time for maximum effect. Well, they certainly achieved that. In my limited understanding, this is what a Kiss concert looks like for the entire show. Paul, Gene and Ace hovering high above the audience while walls of monstrous flames shoot up from out of the stage...sparks flying, smoke bellowing, bombs detonating with every inch of space on that stage covered in the yellowish reddish orange of fire and flames and red and blue and green and white lights flashing and illuminating the entire thing. Peter is somewhere behind his drums as he too is elevated far above stage level. The lighted *Love Gun* stairs, so prevalent to the stage show in moving and trailing shining motion on either side of the drum riser. This is pure over-stimulation of the senses. In my mind, I can hear this photo as I try to imagine.

What song are they playing?

Is this what the end of "Black Diamond" looks like?

Or is it the end of "Rock and Roll All Nite?"

What's happening here?

Holy fucking shit!

Looking at the rest of the Kiss *Alive II* album, Petey and I are increasingly blown away. The cover is no repeat of the first *Alive*. This seems blatant and in your face with the giant red and blue Kiss letters. The small pictures of the Kiss faces are repeated on the back cover but only larger, taking up some 80 percent of the cardboard. Each band member represented majestically... Paul in deep serious reflection, the starshine of a backlit stage reflecting mystically through his hair...Peter, both jovial and tough, a great representation in facial study, almost peering into the Catman's personality. Ace, another study in mystical light that turns his hair into a fiery halo as the parted lips and eternal empty gaze behind the Spaceman's contemplative face is now burned deep into the retina of 1977. And the demon. Blood drips from his mouth and down his chin, his face and hair drenched in a sludgy foreign wetness that accents the glow of a blue light on his face and the dark slick of a motor oil-like substance. The eyes are shifted upward in a spine-chilling stare and whether intentional or not in its magnitude of macabre and ferocity, this famous shot by....remains by far the greatest picture of Gene Simmons ever taken. *Alive II* is packed with surprises, including a booklet titled The Evolution of Kiss, tracing all five years of the band's existence all the way back to 1973. If you're seven, that is a long time ago. I marvel at how the booklet is broken down by year and at how the band's makeup and costumes have evolved...things I was not aware of until now as it becomes visibly evident that Kiss existed in a time before I'd even heard of them, and here it all is for me to discover. Also dropping out of the record sleeves are the usual merchandise order form with new posters and T-shirts available and a set up Kiss tattoos which Petey and I pester our parents to let us try out. They're temporary, so my mom helps me to press onto my arm a tattoo of my favorite

Kiss member, Ace Frehley. From the TV in the corner of the living room, a commercial advertising *Saturday Night Fever* is running on the screen.

"Oh, I wanna see this!" My mom says loudly.

My dad is having none of it.

"Get outta here," he charges boisterously. "I can't stand that John Revolta."

Just past midnight, we ride along the New Jersey Turnpike headed home. All of our presents are in the car trunk, though I hold onto my Kiss album. My little brother and I are both turned toward the back window with our knees on the seat.

"Sit down the right way, both of you," my mom scolds from the front seat. Between the Bayway refinery and the industrial wasteland of Sewaren's landscape, this stretch of New Jersey is littered with an endless array of enormous round oil tanks and smokestacks belching filth and pollution into the sky, though the trail of lights outlining the refinery give it a strange and spooky resemblance to a cityscape. To me and my brother, the oil tanks are giant swimming pools.

"There's the swimming pools," Robert says in a rush because it's a tiny competition thing we do when we ride on the Turnpike and we both try to say "there's the pools" first because whoever says it first, wins.

"I win!" he mocks as we both stare out into the wintery sky searching for Santa Claus with the Bee Gee's "How Deep is Your Love," this week's number one song playing on the radio. The DJ talks about how it's the first song in about three months to knock "You Light Up My Life" out of the number one spot. The song that just simply wouldn't go away is finally starting to move down the charts as the *Saturday Night Fever* soundtrack has taken hold of radio in a big way.

On Christmas morning, I unwrap the second of two AFX tracks, this one left for me by Santa and it's slightly bigger than the one my uncle gave me. My dad sets up both tracks for me in my bedroom, putting both tracks together into one long set that takes up nearly an entire wall. I spend the morning playing with my slot cars and listening to Kiss Alive II on my brand-new record player, taking in every moment of what becomes the best and most memorable Christmas of my life.

25, 35, HELLO BABY (A SORT OF EPILOGUE)

One week later, we're in Elizabeth again and it's New Years Eve. This time the entire family is gathered at my Aunt Teresa's house where my cousins Petey, Angela and Mary also live. In the Seventies this is how our family rides out the year together and rings in the new one. We do a similar Italian dinner as on Christmas Eve, dessert and coffee, and then the adults watch a lot of TV while us kids play in various configurations around the house. For instance, Robert plays with Baby Paul who usually spends a lot of time rolling around on the floor trying to walk. Downstairs in the little foyer area at the entrance to the house, Petey is showing me karate moves and instructing me to kick him, which results in me being flung into the closet doors only to land on my ass after a loud crash.

"Peter, what are you two doing down there?!" Aunt Teresa yells out from the kitchen.

Just up the stairs past the marble naked lady statue is the living room where my cousin Angela sits at the piano. Angela is the oldest of my cousins and she's trying to get everyone to come in and listen to her play.

"Aunt Darlene, I can play 'You Light Up My Life,'" she says to my mom, and proceeds to go into the opening chords of Debbie Boone's unavoidable hit song that always shows up to disrupt the world everywhere the world goes. Downstairs, Mary is carrying up a box of 45-rpm records from the basement to show me as Petey tells her not to bother us, insisting that he's showing me karate moves. Honestly, I want nothing to do with karate moves and would much rather look at the box of records. Mary sits on the floor next to me, digging into the box, pulling out a handful of 45s... "Southern Nights" by Glenn Campbel, "Please Mr. Postman" by the Carpenters, "Kung-Fu Fighting" by Carl Douglas, etc...

Upstairs at the back end of the house is the family room where half the adults are watching TV while the other half remain at the dining room table within earshot of the TV which is showing one of those Year in Review segments on the news. The one thing I notice even at this early age is that there's something about 1977 that's spoken about with a contempt that's not often seen in reference to past years. It's a sense of good riddance. Our TV news is regional, so naturally they show clips from New York City, and every time it's New York City, it's always the Son of Sam and the blackout. Every clip begins with the line "It happened again."

It happened again. In 1965 we didn't think it could ever happen again. But it happened again.

The blackout is a piece of history now, but its remnants are an ongoing piece of the present as the reminders in various clusters of Brooklyn remain...places like Bushwick along Broadway and Gates Avenue where stretches of burned-out buildings are left shuttered. And on the TV the clips inevitably refer back to the events of summer and their immutable consequences. They show the fires and the looting and the Yankees winning the world series. On the national stage, they show the theater lines for *Star Wars* with the theme by Meco playing in the background. They show Kiss and a bunch of kids on the younger end of the teen spectrum at a Kiss concert, all dressed in Kiss makeup. They show rapid flashes of the Son of Sam murder scenes in Forest Hills and Pelham Bay and the crowd outside Valentina Suriani's funeral. They show Berkowitz in handcuffs smiling malevolently and Dead Elvis lying in the casket. The montages always end with the King's procession of white funeral cars. They reiterate in the commentary how it was an especially unusual period of too much happening in succession and the collective feeling of *what's going to happen next*? That was 1977. In modern pop culture, there are rougher times up ahead and years we'd wish to forget culturally and personally, though at this stage in the culture sitting somewhere just past the halfway point in the eighth decade of the twentieth century, it's all sensory overload as the year is talked about as one we'll remember for the rest of our lives, though what influences the culture long term is not solely represented by 1977 but much more contained in a time capsule of 18 months in New York City that begins with the Bicentennial and ends with *Saturday Night Fever*, though *Fever* is its own beginning, albeit the beginning of a prolonged ending. But that's another book.

In the final half hour of '77, we all gather in front of the TV to watch Dick Clark's *New Years Rockin Eve*...a tradition of Clark sitting atop Times

Square intercut with musical guests filmed on a soundstage in Hollywood. The Hollywood portion is hosted by Suzane Summers and John Travolta's *Welcome Back Kotter* co-star and fellow Sweathog, Robert Hedgyes. We watch KC and the Sunshine Band and Crystal Gayle's performances. Gayle performs "Don't it Make My Brown Eyes Blue" while Petey marvels at the TV.

"But her eyes already *are* blue!" he says in confusion.

Everyone laughs. It's something Petey always makes me do. Every time he opens his mouth it's always something very funny or very meaningful.

As the first hour of 1978 is nearing a close, we head home once again down the New Jersey Turnpike, my brother and I assuming our usual positions in the backseat facing out the back window, watching all the cars behind us and staring into the night sky. My dad turns on the radio and shuffles the stations around. On WABC, the news at the top of the hour is on and the guy with the echoey voice is telling us that the Sex Pistols have been granted visas by the Immigration Service in Washington. Turns out their lawyer argued rather effectively that their crimes in the UK amount merely to misdemeanors in the States and stupid male adolescence is understandably ripe for misdemeanors. The Immigration Service has therefore waived the band's ineligibility to enter the country. With only a show or two postponed, the tour will begin in one week. The Sex Pistols in America. What could possibly go wrong?

"Did they say what I think they said?" my mom asks. "Sex *what*?" she whispers, not wanting me to hear.

"Pistols," my dad says.

"Sex Pistols? That's the name?"

My dad shakes his head in disbelief, not answering. Instead, he flips the station again, shuffling around until arriving at the new Bee Gees song, "Stayin' Alive" ...the second hit single from *Saturday Night Fever*. The song is barely on for three seconds before he changes the station again.

"Hey that's the song from that movie," my mom informs him. "Put that back on!"

He switches back.

"This is the Bee Gees," she says. "I like it. They used to make slow songs."

My dad isn't impressed.

"Yeah, now they make this disco crap."

In the back seat, Robert is focused out the side window of the car while my eyes are glued behind us. Along the Turnpike, there's a stretch between Exits 12 and 13 where you can see the skyline of Lower Manhattan. I always look for it when we ride this road at night. It's the World Trade Center's twin towers that have my attention while Robert is quietly awaiting the refinery tanks that sneak up on us until he calls out when I least expect it.

"There's the pools! I won!"

My eyes are so focused on New York City that I didn't even care to wait for the pools to come up.

That's where King Kong is, I thought to myself. *That's where Kiss is!*

Total contemplation now.

That's where the Yankees and the Mets are! That's where Welcome Back Kotter and all the TV channels are!

On the radio, "Stayin Alive" comes to an end and blends right into some new act called Odyssey. It sounds like another disco song, and it is.

My attention inevitably returns to the skyline. Robert is now seated and completely indifferent to anything out the window. He won the swimming pool game, so he's happy.

That's where lots of money is! I think to myself.

That's where all the fun stuff that isn't in New Jersey is!

The calypso beat settles into some female voices...

Runnin pretty, New York City gurrrrl
Twenty-five, thirty-five, hello baybeh
New York Cityyy gurrrrrrrl...

The song sounds like nighttime. It reminds me of the feelings I got this time two years ago when I kept hearing "Nights on Broadway" on the radio. I don't really know what the words are completely about, but it sounds like what I'd imagine New York City to sound like right about now as I watch the skyline from the backseat...taking in every movement of the lights from a distance...observing the outline of the city as if it's one enormous moving living organism. You can actually see it moving.

My God, I think to myself. *What's going on in there? And why can't I be there too?*

I take the song in...every note...every word that I can make out. I'm a fan of rock music, so I'm not sure if I'm supposed to like this song. But I get a feeling from this song. It's a sense of New York City...a feeling that New York is bigger than most things...a place where the music is louder and the lights are brighter, and the movies are movier and the books are bookier and the food is foodier and the sports are sportier and even the stinks are stinkier. The song smells only vaguely like the smells I smelled when I went to New York City for the first time last summer. We went in mid-August just after the Son of Sam was captured and we visited the Empire State Building. Well, that was a steamy hot day with Meco's *Star Wars* theme blaring from the radio as we drove up the Avenue of the Americas. Sitting in stop-and-go traffic we'd hear Rita Coolidge's cover of "Higher and Higher," "Looks Like We Made It" by Barry Manilow, and "I Just Want to Be Your Everything" by Andy Gibb...easily the biggest song of the summer. But that was summer, and as previously noted, the summer city smells are hot dogs, sewage and piss. Then there are the winter smells of New York City...the smells of hot pretzels from a vendor cart and heat coming up from the subway grates along the sidewalks, and no matter how warm you may be, you can still feel the biting chill in the air. The song coming out over the radio that has me entranced as I follow the skyline, sounds the way New York City smells on a cold night. But that's just the city in the senses of a seven-year-old. But here is also New York City as nerve center of the world. It's the Big Apple...the city that never sleeps. And this song I'm hearing along with "Stayin' Alive," is just another song that despite its specific contents, flexes its muscle with the mere image of the city, resting securely in the awareness of its premiere place in American culture and its deep indelible imprint on the rest of the world.

We're in the wee small hours of the morning. It's New Years Day, 1978. The 1970s have peaked. Everything forward will be a direct reaction out of their influence. I turn away from the window and sit back in my seat. Almost home with the car rumbling beneath me I close my eyes into dreamland, still able to see the skyline in the void of black behind my eyelids...that radiant neon outline of New York City...the glory and the tragedy...glowing and burning its way through the mind's eye, imagination, desire and memory.

It's everything you remember.

ACKNOWLEDGMENTS

First, above all, a special thanks to Abbey Suchoski, my co-pilot on these projects, whose insight, guidance and brilliant work have helped make my books a reality from day one.

Bicentennial Chic is a work of pure entertainment, often at the expense of history. Because of the structure of this book which I consider to be a literary nonfiction memoir hybrid as opposed to a work of academic nonfiction, I have omitted the traditional citation styles required of academic texts and allowed myself liberties I would not have dared taken had this book been a straight nonfiction entity seeking to further advance our understanding of these topics, which I make no claims of doing. The information presented has long been well-documented in various forms of media, though most of what I draw from can be easily accessed through newspaper and television archives...many of which are available in a simple Youtube search. These are the quotes of sports managers and politicians whose words are very much part of public record. In the case of some very essential books on my topics... books that are much more detailed and worthy of praise on these subjects than my own, I will mention them here and later include in a separate list. All were accessed as source material. Publications like *Munson: The Life and Death of a Yankee Captain* by Marty Appel and *Billy Martin: Baseball's Flawed Genius* by Bill Pennington were guides in helping me provide a rough sketch of the relationship between George Steinbrenner and Billy Martin and a basic examination of their personalities, flaws and quirks. Reggie's book *Becoming Mr. October* provides a firsthand view from one of our main subject's own perspectives on how he was treated by teammates with regard to race.

Much of this sentiment is echoed in Pennington's book as well as Jonathan Mahler's book *Ladies and Gentlemen, the Bronx is Burning*. The insight into the question of race and Jackson's charges of anti-Semitism was provided in thoughtful detail from differing perspectives in all three of these publications. But believe it or not, sometimes you get more mileage from a *New York Post* headline by using your imagination and conducting your own variation on the who, what, when, where, and why. These are the day-to-day entries against the arc of a baseball season where in the case of the Yankees and of the quoted players in reference to any gameday comments, one need not look too far past the beat reporters. Guys like Murray Class of the *New York Times* who were my firsthand accounts and witnesses to the drama in real time. And speaking of reporters, Phil Pepe's *Ballad of Billy and George: The Tempestuous Baseball Marriage of Billy Martin and George Steinbrenner* were essential in my reconstruction of owner/manager, owner/player interactions. Their quotations of the players in relation to events and to each other was my fodder for dialogue on the rare and few occasions that I used dialogue. As for quoted dialogue from Charles Finley regarding Bowie Kuhn's intervention in June 1976, Joseph Durso's *New York Times* articles cover the daily drama rather effectively and serve as source material here. The coverage is too vast to cite and reads like a daily soap opera, though with today's technology it is easily accessible through digital newspaper archives.

Kiss. Perhaps for the casual fan, a number of things may have been learned on our trip backwards through time. But for the diehard Kiss fan, there is nothing in this book by way of minutia that can't already be found in the timelines of Curt Gooch and Jeff Suh's *Kiss Alive Forever* and C.K. Lendt's *Kiss and Sell.* Once again, the aim of *Bicentennial Chic* with regards to Kiss, was to gather everything we already know from the *Destroyer* tour to the end of the *Love Gun* tour and construct a narrative that weaved itself into the other events that simultaneously took place during this same period.

In the realm of true crime, the shooting of Carl Denaro is recounted based on Carl's own recollection in the numerous interviews he's done over the years. Carl is all over Youtube, take your pick.

ACKNOWLEDGMENTS

The details of Valentina Suriani's life before her murder and the speculation of her relationship with Alexander Esau are conclusions that I have drawn based on podcaster and Son of Sam historian Manny Grossman's interview with Gloria Calilli-Zonghetti. Gloria was a childhood friend of Val's and her insight into Val's personality and character is immeasurable. Manny's conversations with Gary McNerny, another friend of Valentina's also played a vital role in capturing Val's spirit and personality, which I hope I was able to do justice to, given the limited amount of information we've had over the years. The work of Manny Grossman has challenged the long-held myths of the Son of Sam shootings, and he has almost singlehandedly debunked most of them while discovering additional crimes of David Berkowitz and furthering our knowledge on the Son of Sam case. His academic approach to research and meticulous examination of every possible untouched angle cracked this story wide open nearly half a century later. But that's not what *Bicentennial Chic* is about. That story is for Manny to tell if he chooses to. But credit where additional credit is due...we must also include Detective Mike Lorenzo and John Catalano for their insight and contribution to these landmark discoveries with Manny. I was in touch with Manny via Twitter for a short amount of time around the summer of 2022 into 2023. I talked very briefly about my book and that it would only cover the Son of Sam events as a minor background to everything else. Little did I know that I would become attached to the victims and survivors in a way that would inform the path that I'd end up following with this book and that it would become one of my core four topics. Regarding dialogue, the words and accounts of Mike and Rose Lauria are documented by Jimmy Breslin in his June 5, 1977 *Daily News* column, which my chapter 19 narrative is partly constructed from.

The making of *Saturday Night Fever* has been documented ad nauseum. In the age of Youtube and the vast array of interviews with cast and crew as the film reaches anniversary after anniversary every ten years, one could construct their own timeline of Stigwood's project from June 1976 all the way to December 1977.

A few things to note:

The details of Diana Hyland's passing were gathered from Dick Van Patten's personal account as reported by the *Shreveport Journal* on July 19, 1977. Also, the speculation regarding the relationship between Stigwood and Kevin McCormick and the circumstances surrounding the firing of John Avildsen were drawn from writer and director Michael Lee Nirenberg's interviews with Lloyd Kauffman. Nirenberg, a longtime friend who spoke to several crew members for his own book *Cinematic Immunity*, gave me access to his transcripts in 2023 while we were both deep in the weeds of our respective projects.

As for information provided within my portrayal of events such as the blizzard and blackout, I piece together the stories of the people who were there from the actual news reports accessible in radio and television archives which are documented in the text itself. Many come from personal conversations and interviews with people I've known or met who lived through those events.

Finally, with respect to traditional citation, I can take you, the reader, to the door, but I cannot unlock it. It would defeat the purpose of *Bicentennial Chic* as a conscious work of literary nonfiction. Aside from my own personal memories that are sprinkled throughout like a fine seasoning to fuse with the story, there is nothing in this book that can't be verified. If pursuit of origins is a must, the dates of very specific events are all given throughout these pages. Those dates provide their own roadmaps. May you enjoy that journey as much as I have.

An extra special thanks to Annette for being there through this entire ride.

BOOKS FOR FURTHER READING...

Munson: The Life and Death of a Yankee Captain, Marty Appel.
Doubleday, New York, 2009.

Billy Martin: Baseball's Flawed Genius, Bill Pennington.
Houghton Mifflin Harcourt, 2015.

Becoming Mr. October, Reggie Jackson with Kevin Baker.
Knopf Doubleday Publishing Group, 2013.

Ladies and Gentlemen, the Bronx is Burning. Jonathan Mahler.
Farrar, Straus and Giroux, 2005.

Ballad of Billy and George: The Tempestuous Baseball Marriage of Billy Martin and George Steinbrenner, Phil Pepe.
Globe Pequot Press, 2008.

Kiss Alive Forever: The Complete Touring History, Curt Gooch, Jeff Suh.
IP-Verlag, 2003.

Kiss and Sell: The Making of a Supergroup, C.K. Lendt.
Billboard Books, 1997.

Kiss Behind the Mask: The Official Authorized Biography, David Leaf, Ken Sharp.
Warner Books, 2003.

Kiss: The Early Years, Gene Simmons, Paul Stanley. Three Rivers Press, 2002.

Nothin' to Lose: The Making of Kiss 1972-1975, Ken Sharp, Gene Simmons,
Paul Stanley

Face the Music: A Life Exposed, Paul Stanley. HarperCollins, 2014.

No Regrets, Ace Frehley. Joe Layden, John Ostrosky. Gallery Books, 2011.

Kiss and Make Up, Gene Simmons. Crown, 2001.

Makeup to Breakup: My Life In and Out of Kiss, Peter Criss, Larry Sloman. Scribner, 2012.

Hot Stuff: Disco and the Remaking of American Culture, Alice Echols. W.W. Norton & Company, Inc., 2010.

Under My Skin: Drama, Trauma & Rock 'n' Roll, Elise Krentzel. Kumi Consulting and Company LLC, 2022.

Cinematic Immunity: An Oral History of New York Filmmaking As Told by the Crews That Got the Shot, Michael Lee Nirenberg. Feral House, 2026.

The Last Party: Studio 54, Disco and the Culture of the Night, Anthony Haden-Guest. Open Road Media, 2015.

Big Hair and Plastic Grass: A Funky Ride Through Baseball and America in the Swinging 70s, Dan Epstein. Macmillan, 2010.

www.ingramcontent.com/pod-product-compliance
Lightning Source LLC
Chambersburg PA
CBHW070726030726
47601CB00006B/268/J

* 9 7 8 1 7 3 5 4 7 6 7 7 3 *